Unbecoming Blackne

Unbecoming Blackness

The Diaspora Cultures
of Afro-Cuban America

ANTONIO LÓPEZ

New York University Press

NEW YORK AND LONDON

NEW YORK UNIVERSITY PRESS
New York and London
www.nyupress.org

LIBRARY OF CONGRESS CATALOGING-IN-PUBLICATION DATA

López, Antonio M.
Unbecoming blackness : the diaspora cultures of Afro-Cuban America
/ Antonio López.
p. cm.
Includes bibliographical references and index.
ISBN 978-0-8147-6546-3 (cl : alk. paper)
ISBN 978-0-8147-6547-0 (pb : alk. paper)
ISBN 978-0-8147-6548-7 (ebook)
ISBN 978-0-8147-6549-4 (ebook)
1. Cuban Americans—Intellectual life—20th century. 2. Cuban Americans—
Ethnic identity 3. Blacks—United States—Intellectual life—20th century.
4. African Americans—Intellectual life—20th century. 5. American
literature—Cuban American authors. I. Title.
E184.C97L67 2012
305.8968'7291073—dc23

2012009413

References to Internet websites (URLs) were accurate at the time of writing.
Neither the author nor New York University Press is responsible for URLs
that may have expired or changed since the manuscript was prepared.

New York University Press books are printed on acid-free paper, and their
binding materials are chosen for strength and durability. We strive to use
environmentally responsible suppliers and materials to the greatest extent
possible in publishing our books.

Manufactured in the United States of America
c 10 9 8 7 6 5 4 3 2 1
p 10 9 8 7 6 5 4 3 2 1

THE
AMERICAN
LITERATURES
INITIATIVE
A book in the American Literatures Initiative (ALI), a collaborative
publishing project of NYU Press, Fordham University Press, Rutgers
University Press, Temple University Press, and the University of Virginia
Press. The Initiative is supported by The Andrew W. Mellon Foundation.
For more information, please visit www.americanliteratures.org.

To my mother and brother
To Rachel and Maeve

CONTENTS

ACKNOWLEDGMENTS

This book hardly resembles the project I began while in the English Department at Rutgers University, but the confidence John McClure, Brent Edwards, and Bruce Robbins showed in me then has encouraged me ever since. I began researching and writing these pages when I arrived at the George Washington University in 2005, and, since then, I have benefited from the support of Dean William Frawley, Dean Peg Barratt, and Associate Dean Geralyn Schulz. A Junior Scholar Incentive Award and a University Facilitating Fund Award allowed visits to libraries and archives that proved indispensible. The backing of my fellow members of the English Department has been remarkable—in particular, Marshall Alcorn, Hache Carrillo, Patty Chu, Jeffrey Cohen, Holly Dugan, Jonathan Gil Harris, Connie Kibler, Faye Moskowitz, Ormond Seavey, Chris Sten, Linda Terry, and Gayle Wald. Robert McRuer made it his duty to guide me toward publication. Of special significance are my department comrades Jim Miller and Jennifer James, who offered friendship and mentorship throughout. Elizabeth Acevedo, Ricardo Almonte, Kathryn Bibler, Jonathan Chuck, Zak McAdoo, Hilary Moise, Alexandra Moss (who helped research chapter 4), Amanda Nazario, Dennis Perales, Andrew Ratner, Tess Salazar, Trinh Tran, Sonia Valencia, and Laura Warman are on a long list of people I have had the pleasure to teach as this book emerged.

At New York University Press, Eric Zinner demonstrated his commitment from the start. Ciara McLaughlin led me through the review and production stages expertly. I also thank NYU's readers, whose feedback made this so much better.

I appreciate my longtime friends, near and far: Gwen Bradley, Anand Commissiong, Ariel Fernández, Bill de Grummond, Chris Hollingsworth, Luis Iglesias, Thomas Meal, Debra Roy, and Yesenia Selier. The first few years in the District would have been impossible without Lisa Lynch, who brought the Brooklyn, and Tommy Castillo, the Hialeah. Ian Goulston has been a great influence. Talking to him about music and film—collaborating with him—was one of the pleasures of this experience. I am also thankful for the generosity of the families in Miami, Boston, and Los Angeles: Emiko López, Irene Canel-Petersen, Mary McLaughlin, John McLaughlin, Mary Carol McLaughlin, Kaitlin McLaughlin, and Jenny Pearson.

I am grateful to the many people who offered me contacts, sources, and other assistance, including Al Angeloro, Donna Arnold, Mario Barrera, Esteban Luis Cárdenas, Michael Casey, Yasnay Cuesta, Margaret Dakin, Cristobal Díaz Ayala, José Díaz Rodríguez, Marvin Dunn, Jorge Florido, Marilyn Graf, Judge Evelio Grillo, Jr., Pedro Juan Hernández, Leah Jehan, Miriam Jiménez Román, Nicolás Kanellos, Jeff Lemlich, Marquis Lewis, Joseph McNair, Ignacio Mireles Rangel, Lucio Ortigoza, Enrique Patterson, Luis de la Paz, Michael Pounds, Tomás Fernández Robaina, Harold Lee Rush, Manolo Salvat, José Sánchez-Boudy, Nicole Smith, Pam Sporn, Lesbia Varona, Eduardo de la Vega Alfaro, Tony Vélez, and Neva Wartell. Colleagues, many of them friends, offered comments and provided venues for presentation and publication at various stages, including Mónica Ayala, Roberto Fernández, Juan Flores, Jorge Gracia, Ted Henken, Keith Leonard, Iraida López, Manuel Martínez, Suzanne Oboler, and Randy Ontiveros. I especially appreciate Isabel Álvarez-Borland, José Buscaglia-Salgado, Robert Dickson, Raúl Fernández, Rodrigo Lazo, Nancy Mirabal, and José Esteban Muñoz for taking such a strong interest in the work. Ricardo Ortiz, with whom I have been fortunate to share a neighborhood in the District, has been a true advocate and friend; he has led the way for many in Cuban American literary and cultural studies, me included. I greatly value the trust Diana Lachatanere showed in me as I wrote about her mother and father and the many comments she contributed over the past several years. My use of the Rómulo Lachatañeré papers and photographs, without which a large part of this book would not exist, comes courtesy of her. I also thank José Parlá for allowing the reproduction of *Aguada de Pasajeros*.

One of the most rewarding aspects was getting to know the elders: the people whose lives stretched back as far as the 1930s, when, as young men and women, they lived many of the events I describe. It was an honor to talk to Graciela, Melba Alvarado, René Buch, Pupi Campo, Eileen Charbo, Diosa Costello, Evelio Grillo, Simón Jou, Jr., Rosendo Rosell, Max Salazar, and Zoraida Valdés-Holmes.

My mother, Pilar, took care of us in every way, and my brother, Miguel, made me laugh and chill. Anything Cuban American will always begin with them. No one has dedicated more of herself to make this book come true than Rachel McLaughlin. And, even then, she gave still more: to me, a second chance. Our daughter, Maeve, made everything happier. This is for the four of them.

Parts of chapter 5 previously appeared in "Cosa de Blancos: Cuban-American Whiteness and the Afro-Cuban-Occupied House," *Latino Studies* 8.2 (Summer 2010): 220–43.

"In Africa (Fué en el África)," written by Eusebia Cosme, English lyric by Marion Sunshine, arranged by Anselmo Sacasas, © 1945 (Renewed 1973, 2001) Fred Ahlert Music Group (ASCAP)/Administered by Bug Music and Antobal Music Company, all rights reserved. Used by permission. Reprinted by permission of Hal Leonard Corporation.

UNBECOMING BLACKNESS

Introduction

One afternoon late in 1929, two Afro-Cuban men visited the Havana home of an Afro-Cuban woman to conduct an interview for a newspaper article. Nicolás Guillén was already known for his journalism and was on the way to becoming a renowned poet. His companion, Gustavo Urrutia, was a prominent figure in Afro-Cuban social and intellectual life as the editor of "Ideales de una Raza" (Ideals of a Race), a Sunday page on Afro-Cuban topics in *El Diario de la Marina*. Guillén published the interview in "Ideales" as "Señorita Consuelo Serra," a title that revealed to readers his interviewee's connection to Cuban history: Consuelo Serra was the daughter of Rafael Serra, the famous journalist and Cuban independence leader in the United States during the late nineteenth century.[1]

Serra proved a provocative interview, beyond the association with her father. She had migrated from Cuba to New York City when she was seven years old and lived there for fourteen years. She went to public school and graduated with degrees in English from Hunter College and education from the city's Normal School before returning to the island in 1906.[2] This was not lost on Guillén and Urrutia. In the article, Guillén describes how, on the afternoon in question, they come to Serra's apartment, where a "girl, black and smiling" (*niña negra y sonriente*), opens the door. As they wait for their host, they note the very few paintings on the walls, a sign, Guillén says, of good taste. And then Serra arrives, also "smiling." Her speech leaves an impression on Guillén: "despite having lived in the North for fourteen years, her Spanish is pure [*conserva límpido su castellano*], without any of those incriminating Rs [*erres* delatoras], pronounced with a grinding sound [como si se las triturara], that so clearly registers the influence of English."[3] Serra begins to comment on her college career, but Urrutia "interrupts her": "Of course, a college exclusively for people of color [gente de color] ..." "Nothing of the kind," she replies. "For blacks and whites [Para negros y para blancos]." Serra explains that, in her graduating class, six students were "of color" and that she was "the only Cuban," yet she "never felt uneasy [molesta] or passed over [preterida]." This prompts a reply from Urrutia: "So in New York there are no problems," he begins, only before he can specify the kind of problems he has in mind, it is Serra who cuts in: "Oh, I didn't mean to suggest as much! Yes, there are, as is the case everywhere in the Union. Slightly less than in the South, but it exists. What I have tried to point out is the fact that I never had an occasion to get upset [disgustarme] at the college. And on the street ... Well, on the street, whenever I ran into some difficulty, I always had the authorities on my side. But that only happened a few times. I really have no complaints [quejas] about New York."[4]

Consuelo Serra established schools, taught English, and wrote journalism in Cuba during the first decades of the twentieth century, the early years of the republic.[5] In Guillén's narrative, she prompts among "middle-class" Afro-Cubans a tense encounter, a primary reason for which is her seemingly erstwhile Afro-Cuban Americanness: her identity and history as a Cuban woman de color, a negra, living in the United States. For Guillén, this implies a possible impurity, one whose signs he seeks, not surprisingly, in language. Guillén puts the sounds of Serra's speech under surveillance. For Urrutia, it leads to pointed questions regarding her exposure to racial injustice in the United States, the significance of which is fraught, as evidenced by the tacit conversation: nowhere does Guillén show Urrutia or Serra calling these "problems" by name, even as Serra offers examples that leave little doubt in the reader's mind. She notes U.S. racism's geographies and uses her personal experience to place it in institutions such as the unsegregated school, where it may produce bad feelings and jeopardize opportunity, and unsegregated public space, where its effects, now implying a physical menace, call for an intervention by the state. Serra's spoken Spanish was a signifier for her Afro-Cuban American history even earlier still. In 1905, the Afro-Cuban intellectual Miguel Gualba wrote in Havana's El Nuevo Criollo that "Consuelo, despite having taken courses for thirteen years exclusively in the English language [en puro idioma inglés], speaks our language, hers [habla nuestro idoma, el suyo]—the one of the home in which her conscience was formed—correctly and with such naturalness as if she had been studying it in Cuba the whole time."[6] There is in these anxious expressions of an English-free, Spanish-speaking ability (Gualba goes so far as to imagine its power to undo Serra's U.S. migration altogether, transporting her back to the island) a link between femininity and Afro-Cuban Americanness: a Spanish-language "home" in the United States cultivates the class-identified propriety of the Afro-Cuban American woman. Indeed, the final questions Guillén poses Serra in the article are "Are you a feminist [*feminista*], Miss Serra? Are you in favor of the vote?" She says, "Yes, I am a feminist," and begins to recall a lecture she gave as a student in New York on "equal rights for women." But just then the telephone rings, cutting off the conversation. As Guillén leaves the apartment with Urrutia, he again draws attention to that sonic sign for how an Afro-Cuban woman in Havana may, in the end, "really have no complaints about New York": as he walks down the stairs, Guillén hears Serra's voice, now on the telephone, "slowly fading away."[7]

Unbecoming Blackness inquires into expressions across literature and performance of an Afro-Cuban experience in the United States that the apprehensive imagining of an English-sounding Consuelo Serra would invoke. It begins during the period of the *Marina* article, with Afro-Cuban American writers and performers of the first republican genera-tion who migrated to the United States in the 1920s and 1930s, especially to New York City, and continues into the late twentieth century, with those who arrived or were born into a majority white-Cuban exile that, in the aftermath of the 1980 Mariel boatlift, witnessed an increase in the Afro-Cuban population of the United States. The book examines the idea of an Afro-Cuban American voice tainted by the English language in the United States as an indication of broader concerns over the kinds of relations and relationships that Afro-Cuban Americans, as writers and performers, may cultivate beyond the island: relations in trans/national cultures and politics, relationships with fellow Cuban Americans, with other Latinas/os—white, indigenous, and of African descent—and with African Americans. It also sees in the clipped, tacit conversation on racial injustice in the United States and Serra's accompanying admis-sion to having "no complaints about New York" a hint regarding how Afro-Cuban Americans may reside on U.S. soil despite the fact of Anglo and Latino racisms, a choice the book explores as an example of an Afro-Cuban American redefinition of the United States as a space propitious for the pursuit of careers in literature and performance, not to mention the possible achievement of citizenship rights. In poetry, fiction, and the

FIGURE 1. Consuelo Serra in New York, 1905
(From Rafael Serra, *Para negros y para blancos: Ensayos políticos, sociales, y económicos,
cuarte serie* [Havana: Imprenta "El Score," 1907])

essay, in blackface theater, poetry recital, and film—indeed, in artistic
careers often unavailable to them in Cuba—Afro-Cuban Americans
transform the shapes, themes, and concepts of their work in and beyond
racial identity in a body of critically underexamined texts that surface
the importance of aesthetic re-creation in the constitution of Cuban and
African diasporas in the United States.

This book discusses Afro-Cuban American literature and performance as an example of *afrolatinidad*: the Afro-Latino condition in the
United States, which Afro-Cuban Americans share with other Latinas/
os of African descent, including, but not limited to, those with origins in
Puerto Rico, the Dominican Republic, Panama, Colombia, and Venezuela. Central to afrolatinidad is the social difference that blackness makes
in the United States: how an Anglo white supremacy determines the life

chances of Afro-Latinas/os hailed as black and how a Latino white supremacy reproduces the colonial and postcolonial Latin American privileging of *blanco* over *negro* and *mulato* (mixed-race) identities, now on behalf of white Latinas/os who may themselves face Anglo forms of racializing discrimination. Yet, if an Afro-Latino difference reveals how, for Afro-Cuban Americans, encounters with white Cuban Americans may lead to exclusion—to the experience of an older Cuban racism, now become a newer Cuban American phenomenon, heightened by an Anglo-racist United States—it is true that Afro-Cuban Americans may occupy with white Cuban Americans the space of an apparent multiracial inclusion through a shared *cubanoamericanidad*, a Cuban Americanness that, as an ideal of a transnational Cuban belonging, purports an understanding beyond race among Cubans in the United States. Such a shared Cuban Americanness, in particular as cultural and linguistic affinities that bear upon social mobility in the Cuban centers of the country, influences how Afro-Cuban Americans negotiate (if not limit or reject) relationships with other Afro-Latinas/os, not to mention African Americans. And yet, indeed, there are moments in which Afro-Cuban Americans collaborate in solidarity with African Americans and other non-Latinas/os of African descent (those from the Anglophone and Francophone Caribbean, for example) despite the social marginalization such collaboration may entail in Anglo and Latino communities—a risk often deemed worth it, given the opportunity Afro-Cuban Americans may gain from an association with African Americans, measured even against the benefits that Anglo-white and Latino-white hegemonies promise them as foreign blacks and fellow trans/nationals, respectively. To attune a discussion of Afro-Cuban Americans to afrolatinidad in literature and performance is to challenge Cuban America's normate whiteness—to posit, in fact, an *Afro-Cuban America*, one made visible in texts ranging from the Caribbean Latino modernist period, with its turn toward minority rights and anti-imperialism after the exile-directed projects of Antillean liberation at the turn of the century, to the postrevolutionary exodus and founding of a Cuban Miami in the last half of the twentieth century, a span whose latter period is familiar to Latino literary and cultural studies, though less so in terms of the Afro-Cuban American countertradition I offer here.

The Afro-Cuban American writers and performers I discuss represent overlapping Cuban and African diasporas, which is to say that histories of displacement from Cuba and Africa bear upon them simultaneously, with changing, uneven effects on their relations, both material and symbolic, to race and nation, host- and homelands. It is a matter that brings together conversations on the discourse of diaspora in African American and Latino Studies, which I do through the work of Brent Edwards and Ricardo Ortiz. For Edwards, who has historicized the concept among black intellectuals and activists in the twentieth century, diaspora is most useful when it guides us to consider specific contacts between people of African descent across the Americas, Europe, and Africa in a way that attends to difference—"difference not only internally (the ways transnational black groupings are fractured by nation, class, gender, sexuality, and language) but also externally: in appropriating a term so closely associated with Jewish thought, we are forced to think not in terms of some closed or autonomous system of African dispersal but explicitly in terms of a complex past of forced migrations and racializations." Edwards continues that the "use of the term *diaspora* . . . implies neither that it offers the comfort of abstraction, an easy recourse to origins, nor that it provides a foolproof anti-essentialism: instead, it forces us to articulate discourses of cultural and political linkage only through and across difference in full view of the risks of that endeavor."[8] This invitation for criticism and theory to turn toward diasporic praxes in their particulars and, especially, to their "constitutive tension" in nationalism and internationalism[9] resonates with Ortiz's thought in *Cultural Erotics in Cuban America* regarding a possible Cuban diaspora. Working off James Clifford's treatment of the concept, Ortiz shows that any thinking on a post-1959 Cuban diaspora must attend to the ways in which nationalist inclinations urge Cuban Americans to bring to an end their U.S. displacement through a redemptive return to Cuba (however deferred it may be in practice): diaspora as a desire to recover an island-situated national identity against a Cuban American transnational belonging. With the lure of a territorial homeland, one located "nearby" in the hemisphere, Ortiz underscores the importance of recognizing the variety of Cuban departures to the United States—the moment of a post-1959 diaspora's initiation. "Exile" is crucial in this regard for its meaning as an unwilling political (or, against U.S. imperial geopolitics, a willing economic) displacement, although by now there is a history of post–Cold War Cuban departures that, in their most recent form, are very well indicative of a postexile: the back-and-forth movements between the United States and Cuba among recent migrants that trouble the earlier exile's implication of a one-way flow (until such time as a redemptive return). For Ortiz, thinking Cuban diaspora is possible, so long as we account for these limits—limits that touch on sexuality, where the governing of Cuban bodies, on and off the island, impacts who can (or must) leave the country, who can (or cannot) return.[10]

The diasporas of Afro-Cuban America—the African and Cuban— unfold in relation to afrolatinidad. A sign of *African* diaspora appears in the way Afro-Cuban Americans articulate blackness in the black- white spaces of the Anglo United States through (a memory of) Cuban nationalism's postracial and *mestizaje* ideologies: the former emerging during Cuba's nineteenth-century wars of liberation as the privileging of a national, over a racial, form of identification, the latter in the early twentieth century as an ideal of a "mixed-race" nationalism, invoked often as culture, where neither black nor white would predominate. Over the twentieth century, Cuban racial injustice continued despite (indeed, because of) postracial and *mestizaje* nationalisms, which, while provid- ing room for Afro-Cuban mobility, often failed to alter the nation's de facto white privilege, a social legacy the 1959 revolution inherited and revised as a "raceless" revolutionary nationalism—even as its class-based policies helped disproportionately poor Afro-Cubans.[11] A sign of African diaspora appears also in the way Afro-Cuban Americans, in particular those migrating before the revolution, link blackness in the United States with (a memory of) the long-established forms of island-based Afro- Cuban community, which have included mutual-aid societies, religious groupings, and social clubs.[12] Such an African diaspora among Afro- Cuban American writers and performers determines the cultural (and, less often in the texts I discuss, political) "linkages" they establish with African Americans in the un/segregated United States, linkages at times firm and enduring, at times uncertain and fleeting. In the Latino United States, Afro-Cuban Americans twist the meaning of a *Cuban* diaspora by bringing their afrolatinidad to bear on encounters with other Afro- Cuban Americans and white Cuban Americans across the pre- and post-1959 spaces of an unacknowledged white *cubanoamericanidad*—a Latino whiteness that, in fact, may not welcome a possibly "blackening" association with Afro-Cuban Americans under the Anglo-U.S. gaze. Afro-Cuban Americans mark a (white) Cuban diaspora as black, unset- tling its memory, if not practice, of ideological postracial, *mestizaje*, and "raceless" antirevolutionary nationalisms, now transnationalisms—a disruption that, given my period reach back into the early twentieth cen- tury, involves the movements of an Afro-Cuban American diaspora well before, yet carrying through and beyond, the midcentury breaks and migrations associated with the revolution.

A text from this earlier period is the Afro-Cuban American Bernardo Ruiz Suárez's *The Color Question in the Two Americas*, a historico-political essay published in the United States in an English translation in 1922, the tenth anniversary of the killing of thousands of Afro-Cubans on the island by the Cuban government and white militias in the "race war" of 1912, a major event of Cuban racial terror begun after members of the Independent Party of Color, an Afro-Cuban political organization founded to redress racial injustice, had begun to protest and resist the party's banning by the state.[13] Well within memory of 1912—perhaps even commemorating it with the book's publication date—Ruiz Suárez offers another approach to the idea that Afro-Cuban Americans have "no complaints about New York," that, indeed, they may choose to lead a life in the United States, however much such a decision may signify to other Cubans, on and off the island, as unbecoming: as an "unseemly" association with black subalterns (African Americans, fellow Afro-Cuban Americans) in the Anglo-racist United States, and as an *un*becoming of one's island-Cuban black identity, its "becoming," as a revision or even an undoing, Afro-Latino.[14]

In a passage on comparative experiences of racism in the United States and Latin America, Ruiz Suárez writes that the "rough and brutal and contemptuous . . . methods of the Anglo-Saxon" in the United States nevertheless "goad the black [that is, African American] man into a life of activity and, consequently, a life creative of ideals which may in time be realized." He goes on to say that, for an Afro-Cuban American, "it is most gratifying to observe the accomplishments of his congeners in the United States in the development of their own instruments of civilization." For Ruiz Suárez, such a state of affairs contrasts with the conditions in a place like Cuba. In such "Spanish-American countries," the "apparent cordiality" of members of the "white race" works to "conceal their sentiment" of racism, which leads to a "specious national unity" that, for an Afro-Cuban, thwarts the "self-dependence of his race."[15] In the "gratifying" experience of beholding "the accomplishments of his congeners," Ruiz Suárez's narrative exemplifies the diaspora cultures of Afro-Cuban America: in particular, it expresses an unbecoming *desire for* the way in which African Americans belong in the "rough and brutal and contemptuous" Anglo United States—a description here characteristic of the discourse of a violent U.S. inhospitableness that, on the island, often becomes a message delivered to Afro-Cubans (and, in a sign of the Afro-Latino difference, less so, if ever, to white Cubans) to discourage their migration north, a discourse observed across the twentieth century, as an Afro-Cuban Mariel migrant in 1980 Miami demonstrates, recollecting how, "in Cuba, they said dogs were set upon black people here [*que aquí a los negros les echaban los perros*]."[16] In the aftermath of 1912, with its catastrophic failure of an island Afro-Cuban project for "self-dependence," such an Afro-Cuban American desire for African American institutions in the United States makes sense in terms of desire as a complex of always *wanting after*, if never quite achieving, its object, an idea apparent in the translated condition of *Color Question* itself, which comes to us not in the English-language voice of Ruiz Suárez himself—in his achievement of Anglophony—but in the translated echo of his Spanish, the Afro-Latino threat of which, as a possible Anglophone-influenced impurity, we have seen in Serra. There is an implication in all this, finally, that Afro-Cubans are somehow "better off" being in and belonging to an explicitly racist U.S. nation rather than, it turns out, Cuba. This being and belonging is asserted against the "best interests" of a postracial, *mestizo*, even *negro* island-Cuban nation—indeed, against the "best interests" of Afro-Cubans themselves. It is a desire signaling Cuban nationalism as a struggle over the "enjoyment" of a Cuban "way of life" from which Afro-Cubans, often assigned a menacing, excessive enjoyment of the nation, such as in 1912, are now "stealing" themselves (and something of the Cuban nation-myth) away to the Afro-Cuban American United States.[17]

An Afro-Cuban American voice tainted by English in the United States is important for understanding the writers and performers in my study, since such a voice, as a figure for the literary and performance languages in a twentieth-century Afro-Cuban America, emerges as a primary site of racialization: the way in which an Afro-Latino racial identity is "made" in the United States, depending on how one sounds (in writing, in performance) in English, Spanish, or both at the same time. The contemporary Afro-Cuban American novelist H. G. Carrillo makes this point, that the English/Spanish speech, writing, and performance of Afro-Latinas/os, far from being neutral, have a "color," one that bespeaks Afro-Cuban experiences in coloniality. In the novel *Loosing My Espanish*, Carrillo's narrator is a teacher who delivers a long lecture on Cuban history (and thus stands as a performer) before his students: "Miren my hands," he says. "This color on the map, this bit of orange here, Illinois. Chicago stares me in the face every morning when I shave, señores. My face, this color, a subtle legacy of the British Royal African Company, is, as they say in the vernacular, el color of my Espanish."[18] Carrillo's narrator meditates on geography, the body, and language—on the circumstances that have led an Afro-Cuban American's mouth to speak the English-language word "Spanish" in a Cuban-Spanish-accented English, as "Espanish." His narrator is not only resident in the United States—in Chicago: a midwestern Afro-Cuban American—but, in fact, sees himself as the "color" of Chicago. Here we have what Guillén was worried about with Serra, rendered into fictional narrative. The Afro-Cuban American speaks, writes, and performs with an English/Spanish multilinguistic impurity that signifies his blackness not just in (and according to) the Anglo United States but in relation to the other "coloreds" of Illinois, the state's many Latinas/os and African Americans.[19]

To underscore the transhistorical significance of such modalities of race and the multilinguistic, I return to Gustavo Urrutia—now not just a character in Guillén's writing but a writer himself—and another representation of an early twentieth-century afrolatinidad in Afro-Cuban print culture. In a March 1, 1936, "Armonías" column entitled "Imperialismo afrocubano" (Afro-Cuban Imperialism), Urrutia satirizes imperialism, which in the column stands for U.S. designs on global domination ("*imperialismo yanqui*") but also, more implicitly, "black empire," a very different project of black solidarity involving a "global vision of the race" that "shadows histories of empire and colonization in the Americas."[20] Urrutia's satirical starting point is the influence that "Armonías" appears to have on the "North American conscience," for the column, it seems, was circulating, in transamerican fashion, among readers in "the Hispanic-American colony of New York" (*la colonia hispanoamericana de New York*). Indeed, because of the column's presence "on the avenues of Harlem" (*por las avenidas de Harlem*), Urrutia can claim that "our ideals and literature" are being "planted" in the United States and that soon "our vigorous money" will take over "their lands, industries, banks, and press," to be followed by "our warships and marines," all to ensure "our conquests."[21] But what occasions the column and Urrutia's sense of its circulation in the United States—what, in fact, occupies half the column's space in the newspaper—is a brief English-language letter dated February 6, 1936, from the activist, historian, and African-diaspora archive builder Arturo Schomburg in New York City to Urrutia in Havana, a letter reprinted in the column in a Spanish translation. In the English-language original, Schomburg, called by Urrutia in the column an "Afro-boricua" (*afroborinqueño*), mentions possessing "pages from the *Diario de la Marina*" with Urrutia's "articles on 'Ideals of a Race.'" Schomburg states that these pages have now been "mounted on Japanese transparent silk paper and bound with buckram," and he calls the resulting "volume," the description of which has allowed him to revel in the sensuality of the book-making process, "a most remarkable contribution to the Negro race from the Spanish-American angle." Schomburg, in fact, feels "certain that there is no other copy like it any part of the world."[22] What I want to underscore in this text of a (Spanish-translated) Afro-Latino letter within an Afro-Cuban column is Urrutia's attitude toward Schomburg's writing—that is, to his letter-writing in English, an Afro-Latino textual condition that, like Carrillo's novel, confirms the fear of an English-language taint. Urrutia tells readers that "Mr. Arthur Schomburg . . . hardly remembered Spanish" (*apenas recordaba el castellano*), and he emphasizes the point by remarking, just before quoting "the translation of this letter," that it has arrived "written in English," a "detail that urges us to push forward with the reconquest." Here, Urrutia's satire slips from an Afro-Cuban "conquest" of the United States to a "reconquest" of Afro-Latinas/os that, recalling the interview with Serra seven years earlier, would discipline an English-writing/speaking Afro-Latina/o by exposing his or her private writing/speech to the public, "on the avenues of Havana," translated back into its "rightful" language, Spanish. However tongue-in-cheek, in other words, the column would bring under control the linguistic promiscuity of the Afro-Latino United States, which implies not only a "loss" of Spanish among Afro-Latinas/os subject to English-language influences in the United States but the emergence of multilingual Afro-Latino identities, cultures, and politics shaped by contacts with Anglophone, African American history and experience—as was the case, of course, with Schomburg.[23]

The Urrutia-Schomburg text revises the commonplace heard during the early twentieth century that "Spanish-speaking Negroes from Latin America" in Harlem are "distinct because of their language" and have "but little contact with the English-speaking [black] majority."[24] It invites us, in fact, to reflect on how the subjects of such Spanish-speaking "distinctions" are themselves racialized in relation to their "contact," however little or great, with the "English-speaking [black] majorities" in the United States—how, in other words, Afro-Latinas/os manage their racialization by vocalizing themselves in certain ways across the multilinguistic spaces of the United States. "From time to time," for example, "one may see a very dark Negro who will be speaking Spanish more loudly than the rest" because "he does not wish to be mistaken for an American Negro."[25] It is a matter of racialization that involves white *latinidad* as well—the "rest" implied in the passage. For instance, such an Afro-Latino practice of speaking (and, by extension, writing) aloud one's racial identity, only now in an opposite way, is familiar among white Latinas/os: These "light-skinned" Latinas/os "would *avoid* speaking Spanish for fear of being outed" as Cuban American or mainland Puerto Rican, which would carry with it, as I have stated, the menacing possibility of a "blackening" in the Anglo-U.S. gaze.[26] Indeed, in a different way, there were those occasions when silence itself, the absence of spoken language in a social field so plotted by its racial effects, would signify in ways comparable to the Hispanophone loudness of "a very dark Negro," in particular among African Americans manipulating the contradictions of race in the Americas to invest themselves with the privileges accorded by a divide-and-conquer Anglo-U.S. racism to the more "acceptable" blackness of Afro-Latinas/os. Graciela Pérez, the great Afro-Cuban American singer of La Anacaona and Machito and His Afro-Cubans, better known simply as Graciela, tells how, during gigs of the Afro-Cubans in the mid-1940s in Miami and Miami Beach, the baritone saxophonist Leslie Johnakins, an African American member of the band, would respond in silence—"*no contestaba*" (he didn't respond)—when spoken to by Anglo whites, lest he compromise his position as a presumed Afro-Cuban American crossing spaces of U.S. white supremacy otherwise off limits to African Americans. The reason, according to Graciela, was simple: "Tu sabes que ellos no creían que los hispanos son negros, sino que nada más los negros americanos. ¡Mira si eran brutos!" (You know they didn't think Hispanics were black, only black Americans. How stupid they were!).[27]

These embodied expressions of race and the multilinguistic, in and of themselves and as figures for the literary and performance voices of Afro-Cuban Americans, frame my work in the following pages. They demonstrate the mutual instantiation of Afro-Latino, African American, and white-Latino identities in the context of hemispheric logics of white-supremacist, colonial domination: whether one is white enough or the right kind of white, or less black or the right kind of black, to receive or be denied rights and advantages, based on how one speaks (or does not) in English, Spanish, or both. When Guillén frets over Consuelo Serra's possible English-influenced vocality deriving from her time in the United States, when the Afro-boricua Schomburg writes a letter in English from Harlem to the Afro-Cuban Urrutia in Havana, who then translates it into Spanish—when these things happen, something of the racializing logic of the multilinguistic, scriptive now and sonic, underlies the exchanges. Indeed, a text such as "Imperialismo afrocubano" suggests the possibility that an Afro-Latino in the United States, writing in English, will be "mistaken for an American Negro," while an Afro-Cuban in Cuba, writing in "Spanish more loudly than the rest," will not. The great Afro-Cuban musician and brother-in-law to Graciela, Mario Bauzá, crystallizes the experience of Afro-Cuban Americans in such modalities of the multilinguistic. Like Graciela, he arrives on the page through the genre of the tape-recorded interview. Speaking in English, Bauzá recalls a return to Cuba from New York City during the early twentieth century. He had gone to the U.S. consulate in Havana to obtain a visa for his wife. Upon hearing him speak, the (presumably Anglo-white) consular representative remarked, "You don't sound like a Cuban. You sound like a Cuban from Harlem." Bauzá's response: "That's exactly where I learned my English. On the streets of Harlem."[28]

Unbecoming Blackness contributes through Latino and African-diaspora literary and cultural studies to the critical conversation on Cuban racial identity on the island and in the United States across a variety of disciplines. It pushes this conversation further with its attention to the importance of afrolatinidad; its recovery, through performance texts, of an Afro-Cuban American modernism; and its highlighting the techniques of a post-1959 Cuban American literature in the representation of race as both Afro-Cuban American and white Cuban American. In history and social science, there is a longstanding commitment to the analysis of Afro-Cuban conditions on the island that I hope this book will complement.[29] Another area of dialogue is the tradition of Afro-Hispanist literary criticism, which emerged in the United States during the civil-rights and black cultural-nationalism eras among African American, Afro-Caribbean, and Afro-Latino critics who sought an idiom to discern the aesthetic and political differences between the works of Afro–Latin American and white Latin American writers on racial "themes," a project that, informed as well by an earlier _Négritude_, often asserted a "black" Latin American literary culture over the claims of _mestizaje_ and "_negrismo_," the tradition of white writers representing black subjects. In many ways, a discussion of afrolatinidad remembers the high era of Afro-Hispanism in the 1970s, even as the U.S. location of our Afro-Latino texts shifts our conversation beyond black/_mestizaje_ cultural oppositions in Latin American nationalism toward a recognition of how Afro-_Latinas/os_, as writers and performers in English, Spanish, or both represent the simultaneity of their racialization in the Anglo and Latino United States: in the case of Cubans of African descent, their (un)becoming Afro-Cuban American(ness) in relation to African Americans, other Afro-Latinas/os, and white Latinas/os, a condition of U.S. racial, "ethnic," and "minority" experience that may yet engage island-based *mestizaje*/postracial nationalisms, now as a memory (if not a revision) proper to a transnational Afro-Latino culture.[30] To be sure, Afro-Hispanism engages a tradition of literary criticism on island Afro-Cuban writers by island Afro-Cuban intellectuals after the revolution whose arguments, while committed to the nation-state, are hardly reducible to postracial, *mestizaje*, or "raceless"-revolutionary apology.[31] Meanwhile, a growing area of study, one in which this book situates itself directly, concerns the place of Afro-Cubans in the United States. Leading the way have been scholars in history and social science, with the early 1970s essays of Lourdes Casal serving not just as a backdrop here but as a stimulating point of reference for recent work by Nancy Mirabal, Susan Greenbaum, and Frank Guridy.[32] Related to this is the research on Afro-Latinas/os in U.S. music and sports cultures from the early twentieth century to the present.[33] These inquiries into Afro-Cuban Americanness all relate to recent announcements of an overt Afro-Latino commitment in an array of multidisciplinary scholarship, none more so than in Miriam Jiménez Román and Juan Flores's *The Afro-Latin@ Reader: History and Culture in the United States*, a volume that extends Flores's longstanding effort in the area, characterized well, for the purposes of this introduction, in his recognition that the "Cuban–Puerto Rican continuum . . . is intimately associated with blackness in the U.S. context."[34] Finally, as a work also in Cuban American literary and cultural studies, this book foregrounds the other experience of an Afro-Cuban American literature and performance to add to the insights of Rodrigo Lazo, Ricardo Ortiz, and Laura Lomas in their recent publications on the movements—around the hemisphere, within the United States—of Cuban American literary and print cultures in the nineteenth and twentieth centuries.[35]

In the first part of the book, I present archival research to evidence an Afro-Cuban American modernism in performance. I draw on perspectives in African-diaspora studies regarding the archive, whose material and discursive conditions, in the context of the plantation system in the Americas, Édouard Glissant limns: "The obligation to get around the [plantation's] rule of silence," he writes, "gives rise everywhere to a literature that has no 'natural' continuity, if one may put it that way, but rather bursts forth in torn-off fragments [*fragments arrachés*]."[36] Such *fragments arrachés* are material, seen and felt in the manuscripts of an archival box, heard in the sounds of a performance recorded on tape. They take immaterial form, too, in that they intimate the "discursive system that governs and regulates the production and appearance"[37] of African-diasporic knowledge across the slavery and postslavery institutions of the Americas. Chapter 1 discusses the *fragments arrachés* of Alberto O'Farrill, the blackface actor and writer who appeared on the *teatro bufo* (Cuban minstrelsy) stage at the Apolo and Campoamor theaters in Harlem and in the New York City Latino newspapers *La Prensa* (as a subject of reviews) and *El Gráfico* (as a writer) from the 1920s to the 1930s. I tell the story of O'Farrill's arrival in the United States via Key West and how it appeared to allow him a career (otherwise closed off in Cuba) in the transnational *teatro bufo*—by then a belated, however popular, form of troubling racial representation. The traces in *La Prensa* of O'Farrill's "*negro*-on-*negro*" performances in Cuban American versions of the *teatro bufo* at the Apolo evince an awareness of his afrolatinidad. In his own autobiographical-fictional writings in *Gráfico*, an important Latino publication of the period, O'Farrill goes further: he produces an Afro-Latino "blackface print culture" that conflicts with the culturalist, postracial assumptions of a *raza hispana* (Hispanic race), the pan-Latino ideology of the day. I finish the chapter with a reflection on O'Farrill's performance in *No matarás* (Thou Shalt Not Kill), a 1935 film that emerges from his work on the Campoamor stage and offers a rare glimpse of his moving, speaking, indeed, singing and dancing body. Chapter 2 recovers Eusebia Cosme, the poetry performer and actress. By 1938, Cosme was famous in the Hispanophone Caribbean for her stagings of *poesía negra* (black poetry), the verse of predominantly white and mixed-race men that sought to represent the popular cultures and identities of Afro–Latin Americans. Yet, in August of that very year, Cosme migrated to the United States, where she spent the majority of her life, a sign, I suggest, of the way in which an Afro-Cuban woman such as herself dealt with the scarcity of career opportunities on the island. Her performances in the United States pushed *poesía negra* beyond its own belated situation over the course of the 1940s, which I recollect in radio scripts and the trace of a sound recording—a career that benefited, in particular, from Cosme's contacts with African Americans through print-culture spaces such as the *Chicago Defender*, relationships with such figures as Langston Hughes, and in venues such as the auditorium of Washington, DC's Armstrong High School, all of which occasioned Cosme's afrolatinidad, in tension with island-Cuban representations of her racial identity, including Fernando Ortiz's "*mulata*" appellation. To emphasize the history and politics of my critical recovery, I offer the remarks of the Anglo-white woman who "discovered" a poststroke, disabled Cosme in Mexico City and was responsible for gathering her effects and sending them to the Schomburg Center for Research in Black Culture, at the New York Public Library, an itinerary I follow as well in the alternative path that Cosme's own body took to Miami, where she died in 1976. A major element of Cosme's biography is her admission into a film career late in life, first in Sydney Lumet's *The Pawnbroker* and later in Mexican productions, most famously in *El derecho de nacer* (The Right to Be Born), which I attend to as examples, however loaded, of Cosme's admirable commitment to finding and doing work in the arts, against the odds.

In the subsequent three chapters, the second part of the book, I examine the signs of race in Cuban American writing and popular culture after the midcentury. Chapter 3 sees in the way Afro-Cuban Americans identify—indeed, pass—as mainland Afro–Puerto Ricans still another turn in the discourses of afrolatinidad. Central here is how such "boricua identifications" appear in the secondary works of major Afro-Cuban American figures or in secondary ways of reading their most recognized works: the elements of a "supplementary career." Thus, the 1940s publications on Afro-Cuban religion by the anthropologist Rómulo Lachatañeré become significant in a new way when seen through the archival remnants of their voyage through the peer-review process, where Lachatañeré manages the U.S. institutions of an anthropology on the African diaspora in a way that gestures toward his afrolatinidad. With Lachatañeré, an Afro-Latino identity and professional interest become increasingly associated with mainland Puerto Ricans, culminating in his secondary career in photography, particularly in the photographic documentation of Puerto Ricans in Harlem and on the island of Puerto Rico itself, the journey to which ended in a tragic boricua identification: Lachatañeré's death in an airplane crash off San Juan in 1952. As literary narrative, a boricua identification intensifies in *Down These Mean Streets* by Piri Thomas, whose Afro-Cuban American father appears in the text as a mainland Afro–Puerto Rican, a sign of the exigencies of the 1960s "ethnic-literature" book market and of U.S.-imperial relations between Cubans and Puerto Ricans, marked by amicability and enmity. Chapter 4 turns to the period and texts around 1979 in Miami and the overlapping histories of the illicit drug trade, African American uprising, Mariel migration, and my family. In a personal-critical narrative, I consider how the presence of Afro-Cubans in the Mariel migration panicked the old-guard Cuban exile regarding its (purchase on) Cuban American whiteness. A spicsploitative response to Mariel appeared in the 1983 film *Scarface*, which put its lead actor, Al Pacino, in brownface, as the Mariel migrant Antonio Montana, a minstrel moment whose lineage involves the Jewish American Paul Muni's Italianface performance in the 1932 version of the film and, moving forward in time, African American and Afro-Cuban American appropriations of Montana in rap music, which amplified the Cuban exile's original fear. These acts of a *Scarface* minstrelsy, as the seeming idolizing of the drug-violence corpse of Antonio Montana, commemorate other corpses as well, such as that of Arthur McDuffie, the African American whose murder by the police led to the 1980 African American "riot." Cuban American whiteness is the focus of chapter 5, in which autobiographical narratives of a voyage back to Cuba during the post-Soviet 1990s by white, middle-class, Cuban American academics lead to a return to the family house left behind, now lived in by island Afro-Cubans. This trope of the "Afro-Cuban-occupied house" seems to leave us with yet another representation of Afro-Cubans in the white Cuban American text; in fact, it discloses Cuban American whiteness and its basis, textured here by the complexities of the autobiographical plot, in social and economic privilege. A counternarrative of an Afro-Cuban American return to the island, the video *Cuban Roots/ Bronx Stories*, further frays the edges of going back in the Cuban American imaginary. In the conclusion, I look to someone who very much has become a recognizable figure in our discussions of Afro-Cuban American literature, Evelio Grillo, the author of *Black Cuban, Black American: A Memoir*. With my interview of Grillo, and with an examination of the unheralded antecedents of his book, I suggest what may remain as we search forward and back in afrolatinidad.

1 /   Alberto O'Farrill: A *Negrito* in Harlem

In an April 1929 edition of the *Diario de la Marina*, two essays appeared side by side in "Ideales de una Raza": "El teatro cubano" (Cuban Theater), published by Gustavo Urrutia in "Armonías," and "El camino de Harlem" (The Road to Harlem) by Nicolás Guillén. In "Teatro," Urrutia calls for a "modern Cuban theater" in which actors and actresses of "our race" (*nuestra raza*) would appear in roles as "cultured and patriotic blacks [*negros cultos y patriotas*], full of dignity." Urrutia hopes such a theater would challenge not only the contemporary Cuban blackface stage but also the influence of other dramatic works whose settings "in slavery" seem particularly "belated" (*tardía*) and possibly even "harmful to the harmony of the two Cuban races [*las dos razas cubanas*]." Advocating on behalf of "Cuba's colored race" (*la raza de color en Cuba*) is also the idea behind Guillén's "Camino." Guillén cites incidents across the island in which "whites and blacks [*los blancos y los negros*] stroll on public streets" within separate spaces, the "violation of which by anyone," but "most of all by blacks, gives rise to true conflicts." Cuba, he warns, might soon develop a specific, unwanted characteristic of "certain Yankee regions [*ciertas regiones yankees*]," a "'black neighborhood' ["*barrio negro*"]" in each of its cities and towns. "That," he concludes, "is the road to Harlem": a movement toward U.S.-style segregation, the notion of which is intensified in the translation of "El camino *de* [*of*] Harlem" into "The Road *to* Harlem."[1]

The link between race, modern theater aesthetics, and hemispheric space matters in Urrutia and Guillén introduces the broad theme of the first part of this book: the movement of performance and print cultures from Cuba to the United States among Afro-Cubans between the 1920s and 1940s. Afro-Cuban actors, poetry reciters, and literary journalists in the United States challenge Guillén's "*barrio negro*" as a primary metaphor for the Afro-Cuban apprehension of segregated Anglo-U.S. geographies, producing instead their own Afro-Latino representations of the experience of race (and spatialization) in the United States, one in which they risk an identification as African-diasporic subjects. The texts of a U.S. "*barrio afrolatino*," against Guillén's island-oriented *barrio negro*, invoke the spatial and temporal multiplicity specific to the modern performance and print cultures of Afro-Cubans in the United States: the many overlapping periods and barrios of African American, Afro-Latino, and Jewish Harlems, as we shall see, along with their institutional locations in theaters, social clubs, and university halls, as well as in print genres such as the newspaper review and the chronicle.[2] In such an Afro-Latino reconception of the *barrio negro*, the multiple negros/as of African diaspora in the United States overlap with early twentieth-century discourses on Cuban race: postracial notions of a Cuba in which "racial differences [are] irrelevant," counterstrategies among "black and mulatto activists [and intellectuals]" of using "'blackness' as a political category," and *mestizaje* ideas "in literary, artistic, and touristic circles."[3] In a U.S. *barrio afrolatino*, in other words, Afro-Cuban writers and performers articulate Cuban race and nation—and, in particular, the Cuban *negra/o, mulata/o,* and *raza de color*[4]—with the U.S. Negro, colored, and black; the "West Indian"; and other *afrolatinidades*, in particular that of mainland Afro–Puerto Ricans.

Afro-Cuban writers and performers were a part of the larger Cuban migrations of the 1930s and 1940s to the United States, migrations that "were smaller in number than the pre-1898 and post-1959 migrations" yet "significant . . . because they attracted not only Afro-Cuban political migrants but also economic migrants who tended to settle in large urban areas like New York City."[5] These Afro-Cubans left the island around a time of ongoing struggles over racial justice that overlapped with the Great Depression and the violence of the Machado dictatorship (including its overthrow with the revolution of 1933), and they encountered on arrival in New York City a shifting Latino scene: whereas at the turn of the century, Puerto Ricans, Cubans, Spaniards, and others of Latin American descent lived in the vicinity of cigar factories in the Lower East Side and Chelsea, by the middle of the 1920s, Latino New York City was primarily Puerto Rican and working class in population, with communities located along the Brooklyn waterfront and, in "the largest and most significant of all the inter-wars settlements," in Harlem, from 110th Street to 125th Street between Fifth Avenue and Manhattan Avenue, including blocks on the East Side stretching down to 90th Street.[6] Latinas/os in New York City participated in local labor and civil-rights activism, and they engaged in global politics critical of the Machadato in Cuba and of U.S. imperialism in Puerto Rico and Nicaragua. Support among them for the Republican side during the Spanish Civil War was significant, too.[7]

In what follows, I discuss the careers of two figures in the performance and print cultures of Afro-Cubans in the early twentieth-century United States: Alberto O'Farrill (in the present chapter) and Eusebia Cosme (in chapter 2). O'Farrill was a blackface actor in the *teatro bufo*, a genre of Cuban theater in which he performed in New York City, beginning in the mid-1920s. O'Farrill himself wrote *bufos* and was a contributor of literary-journalistic writing to the Harlem-based, Spanish-language weekly *El Gráfico*, of which, for a time, he was a director. He also appeared in the 1935 film *No matarás (Mi hermano es un gangster)* (Thou Shalt Not Kill [My Brother is a Gangster]), produced on location in Harlem and in studios in Hollywood by Miguel Contreras Torres, the Mexican director. Cosme was a major performer of *"poesía negra"* (black poetry), a poetic movement emerging in the late 1920s whose writers, predominantly *mulatos* and white men from the Hispanophone Caribbean, drew on representations of musical, religious, and spoken-language expression among working-class Afro-Cubans (and other Hispanophone, African-diasporic people) to imagine a poetry both modern and "authentic" to the region. Cosme arrived in New York City in 1938, and she continued performing *poesía negra* and other verse forms, both on stage and over the radio across CBS's Cadena de las Américas (Network of the Americas). In later years, she had roles in theater and film, including Sidney Lumet's *The Pawnbroker* (1965).

I argue in these two opening chapters that the careers of O'Farrill and Cosme, once lost but now the objects of recovery through the archive, research, and publication, reveal a late, untimely logic—a "belatedness"— that constitutes the literary and performance cultures of Afro-Cubans in the United States in the early twentieth century. Such a genealogy of Afro-Cuban American literature and performance between 1898 and 1959 reflects a postcolonial understanding of temporality: of the way in which the colonized, imputed a premodern "pastness" by the colonizer, responds with a consciousness of his or her own alternative historicity, one that exists in a coeval (and, thus, critical) relation with the modernity and coloniality of time.[8] The *fragments arrachés* of O'Farrill and Cosme, collected in the archive, engage belatedness in ways that depart from Urrutia's claim in "El teatro cubano" that the representation of slavery on the Cuban stage is negatively *tardía* and thus worthy of rejection. For O'Farrill, it is blackface theater's very belatedness during the period, politically and artistically, that, far from rejecting, he engages—an engagement influenced by O'Farrill's limited career prospects as an Afro-Cuban actor and refracted in his writings in *Gráfico*, which emerges as a site of what I call an Afro-Cuban *blackface print culture*, a material and discursive space in which O'Farrill explored the limits of a *raza hispana* (Hispanic race) ideology. For Cosme, engaging *poesía negra*, itself belated politically and artistically after 1938, indexes her own professional vulnerability as an African-diasporic woman working in performance; it structures, too, the commonplace that she was the greatest *intérprete* of *poesía negra*, which underscores a tension in the Spanish-language definition of "interpreter" between Cosme's role, on the one hand, as a *performer* of the poetry of *mulato* and white men and, on the other, as a *hermeneut* with the authority to analyze and revise the texts of these self-same poets—a tension with Cosme around race, gender, interpretation, and authorship that, as we shall see in the next chapter, well describes the scholar's fraught encounter with the *fragments arrachés* of her archive at the Schomburg Center for Research in Black Culture. Now, however, I consider in detail such issues in an Afro-Cuban American literary and performance history by turning to the career and texts of Alberto O'Farrill, beginning with the circumstances of his U.S. arrival.

The "African," the *Bufo*, and Blackface Print Culture

In September 1925, Alberto Heliodoro O'Farrill Gavito arrived in Key West, Florida, from Havana, Cuba, aboard the SS *Governor Cobb*. Several decades removed from Key West's history as a Cuban center with an active role in the independence movement, it was still a town with a Cuban presence. The ship's "List or Manifest of Alien Passengers" states that O'Farrill was a twenty-six-year-old man from the town of Santa Clara; his "nationality (Country of which citizen or subject)" was "Cuba." O'Farrill was one of only two "alien" passengers on the ship that day. His "calling or occupation" was "photographer," which was written in hand over the typed word "mer[chant]." The manifest also attested to his literacy: he could read and write in Spanish. O'Farrill's last permanent residence was on the Calzada de Jesús del Monte in Havana, and his final destination was New York City. Also in the manifest was a column entitled "Race or people," which included a footnote: "List of races will be found on the back of this sheet." The other "alien" passenger aboard the *Governor Cobb* that day, himself a "citizen or subject" of Cuba, was a certain Luis Alfaro, who was identified under "Race or people" as "Cuban." The way in which O'Farrill, also a "citizen or subject" of Cuba, was himself identified under "Race or people" is another matter, one which invests his very arrival in the United States with the contradictions of race and nation in the Americas: under "Race or people," the manifest listed O'Farrill as "African."[9]

Upon O'Farrill's Key West arrival, therefore, he encountered U.S. racialization as an African-diasporic migrant from Cuba. Unlike his fellow passenger, a "Cuban" twice over in terms of "nationality" and "race or people"—a doubling with multiple implications: it subsumes Cuban whiteness under "Cuban race"; it affirms, however unintentionally, the notion of a postracial "Cuban people"—O'Farrill's identity is both Cuban and excessive to Cuba: he is a "citizen or subject" of the Cuban nation-state who also belongs to an "African race," an "African people." As an "African," O'Farrill's identity aligns with African American histories of U.S. "naturalization," particularly those in which the term "African" signifies identities in legal regimes such as the postbellum Nationality Act, which granted "the right to naturalize to 'persons of African nativity or descent,'" even as such "persons" continued to live with "the social stigma and unequal status associated with blackness."[10] An "African" identity thus invokes histories of (il)legal U.S. inclusion and exclusion framed by the way "race and nationality disaggregated and realigned in new and uneven ways" during the period.[11] It is such an "African" identity that marks O'Farrill's difference as an Afro-Cuban migrant in the United States.

Also coming to Key West that September was the Arango-Moreno theater company, led by two white men, Guillermo Moreno and Rafael de Arango. The Arango-Moreno was a Cuban blackface company. The coincidence is striking. In the 1930s, O'Farrill would appear on the New York City stage with Moreno. Now, however, having just arrived in the United States—in all likelihood to improve his chances of working in Cuban blackface—O'Farrill would have found in the visiting Arango-Moreno an occasion to consider the relation between Cuban racial identity and theatrical career opportunities, particularly if he came across a copy of *Florida: Semenario Independiente,* a Key West newspaper touting the upcoming performances with a full-body photograph of de Arango himself, in blackface, with a caption inviting "the people of Key West to the big event tomorrow, Sunday, at the San Carlos" hall.[12] De Arango was an important Cuban blackface actor of the early twentieth century, belonging in a list that begins with Arquímedes Pous and includes, among others, white Cuban men such as Sergio Acebal, Ramón Espígul, and Enrique "Bernabé" Arredondo.[13] Indeed, blackface roles in Cuban theater were almost exclusively "played by white actors," an element in the political economy of Cuban blackface inseparable from the way in which Afro-Cubans "were systematically denied employment in the theater" during the early twentieth century, well into "the 1950s," and "even today."[14] The *Florida* photograph of de Arango, advertising his company's run at the San Carlos, is a multilayered, transnational Cuban text that complements the "List or Manifest of Alien Passengers," locating O'Farrill's U.S. arrival in the context of Cuban blackface professional practices, in which white faces, much more than black, *mulato,* or "African" ones, were able to earn a living covered in cork.[15]

Alberto O'Farrill was a nearly unknown figure in critical history until his appearance in Nicolás Kanellos's field-defining research in the areas of Latino theater and periodicals. In *A History of Hispanic Theatre* and *Hispanic Periodicals in the United States, Origins to 1960,* Kanellos's extensive reading of the New York City Latino press reveals how O'Farrill was a "ubiquitous" blackface performer in "all the major Hispanic stages in New York's stock and itinerant companies" and worked on *Gráfico* as an editor, writer, and even cartoonist.[16] Such scholarship has brought O'Farrill into the orbit of the Recovering the U.S. Hispanic Literary Heritage Project—in particular, his appearance in *Herencia: The Anthology of Hispanic Literature of the United States* (2002). *Herencia* includes a *Gráfico* column of O'Farrill's. The accompanying biographical note, however, fails to mention his Afro-Cuban identity or role in blackface, thereby missing an opportunity to reflect on how O'Farrill's representation of "the social and labor conditions of Hispanic immigrants in the city" also involves Anglo and Latino histories and conceptions of race.[17] Kanellos's critical work recognizes O'Farrill's Afro-Cuban identity and career in blackface and speculates on his interest in "Afro-Cuban culture, religion, and music."[18] Ultimately, however, Kanellos treats Afro-Cuban history and identity in O'Farrill as a thematic concern, an approach which casts race and nation in the Americas, at best, as a topic that comes and goes in the work. My focus, informed by the Key West convergence of an

"African" O'Farrill and a blackface de Arango, demonstrates how race and nation in the Americas, more than just a theme in O'Farrill's work, in fact constitute it. In this light, I understand O'Farrill's newspaper writings and theater performances in the United States as phenomena of an Afro-Cuban *blackface print culture*, a term that describes how blackface logics shape O'Farrill's print forms—their production, content, and circulation. Of significance, too, is how such interrelated theater and print texts mediate understandings of Cuban American race specific not only to a dominant Latino public but also to an Afro-Latino counterpublic, one with a possible critical relation to power.[19]

O'Farrill's Afro-Cuban blackface print culture turns on the Cuban *teatro bufo* (comic theater), the primary location of Cuban blackface expression. Emerging in the mid-nineteenth century, the *teatro bufo* derives from popular Spanish theater forms and the realist literature of *costumbrismo* (local custom), with influences from U.S. minstrelsy; it incorporates acting, music, and dance in its "parody of blacks and black street culture," including forms of "improper" Afro-Cuban speech.[20] Jill Lane shows that the *bufo*, "as a central vehicle for the expression of *mestizaje* as national ideology," shaped anticolonial politics between 1868 and 1895, a peak era of the genre, during which it exhibited "a coherence organized around a discourse of race, nation, and colonial power that is absent from other forms of vernacular theater."[21] The *bufo* featured three main characters: the *gallego* (Galician), a Spanish-immigrant man, often a policeman or merchant, typically portrayed with a thick, Spanish accent; the *mulata*, "at once a pathologized figure of dangerous racial encroachment ('Africanization'), a miscegenating temptress, and a symbol of the innocent, tropical Cuba to be rescued from the lascivious Spanish imperialist"—the aforementioned *gallego*; and the *negrito*, "a manifestly racist caricature of black people by white actors" and the "most popular stage character in the nineteenth century and well into the twentieth."[22] The diminutive suffix *-ito*, added to *negro*, renders *negrito* ("little black man"), "a common racialized epithet" suggestive of an "endearment between white and especially black Cubans," one that is "never free of the infantilizing, patronizing connotation that 'little' carries when applied to an adult black male."[23] In *bufo* performances, often in the form of a *sainete* (one-act play), the "*negrito* is typically depicted as a hustler, trying to cheat customers and making sexual advances to all *mulatas* and light-skinned women." The *negrito*, therefore, "his occupation depicted as subservient, criminal, or nonexistent," "occupies the lowest social and cultural rung relative to other figures, even in twentieth-century productions."[24] It is such a figure of Afro-Cuban masculinity that in the late nineteenth century "came to stand in for a national sentiment whose primary attribute was a celebrated racial diversity" and that in the early twentieth led the way for the bufo's "political commentary" critical of successive Cuban governments.[25]

By the time O'Farrill began performing the negrito on the New York City stage in the mid-1920s, the belatedness of the teatro bufo in Cuba, in terms of its viability and politics, had become apparent. While performances in the genre did indeed continue—and while elements of blackface have endured in other Cuban expressive contexts across the twentieth century and into the present—it was evident that during the 1930s the bufo seemed about "to succumb," when it was "only traveling companies in the interior of the republic" that seemed to be performing it.[26] By "the beginning of 1930," writes one critic, with the Machadato, the Great Depression, and the consolidation of radio and sound cinema, bufo works had begun losing their "encanto criollo" (national enchantment).[27] Writers and intellectuals of the period reflected an awareness of this. In 1935, the white Cuban poet Emilio Ballagas stamped bufo performances as out-of-date, remarking that "only ten years ago the black man was a beauty mark in bufo works [el negro era un lunar decorativo]," in contrast to current (and "better") representations of Afro-Cubans in the subsequent poesía negra. Consuelo Serra, meanwhile, challenged the representation of the "eternal negrito catedrático," proclaiming in 1935 that to endorse a bufo-inspired national culture was not how one "uplifts a race or builds a nation" (ni se eleva una raza ni se construye patria).[28] In the case of Havana's most famous bufo venue of the time, the Alhambra theater, the lapse was literal: the Alhambra building, a male-only space, collapsed in 1935, marking an end to its particular brand of bufo, which extended the genre's racial, gender, and sexual dynamics through the use of "burlesque and sometimes pornographic" elements.[29]

O'Farrill's career in New York City is attributable to the bufo's belated condition. As an Afro-Cuban man seeking work in the theater, his migrating to the United States was likely a reprieve from chronic unemployment on the island. Indeed, O'Farrill's stage negrito in New York City, together with the character's print counterpart in Gráfico, exploits the very belatedness of bufo performance, setting back O'Farrill's career even as it moves forward. This is to say that, in New York City, the bufo's tardy, island incarnation becomes an emerging Latino form, one in which, as Raymond Williams has observed of the emergent, "new meanings and values, new practices, new relationships and kinds of relationship are continually being created."[30] The music historian Ruth Glasser details such emerging creativity in the *bufo*-centric New York City Latino performance cultures of the 1920s and 1930s. The "theatrical forms best known to the primarily working-class" Latino groups, she writes, "were not the zarzuela or the Spanish drama but the *bufos cubanos*." She continues, "While they sometimes featured companies visiting from Cuba, the *bufos* also incorporated a variety of Latino artists, including dancers, acrobats, magicians, *conjuntos*, *orquestas*, and a surprising number of operatic singers." They also "used local talent, drew upon *older forms* familiar to at least Caribbean Hispanics, and provided an opportunity for New York's Spanish-speaking population both to unite physically and to humorously comment upon the divisions and power relations between them."[31]

O'Farrill's blackface work exemplifies such an emerging, localized culture of Latino performance in the way it references prior Cuban *bufo* forms to project the racial dimensions of *latinidad* in early twentieth-century New York City. Important here is the signal irony of O'Farrill's performance: his identity as an Afro-Cuban man in blackface. Approaches to "black-on-black minstrelsy" in the United States, especially in discussions of Bert Williams, born in Nassau, the British West Indies (today the Bahamas), acknowledge a critical tradition of rejecting the practice as "pathological" or politically regressive, even while recognizing how it "mediates and silently complicates the institutionalized dynamics of black and white through a form of intra-racial and cross-cultural signifying."[32] In the Anglo United States, in other words, black-on-black minstrelsy heightens the situation of African American performance in the nineteenth and early twentieth centuries generally: it "was often a product of self-commodification, a way of getting along in a constricted world," one that, in terms of performance markets, was marked by Anglo whites' "greater access to public distribution (and profit)."[33] In the Latino United States, the practice of a "*negro*-on-*negro* *bufo*" betrays its own, not entirely unrelated, dynamics, a way into which is offered by Rosendo Rosell, the white Cuban performer, composer, and writer who was active in radio, stage, television, and film in Cuba before 1959 and, later, in Miami. Remembering Afro-Cuban actors in blackface during the 1940s and 1950s "such as Roger Liver, the *negrito* Giovanni, and the *negrito* Silva," Rosell remarks that they were all "real *negritos*" (*negritos de verdad*), "but they painted themselves with burnt cork to come out on stage ...?" (*pero se pintaban con corcho quemado para salir a escena ...¿?*).[34] The ellipsis and question marks, original in the text, suggest that the notion of *"negritos de verdad"* is most generative in its seeming incomprehensibility. For one thing, the punctuation marks recall that Cuban racial identity, as a social and political construct, exists *"de verdad"* (really, in truth) only en route to performance, *"para salir a escena,"* which is to say, it is *de verdad* only to the extent that its orientation is also *"de mentira"* (fake, a lie). Further, like Urrutia in "El teatro cubano," Rosell clarifies an aspect of Cuban theater in general and the *bufo* in particular across the twentieth century: namely, that a *negrito de verdad*, one not covered in burnt cork, would likely find it difficult, if not impossible, in market and ideological terms, to land a role either within or beyond the *bufo* sphere. Indeed, with respect to white Cuban performers and Cuban whiteness, Rosell's punctuation marks sound a note of alarm over the possible loss of market and ideological supremacy in relation to the semiotics of Cuban race should an Afro-Cuban actor worry the boundary between *de verdad* and *de mentira* by performing the *negrito*—or any other role—without burnt cork. Even as O'Farrill's performances resolved these Cuban "institutionalized dynamics of black and white," they prompt, by virtue of his U.S.-situated Afro-Cuban blackface persona, an Afro-Latino revision of the argument regarding white-Cuban blackface: that, "in Cuba, whites occupy the space of blackness to imagine their nation as mestizo."[35] In the United States, rather, the Afro-Cuban O'Farrill occupies the space of blackness not so much to imagine the Cuban nation as *mestizo* or even *negro* (two possibilities nevertheless) as to invoke a Cuban blackness beyond the symbolic exigencies of Cuban nationalism, articulating it, instead, with formations of an early twentieth-century U.S. *latinidad*—its multiple audiences, cultures, markets—which O'Farrill thereby marks, in the *negrito* aftermath of his migration to the United States, as "African," Afro-Cuban, Afro-Latino. To consider the details of O'Farrill's blackface print culture, I turn now to his early years on the New York City stage and his writings in *Gráfico*.

Moreno Moments

From the summer of 1926 to the spring of 1931, O'Farrill performed in blackface in over fifty different plays in Harlem. Most of these were *bufos*, with O'Farrill playing the *negrito* opposite the *gallego* and the *mulata*, though often he appeared just in duets with one or the other of the characters. He also acted in blackface in zarzuela and *revsita* (revue) productions.[36] The most important commercial-theater space in which O'Farrill performed during these years was the Teatro Apolo. It was the Apolo, which had begun "featuring Hispanic comedies, variety, and Cuban musical farces intermittently on Sunday in March 1926," that "was to fix and systematize what became distinctive of New York Hispanic theatrical culture: balancing the theatre and entertainments of the diverse Hispanic nationalities for the working-class audiences," which involved "alternating Spanish, Cuban, and Puerto Rican shows" and "integrating lyric theatre with vaudeville and musical revues."[37] Of further significance is the Apolo's location itself on 125th Street, a key place in the shifting relations among African Americans, Latinas/os, and Anglo whites in the entertainment industry. Ruth Glasser writes that the "Spanish-language shows started at a time when the major movie and stage show theaters of Harlem were owned by a handful of white, mostly Jewish men who were battling for dominance of the local entertainment scene." In the absence of white performers, who in increased numbers had begun working on Broadway with its higher salaries, theater owners on 125th Street turned to African American artists and audiences. The street thus changed from a mostly "Irish strip" to, by the early 1930s, an African American and Latino space of the entertainment industry.[38]

The Apolo-era *bufo*, in the form of scripts or sound recordings, is lost, to the best of my knowledge, but its effects in print culture remain, offering a glimpse of O'Farrill's stage *negrito*. For *La Prensa*, founded in 1913 "to serve the community of mostly Spanish and Cuban immigrants in and around Manhattan's 14th Street,"[39] O'Farrill's *negrito* was disruptive of the idea behind the newspaper as "el órgano de la raza" (the organ of the race), a key discursive site of *latinidad* during the period.[40] The *raza* in question—the *raza hispana* (Hispanic race)—is "the widespread notion of a single Ibero-American race," which "gained currency" "in the wake of the Spanish-American War of 1898," emphasizing "Latin-related cultural values in opposition to the Nordic tradition that the U.S. presumably represented."[41] *Raza hispana*, in short, represented a "view of race . . . more akin to ethnicity, culture, or national origin."[42] However, like *gente de razón* (people of reason), a forerunner concept that in preindependence Mexico could "accommodate the heterogeneity of the colonial population" under a label of "politics and culture," even as "stigmatized racial categories" such as "the Indian" endured,[43] the unresolved raciality of an early twentieth-century, culturalist *raza hispana* was often configured to forms of tacit, Spanish-derived whiteness (*hispano* as white), while other possible Hispanophone *raza* signifiers, including the *raza negra*, continued to be "stigmatized." An example of this appears in the particular way in which *La Prensa* represents O'Farrill's *negrito* performance in the Apolo-era *bufo*: In a significant twist, the role is identified in the early coverage not as the *negrito* but as the "*moreno.*" For example, in a piece on the revue *Mientras Nueva York duerme* (While New York Sleeps), O'Farrill is credited as the play's "*morenito.*"[44] In another, on the "zarzuela bufo cubana" *Bronca entre latinos* (Quarrel among the Latins), he is acknowledged for "the naturalness he stamps upon the types of the Cuban *moreno.*"[45] By the end of his first summer on the Apolo stage, appearing in his own written work, *Los misterios de Changó* (The Mysteries of Changó), in which he "played one of the principal roles," "the already famous 'morenito' O'Farrill . . . made an audience that much enjoys" his "doings and jokes roar with laughter."[46] Indeed, by that time, O'Farrill was "already so popular in Harlem for his performances of the Moreno Cubano . . . that in [the Latino] colony he is already called the successor of Arquímedes Pous."[47] While eventually *La Prensa* would identify the role as that of the *negrito*, as late as May 1927, it continued to call O'Farrill's blackface character "the *moreno.*"[48]

Moreno is a euphemism for the way in which O'Farrill's *negrito* invokes "African," Afro-Cuban, and Afro-Latino identities excessive of both *bufo* and *raza* logics. Indeed, *moreno* is implicated in the very "distasteful" thing it would substitute. The term comes from *moro*, the word for Moor, and it "was originally used, as it is still, to describe a black horse." By "the sixteenth century *moreno* became the general term used to refer to blacks and mulattoes alike"—and thus a category for identities threatening to colonial and Christian power in the Spanish-controlled Americas.[49] A nineteenth-century Cuban dictionary, Esteban Pichardo's *Diccionario provincial casi razonado de vozes y frases cubanas*, offers a point of entry into the Cuban complexities of *moreno*. Looking up *moreno*, one is immediately led elsewhere by the dictionary: "See *trigueño*," it says.[50] The entry for *trigueño* reads thus:

> Trigueño, ña.—N., Adj.—By definition, a person of darkened color [*el color algo atesado*] or like the color of wheat [*trigo*], just as Blanco is said of the lightest person [*más claro*] who tends toward the milky with something of the pink. *Trigueño lavado* [Washed Trigueño], a little lighter and more even than the Trigueño. When dealing with races, the word Blanco is used, even if a person is Trigueño, to differentiate from Negro and Mulato; even though among the latter there are some of whiter color [*de color más blanco*] than many of the white race [*la raza blanca*]. Moreno is a synonym of Trigueño; but the Negro is also called Moreno to

sweeten the expression [*para dulzificar la espresión*] and never Trigueño; just as the Mulato is called Pardo. As a group, Negros and Mulatos are *Gente de color* [People of Color]. The Asiatics [*Asiáticos*] are officially counted among the Blancos.[51]

The *Diccionario*'s evasive treatment of *moreno* is remarkable, and it indicates something of the stakes involved in representing O'Farrill's Apolo-era blackface performance through the term. The evasion begins with "See *trigueño*," which sends one to a word that, upon consultation, is itself elusive, referring to an identity of "color," except, of course, when it does not: when instead, in its place, "the word Blanco is used," thus reassuring, through its paradoxical circulation among subjects of "color," white Cuban power. That the *Diccionario* finally gets around to defining *moreno* only as a "synonym" of *trigueño* further suggests evasion: what *moreno* means is that to which, whatever it is, *trigueño* alludes. The *Diccionario* posits Cuban racial synonymity nearly in terms of a critique of racialization; the *moreno* is similar to the *trigueño*, which is itself similar to the *blanco*, which recalls how there are some "whiter/ *más blanco*" people among the *negros* and *mulatos* of Cuba than among "many of the white race," whose power is again reassured through the "official" inclusion of still others in its ranks, the Chinese indentured workers. Seemingly to forestall the critique, the lexicographer—who, significantly, was also a renowned cartographer—notes the synonymous *moreno*'s different "shade" of meaning: unlike *trigueño*, which "never" does, the *moreno* can mean *negro*. The metaphor here, "*para dulzificar*," is another remarkable element of the entry, both an admission of euphemism and its unraveling: to enact the substitution of the "distasteful" *negro*, a word is used, "sweeten," that links *moreno* to the violence of the Cuban sugarcane plantation.

In *La Prensa*, *moreno* would "*dulcificar*" *negrito*, but, in fact, as is the case with its "sweetening" of the "expression" *negro*, it succeeds instead in articulating the fraught histories and racial categories of Cuban coloniality. O'Farrill's *moreno/morenito/negrito* thus casts the Apolo stage as a space of dramatic simultaneity: it is at once a comforting *bufo* space, with the *negrito* performing a racist stereotype, and an unintended example of Urrutia's "modern Cuban theater" featuring actors and actresses of "our race"—in this sense, a discomfiting example, for O'Farrill's *moreno* is less a representation of Urrutia's "cultured and patriotic blacks" than a figure for the "synonymous" relations between *trigueño*, *moreno/negro*, and the violence of the plantation. The *moreno*, in short, suggests how

O'Farrill may have preserved elements of—even as he surpassed—the belated *negrito*, hinting at a manipulation of racialized social and stage meanings. To the extent that his performance confuses Cuban racial categories, O'Farrill's *moreno/negrito* points to a prevalent, corresponding concern regarding the Harlem *bufo* in general: that it not be confused with other dramatic genres in New York City or with its Havana *bufo* counterpart. For example, a play entitled *¿De quién es hijo el negrito?* (Whose Son Is the Negrito?), a "Spanish zarzuela," might trick readers into thinking it was "a play of the Cuban *bufo* genre." Whoever "thinks thus," however, "makes a huge mistake," for the "play has everything except the *bufo* genre."[52] Meanwhile, the fragment of a faux letter to the Asturian-born Regino López, the famous director of Havana's Alhambra Theater, offered a complaint: "How they ride roughshod over the *bufo* genre in New York!"[53] Such theatrical integrity, or lack thereof, in its moral register was an issue regarding *bufo* audiences, too. Addressing audiences who disrupted performances with "shouts" and "insinuations in poor taste," *La Prensa* claimed that when "those same individuals find themselves in an American theater [*teatro americano*], they behave with decency and manners, but when it comes to a *raza* show [*un espectáculo de la raza*], they conduct themselves in a manner ill befitting our gentlemanliness."[54] The *bufo* audience's "distasteful" behavior, like O'Farrill's *moreno/morenito/negrito*, compromises *la raza*, linked here to a "gentlemanly" masculinity. Indeed, the implication of the *"teatro americano"* is that Latino audiences in such spaces may be subject to the varieties of Anglo racialization as a consequence of their public use of Spanish or "Spanish-sounding" English—their Latino performance of the linguistic, in short, whitening or blackening them in the Anglo imaginary. Susceptible to Anglo racialization, the (in)decent *raza* audience member resembles O'Farrill's *moreno/morenito/negrito*, who, at any moment, in terms of U.S. racial logics, may also signify as "African."

Photo/*Gráfico*

During the beginning of *Gráfico*'s run, in ways that countered *La Prensa*'s *moreno* appellation, this illustrated Sunday newspaper called O'Farrill's character, in no uncertain terms, *negrito*. He was the *"negrito* who cracked up the public."[55] He was not only the "original *negrito*" but "the '*negrito*' of the Apolo."[56] *Gráfico*, in other words, displayed O'Farrill's *negrito* "as such" to the public in print, reflecting how O'Farrill himself performed the *negrito* "as such" to the public on stage. Yet *Gráfico* still sought to manage the possible distaste of exhibiting O'Farrill's *negrito*, offsetting that with representations of the "real," "private," non-*negrito* O'Farrill, the actual subject seamed up with the role. Such a figure of blackface print culture in *Gráfico*, the stage-*negrito* O'Farrill/actual O'Farrill, was suggestive, not unlike the *moreno/morenito/negrito* in *La Prensa*, of histories and categories of "Cuban color" (and, in the United States, of their possible "African" signification) that disturbed the composure of *raza* configurations.

Indeed, *Gráfico*, which appeared in tabloid form, styled itself a medium for both Latino theater publicity and *raza* solidarity during what I consider its first period, which lasted from the newspaper's inaugural issue on February 27, 1927 (the occasion of the forty-seventh Spanish-language performance at the Apolo),[57] to the July 10 edition of that year. During this four-month stretch, when O'Farrill was listed as *Gráfico*'s managing editor, its office was located on 115th Street, just off Lenox Avenue; its motto was "Semanario Defensor de la Raza Hispana" (Weekly Defender of the Hispanic Race). Moreover, as its first editorial indicates, *Gráfico*'s *raza* interest was inseparable from its satirical mission: "The constant increase of the Spanish and Ibero-American colony [*la colonia española e ibero-americana*] that daily, in ever more significant proportion, extends across all the neighborhoods [*barrios*] of the city of New York has impelled us to publish this weekly, *Gráfico*, that without losing sight of its defining characteristic—satire—comes to work together on behalf of everyone forming the great Hispanic family [*la gran familia hispana*]."[58] During those first four months, coverage of the theater world appeared next to anonymous or pseudonymous essays poking fun at its actors, audiences, and impresarios. Readers found pages devoted to reports on the world news, reproduced not without ridicule, and announcements on the activities of social clubs. A personals column appeared next to a resolution of the Liga Portorriqueña e Hispana (the Puerto Rican and Hispanic League), while a mocking report on the Cuban president Gerardo Machado's visit to the United States included a cartoon by O'Farrill that represents Machado ogling the Statue of Liberty.[59] This is not to suggest that everything in the newspaper was threaded with the comic. A column in March, "Los portorriqueños," decried the discrimination and violence faced by Puerto Ricans in New York City and the failure of the state to come to their defense despite their U.S. citizenship, while another piece expressed solidarity with Sacco and Vanzetti.[60] The newspaper's predominant tone during this period, however, was satiric.[61]

On July 24, 1927, Bernardo Vega inaugurated *Gráfico*'s second period by becoming its editor and president.[62] A white Puerto Rican from the town of Cayey, Vega was a major figure in Puerto Rican politics and culture on the island and in New York City. He was a tobacco worker, wrote for newspapers, and was a participant in movements on behalf of working-class liberation and Puerto Rican independence. His book *Memorias de Bernardo Vega: Contribución a la historia de la comunidad puertorriqueña en Nueva York* (Memoirs of Bernardo Vega: A Contribution to the History of the Puerto Rican Community in New York) "is widely recognized as the single most important documentary source about the early Puerto Rican community in New York," with its "wealth of factual information and running analytical and personal commentary."[63] Vega's leadership was linked to the participation in *Gráfico* of another great political and cultural figure of the Puerto Rican diaspora: the Afro-boricua Jesús Colón. Under the pen names Miquis Tiquis and Pericles Espada—and under his own name, too—Colón published essays and a handful of poems reflecting on the migrant and U.S.-born Puerto Rican and Latino experience.[64] In Vega's first issue as editor and president, *Gráfico* published a letter of Colón's, "Palabras de aliento" (Words of Encouragement), in which Colón expressed support for the newspaper's "principal policy of defending our Colony."[65] While Colón's "*Colonia*" was arguably that of the *raza*, a notion still alive in the newspaper's newly modified motto—"Semanario Defensor de la Raza," the modifier "*hispana*" now missing—the presence of Vega and Colón gave *Gráfico*'s *colonia* and *raza* references a greater Puerto Rican meaning, something that, in retrospect, Vega himself acknowledged, writing that the newspaper was "the best" publication "of the Puerto Rican community up until that time."[66] The shift was apparent in *Gráfico*'s editorials, which, under Vega, began including side-by-side English versions, a sign of the newspaper's interest in communicating with Anglophone readers. One editorial condemned in Spanish how certain "*políticos boricuas*" in "*la colonia*" were leading astray "*los puertorriqueños en Nueva York*" regarding how both Democrats and Republicans were both ultimately in support of "*el imperialismo americano en la América Latina*" (*Gráfico*'s English versions for these phrases read "Porto Rican politicians," "the Colony," "Porto Ricans resident in New York," and "American imperialism in Latin America"). The editorial urged *los puertorriqueños en Nueva York* to struggle for national and international justice by rejecting such kinds of "*organización política*" (in the English version, "political organization"), advocating instead for a project in which "*nos incorporamos a lucha industrial del país*." This last clause, which I would translate as "we incorporate ourselves into the industrial struggle of the country," appeared thus in the English version: we "fight our battle to defend our economic betterment."[67] There is a strategic difference between the Spanish and English versions, with the radicality of the Spanish "*lucha industrial del país*" (here suggestive of "Porto Ricans resident in New York" who would transform an Anglo-U.S. *país* through a Latino-inflected class struggle) replaced by the more accommodating, upwardly-mobile-sounding (if still martial) "battle to defend our economic betterment." The importance of the English-language editorial to *Gráfico*'s second period is emphasized by an English-language call for advertising, one which links *Gráfico*'s bilingual maneuvering to "ethnic marketing": "This weekly Spanish publication is the most read in the neighborhood. Sold all over the section. Nine out of ten of the Spanish Speaking inhabitants of Harlem read *Gráfico*. Advertise in this Spanish weekly. Read the English editorial column of this publication and become acquainted with our policy."[68]

Another development in *Gráfico* during Vega's editorship was a decline in its self-referential, 125th Street, *farándula* (show business) coverage. Such coverage, a hallmark of *Gráfico*'s first period, seemingly fell into disfavor. In its second-period incarnation, for instance, the newspaper attributed to "various readers" the impression that "*Gráfico* is better off now, with its new look," which it contrasted with the earlier period, during which, in its harsh assessment, *Gráfico* had resembled "a theater program, an announcement of *tutti le mundi* that wanted to call itself artistic and was paid for with its editors' money."[69] There was a difference of opinion over the matter, and it was public, acknowledged in the newspaper's very pages. One column stated that "something you won't see" is "O'Farrill and Simón [Jou] resign themselves to *Gráfico*'s new policy" or "artists resign themselves to the absence in *Gráfico* of long encomiums on their work."[70] The issue found its (indirect) way into an editorial on the need for collective action on behalf of better housing for the "*población hispana*" (Hispanic population); it stated that spending time on the "*farándula*" and the "frivolities of life" would "never earn respect for our racial group [*nuestro grupo racial*]."[71] The accompanying English version of the editorial, however, elided the *farándula* reference, a gesture keeping the discussion of the cultural politics of Latino show business in-house. During this second period, *Gráfico*'s masthead listed O'Farrill as a member of its board of trustees and, eventually, as a contributing editor, a title under which he appeared until January 8, 1928, the last date of his public connection to the newspaper's management. A year later, Vega's *Gráfico* editorship came to an end.

The representations of the stage-*negrito* O'Farrill/actual O'Farrill span the two periods of *Gráfico* just described. Important among "actual O'Farrill" representations during the newspaper's first period are two photographs of him out of blackface. One showed O'Farrill standing among a group of other actors and singers who had taken part in a popularity contest. O'Farrill wears a suit and bow tie and appears from the waist up; he is the only Afro-Latino in the image. The caption calls him "our diligent Administrator" and lauds his work on the contest: he "has worked tirelessly" and "deserves our most sincere congratulations." Another was a headshot of O'Farrill set among publicity photographs of other performers. The spread commemorated a show at the Park Palace that night. Again, O'Farrill was the only Afro-Latino in the group.[72] The significance of the photographs as examples of an "actual O'Farrill" always in relation to his *negrito* performance is evident in a comment in the column "Chismes de la Farándula" (Show-Business Gossip) regarding the first photograph appearing in the newspaper: O'Farrill *"ya se retrató fuera de carácter"* (has already been photographed out of character).[73] A series of throwaway lines in other columns also referenced O'Farrill's off-stage identity. One quotes a police officer who had apparently "searched O'Farrill's suitcase" on the street. The officer asks him, "are you a bootlegger or a rag vendor?" Another puts O'Farrill on the street, "stepping off a scale and addressing himself to a group of people: 'How annoying! I haven't gained a pound.'" And still another attributes to O'Farrill the admission that "if nature had been more prodigious on his behalf, he would have nothing to envy John Barrymore and Lon Chaney."[74] In each throwaway line, there is an aspect of performance—and a connotation of the *negrito*—in the glimpse of the "real-life" O'Farrill, with the police officer displaying his "wardrobe" and mockingly wondering how to fix O'Farrill's identity; with O'Farrill himself stepping off the street-corner scale and calling his audience's attention to the condition of his body; and, finally, with his self-deprecating admission of his failure to meet the standard of a Barrymore or a Chaney, the latter of which, of course, was renowned for his use of makeup.

Simón Jou, who was more than just a colleague of O'Farrill's, but a friend, was also active in creating such representations. During the newspaper's first period, Jou wrote, "A few nights ago, we were surprised to see O'Farrill weigh himself on a street-corner scale and heard him exclaim with feeling, 'I've lost four pounds!'" Jou responds by saying,

"Calm down, Albertico."[75] Jou continued writing about O'Farrill's everyday life in the vein of performance well into *Gráfico*'s second period. He not only continued to imagine O'Farrill as a body on display on street-corner scales but suggested that, in the absence of steady theater work, O'Farrill had fallen on hard times: "In order to make ends meet," "Gavito" (O'Farrill's maternal last name) "is working as a mechanic, and it seems to suit him well because the last time he stepped on a street-corner scale, he found he had gained seven pounds."[76] The final two references to O'Farrill in *Gráfico* were Jou's, and they extended the idea of O'Farrill as an everyday man caught in a struggle against economic (and now psychological) depression. Jou called him "Alberto (the worried one)" in the penultimate reference, thus calibrating O'Farrill's public exposure (as was the case with the use of "Gavito") by revealing only a part of his name. In the last reference to O'Farrill in *Gráfico*, Jou addressed him significantly as "Gavitofa," one of O'Farrill's *Gráfico* pseudonyms: "We received a telephone call from Gavitofa, who tells us that" he found a job he likes and "got a raise, gained some weight, got some more suits, and hopes to increase his savings."[77] Jou's micronarratives on "O'Farrill," "Albertico," "Gavito," "Alberto, *el preocupado*," and, especially, "Gavitofa" tile O'Farrill's "actual" and (literary) performance identities, occluding and exposing each to varying degrees. The Gavitofa identity does so more than just by blending within a pen name the two last names, O'Farrill and Gavito; as O'Farrill's pseudonym for "Se dice que a mí no me importa" (They Say I Don't Care), a column combining mordant observation with a kind of theater criticism, Gavitofa dismisses the claim that some actors (he cites two *bufo* colleagues, Juan Rivera and Álvaro Moreno) "know who *Gavitofa* is," stating, in fact, that Gavitofa "still hasn't revealed himself" and that "each time he sneaks into theaters, he pays his own way for the right to tell the truth to whoever is no good."[78] Gavitofa turns the tables: less a (performing) body on public display on a street-corner scale, he is an anonymous, and later a pseudonymous, purveyor of judgment on the theater, a role that is compensatory, since, as I have suggested, what prompted O'Farrill's migration to the United States in the first place was likely the difficulty of finding work as an Afro-Cuban man on the Cuban stage, a fate that, in a way, seems also to have befallen him in New York City.

Simón Jou's figure of a stage-*negrito*/actual O'Farrill only alludes to the latter's appearance in blackface. In contrast, a comment from the first period of *Gráfico* under the title "Things That Stood Out at the Park Palace Festival" offers an actual description, doing so in a way that foregrounds the performative: it is the "gloves and wig of O'Farrill" that stood out at the performance that night—his costume of Cuban blackness.[79] Significantly, in the papers of Erasmo Vando, the Puerto Rican actor, writer, and activist, a depiction of O'Farrill in blackface survives: a *fragment arraché* of Afro-Cuban culture in the United States that, located in the Archives of the Puerto Rican Diaspora at the Center for Puerto Rican Studies, Hunter College, the City University of New York, represents Cuban–Puerto Rican cultural exchanges in Harlem as an unsettling archive effect. It is a 5¾-inch-by-3¾-inch, black-and-white, full-body portrait photograph of O'Farrill as the *negrito* (see fig. 2).[80] The photograph is damaged in parts, fragile. It shows O'Farrill standing in front of a blank wall. He wears a boater straw, a jacket with a vest and bowtie, slacks worn high above the waist, and what appear to be tap shoes. His arms are close to the side, but his hands—gloved—are active, with both index fingers pointing outward. O'Farrill's stance is wide, while his shoulders are much more narrow, drawing the gaze upward, from feet to fingers, torso to head. O'Farrill's face is painted black, setting off a rictus and wide-open eyes that stare at a spot above the camera. Across the lower quarter of the photograph, in a diagonal line of cursive script, the name "Alberto O'Farrill Gavito" appears. On the back, in handwriting, are the words "El Trópico," a possible reference to a theater or play. While it is difficult to date the photograph with precision, I place it around the Apolo era or shortly thereafter. The mood of the photograph is complex. The *negrito* suggests hilarity and entertainment, which O'Farrill's "real" name extends into publicity: getting the word out about the actor playing the role, the actual O'Farrill. Yet the *negrito*'s mouth and eyes unnerve. In an attitude of frozen mirth, they bestow on the blackface visage— and on the performance of the *negro*-on-*negro bufo*—something of the insensible: the *negrito* looks unmoved, indifferent to feeling, despite the show of popular merriment.[81] In the context of the many missing materials of the Apolo era, this photograph of O'Farrill in the Vando Papers, which both stages and undoes the idea of a *bufo* hilarity, arrives as a key text of a modernist *afrolatinidad*.

Animality, Jews, and the "Pegas Suaves"

Of primary significance to the itinerary of O'Farrill's *negrito* is "Pegas Suaves," O'Farrill's primary writing contribution to *Gráfico* during its first period. The noun *pega* comes from the verb *pegar* (to hit) and the word *suave* means "soft." In O'Farrill's context, *pega* is

FIGURE 2. Alberto O'Farrill in black-
face, c. 1930 (Box 5, Folder 9, Erasmo
Vando Papers, Archives of the Puerto
Rican Diaspora, Centro de Estudios
Puertorriqueños, Hunter College, City
University of New York)

a term for "job," while *suave* suggests the kind of job under discussion: an easy one. Signed in a pseudonym, "Ofa," that further layers
negrito/actual O'Farrill identities, the "Pegas Suaves" are realist, first-
person narratives ranging from five hundred to six hundred words.
In the twenty-one installments that appeared from February to July
1927 (the last "Pegas" coincided with Vega's inaugural issue), O'Farrill
meditates on the conditions of Latino labor and migrancy around
the Depression, satirizing the injunction to productive labor and the
generation of surplus value in a protagonist who spends as much time
looking for work as he does evading any and all kinds of it—*suave* or

otherwise. Indeed, in his critical aversion to work and his marginality even to a working-class identity, the "Pegas" protagonist is a kind of *lumpenproletariat* figure whose modern, Manhattan-island location links him to the "vagabond," African-diaspora internationalisms particular to the colonial-center, port-city metropoles of Europe.[82] In related fashion, the "Pegas" represent the *barrio afrolatino* as a space of masculine, nocturnal wandering, with the narrator beginning every story in his boarding-house room at three in the morning, about to set out in search of work, and later walking the empty streets, riding the subway, or hitching a ride on the back of a truck en route to a factory or warehouse. Accompanying him always, his motif, is a "*valsesito*" whose melody he sings or whistles—a "little waltz" entitled "Son las tres de la mañana" (It's Three in the Morning).[83]

In the connection of the "Pegas Suaves" to dance and musicality, in the persona of an "Ofa" narrator, and in the production of nighttime, public performances of (looking for) work, they allegorize O'Farrill's *negro*-on-*negro bufo* experience during the Apolo era, revealing the concurrent production and constitutive relation of literary-journalistic narrative and stage *negrito* performance, all of which defines an Afro-Latino blackface print culture. In this respect, it will not do to call the narrator of "Pegas Suaves" a "mulatto *pícaro* [roguish mulatto]," as Nicolás Kanellos does.[84] Not only is there no evidence in the "Pegas" of a "mulatto" self-appellation; to ascribe it to O'Farrill's narrator is to reproduce, rather than inquire into, the categories of modern Latino race present in such print-culture spaces as *Gráfico*. I propose instead that what converges in the narrator of "Pegas Suaves" are the identities of the *moreno* and the *negrito*, as reimagined by their possible "African" author, the Afro-Cuban/Afro-Latino "Ofa."

Two "Pegas" are relevant to the discussion here. In the first, published on July 10, the narrator describes a job he found in Brooklyn:

> The job that turned up came about through all the many influences I have in this country, all due, no doubt, to my way with the words of a crude vocabulary that sprouts from my hard little *chola* [in original; "head"],[85] covered in tangled, bundled-up hair [*una pelambre y recopilada cabellera*].
>
> Before anything, I want you to know that I get paid FIFTY-FIVE dollars a week. All I have to do is play a few roles in Coney Island, where animals of every species are exhibited. I, among them, merely put myself in view of the public.

It's therefore a job worth having, despite appearances. Even though we're all together, we aren't mixed up, because each of us is in his own apartment, luxuriously decorated and protected by iron bars, but only so the curious won't get the urge to touch and annoy—or better said, so we'll be within sight but not within reach.

We stay there from 3 to 12. They give us an hour break between 5 and 6, and, what's more, they offer us the same apartment to sleep in if we want to save money on renting a room.

Don't think my job is that easy. To do this, you need a man with many intellectual resources, which is why they always thought I was the only one in New York who could do it, which I am.

I have to imitate the roar of the lion, the tiger, and all the songbirds, which is the only thing I'm really afraid of, because at the beach, stuck inside a cage, I can very easily *coger un airecito y quedarme con el pescuezo jorobado* [in original].[86] And I've got a clean conscience; I'd rather keep playing the . . . I don't know what role I'm playing inside a cage, but, in reality, I prefer it to walking around, flapping my arms with a crooked neck.

Then, naturally, I have to give the person who got me the job twenty-five percent of my wages, twenty-five percent to the *boss* [in original] and a good tip to the person who takes care of my apartment so he'll keep it clean.

I don't care about any of this because there's enough to go around. It's the case that I have a good job and earn a good salary, and even though I don't take everything home, they pay me fifty-five dollars every week.[87]

The caged narrator performs his roar and singsong in a way that stages the boundary between the human and nonhuman animal. In light of the discourses of modern racist primitivism, in which the "ape was the Negro [and the Afro-Latino *negro*] unmasked,"[88] the Coney Island "Pegas," like racist primitivism, blurs such boundaries, here to turn a profit: acting like an animal earns the narrator a wage. Furthermore, Coney Island as the site of such a performance of racialization allegorizes the period's primary institution of Latino racial performance, the Teatro Apolo. Over the weekend, a theatergoer could witness O'Farrill as the stage *negrito* and then, as a *Gráfico* reader, reencounter him on the page (in the same medium that advertised the Apolo) as a literary character satirizing the very discourses and professional conditions constitutive of his *bufo* career. The description of the body in its animality is still another sign of O'Farrill's blackface print culture in the Coney Island "Pegas": the narrator's unruly head of hair suggests the *negrito's* wig, which, in fact, is implied in the word *cabellera*, while *pelambre* can also mean the hide of an animal; this is also the case with *pescuezo*, which popularly means "neck" but more properly signifies "scrag"—the neck of an animal.

The convergence of animality, race, and performance in the Coney Island "Pegas" draws attention to the fissures in a *raza hispana* ideology at other important moments in *Gráfico* in 1927. The very first editorial under Bernardo Vega, for instance, laments that for the "common American [*vulgo americano*]," there are "only Toltecs, Mayas, *cholos*, and *gauchos*"[89] who "inhabit the countries south of the Río Grande, living in a savage state," which leads them to consider those countries as "incapable of living the civilized life of our century."[90] A column later that summer, called "Palpitations of National Life," went even further in its elaboration of the Latino white-supremacist subtext of the *raza hispana*, using a report of Irish American protests against the film *The Callahans and the Murphys* (1927) to suggest that if Latinas/os protested in a similar way against U.S. cinematic depictions of "lions in Cuba, alligators in Puerto Rico, and barefoot and naked *negritos* climbing coconut trees [*negritos descalzos y desnudos subiendo a las palmas de coco*]," one would invite an Anglo-racist "anti-Latino" backlash: "in all the major dailies there would be" a confirmation "of the savages, of the Indians, and of the blacks of Hispanic America [*de los salvajes, de los indios y de los negros de la America Hispana*]."[91] In *Gráfico's* depiction of a colonized, Americas indigeneity (*toltecas, mayas*), a European/indigenous-Americas "miscegenation" (the *cholos*, the *gauchos*), and a colonized but now seemingly U.S. "white," European-immigrant indigeneity (the Irish), the newspaper would anthologize identities and subjects of the "*salvaje*" that, across the Americas (and the British archipelago), the *raza hispana* (or the *raza anglosajona*) would subject to violent "assimilation." "Barefoot and naked *negritos*" are implicated here, too, of course, only in a curious way: they are "fictitious"—like Cuban lions and Puerto Rican alligators, the mishaps of an Anglo-racist imaginary. Yet, when figured as the "blacks of Hispanic America," these "*negritos*" are also real, perhaps too real, for *Gráfico*, as are the "unassimilated" "Indians." It is such a fissure in *raza hispana* ideology that, earlier in 1927, the Coney Island narrator of "Pegas" exploited through his narrative of animality and racial performance. What this *Gráfico* article displaces in such an antsy way on the Anglo imaginary—the fictitious "*negritos*," aligned with nonhuman animals—is what O'Farrill's narrator critically embraces: not only is the a narrator a *negrito* himself, on stage and in print; he is a Cuban lion, roaring. The "savage-animal" condition of the Coney Island "Pegas" narrator, in short, resituates the "barefoot and naked *negritos*" of the *Gráfico* article from a Latin American elsewhere ("south of the Rio Grande") to the Latino United States itself. The *"negritos"* of the *Gráfico* article inhabit Harlem, O'Farrill's narrator says, and, if not "barefoot and naked," they are covered in cork, contending with "African," *moreno*, and animal identities.

The other "Pegas Suaves" I wish to discuss was published on June 11, 1927, in the same issue of *Gráfico* in which O'Farrill's head shot appeared. It, too, meditates on otherness and performance. The narrator, as usual, is up at three a.m. He sings his *valsesito*, which prompts the boarding-house landlady to ask him to end his song: "porque a los vecinos les agrada ir al teatro pagando su dinero, y . . . yo les estaba dando una función gratuita" (because the neighbors like paying money to go to the theater, and . . . I was giving them a free show). With the theater-motif connection now openly admitted in the narrative, the "Pegas" manages Cuban blackface and *raza hispana* ideas through a crucial subject of Latino modernism in New York City: the Jew.

> Taking into account what that good woman said to me, I headed out really early in the direction of Central Park. Arriving at the lake, I stopped and contemplated the ducks playing in the water. It made me feel so jealous, and unable to resist and thinking I could serve as an example and be the first one to do it, the happy thought occurred to me, of course, to wash myself down in that water, which, despite its appearance to what a Jew sheds after taking a bath, due to its clear black color [*que aunque parecía la arrojada por un judío después de darse un baño, por el color de negro cristalino que le dejan*], I couldn't resist (and, naturally, I wasn't prepared for it). I took off my clothes, down to my BVDs, dove into the water, stuck my face [*caricatura*] out quickly, and soon there were more than four hundred curious onlookers, watching me and full of envy. But since they're such cowards, none of them decided to jump in. I was already considering myself a hero. I thought I would be given an award, like the aviators who went to Paris, when I noticed someone going for my pants. Thinking that the gentleman wanted to steal the nickel I carry around to trick others, I shouted at him, and since he wouldn't let go of my clothes, I swam to the edge. I saw

ALBERTO O'FARRILL / 43

him rush toward me, and as his jacket flew open, I saw that the guy had a badge. I turned around and swam with hurried strokes to the other side, while everyone yelled, "*Quick!*" [English in original.] I got out and immediately I smash full-speed through the park, taking a tremendous lead on the guy. But I failed to realize that I was in my BVDs and that, of necessity, I would have to pass a policeman. And it wasn't long, in effect, before one stopped me. I was already seeing two blows to the ribs with a nightstick, when he said, "Oh! You're a boxer and you're in *training* [English in original]." I let out a big, startled *yes* [English in original], which he wouldn't have believed if it weren't for all the running I'd done. And that's how I was able to go free. But when I got home—oh, Lord!—what a huge mess [*titingó*] I got into with the landlady. She got it into her head [*cayuca*] that I was crazy and tried at all costs to find a policeman to put me in the hospital.[92]

O'Farrill's Harlem Meer comments on his situation in the *negro*-on-*negro bufo* through the anti-Semitic figure of a Jew off whom runs water the color of a "*negro cristalino*" (clear black), a sign of Jewish "pollution" suggesting blackface paint itself and, by extension, early twentieth-century U.S. Jewish minstrels such as Al Jolson, Eddie Cantor, and George Burns.[93] The narrator's immersion in the *negro cristalino* run-off before hundreds of onlookers represents not only performance in general but a special kind of blackface routine, one in which the narrator's blackface paint failed to take, leaving him exposed. The routine thus suggests a comparative canon of ethnicized, racialized minstrel practices in the early twentieth-century United States—the Jewish American *judío* on black, the Afro-Latino *negro* on *negro*—and, for the narrator, the difficulty of (imagining) movements between the two. His is not the fraught career in minstrelsy through which Jewish American performers managed an "assimilation" of their ethnicity in the anti-Semitic Anglo United States; at the same time, for the *raza hispana*, his immersion in Jewishness, however endorsed by an anti-Semitic feeling, suggests a problematic likening of the Afro-Latino with the Jewish, given how Jewish identity fissures the *raza hispana* in relation not only to the anti-Semitism of early-modern Spain but to the more recent conflicts between Latinas/os and Jews in Harlem during the Apolo era itself. If, for O'Farrill, the *negro*-on-*negro bufo* promises to tighten, but in fact loosens, his bond with the *raza hispana*, his association with the figure of the Jew troubles matters even more.

The Harlem Meer "Pegas," set in and around that particular liminal zone of Central Park and Harlem, invokes the relations among the
Latino and Jewish barrios during the 1920s. The latter's population was
in decline by the end of the decade, particularly in East Harlem, where
the Jewish population (poorer and more working class than the Jews
of Central Harlem) had begun migrating to the Bronx, leaving behind
"vacated tenements [that] were soon occupied by New York's newest
immigrants—the Puerto Ricans."[94] Among the connections between
the Jewish and Latino barrios was violence, particularly in the summer of 1926, when the "ill-feeling of recent weeks between young Porto
Ricans and others of Spanish blood who have been moving into Harlem
in large numbers recently and the older residents of the district broke
out . . . in an attempt at riot, which was quelled by police reserves of four
precincts before it got well started."[95] The "ill-feeling" among Latinas/
os and Jews in Harlem, according to observers of the period, was the
result of "commercial rivalries" involving "disputes and bloody fights"
and "much difficulty in renting shops,"[96] although others narrate Latino-
Jewish amicability and coexistence, stating, for example, "we became
friendly neighbors with Jews" and "the Hebrews or Jews" were the "race
with which we, the *boricuas* [in original] coexisted for a brief time,"
partly because of their being "persecuted and discriminated against as
we were."[97]

O'Farrill's *negro cristalino* run-off is significant for the way it ori-
ents *bufo* elements with anti-Semitism as a form of ideological consolidation.[98] For a *raza hispana* ideology in the Latino United States, the
negro cristalino projects the social as constituted not simply by *negros*
and *indios* "*salvajes*," but by *judíos*, too: the Sephardim diaspora of
New York City, which had migrated from the former Ottoman Empire,
whose ancestors the Spanish Crown had expelled in 1492, and whose
Ladino language, "based on early modern Castilian, with admixtures of
Hebrew, Aramaic, Portuguese, Italian, Greek, French, and Arabic, and
traditionally written in Hebraic letters,"[99] transforms further the racial
politics of Latino language practices, representing here a "Spanish" that,
in the form of a Hebrew alphabet, recollects an earlier, Peninsular *raza
hispana* ideology itself stressed by "vile casts"—that "of the Jews and
Muslims."[100] The cultural signs of a *negro cristalino* at the time were multiple. At the Apolo, a *bufo* entitled *Terremoto en Harlem o conflicto entre
judíos e hispanos* (Earthquake in Harlem or Conflict between Jews and
Hispanics) featured O'Farrill himself and engaged the "recent conflict
between Hispanics [*hispanos*] and Hebrews," which the *bufo* represented

as "a purely commercial issue" that, according to *La Prensa*, should motivate "all Spanish speakers [*a todos los de habla española*] to come and work together to elevate our race and avoid friction and unpleasant occurrences."[101] In *Gráfico*, O'Farrill contributed a drawing (called a "photograph" in the following quote) of a "Jew" in a discussion of the proliferation of venues for Spanish-language theater: "Alberto O'Farrill, our editor-photographer, armed with his camera, went to 125th Street and 7th Avenue and took the photograph we include here, which shows a Jew who, unable to find a theater in which to offer Spanish performances [*representaciones españolas*], goes to the *roof* [English in original] at the abovementioned corner, with the aim of renting it in order to put on Hispanic shows [*funciones hispanas*]."[102] The drawing is of a corpulent man, seen from the back, who wears a checkered jacket and a straw boater, carrying a valise and smoking a cigar. The point of the piece, which may well have been written by O'Farrill himself, was that everyone was trying to get into the Spanish-language theater business, including "Jews." The tone of a line in the following week's *Gráfico*, however, was darker: "Spanish theater [*El teatro Español*] must, should, and will be the property of Hispanics [*hispanos*], for Hispanics, and by Hispanics. *Never for the Jews* [*Nunca para los judíos*]."[103]

But it was in *Gráfico's* Spanish-English editorials that such Latino-Jewish signs were most strikingly apparent, revealing a *raza hispana* under stress. Consider the following example: "One of the arguments that our detractors use constantly with the intention of insulting us," a 1927 editorial begins, "is to accuse us of belonging to the colored race [*raza de color*]. According to the opinion of these enemies, it is only Indians and blacks [*indios y negros*] without culture and education that exist in Cuba, Puerto Rico, and other Hispanic countries [*países hispanos*]." The charge of being "*de color,*" according to the editorial, arises from the way in which "we Spanish speakers [*los que hablamos español*]" have a "spirit of tolerance" and "don't distinguish among ourselves on account of race hate [*odio de razas*] in the neighborhoods and towns where we live. . . . There are in all our countries whites and blacks [*blancos y negros*], just as in the United States," and "if on account of having this liberal, altruistic, and human feeling we should be considered as blacks [*hemos de ser considerados como negros*], then let it happily be so." What begins with the promise of an acknowledgment of an Afro-Latino identity concludes instead with a figurative admission: that the newspaper's Latino voice considers itself, in fact, "*como negros*" (as blacks), which thus instances *afrolatinidad* as an attitude *toward* Afro-Latinas/

os, the practice of which, as a "feeling" (*sentimiento*), constitutes here an element of *raza hispana* ideology. In the English version, the first paragraph reads differently from its Spanish counterpart, dropping "*negro*" entirely and replacing it with "colored race": "One common argument heard often among some individuals in Harlem," begins this English-language version, "is that all Porto Ricans, Cubans and South Americans are either uncivilized Indians or people belonging to the *colored race*. But what moves us to a good healthy laugh is the fact that this argument is used as a sign of race superiority by people who are as discriminated in the United States as the Porto Ricans or the *Negroes* are."[104] The English-language editorial works along tacit lines. Jews are invoked not by name but by indicating a history of discrimination specific to an unnamed "people." The word *negros*, meanwhile, cut out, thus obviates the translation (and admission) of this category of Latino blackness into English.[105] In fact, what *negros* signified in the Spanish text appears in the English as "colored race," a phrase that suggests "*raza de color*," the island-Cuban "uplift" category for *negras/os* and *mulatas/os*. To an English-language reader, however, "colored race" may also include African Americans. In order to hinder such a possibility, with its troubling suggestion of the African Americanizing of a *raza hispana* (the very threat that led to the editorial in the first place), *Gráfico* turns to the word "Negroes," here representing African Americans, who are thereby segregated in print from Afro-Latinas/os (who "aren't" Negroes), even as such "Negroes" share with "Porto Ricans" and other unnamed "people" an experience of structural oppression. The text thus forestalls both an Afro-Latino and African-diaspora identity among its readers, all in response to a (tacitly Jewish) accusation of the community's *afrolatinidad*. In this way, *Gráfico*'s editorial, like O'Farrill's Harlem Meer "Pegas," encounters the limits of a *raza hispana* ideology in its engagement with a Harlem "Jew."[106]

One of the final traces of O'Farrill in print around the Apolo era is an advertisement in *La Prensa*, and it is fitting: "¡Una noche sólamente! ¡Sensacional! ¡Emocionante! Concurso de rumba con los campeones mundiales, Alberto O'Farrill y Margot Guerra. Fama, fortuna, y gloria. Savoy, el mejor salón de baile en el mundo" (One night only! Sensational! Exciting! *Rumba* contest with the world champions, Alberto O'Farrill and Margot Guerra. Fame, fortune, and glory. Savoy, the best dance hall in the world).[107] O'Farrill's hosting a *concurso de rumba* at the Savoy is a symbolic event. The typical *bufo* during the period still ended with a "final *rumba* [in original]" in which "all kinds of [plot] contradictions are resolved."[108] O'Farrill's *concurso de rumba* is the "finale," in a way, of his hot-and-cold career on the blackface stage during the Apolo era. Less a resolution, however, of the contradictions of that career, the *concurso*, in fact, reiterates them. For one thing, resorting to hosting a *concurso* was a sign of his falling on hard times, a general condition during the Depression, to be sure, but also of specific meaning to an Afro-Cuban man seeking work on the stage in the early twentieth century—and particularly to an Afro-Cuban like O'Farrill, who, less than five years earlier, was likely greeted upon his arrival in Key West with a reminder, in the Arango-Moreno company, of his white-Cuban competition in the Cuban and (now) Latino U.S. markets of racial performance. Another important fact of the contest involves the space itself: the Savoy Ballroom. The Savoy performance links O'Farrill's career to a particular history of Latino, Afro-Latino, and Afro-Cuban uses of that African American–identified venue. By the time of O'Farrill's contest, the Savoy Ballroom, like the Cotton Club, Small's Paradise, and Connie's Inn, was a "success-ful jazz" space.[109] It was where, in the 1930s, Alberto Socarrás would play "jazz and blues" before heading to the Park Palace or the Campoamor theaters (which were also *bufo* spaces) to play Cuban music;[110] where, during the same period, African Americans, Puerto Ricans, and other Latinas/os would dance jazz "from 3 to 7 p.m., then go to the Park Palace at 5th and 110th from 7 p.m. to 1 a.m." to dance Cuban and Puerto Rican music;[111] and where, in the following decade, Machito, Graciela, and Mario Bauzá would play Afro-Cuban jazz. The figure of O'Farrill as a dancing Afro-Cuban man who sits (or dances) in judgment of other dancing men and women at the Savoy suggests still other possibilities for his "African" identification: a sharing of space, at times alternating, at times simultaneous, among Afro-Latinas/os and African Americans.

Screening Harlem Uprising

I turn now to a time around 1935, a moment of great professional success for O'Farrill. He performed regularly at the Teatro Campoamor on 116th Street and Fifth Avenue with Alberto Socarrás and his orchestra; he appeared in Contreras Torres's *No matarás* (Thou Shalt Not Kill), filmed in New York City and in Hollywood; he enjoyed an homage in recognition of his theater work dating to the Apolo era; and, finally, he returned to Havana for a season to produce and perform in his own stage show. Two seemingly unrelated events in the histories of race in the Americas—both occurring within a month of each other—converge in this career narrative. The first was the "Harlem Riot" of March 1935, which began at an E. H. Kress and Company store on 125th Street, across from the Harlem Opera House (the Teatro Apolo) and the Hurtig and Seamon (the Apollo Theater), when an Afro–Puerto Rican named Lino Rivera, described in the city's subsequent report as "a 16-year-old colored boy," was detained and accused of theft.[112] The other was the collapse in February 1935 of the Teatro Alhambra building on the corner of Virtudes and Consulado Streets in Havana, an event that the theater critic Eduardo Robreño saw as a physical manifestation of the Alhambra's (and its *bufo's*) "decadence," the signs of which had already been apparent "around the year 1930."[113] The "gangster" violence and *raza hispana* ideas represented in *No matarás*, O'Farrill's "straight" and blackface performance in the film, and its close association with the Teatro Campoamor (where it premiered) suggest a modern Latino popular-cultural text in dialogue with the African American uprising of 1935 and, in particular, its "accidental" protagonist: the Afro–Puerto Rican "colored boy." It was O'Farrill's work in *No matarás* that he parlayed into a stage production in Havana at a theater located two blocks from the ruins of the Alhambra, thus exporting "in triumph" his "straight" and *negrito* performance in the film into the vacuum of Cuba's collapsed *bufo* establishment.[114]

The Teatro Campoamor opened in 1913 as the Mount Morris Theater. By the summer of 1932, it was featuring Latino stage and musical performances.[115] In 1934, the Puerto Rican Marcial Flores, "a wealthy *boletero* (numbers runner), . . . rented the closed Mount Morris" and "renamed it El Campoamor" after a Havana theater.[116] Flores's interest in the entertainment business had a precedent: He had earlier opened the Cubanacán, an important club on 114th Street and Lenox Avenue. With Alberto Socarrás leading its orchestra, the Cubanacán featured a "nightly show [and] Cuban music [*música criolla*]." It was the Cubanacán orchestra under Socarrás that became the house band at the Campoamor. The theater's artistic director, Fernando Luis, was, in the words of Socarrás, "Cuban, a little white guy."[117] Luis, who, according to Diosa Costello, had entered show business "*a la cañona*" (by force),[118] was previously the artistic director of the Teatro San José/Variedades in the early 1930s, where he had produced shows in which O'Farrill performed. Luis incorporated chorus lines into the Variedades's revues and emphasized the screening of Spanish-language films, two innovations that, characteristic also of his Campoamor work of the mid-1930s, shifted the experience of Latino theater culture during the period.[119] It was Luis's efforts as theater manager and director that led to the renovation of the Campoamor and its reopening in the summer of 1936 as the Teatro Cervantes. The theater's

motto was "Por el Arte y por la Raza" (For Art and the Race), with offer-
ings that continued to include Spanish-language films, chorus lines, and
stage shows.[120] The Cervantes was short-lived. By the following summer,
the Mount Morris/Campoamor/Cervantes "was again metamorphosed
into another Hispanic house. This time the name would live on into the
1950s: El Teatro Hispano."[121]

The significance of the two Albertos' collaboration at the Campoamor
around 1935—O'Farrill and Socarrás's—cannot be overstated. A glimpse
at Socarrás's biography reveals why: the two share an experience of
Cuba's Pous-era *bufo*, with Socarrás, unlike O'Farrill, thriving in it, and
of a migration to the United States, likely a result of Cuban racist practices in the culture industry. Socarrás was a master flutist, but he also
played the clarinet and alto and soprano saxophones. He was born in
the town of Manzanillo, Oriente, in 1903, and he was a prodigy. He performed musical accompaniments to the silent movies at a Manzanillo
theater, where he was discovered by Pous in 1920. Pous hired him to play
in his company's orchestra. Socarrás's earliest professional experiences,
then, were linked to Cuba's early-republican *bufo* cultures—and not just
any, but its most successful. Socarrás not only played for Pous's stage
shows; he eventually began arranging pieces. He traveled with Pous from
Manzanillo to Santiago, and from there to Havana, remaining with the
company for nearly three years.[122] In Havana, among his gigs, Socarrás
played in Moisés Simóns's band at the Plaza Hotel. During this time,
he recognized racism in music hiring practices. "I noticed about some
places where they don't want in this house, *negro*," Socarrás said in an
interview. "They start all those things, Cubans."[123] Socarrás resolved to go
to New York, where he arrived in 1927, at the height of the Apolo era. He
was met at the pier in Manhattan by Justo Barreto, an Afro-Cuban musician. The two rode the IRT together to Harlem, getting off at the 125th
Street and Lenox Avenue station, where Socarrás was amazed by the
majority-black population.[124] One of his first jobs was with the orchestra
of the white Cuban Nilo Menéndez at the Harlem Opera House, where
the Teatro Apolo was located.[125]

Early on in New York City, Socarrás rented a room with an African
American family in Harlem to learn English and immerse himself in the
everyday cultures of jazz.[126] His career in African American music and
among African American performers during the 1920s and 1930s is well-
known: he recorded with the Clarence Williams orchestra, including
what is considered the first-ever jazz-flute solo in "Have You Ever Felt That
Way"; he was in the orchestra of the *Rhapsody in Black* and *Blackbirds*

revues; he played with King Oliver, Sam Wooding, Allie Ross, Cab Calloway, Duke Ellington, and Dizzy Gillespie; and he led orchestras of his own at the Savoy, the Cotton Club, Small's Paradise, and Connie's Inn. He was "also playing Cuban music at El Campoamor, El Cubanacán, and [the] Park Plaza."[127] It was a career not only with origins in the island-Cuban *bufo* circuits of Arquímedes Pous, therefore, but unfolding still in the cultures of the belated *bufo* of New York City. Socarrás was Marcial Flores's personal choice to direct the Campoamor orchestra; "he want me there, because he want to have show from Mexico, American shows, from everywhere," Socarrás said, "and he didn't have a conductor there," so "he send somebody to talk to me."[128]

Nearly every performance of O'Farrill's at the Teatro Campoamor around 1935 happened to the accompaniment of Socarrás's band, as *La Prensa*'s theater coverage between December 1934 and December 1935 demonstrates. As the theater's "popular and applauded *negrito*," O'Farrill, it seems, had expanded his repertoire in *negrito* characterization at the Campoamor; in one instance, not surprisingly, he did so through still further racial performance, in relation to a stereotype of gender and Chinese identity in a Warren and Dubin song: the "likeable *negrito* Alberto O'Farrill again steals all the applause, especially in a parody of 'Shanghai Lil,' with an appropriate lyric [*poesía*], in which O'Farrill shows himself as a magnificent character actor."[129] In another show, he appeared with Antonio Machín, "the theater's chorus, and the orchestra of Alberto Socarrás."[130] Finally, in what was again an instance of ideologies of circum-Pacific race informing Latino performance, he appeared in a Fernando Luis production called *Hawaiianerías* (Hawaiianities) alongside the *gallego* of Guillermo Moreno—formerly of the Arango-Moreno.[131] O'Farrill's collaboration with Socarrás thus represented a palimpsest of Pous-era, Apolo-era, and now Campoamor-era *bufo* expression, theatrically and musically, which Moreno's contributions inscribed further in relation to the memory of O'Farrill's Key West arrival.

The African American uprising in Harlem of March 19, 1935, that resulted in the deaths of three African Americans matters here as well, as text and context of the racial performance of the O'Farrill-Socarrás Campoamor. In the experience of the Afro–Puerto Rican Lino Rivera, the uprising contained an implication of the *negro*-on-*negro bufo*: that Afro-Latino blackface performance signifies how an "African" identity in the United States exposes Afro-Latinas/os to Anglo-white violence, including lynching. *La Prensa* identified Rivera as both a "Puerto Rican youth" (*joven puertorriqueño*) and a "Hispanic young man" (*muchacho hispano*), side-stepping his African diasporic identity. Yet the newspaper had to come to terms with it somehow. It did so by "quoting" the African American woman who, as a witness to the detention of Rivera, "mis-recognized" him: what began the "riot" was "the shout of an alarmed woman of the colored race that 'they're beating to death a colored boy [*un muchacho de color*] in the basement of this store!'"[132] Bernardo Vega uses a similar approach in his account of the uprising in the *Memorias*: Rivera was a "young man" (*un muchacho*) whom "various women . . . took for a young black North American [*joven negro norteamericano*], even though he was Puerto Rican."[133] Both narratives burden African American women with an "African" and African-diasporic mis/recognition of Rivera, a racialized and gendered division of representational labor that offers *La Prensa* and Vega a subsequent opportunity to disabuse their informants of the idea.

The mis/recognition of Rivera's *afrolatinidad* explains, in part, the dismissive attitude noticeable initially in the press regarding the uprising's beginning at the Kress on 125th Street. Accounts of Rivera's detention as a "simple incident" and an "incident of no importance," and of the uprising as a result of "deceitful circumstances"[134] and a "false report,"[135] reflected the apparent facts: that Rivera's brief detention for shoplifting had somehow become, in the imagination of African American women, an act of police brutality and murder. In fact, such a coding of the uprising's origins implicates the mis/recognition of Rivera itself: what was dangerously "false" and thus in need of a hasty dismissal was the Afro-Latino Rivera's interpellation as an African American. Such was the power and perplexity of the mis/recognition that some believed Rivera "had been substituted for the Negro boy" who, according to rumor, had actually been murdered.[136] The performance logic particular here to Rivera imagined as an Afro-Latino stand-in for an African American corpse was reproduced in more general terms in Alain Locke's "Harlem: Dark Weather-Vane," his account of the uprising that appeared in *Survey Graphic* eleven years after his editing and publishing the New Negro materials in that same journal. Locke, calling Rivera "a Negro lad of sixteen," described the uprising as "the first scene of the next act," a "curtain-raiser," and a "dress rehearsal" for Harlem's future.[137] The stage language also signified literally: "The publicity [Rivera] received from the riot has brought him two offers to go on the stage, his friends revealed."[138]

Miguel Conteras Torres's *No Matarás* and O'Farrill's performance in this Campoamor-centric film invoke the 1935 Harlem uprising in a *raza hispana* narrative of belated bloodshed (here in the film's Prohibition-era setting and bootlegger plot) that would seal off the film from the violence and racial mis/recognition of the recent uprising. The film was very much a primary text of the Campoamor. Not only did it premiere at the theater in November 1935 (and, as we shall see, include its exterior in an opening scene); it featured two of the Campoamor's primary figures, O'Farrill in a supporting-actor role and Fernando Luis in a smaller part, in addition to two amateur performers who had won a contest sponsored by the theater. For O'Farrill, appearing in *No matarás* was likely the highlight of his career. He was credited third, after the film's two stars, Ramón Pereda and Adriana Lamar, and he played a character that, "straight" and in blackface, won over the public at the Campoamor—a character that reprised the limits and possibilities of O'Farrill's nearly decade-long career in *negro*-on-*negro negrito* performance in the United States.

No matarás was "the second and final 'Hispanic' film" (that is, film set in the Latino United States) of Miguel Contreras Torres's career, which dated to the early 1920s; Contreras Torres was its writer, director, and coproducer.[139] The film was made in August and September of 1935, on location in New York City and at the Talisman Studios in Hollywood; it was produced by Hispano International Film Corporation and distributed by Film Selectos and 20th Century Fox.[140] The cast included the Spanish-born Pereda, its leading man; the Mexican Lamar, his wife and leading woman; and, in a supporting role, the Argentinean Paul Ellis.

No matarás begins in Spain, with views of Madrid, where the brother of the film's protagonist muses on the "one hundred million souls of the same race [*misma raza*]" that inhabit the Americas.[141] The protagonist himself, Antonio Guerra (Pereda), is one such soul, a Spanish immigrant in New York City, and he is down on his luck. On the street one day, he meets Edmundo (O'Farrill), an Afro-Cuban shoeshine who takes him in. Antonio ends up bootlegging, despite Edmundo's reservations. To protect his identity, Antonio changes his last name, going as Antonio "López." Antonio eventually rises in the criminal organization, supplanting the boss. The rise, however, was a ruse: Antonio's promotion was orchestrated by the gang in order to make him the fall guy, with the boss now working behind the scenes. It is only after the boss is murdered that Antonio truly ascends in the organization. Meanwhile, he woos Amapola (Lamar), a Mexican singer at a Spanish-immigrant-owned nightclub managed by a Cuban, Fernando (Luis). Amapola spurns Antonio at first, suspicious of his illegal activities. Eventually, though, she grows fond of him. With Edmundo confiding in her, she learns of Antonio's participation in a kidnapping plot and alerts his brother, who comes from Spain to rescue Antonio from a life of crime. Amapola also helps Edmundo find a job with Luis's nightclub, where he performs a "rumba" in blackface. The climax sees Antonio nearly going through with the kidnapping, only to be prevented by his brother, whom he nearly assaults. Appalled at his own behavior, Antonio has a change of heart. The final scene shows him aboard a ship bound for Spain with his brother. They are joined by Amapola, who is embarking on a performance tour of the Spanish peninsula, and by Edmundo, now her *"empresario."*

The production and release of *No matarás* were very much identified with Latino Harlem and, in particular, the Campoamor. During the summer of 1935, Contreras Torres appeared there during a showing of an earlier film, *Tribu*, announcing that he would soon be directing a new film with an "inter-Hispanic flavor [*sabor intra-hispano*], for which he wishes to cast actors of all nationalities, and, naturally, he hasn't forgotten about New York."[142] The Campoamor-sponsored contest to "find young people of both sexes" to appear in the film even spilled onto the Campoamor stage, with some of the contest participants appearing in a *bufo* with O'Farrill himself.[143] It seems likely that Contreras Torres "discovered" O'Farrill and cast him in the film during this time; it is likely he even wrote the part of Edmundo specifically for him. By the film's Campoamor premiere in November 1935, *No matarás* was known as the film with "the soul of the Hispanic-American colony of New York [*la Colonia Hispano-Americana de New York*]" and as the "magnificent film on the life of the Hispanics [*los hispanos*]" in the city.[144] Its reception underscored the importance of technology matters to understandings of Hispanophone cinema during the period. The film programming at the Campoamor had already prompted discussions regarding the technological successes of the film industry in Spain, which had improved in "lighting, photography, and sound."[145] With the release of *No matarás*, such discussions continued, weaving together in praise the film's technological features and Latino-Harlem content: *No matarás* was claimed as the "Spanish-language film that has surpassed the precedents established up until now in its impeccable technology and the way in which, in the film, the real character of the Hispanic colony in New York vibrates."[146] The Anglophone press, with little advocacy interests in the representation of Latino Harlem, offered a response more attuned to elements of the film as a text of the 1935 uprising: its violence and belatedness. *No matarás* was a "well-made gangster picture," "shot in New York and assembled in Hollywood," that "is outdated by being timed during the last months of the dry era and dealing with the activities of bootleggers instead of policy racketeers and the like"—"policy racketeers," one hastens to add, such as Marcial Flores.[147] In another review, *No matarás* was a film in which "some good acting and a satisfactory production offset the rather outdated theme."[148] Such a lag would have been apparent to O'Farrill, if for only one reason: nearly ten years earlier, during Prohibition, he had appeared on the Apolo stage as the *negrito* in a *bufo* entitled *En el país de los secos, o el efecto de la prohibición* (In the Country of the Dry, or the Effects of Prohibition).[149] Finally, the attention and praise received by O'Farrill for his performance in the film was noticeable. His return from California was hailed as "triumphant," and an advertisement for the premiere (which included an O'Farrill *bufo* and the regular performance of the Socarrás orchestra) featured a still of him in blackface next to Adriana Lamar.[150] Indeed, in a review of *No matarás*, *La Prensa* remarked how O'Farrill, the "popular *negrito* and idol of the Hispanics [*los hispanos*], nearly 'steals' three quarters of the film." "Never before had he played a part in films," it remarked and then added, in a comment of unintentional, bitter irony regarding the situation of theater (and now film) work among Afro-Cuban performers, "yet he acts as if he had been working on screen for years."[151]

O'Farrill's performance as Edmundo in *No matarás* both revisits and goes beyond his earlier print and performance *bufo* work. Edmundo, for example, appears out of blackface for a majority of the film, which thus imagines him as a Harlem Afro-Cuban identified with servant work and hard times, with the latter representation reminiscent of Simón Jou's *Gráfico* micronarratives of O'Farrill's lean years during the late 1920s. It is also out of blackface that Edmundo briefly participates in the plot's criminality and violence. His one blackface scene, which takes place at Fernando Luis's cabaret, suggests a metacinematic moment: Edmundo appears in a film image that, at the premiere, was projected on a screen above the actual stage on which O'Farrill performed regularly as the *negrito*. Meanwhile, from start to finish, *No matarás* draws on a *raza hispana* ideology that, with Edmundo's trip to Spain at the end, is rendered literal: the Afro-Latino is finally "back" in *Hispania*/España.

In fact, in the film's opening Madrid scene, what prompts the protagonist's brother to muse on the "one hundred million souls of the same race" that inhabit the Americas, and on the possibility of "uniting [them] with Spain . . . on practical, moral, and racial foundations," is an altogether different project, one that hinges on a kind of *raza* uncanniness:

that of "uniting Spain and Africa," which the plot implies is strictly a business proposition, involving the construction of a physical link between the peninsula and North Africa. Such "African" refractions of *raza* carry over into a following scene, Edmundo's first, which features him plying his trade on a Harlem sidewalk—in front of the Teatro Campoamor itself, at 1421 Fifth Avenue—and calling out in English to a passerby who happens to be the protagonist, Antonio: "Shine? Shine? Shine, mister?" The first words we hear O'Farrill speak in the film are in English; after encountering him for so long on the print-culture page, it is a moving experience to hear his voice. The English-language utterance renders Edmundo's *afrolatinidad* uncertain: is this shoeshine an African American, or is he an Afro-Latino who learned English? Edmundo soon clarifies the matter, speaking in a Cuban-accented Spanish that facilitates a public show of Latino racial (and national) identification. He begins by confirming Antonio's white *latinidad*, telling him, "Usted parece español" (You look like a Spaniard), before asking him, "¿De dónde es Usted?" (Where are you from?). In that same scene, Edmundo also mocks the film's *raza hispana* inclinations, here as a concept deriving from Spain as the "motherland." Having gotten Antonio to say that he comes from Castilla la Vieja (Old Castile)—a historic region of the Medieval Kingdom of Castile, which thus intensifies the script's Hispanicity—Edmundo replies, "¿La vieja? ¿Qué vieja?" (The old woman? What old woman?). It is a reply in which Edmundo disrupts Castilla la Vieja's possible grandeur, and he takes it further still: "¡Entonces somos casi paisanos! Yo también soy de Santiago. Santiago de Cuba. Pero mi padre era catalán. Catalán, ya Usted ve. Casi callestano [*sic*]" (Then we're almost compatriots! I'm also from Santiago. Santiago de Cuba. But my father was a Catalan. Catalan, you see. Almost *callestano* [in original]). The play of Edmundo's Cuban-accented voice—the *"catalán"* is *"casi"* the *"castellano,"* which, in fact, Edmundo "corrupts" further, as *"callestano"*—not only further disrupts Hispania, satirically disintegrating Spain and its modern, disparate provinces in an ominous gesture on the eve of the Spanish Civil War; it invokes, too, the Afro-Latino uncanny in *raza hispana* ideology, with Edmundo revealing himself as an Afro-Cuban from Santiago, even as he assumes a Spanish identity through a Catalan father—a form of Cuban colonial-plantation filiation typical for its strategic elision of a mother figure (possibly African diasporic, possibly the subject of sexual violence) in favor of a white, Spanish father.

Central to *No matarás*'s characterization of Edmundo is his servant identity. Yet the film complicates this, too, imagining a servant

Edmundo as a possible Afro-Latino agent of violence through his very service to Antonio. This happens in an important sequence. Antonio has just embarked in organized crime and comes to share the news with Edmundo, greeting him in English: "Hello, boy!" The Spaniard-as-white-Latino Antonio (the *gallego*, as it were) adopts an Anglo-white form of belittling, racist address in his greeting of Edmundo (the "*negrito*"), a complement to the latter's own Anglophone "shine, mister" in the opening scenes. Indeed, "boy" resonates with the phrase "Negro boy" used for Rivera as well as the diminutive -*ito* in *negrito*. Distressed at the news, Edmundo responds with a plea: "I'll be your driver, your servant [*criado*], your shoeshine, but take me with you." Later, Edmundo decides to make a bomb to protect Antonio. "How to make a dynamite bomb," he reads from a book, as he dissolves black powder in water, here calling to mind the *negro cristalino* of the Harlem Meer "Pegas." The film then trades in the comic value of the scene: Edmundo lights a cigarette, which, in a minor flash, sets off the explosive, thereby defusing for now the servant "boy's" violent practice. Shortly thereafter, Edmundo interrupts a meeting between Antonio and the other gangsters by producing the fully made bomb. It turns out to be a coconut with a fuse sticking out—an exoticist prop that, yet again, relegates Afro-Latino violence to the place of comic relief. Edmundo goes on to demonstrate the "bomb's" capability by setting off still another minor flash. Antonio asks him where he got the bomb. "Oh, I make them," Edmundo replies. "I'm preparing to become an anarchist." It is a joke that works because Edmundo's threat of political violence appears so unrealistic.

In the judgment of the New York Motion Picture Division, however, it was not so unrealistic. The division decreed that among the "eliminations . . . to be made in all prints to be shown in New York State" of the film were "all views of Edmundo making bomb, all views of the bomb, and the explosion." The reason, it stated, was that such scenes "would tend to incite to crime."[152] The elimination of the threat of Afro-Latino violence in *No matarás* represents a practical application of a kind of cultural theory on the part of the state, which deems the relation between the cinematic staging of a bomb-making Edmundo and the scene's reception determinative: seeing the bomb-making Edmundo on screen would "incite" the people, with effects the state presumes are criminal. The censored scene thus shares a political occasion with the arrest of Lino Rivera at the Kress on 125th Street: Edmundo's criminality and *afrolatinidad*, not unlike Rivera's mis/recognized criminality and *afrolatinidad*, threaten to "stir up" Harlem, a possibility that the state (as the police, as the Motion Picture Division) would prefer to eliminate.

Edmundo's appearance in blackface in *No matarás*, as I suggested, comments on O'Farrill's career in the *negro-on-negro bufo*. Set in a cabaret managed by Fernando Luis, the scene imagines an origin for O'Farrill's career—one that, no doubt, amounted to an in-joke for the audience at the Campoamor, accustomed as it was to seeing him as a veteran performer at that theater over the past year and even earlier in other venues. Amapola tells Edmundo, "you could be a performer [*artista*], too," and introduces him to the Spanish-immigrant cabaret owner as "a great dancer." Edmundo seizes the opportunity, though not without again revising the *raza hispana*, telling the owner that he "*parece gallego*" (looks like a Spaniard/Galician/*gallego*), to which the owner responds, in a huff, that, in fact, he is "a Spaniard." The owner then adds, "How can you tell I'm a *gallego* [in original]?" The exchange foregrounds how Edmundo throws into crisis the matter of a Spain-derived *raza hispana*, making it a matter of Hispanicity's own unresolved internal differences (as *gallego, español*), here provoked (and, what is more, uncustomarily rendered as an object of discourse) by the Afro-Latino character: indeed, appropriately enough, by the film's would-be *negrito*. Edmundo's reply to the owner—"Oh, I know a lot about that, quite a bit. You see, my father was a *gallego* [in original]"—signifies yet again on the *raza hispana*, showing Edmundo as he plays the part of the self-denying Afro-Cuban American in an even more incredible (which is to say, unbelievable) way, as he presents himself now not as the son of a *catalán*, as he did in the earlier scene, but as the son of a *gallego*. Here, in other words, the Afro-Latino's assimilation to a *raza hispana*—an assimilation necessary for Edmundo to receive a job offer in performance—is made a mockery of: the Afro-Latino, in fact, interrupts a *raza hispana* identification at every turn.

When Edmundo finally appears in blackface, he revisits elements of O'Farrill's earlier *negrito* work in print and performance. Back at the Fernando Luis cabaret, he peeks into Amapola's dressing room and asks her, "Do you recognize me?" Edmundo's face is covered in blackface paint, down to his neck. He wears a wig underneath a fedora, which is on backward. His costume suggests a stylized stage "rumba" outfit, with a scarf, sash, and many-ruffled shirt. "How funny," Amapola replies. "You look like a Cuban Al Jolson." Edmundo affirms that, yes, "that's exactly who I want to be like. All I need now is the voice. But—I don't know. I'm nervous. I'm not sure if people will like me." Luis then introduces

Edmundo to the audience: "I now have the pleasure of introducing to you a new performer, a creator of Cuban dances, who with his partner, Estrella, is going to dance a hot *rumba* [*rumba sabrosa*]." Edmundo appears on stage with his partner, a white Latina named Estrella, herself wearing stylized stage "rumba" attire, including a dress with a long, ruffled train and a scarf around her head. Edmundo begins by singing the verse of a *son* about a slaughtered goat, accompanied by a quartet (violin, piano, bass, accordion), and then, with the *montuno* section, he dances the "rumba" with his partner: a dance suggestive of the mannered, often commercialized version of that popular Afro-Cuban dance form.[153] Edmundo's *negrito* is limited here to performing a version of the *bufo's* "final rumba" with Estrella, who was played by Estrella Segarra, a winner of the Campoamor contest. Appearing with such a local-girl-done-good intensifies the Latino-Harlem associations of the *negrito* Edmundo, whom the audience already knew, of course, as the *negrito* O'Farrill. But it is the likening to Al Jolson that most significantly renews the film's and O'Farrill's relations with a Latino-Harlem locality. A "Cuban Al Jolson," here in the film's belated Apolo-era/Prohibition setting, figures anew the central image of O'Farrill's Harlem Meer "Pegas Suaves." In his big, blackface break, identifying with a renowned Jewish-blackface performer, Edmundo is awash, like the "Pegas" protagonist, in the *negro cristalino* run-off of a Jew—an identification that, again, compromises the *raza hispana*.

It is no surprise, then, that *No matarás* concludes with the principal characters aboard a ship bound for Spain. It is an Americas-phobic ending that would take the cast to the Hispanic "source" of the *raza* (in the case of O'Farrill, as a maritime "Hispanic" departure that reverses the meaning of his "African" Key West arrival on the *Governor Cobb*). Yet, because the film gives Edmundo the last word, the ending takes a different course. At one point, Edmundo claims to have seen a whale and is accused of having "visions." "And what is life?" he replies. "A vision." He then paraphrases a few lines from the poem "Dolora XXXV: Las dos linternas" (The Two Lanterns), by Ramón de Campoamor, the nineteenth-century Asturian poet. A sign of Campoamor's popularity at the time, Edmundo's reference is also more: as the namesake of the theater on 116th Street and Fifth Avenue—even as the film abandons Harlem and the Americas—Campoamor allows O'Farrill to pay tribute to the theater, the site of his greatest professional success.

Off screen, where O'Farrill ended up was a different story. Most immediately, in late November 1935, he was the subject of an homage at the

Club Atlético y Social Pomarrosas on Eighth Avenue between 116th and 117th Streets: "No one deserves such a tribute better than Alberto after triumphing in his first film, *Mi hermano es un gangster.* O'Farrill's work has been well appreciated by the public wherever he has performed, and tomorrow night a supportive crowd will applaud the honoree, offering thanks for the happy moments he has spread throughout the city's Hispanic theaters [*teatros hispanos*]."[154] Among the scheduled participants were Alberto Socarrás, Marcial Flores, and Fernando Luis, together with the Campoamor chorus. Augusto Coen and his orchestra and Davilita were also scheduled to appear, along with Guillermo Moreno and Antonio Machín. The Puerto Rican poet Ángel Manuel Arroyo was also in attendance, and Erasmo Vando served as the master of ceremonies. The event, billed as a "dance-show [*función baile*]" on behalf of the "popular '*negrito*'" and "great Hispanic actor [*gran actor hispano*]," went off in an "atmosphere of great warmth," lasting until well after two in the morning.[155]

Return to Havana, 1936

But soon O'Farrill ended up still farther away: not in Spain but in Cuba. In February and March 1936, a year after the Harlem uprising and the collapse of the Alhambra, O'Farrill parlayed his success with *No matarás* into producing, directing, and performing in *The O'Farrill's Scandals* (in English in original), a revue at the Teatro Prado on the corner of Trocadero Street and the Paseo del Prado in Havana, two blocks from the site of the Alhmabra. The Prado was not on the list of "the most prominent theaters in Havana" during the period—a list that included the Nacional, the Regina, the Principal de la Comedia, the Martí, the Encanto, the Fausto, and, of course, the late Alhambra[156]—which is in keeping with O'Farrill's hardscrabble career narrative in literature and performance between 1925 and 1935. Clearly modeled on George White's Broadway *Scandals, The O'Farrill's Scandals* traded on, among other things, O'Farrill's recent experience in the film industry and familiarity with popular African American music and dance. Likely performing in blackface, O'Farrill was billed as "the star of the film *No matarás*," and the initial week of the *Scandals* featured a series of "Hollywood Revues" (in English in original), with sketches such as "Mi vida en New York y Hollywood" (My Life in New York and Hollywood), "Lindy-Hoop" (*sic*; Lindy Hop), "De México a Hollywood" (From Mexico to Hollywood), "La boda de Minnie de Mooker" (*sic*; The Wedding of Minnie the Moocher), and "En un studio de Hollywood" (In a Hollywood Studio).[157] The *Scandals* cycled through two other original stagings during its month-long run at the Prado, where O'Farrill was described as "keeping the audience constantly roaring with laughter" and even engaging it personally "on the origin of the dances" appearing in the show.[158] It was the return to Cuba (if not triumphant, then at least with a professional project of his own design) of the *barrio afrolatino negrito*, here outliving the early twentieth-century Havana *bufo* at its most institutional: the fallen Alhambra. O'Farrill returned to New York City soon after the *Scandals* closed, and it was another ship's "List or Manifest of Alien Passengers"—the *Pennsylvania*'s this time—that again identified him officially upon his rearrival in the United States. Now, under the column "Race or People," O'Farrill was not called "African," as was the case in Key West ten and a half years before. Rather, his "Race or People" was "Cuban." The Afro-Cuban American *negrito*, once and still an "African," could now add "Cuban" to his repertoire of racial and national performance in the Americas.[159]

In a crypt in the Sunset Mausoleum of the Flagler Memorial Park on Flagler Street and Fifty-Third Avenue in Miami rest the remains of one of the most important Afro-Cuban women cultural figures of twentieth-century Cuba and its U.S. diaspora. The crypt plate offers an identification: "Eusebia Cosme, Vda. de [widow of] Laviera, 'Mama [*sic*] Dolores,' Marzo 5, 1908–Julio 11, 1976." Born in Santiago de Cuba, Eusebia Cosme had been living at the Miami Convalescent Home since early 1974. She had arrived there from Mexico City, her body partially paralyzed by a stroke. It was another stroke that eventually ended her life: she died at the Jackson Memorial Hospital, and over three hundred people, including many Cuban American artists and performers, attended her wake at the Caballero Funeral Home on Calle Ocho. Nearly four decades earlier, right around the time Alberto O'Farrill had begun disappearing from print accounts of the Harlem theater scene, Cosme arrived in New York City. It was August 1938. Already, in the Cuban cultures of *poesía negra* (black poetry)—viewed by many people as a legitimate alternative to the *bufo* in its representations of Afro-Cubans—Cosme had achieved in her recital performances an international renown unlike anything O'Farrill had ever experienced. She was hailed on arrival as "the celebrated Cuban reciter [*declamdora cubana*]," and, by the end of the year, she had made her U.S. debut at Carnegie Hall in a performance attended by thirty-two hundred people, including many from the Cuban and Latino communities of Brooklyn and Harlem, where tickets for the event had been sold.[1]

Yet the line between Cosme's career in *poesía negra* and O'Farrill's in the *bufo*—a class line, among others, with her audiences coming from middle-class and elite zones, in contrast to O'Farrill's more working-class spectators—is blurred. A Miami obituary text suggests as much in its remembrance of her as "*la negrita*," a term that, despite its lack of a formal *bufo* meaning, comes close to *negrito* in its figuring a belittled, Afro-Cuban femininity.[2] Cosme's crypt offers another point of contact between her and O'Farrill in its reference to "Mamá Dolores." Dolores was Cosme's character in the film *El derecho de nacer* (The Right to Be Born; 1966), a role that later in life brought her renewed fame (and career prospects), particularly in Mexico. What this cryptic movie-role reference conceals is Cosme's lifelong professional challenges—not unlike O'Farrill's—as an Afro-Cuban woman in the twentieth-century Latino and Latin American theater and film industries. Her career in *poesía negra* performance, in other words, developed in large part because of the near impossibility for Cosme, except toward the end of her life, to find work as an actress. Linking her, too, to O'Farrill is an Afro-Cuban experience of uneven U.S. racialization, exemplified in the official discourses of U.S. arrival: in 1938, at the port of New York City, a "List or Manifest of Alien Passengers" called her "race" "Cuban." Just a few years later, however, Immigration and Naturalization documents written in Laredo, Texas, called her "African black."[3]

In this chapter, I offer a critical account of Cosme's life and work from the early 1930s in Cuba to her final days in Miami in the mid-1970s. Cosme is exemplary of the modern Afro-Cuban literary and performance cultures of the United States. As we shall see, one reason involves her various collaborations, both ephemeral and enduring, with African American cultures and institutions—collaborations only hinted at in the O'Farrill record. In one way, Cosme's connection to African Americans resulted from the accessible meaning (as signs of uplift) that her *poesía negra* performances held for middle-class African American audiences in the early twentieth century. In another way, Cosme's African American contacts in the United States resulted from a conscious effort on her part, one that illustrates the Afro-Cuban American difference: being an Afro-Cuban migrant woman in the United States—an Afro-Latina—put Cosme in the position to conceive of and benefit from a relationship with African Americans in terms of improved career prospects, friendship, and, most elusively, perhaps even African-diasporic solidarity despite (and, in some ways, because of) the social risks such an identification in a white-supremacist, Anglo United States involved.

Central to my discussion as well (and, indeed, related to Cosme's African American contacts) is the condition of what I call the "Cosme text": the many Cosme *fragments arrachés* that, in the absence of a definitive master object of critical attention (a novel, for example), make the enterprise of writing about her both a challenge and rewarding. The Eusebia Cosme Papers at the Schomburg Center for Research in Black Culture at the New York Public Library stand as just such a collection of *fragments arrachés*—an archive of the lost, now recovered, major figure whose primary texts were authored (and, indeed, *arrancados*) often by hands other than her own and are today housed in a key institution of African American and Afro-Latino culture. The Cosme text invokes the experiences of Afro-Cuban women in overlapping literary and performance cultures in Cuba and Cuban America during the early to mid-twentieth century: their general professional absence from such cultures, their sometime (and often troubling) presence therein, in ways that involve belatedness as both a politics of institutional recovery and (in Cosme's case) the aesthetics of her performance object, a "late" *poesía negra*. Cosme's life is a remarkable instance of Cuban American cultural practices as Afro-Cuban American, encompassing as it did the Machadato and the classic Miami Cuban exile. In this chapter, I hope to do right by such a life.

"The Effects of a Negro Actress": Creating the Cosme Papers

In a discussion of the 1920s and 1930s in Cuban literary history (the *vanguardia* period, or Cuban modernism) and its poetic interest in the "black theme" (*tema negro*), the Afro-Cuban poet and critic Nancy Morejón cites "the reciter [*recitadora*] Eusebia Cosme" as the only woman in a movement that was "all men." Indeed, she continues, "I know of no work by a woman in which . . . the historical experience of slavery or even of the violation of women's civil rights or of women's sexuality is represented or at least analyzed."[4] Vera Kutzinski also attends to the gender politics of Cosme: the *recitadora* was the "only woman associated" with the literary cultures of the *tema negro* during the period, yet her "participation . . . was limited to lending her voice to the poetry of her male compatriots."[5] In these arguments, Cosme's presence is symbolic of the absence of Afro-Cuban women writers during Cuban modernism—and of the absence, in general, of Afro-Cuban women from the spheres of social and economic capital on the island at the time. What is more, that Cosme was a migrant Afro-Cuban woman in the United States for the majority of her career complicates even further her relation to the masculanist island-Cuban canon (and the experiences of island Afro-Cuban women). A discussion of Cosme's life and work as interventions in Cuban canon formation thus engages a key idea of Carol Boyce Davies: that central among the projects of African-diasporic women writers and intellectuals is work that "re-connects and re-members" and "brings together black women dis-located by space and time," even as it confronts canonicity's own nationalist, completist fantasies with the political and cultural "slipperiness, elsewhereness" of African-diasporic women's subjectivity, which, in the case of Cosme, involves her Afro-Cuban American experience.[6] Such a complex emerges in a particular, insistent construction of Cosme over the years—that she is the greatest "*intérprete de la poesía afro-antillana*"[7]—a compelling construction, for *intérprete* (here of "Afro-Antillean poetry") means both "performer" and "interpreter," with nuances corresponding to the politics of "interpretation" itself: Cosme the *intérprete* as "performer" is the object of interpretation by others, who interpret not only her body and voice but also the poem she embodies in performance; Cosme the *intérprete* as "interpreter," on the other hand, is the agent of interpretation, a hermeneut invested with the power of interpretation over the poetry of white and mixed-race Cuban men and, indeed, over her own performing body.

The Cosme text is also a material, institutional object: the Eusebia Cosme Papers, 1927–1973, in the Manuscripts, Archives, and Rare Books Division at the Schomburg Center for Research in Black Culture at the New York Public Library. That the Cosme Papers reside at the Schomburg Center on 135th Street and not, say, at the Biblioteca Nacional José Martí in Havana or the Cuban Heritage Collection at the University of Miami in Coral Gables locates Cosme's archive effects in a library and public-memory space where the Afro-Latino and the African American overlap. The Schomburg Center is also representative of the library as a gendered space: in particular, as a site of struggle over African-diasporic women's professional participation in matters of who and what gets collected (and hence recollected) as black culture. It is not insignificant that the archivist who began working on the Cosme *fragments arrachés* at the Schomburg Center in early 1980 was Diana Lachatanere, the New York–born Afro-Cuban woman who today is curator of manuscripts, archives, and rare books. Lachatanere's family knew Cosme: her parents kept photographs of Cosme, and her aunt was Cosme's dresser. (Lachatanere's father, Rómulo Lachatañeré, the Afro-Cuban ethnographer and photographer, is among the subjects of chapter 3.) Because the Cosme *fragments arrachés* were the first items Lachatanere ever cataloged as a

Schomburg archivist, her professional beginning situates her as Cosme's collaborator, one whose work "brings together black women dis-located by space and time."[8]

In fact, the arrival at the Schomburg Center of the Cosme *fragments arrachés* is itself a historical narrative of African-diasporic (and Anglo-white) women's professional collaborations in and beyond library spaces. Of the two figures central to this narrative, one is Jean Blackwell Hutson, the longtime African American curator and chief of the Schomburg Center.[9] The other is an Anglo-white woman named Eileen Charbo. Charbo was a researcher and writer who, among other pursuits, worked with the Kansas Historical Society. Like Blackwell Hutson (1914–1998), Charbo (born in 1911) belongs to Cosme's generation. The details of Charbo's encounter with Cosme in Mexico City in the mid-1970s, her recovery of Cosme's belongings, and her shipping them to the Schomburg Center are constitutive of the belated (and vulnerable) condition of the Eusebia Cosme Papers—and of the modern literary and performance cultures of Afro-Cubans in the United States.

In 1975, Eileen Charbo sent a letter from Mexico to Blackwell Hutson, who had known Cosme through Langston Hughes.[10] It was apparent that Blackwell Hutson and Charbo had been in contact before. "I am now living in Mexico and have come on material I wonder if your library might like," writes Charbo.

> If you do want it, may I mail it collect to you from Texas, where some friend who would take it out of Mexico would send it to you from Stateside . . . ? . . . In working with the board of the American Benevolent Society here, I have gone through the effects of a Negro actress, Eusebia Cosme. She was a naturalized American, living in New York for years, [and] her early passports show she was born Cuban of a German father and Island (Negro) mother. . . . I think she was in the Follies Bergère in the 1930s. She is well known and much admired down here, particularly for her starring role in *Mamma Dolores* [sic] and *The Right to Be Born*. She appeared with Rod Steiger as Mrs. Ortiz in *The Pawnbroker* and in other films. Her old showbills and news clips show she read poetry at Town Hall; Columbia; appeared with Marian Anderson and other notables; did a show or two at Yale; and on CBS with Langston Hughes. . . . I will enclose a few samples of the things—destroy if you do not want.[11]

A few weeks later, in another letter, Charbo continued the conversation:

When I'm next in the States, will send a package of things from Eusebia Cosme's effects. Destroy what you do not want. She is now in Florida in a nursing home—where quite a group of old actors can visit and attend her. She had a crippling stroke here about four years ago and was in the care of the American Benevolent Society (speechless and paralyzed on one side). A prominent U.S. actor "picked up the tab" for her night nurse and eventually arranged for her to come to Florida. She took all of her belongings that she wanted and left a trunk of costumes and old pix and showbills for disposal by the Society. Of course, it seems wrong to not disperse them where they should go. Her costumes went to the civic theater here. . . . I think her father was named German [*sic*] and her mother Cosme. She was married to a man named La Viera who was, I think, killed in an accident. . . . I did see her in *The Pawnbroker*. I think she was the woman who sold the baby clothes to Rod Steiger. . . . P.S. I regret that the pictures are unidentified. . . . I can recognize Langston Hughes . . . , but haven't a clue to many others.[12]

Charbo only ever saw Cosme bedridden, looking "real brittle." The American Benevolent Society had asked her to take charge of Cosme's possessions, brought to her in garbage bags, and to examine and, as the case may be, "dispose of" them. Charbo donated Cosme's "plain dresses" to the Daughters of the American Revolution in Mexico, and she contacted the Smithsonian Institution (to no avail) about their possible interest in Cosme's costumes. Charbo also recalled, finally, that Cosme had expressed a preference for "going back to Florida."[13]

Charbo's letters to Hutson locate the "loss," "recovery," and archival arrival of Cosme's *fragments arrachés* in terms of cultural materiality and the abject. Placed in trash bags, Cosme's newspaper and magazine clippings, radio and film scripts, performance programs, photographs, and more were (laid) waste, a condition also associated with the body of Cosme herself, here in a state of partial mobility and seeming silence that invites a critical reflection on her prior states as a "fully" moving, "fully" speaking body in performance. Charbo's letters reproduce in other ways the constitutive partiality of the body and its "effects" in (and prior to) modalities of recovery. The letters recognize how "well known and much admired" Cosme was in Mexico, where she had been living since 1966, working in film, television, and theater, until she was hospitalized in 1973 with a stroke.[14] Yet, in details, the letters also err: Cosme's father was not a German, for example, but a Cuban named Germán Cosme (as Charbo later realized), a veteran of the Liberation Army of 1895; Cosme never did perform with the Follies Bergère; and her role in *The Pawnbroker* was that of Mrs. Ortiz, as Charbo first recognized.[15] The 1970s geographic separation of Cosme from her effects is itself indicative of recovery's partiality, here in another sense: Cosme's body, "speechless and paralyzed on one side," favors Miami, which identifies Cosme's physical recovery with the post-1959 Cuban exile; her effects favor the Schomburg Center, which identifies their archival recovery with the past of the *barrio afrolatino* and its present in the soul, salsa, and early hip-hop cultures in and around Harlem.

Declamaciones

Cosme's *fragments arrachés* signify in and beyond the *poesía negra* cultures of early twentieth-century Cuba—cultures whose belated logics and professional-career politics, comparable in many respects to those of O'Farrill's *bufo*, influenced Cosme's experience as an Afro-Cuban woman performer. *Poesía negra*—known also as *poesía mulata* (mulatto poetry), *poesía afrocubana* (Afro-Cuban poetry), and *poesía afroantillana* (Afro-Antillean poetry)—was a literary phenomenon of the 1920s and 1930s with origins in the Hispanophone Caribbean. In the poetry of predominantly white and mixed-race Cuban men, elements of the Afro-Cuban popular in music, speech, and religion were invoked as content and form, with a particular emphasis on the sonic and rhythmic. Critics have recognized *poesía negra*'s articulations with *vanguardismo*, *afrocubanismo* (especially in its musical elaborations), European primitivism, and the interwar cultures of the African diaspora; in terms of its ideological vectors, *poesía negra* drew on eroticized figures of mixed-race femininity to imagine national belonging as masculine and multiracial, all in the context of U.S. imperial relations with the island.[16] Among the Cubans identified with *poesía negra* production during the period were the white Emilio Ballagas, Nicolás Guillén, and the Asturian-born Alfonso Camín, while the white Puerto Rican Luis Palés Matos is considered the movement's original figure.[17] *Poesía negra*'s place in relation to Cuban *vanguardismo*, according to one critic, was itself "more or less belated" (*más o menos tardía*), while Ballagas, writing at midcentury, recalled *poesía negra* as an "exaggerated enthusiasm" that "lasted ten years: more or less from the publication in Havana of a poem by the Puerto Rican writer Luis Palés Matos (1927) to 1936 [*sic*], when Ramón Guirao collects in his anthology the movement's most interesting manifestations."[18] Here, in other words, is *poesía negra*'s belatedness, and it involves Cosme: her 1938 arrival in New York City coincides with the latter end of Ballagas's ten-year frame, marking her U.S. career as a countercurrent to *poesía negra*'s "official" wane.[19]

Cosme's interest in conceptualizing her *poesía negra* practice was keen, especially in relation to its social significations—what critics at the time called *poesía negra*'s "sociological, extrapoetic levels."[20] In the early 1950s, Cosme expressed an understanding of and *feeling for* the way in which the historical and everyday experiences of the African diaspora in Cuba had mattered to her work: "I feel deeply the tragedy of my race [*tragedia de mi raza*] and pour all my heart into its heartrending lament of anguish. It's the ancestral that comes out into the open for me. Nevertheless, as part of my very Cuban heritage, I also like the *cumbanchero* [in original], the spell of Cuban music with its Afro-modalities [*modalidades afras*]. The comical is pleasant with a true imprint of the things that occur daily among our people [*nuestro pueblo*]."[21] Years earlier, on her arrival in New York City, Cosme had drawn a link between her work, African American culture, and the memory of slavery in a discussion of performing *poesía negra* in the United States.[22] She also offered insight into the staging of her performances in the 1930s and 1940s, particularly in terms of their *afrocubanista* stylizing of Afro-Cuban popular expression: "A bit of dance, something of song, from time to time black instrumental [*instrumental negro*], diluted, subordinated to the most noble art of *declamación*. Actually, I'd say they're complementary suggestions. A *recitadora* [in original], above all, has to recite. Of course, wardrobe, traditional costumes, little things like that."[23]

Such critical self-reflection further shapes the hermeneut-performer dialectic in Cosme's *intérprete* identity, revealing her also as a theorist of her own *poesía negra* practice. Andrés Iduarte, the great Mexican intellectual living in New York City at the time of Cosme's arrival, adds still another element to the discussion, imagining Cosme as an "author" of the *poesía negra* texts she performed. "A true artist," writes Iduarte, "the young Cuban woman has not only known how to perform [*interpretar*], but has created a new genre, and she is, together with those who wrote the poems she recites, the author [*autora*] of a new emotion."[24] These figurations of Cosme—the critic-theorist, the author-performer—not only indicate the multiplicity of her vocation; they resolve in her a history of the gendered, racialized inaccessibility of modern, literacy-intensive institutions such as criticism, authorship, and stage performance for Afro-Cuban women.

Cosme's experience of professional-career politics is particularly compelling as it appears in the dis/continuities between *declamación* and acting. As Magali Roy-Féquière suggests, Cosme's career in *declamación* implied her exclusion from the theater: during the period in Cuba, "to become an actress in the serious theater arts one had to be white."[25] Yet, over the course of her career, it is evident that *declamación* and theater practices converged for Cosme through performativity. Relevant in this regard are her origins in the particular gendered, racialized cultures of *declamación* in the early twentieth-century Americas.[26] The road to *declamación* for Cosme began with music. She attended the Conservatorio Municipal de Música de la Habana in 1926 and 1927, from which she earned a diploma. Around graduation, she made her professional debut at the Teatro Neptuno as a *cupletista*—that is, as a performer of the *cuplé*, a Spanish popular song form of the early twentieth century whose stagings in theater and cabaret spaces by solo women performers linked ideological femininity and sexuality to the "dramatic arc, form of address, reliance on gesture, costume, and corporealization" of the melodramatic.[27] In 1931, Cosme returned to the Municipal to study at its Academia de Declamación under the writer and performer Graziella Garbalosa, a figure of the Cuban *vanguardia* and the Academia's founder and director. There, among the girls and young women in her *declamación* class, Garbalosa "noticed that the *negrita* [in original] Eusebia Cosme Almanza had a theatrical temperament." As she mentored Cosme, a "few marble-skinned students with light-colored eyes and blonde hair were put off by my favoring the *negrita* [in original] who back then had a faint voice and no political influence." Garbalosa recalled a performance at the Academia in which four students each portrayed "a different genre of declamation," with Cosme doing "*lo afrocubano*." "Cosme's set consisted of a black backdrop with three plantain leaves painted on transparent paper from one end of the stage to the other," Garbalosa writes. She then describes Cosme's appearance: "A sleeveless, red-silk costume with a long train, gold earrings, gold-hoop bracelets, gold fingernails." According to Garbalosa, Cosme's performance was the "program's greatest novelty for her being black [*ser negra*] and for reciting Africanoid or Afro-Cuban poems [*poemas africanoides o afrocubanos*]."[28]

In Garbalosa's account, theatricality structures Cosme's beginnings in *declamación* (as it did in the *cuplé*), and, as she mentors her pupil against the currents of Cuban whiteness, Garbalosa does so by positing an identity, the *negrita*, that only further underscores theatricality in its suggestion of *negrito-bufo* performances, which, of course, loops Cosme again into white-Cuban imaginings of race. This is to say that Cosme's *declamación* career was never simply compensatory for a theater career; in fact, in keeping with "slipperiness, elsewhereness," Cosme's spoken, embodied poetry performances were participatory commentaries on the status of Afro-Cuban women in performance professions such as the theater, thus revising, to an extent, reflections such as Urrutia's on a hoped-for, "modern Cuban theater" or, in 1938, Fernando Ortiz's on how "what is still needed is a Cuban theater on black-white dilemmas [*dilemas blanquinegros*] in which the dark personification [*oscura personificación*] isn't only that of the white comedian in a mask of the boastful, roguish *negrito*" but "a stage where the black man [*el negro*] speaks for himself, 'what comes from inside,' and speaks it in his own language, manner, tone, and emotions, even the most sorrowful ones."[29] What such future-oriented discussions of race and Cuban theater were in danger of losing sight of, of course, was how Afro-Cuban women such as Cosme were already performing a "modern Cuban theater" outside its expected institutions and roles through the theatricality of such gendered, racialized genre spaces as *declamación*. In this light, Cosme's expressions of regret about the theater, of which there were many, emerge as the moving, knowing reflections of an Afro-Cuban woman on her life in the theatrical profession. Cosme recalled seeing "comedy and drama performances" as a child and saying to herself, "soon you'll get there, too," but then thinking, "being a black girl [*niña negra*], I would never be able to step foot on those stages."[30] In 1950, she recalled, "I had to struggle uphill to gain the humble position I occupy in art," and stated, regarding her prospects, "I am looking for a way to do a play [*obra teatral*], bringing to the stage my style and character."[31] In this regard, I find an exchange between her and Langston Hughes in the late 1950s particularly meaningful. Cosme had just seen Hughes's *Simply Heavenly* off Broadway as his special guest, and she wrote him to say thanks. The letter was entirely in Spanish, with Cosme referring to Hughes throughout in the formal *usted*. She did, however, write one sentence in English: "The only thing I am worrie about is what I am not in the cast."[32] Cosme pokes fun at Hughes: she is not really "worrie" about not acting in the play because, in all likelihood, she never had an expectation of appearing in it in the first place, despite the authorship of Hughes, a friend. In another way, "the only thing I am worrie about is what I am not" is written in all seriousness: it is a text in which Cosme testifies about *what* (and *who*) she was not, here in terms of her identity, that conspired to make her not "an actress," a testimony whose English-language form (with its "errors") bespeaks, like Edmundo's "shine, mister," Cosme's *barrio afrolatino* location.

The Phonograph and the Lyceum

An important opening into the meanings of Cosme's early *declamación* career is the representation of her 1934 performance at the Havana Lyceum by Fernando Ortiz in "La poesía mulata: Presentación de Eusebia Cosme, la recitadora," an essay in the *Revista Bimestre Cubana*. *Presentación* can mean Ortiz's introduction of Cosme to the Lyceum's public but also Cosme's own public "presentation": her *recitadora* performance that day. The enfolding of patronage and self-performance evident here leads back to Cosme's origins in Santiago and the details of her early career in and beyond Havana. Before turning to Ortiz's "Presentación," I discuss that history.

The historian and journalist Nydia Sarabia states that Cosme's mother was the cook of Luis Fernández Marcané, a senator and "senior United Fruit counsel in Cuba."[33] The Fernández Marcané family participated in Cosme's upbringing and education, thus linking Cosme to longstanding experiences of servitude and white mentorship in the African-diaspora Americas.[34] In Garbalosa's account, Cosme was still living under the patronage of the Marcané family in early 1930s Havana. Garbalosa convinced Cosme to stay in the capital after the family decided to return to Santiago. Cosme rented an apartment, where she lived with an older aunt and worked as a "little neighborhood teacher," earning between ten and twenty cents per week for each pupil. During this time, Garbalosa continued mentoring Cosme in *declamación*, including at her own home, where one day, Francisco Ichaso saw her perform Guillén's "El velorio de Papá Montero" (Wake for Papá Montero), Camín's "Macorina," and Ruben Darío's "La negra Dominga" (The Black Woman Dominga).[35] Regarding this period, Gustavo Urrutia reflects on Cosme's "tenacious self-education" and the role that the "loving Graciela [*sic*] Garbalosa" played in bringing Cosme into "public light."[36] However, another history of Cosme's professional origins in "tenacious self-education" and mentorship, one that Cosme herself repeated in interview after interview, involved her "discovery" by the Málaga-born reciter and actor José González Marín at the house of the Cuban poet, playwright, and lyricist Gustavo Sánchez Galarraga. González Marín, a performer of modern Spanish poetry, met Cosme at Galarraga's through the involvement of two major Afro-Cuban performers of the period, Rita Montaner and

FIGURE 3. Eusebia Cosme and Nicolás Guillén, c. 1930 (Eusebia Cosme Photograph Collection, Photographs and Prints Division, Schomburg Center for Research in Black Culture, New York Public Library, Astor, Lenox and Tilden Foundations)

Ignacio "Bola de Nieve" Villa. González Marín brought Cosme to the Teatro Payret, where he was giving a farewell performance. She recited at the Payret on that occasion, later calling the performance "no more than a rehearsal, serving as an introduction [*a manera de presentación*]."[37] Garbalosa expressed disappointment at the Cuban press's recognition of González Marín's mentorship of Cosme at the expense of her own, calling it an "injustice."[38] While absent from such narratives of early mentorship in the Cosme text, Guillén was very likely a presence in her life during the late 1920s and early 1930s; a photograph-postcard among the materials that Eileen Charbo recovered shows a young Cosme arm in arm with a young Guillén.

The summer of 1934, which saw Cosme's performance at the Lyceum and another at the Teatro Principal de la Comedia (her first major show), was her breakthrough moment, preceded by a lull during the revolutionary crisis of 1933 and followed by performances to acclaim across Cuba, in Puerto Rico, and in Venezuela—a roughly four-year period that was the sum of Cosme's time in *poesía negra* performance in Cuba and the Caribbean, culminating in her August 1938 migration to New York City, a migration that, despite the acclaim, signaled Cosme's need to improve on her career and personal prospects with a voyage to the United States.

A survey of Cosme's performances around this time reveals their range. At the end of 1932, she performed *declamación* in a hurricane benefit at the Unión Fraternal, the Afro-Cuban club and mutual-aid society in Havana, appearing on the program with Ignacio Piñeiro and his Septeto Nacional.[39] In 1934, she performed in a theater in the town of Camagüey, where, around the same time, a controversy occurred involving white university students protesting the appointment of an Afro-Cuban professor.[40] Later that year, Cosme appeared at the Lyceum, the important women's civic and cultural institution with a white, middle-class and elite membership and origins in the 1920s avant-garde. In August, at the Principal de la Comedia, she gave her first "recital completo," a performance that she said was completely her responsibility.[41] Also in August, Cosme performed at Havana's Sociedad Pro-Arte Musical, the island's most important institution of classical music and dance.[42] Cosme's performance of Guillén's "Sensemayá" was such a success that evening that she performed it twice.[43] She also appeared on the radio, an important example of which was the *Hora Sensemayá* on CMCG in Havana.[44] By the middle of the decade, Cosme's imprint on Cuban culture was definite. The poet and critic Cintio Vitier recalled 1936 as the year of "those innocent recitals of Eusebia Cosme in a Havana full of illusions."[45]

Indeed, 1936 was a year of significant professional activity for Cosme; her venues suggested someone branching out, in search of greater professional opportunity. She performed at such elitist institutions as the Casino Español.[46] And, around the time of *O'Farrill's Scandals*, she was at the Teatro Martí, a *bufo* space, appearing in an homage to the actress Alicia Rico, who had performed on the Latino stage in Harlem.[47] It was this year that the Sociedad de Estudios Afrocubanos was founded, with Cosme listed as an associate in its first journal issue. She then embarked on a tour through Puerto Rico, the Dominican Republic, and Haiti that ran through July—her first time abroad. Cosme's recital at San Juan's Teatro Municipal on April 5, 1936, concluded with a series of four Palés poems.[48] Her initial contract at the Municipal was for four performances; eventually, she appeared in twenty-two, with shows elsewhere on the island, including at the Teatro Broadway in Ponce.[49] Cosme's work in the Dominican Republic, where she was introduced by the writer Tomás Hernández Franco, was less extensive, with five stagings, while the performance in Haiti seems to have been restricted to an official audience.[50] Upon returning to Cuba, Cosme took a few months off, before appearing before audiences again, "her emotions rested from the trip," in a performance at the Principal de la Comedia in November 1936.[51] The following month, as the "best *declamadora* [in original] in Cuba," she was honored by the city of Santiago with the title of "Hija Predilecta" (Favorite Daughter) at a ceremony attended also by Guillén.[52]

By early 1938, Cosme was on the verge of another voyage: to Venezuela. In April 1938, she performed at the Teatro Baralt in Maracaibo, where she was billed as the "Ambassador of Negroid Poetry [*Poesía Negroide*]" on a "cultural mission" of the Cuban Ministry of Education. During this trip, she met the great writer Andrés Eloy Blanco, who introduced her at the Teatro Nacional.[53] A few months later, in July, she was back in the Antilles—but not in Cuba. With a performance at the University of Puerto Rico in Río Piedras, Cosme had returned to Puerto Rico. She performed eighteen times during this—her second—visit to the island, spending time in Loíza Aldea, a center of Afro–Puerto Rican history and culture, and in the Machuchal neighborhood of Santurce, where she recalled watching a *bomba* performance.[54] It was during the stay in Puerto Rico that Cosme decided to travel to the United States. She embarked from San Juan aboard the *Coamo* and arrived in New York City on August 22, 1938.[55] Cosme did not return to Cuba until the early 1950s.

Returning now to the representation of her performance at the Havana Lyceum in 1934, Ortiz's "La poesía mulata: Presentación de Eusebia Cosme, la recitadora" is characteristic of how Cosme's body and voice were configured to Cuban discourses of *mestizaje* during the stretch of her career I have just detailed, particularly among white Cuban audiences and intellectuals. In this light, Miguel Arnedo-Gómez rightly argues that Ortiz's essay stands for the "desire to produce an image of harmonious unification between Cuban blacks and whites," but he ignores the way the presence of Cosme complicates Ortiz's endeavor, turning it into a negotiation with Afro-Cuban femininity, sexuality, and national belonging, all in the context of an institution, in the Lyceum, identified with elite white Cuban women and the politics of the avant-garde *minorista* social movement.[56] Ortiz's title encodes such complications in the way *"poesía mulata"* (mulatto poetry) links categories of literature and embodied identity (the eroticized, mixed-race femininity of the *mulata*). Meanwhile, in the essay's central claims, it recalls the assessments that, over and over again during the period, other Cuban critics rendered of Cosme. She knows how "to collect the beauty of the new poetry and transmit it in pure form to the multitude," Ortiz claims. "This is her contribution to the history of Cuban art."[57] Cosme, he continued, represents "a new moment in our country's history of aesthetic expression." Finally, and most resoundingly, her performance advances an "integrated nationalism [*nacionalismo integrativo*]" (206, 211).

As Ortiz posits a paradigmatic Cuban *poesía/mulata* in the figure of Cosme, he struggles with the physical presence of Cosme herself. One reason is his possible identification with her, at the level of performance: like Cosme, Ortiz is also doing a reading, since "La poesía mulata: Presentación de Eusebia Cosme, la recitadora" is not just an essay he published in the *Revista Bimestre* but a print-text remnant of the words he uttered before the audience gathered for Cosme's performance "at the Havana Lyceum on the 23rd of July, 1934" (205). The recital, in other words, and the sonic performance of a gendered, racial Cuban identity were also Ortiz's that day—he as the masculine, white Cuban arbiter of Cosme's performance. The implications of such an identification with Cosme— judging, as we will see, by Ortiz's use of a particular metaphor—were unsettling. Even at the start, things seem awry. Ortiz opens by asking, "Who is Eusebia Cosme? I will try to tell the women members [*socias*] of the Lyceum, who have invited me for that reason. Perhaps I will have to tell her herself, whose own sincerity she feels, knows, and lives without being able to explain" (205). Ortiz makes a show of his critical vocation, drawing attention to its workings, rather than simply enacting it: he *says* that he is going to tell his audience who Cosme is—and, in a revealing, condescending gesture, he will tell her, too—before doing any of the actual telling. It is a self-presentation of sorts, a way of marking off his own performance as critical and self-aware: his role as different, in other words, from what Cosme was about to do on stage. When Ortiz finally tells the Lyceum (and Cosme) who she is, he ends up restating (actually, intensifying) the *poesía/mulata* articulation. She is "a *mulata* [in original] born in an instance of peaceful synthesis in the dialectic of the races" and, what is more, "a saucy, witty [*sandunguera*] *mulatica* [in original; little *mulata*] before a most cultured, feminine society, reciting with art *mulato* [in original] poems that tell of things that happen to and move the mixed strata [*capas amalgamadas*] of society" (205, 206). Among the problems of Ortiz's *poesía/mulata* articulation here, as Vera Kutzinski's *Sugar's Secrets* has shown with *poesía negra* in general, is its association with a history of slavery and postslavery sexual violence against Afro-Cuban women that *mulata* figures would resolve. Another is that Ortiz would ascribe a *mulata* identity to Cosme at all, however figuratively. In doing so, he elides her *negra*, or black Cuban woman, identity, underscoring the difficulty that blackness creates for Ortiz's "Presentación," in which he doubts that the "recent stream of poetry" "is black" (*sea negra*). Instead, he argues, it is "simply *mulata* [in original], daughter of an inextricable embrace between Africa and Castile in emotion, rhythm, word choice, prosody, syntax, concept, tendencies . . ." (210; italics and ellipsis in original). Ortiz's *poesía/mulata* re/presentation of Cosme is, in ideological terms, a success, using Cosme, a *mulata* figure, to screen an erotic, asymmetrical, public encounter between an elite white Cuban man (Ortiz) and the elite feminine Cuban audience of the Lyceum, whose whiteness is coded as "most cultured" (*cultísima*).

The distress of introducing Cosme to the Lyceum appears in a particular metaphor in the "Presentación." Discussing how to make the poetry of Emilio Ballagas or Nicolás Guillén "sound well," Ortiz says it is necessary "that the reciter dance it for us, move it for us, with that garrulous gesticulation [*mímica parlera*] that completes the act of saying, without which such poetry would of necessity descend to the category of a poem emitted by a phonograph hidden inside the hollow abdomen of a statue [*poema emitido por el fonógrafo disimulado en el vientre hueco de una estatua*]" (212). The phonograph manages for Ortiz anxieties related to the graphic, the phonic, and mechanical reproduction as elements of a post/colonial Cuban literature and performance. Alexander Weheliye recalls how the phonograph exposed "the materiality and iterability of the voice," disrupting associations between "human vocalization" and "unmediated presence." Weheliye extends here Derrida's well-known formulation of the *pharmakon* of writing to draw attention to "the writingness of all vocal acts and their differently calibrated sonic iterability through the technology of the phonograph." In terms of the phonograph and race, a distinction of the African-diasporic cultures of the Americas, with their fraught slavery and postslavery relation to writing-based literacy, is that "the phonograph did not cause the same anxieties in black cultural discourses" as it did in the dominant culture. Indeed, it is the "coupling of the graphematic *and* the phonic" that "represents the prime achievement of black cultural production in the New World."[58]

These ideas about technologies of sound, writing, and race bear on the "Presentación." Ortiz needs a moving, dancing Cosme—a Cosme that is foremost a body—to spare him what the phonograph (and the haunting statue) admits: that what he hears in the *poesía/mulata* of Cosme's voice is its iterability, which it shares with both the written poetry it sounds and Ortiz's own *presentación*, soon to be published in the *Revista Bimestre*. (Indeed, Cosme's visibly moving, dancing body emphasizes how "the *phono* and the *optic* cannot materialize without each other.")[59] Iterability challenges the authenticities of the *poesía/mulata* articulation—the *poesía*'s fidelity to Afro-Cuban expression, the *mulata*'s to Afro-Cuban femininity, both emerging here as objects/subjects of reproduction—a challenge that extends also to the *poesía/mulata*'s ideological subtext: the authenticity of an "integrated nationalism." The phonograph also admits the materiality, and hence the historical-material condition, of Cosme's voice: its emergence from the "mute world of the Plantation," as Glissant puts it, in which "oral expression, the only kind possible for the slaves, was organized in a discontinuous manner."[60] The connection between the postslavery Americas, muteness, and a discontinuous, sonorous orality will return in the conclusion of this chapter with the poststroke, speech-disabled body of Cosme sitting in the audience at the Teatro Lecuona in Hialeah, Florida, in 1975. For now, the "mute world of the Plantation" historicizes the record, as it were, of Ortiz's "Presentación": in a suggestion of the kinds of literacy divisions characteristic of Cuba as a plantation space—where the white masculine subject of writing leaves something behind, the Afro-Cuban feminine subject of discontinuous orality "nothing"—it is not the sound of Cosme's voice at the Lyceum, "unmuting" the "world of the Plantation," whose record we hear (her sounding of a "plantation orality") but that of Ortiz's written metaphor, the "fonógrafo disimulado," read aloud in the critical enterprise.[61]

Courier/Adelante

The representation of Cosme's Lyceum performance in Ortiz's essay contrasts in important respects with comparable accounts in Afro-Cuban print culture during the period. *Adelante*, a journal associated with an Afro-Cuban club of the same name, offers one such example. As Alejandro de la Fuente shows, the Club Adelante (Forward) was among the Afro-Cuban organizations "that emerged after the fall of Machado"

FIGURE 4. Eusebia Cosme, c. 1935 (Eusebia Cosme Photograph Collection, Photographs and Prints Division, Schomburg Center for Research in Black Culture, New York Public Library, Astor, Lenox and Tilden Foundations)

to support equality for Afro-Cubans with a progressive agenda. Among its strategies was a politics that "condemned gender discrimination," which was significant since, "traditionally, the directors of the Afro-Cuban clubs had sought to limit the role of women to charitable work and the organization of 'ladies' committees.'"[62] *Adelante* was a remarkable publication for its transamerican, African-diasporic reach (essays on Du Bois and Paul Robeson, Spanish translations of Langtson Hughes); its commitment to research and writing on Afro-Cuban history and culture (essays on Antonio Maceo, Juan Gualberto Gómez, and the poet Plácido); and its inclusion of women contributors, including Consuelo Serra.[63]

The November 1935 issue of *Adelante* devoted an entire page to Cosme. Entitled "Eusebia Cosme," the page featured three photographs of her in costumed poses, and it included text:

> Not a note of criticism, not an artistic profile. This is, simply, an homage and a statement of pride. For the public at large, Eusebia Cosme can be—and no doubt is—a brilliant *recitadora* [in original]: the most personal, spontaneous, and profound of performance

sensitivities of verse to have come across our stages. The public at large will say that, and it will be true. For us she is something more [*algo más*]. She is black emotion, voice, and rhythm [*la emoción, la voz y el ritmo negros*], harmoniously vibrating in the flesh and grace of a woman. From the natural, infectious laughter to the deep, whipping pain of injustice or the tragic, tempestuous cry, all black emotion [*emoción negra*] burns and cries out in Eusebia with deep fullness. That is why the dedication of this page is an homage to her merits, which *Adelante* proudly pays her.[64]

The contrast with Ortiz's "Who is Eusebia Cosme?" is striking. *Adelante* intends *not* to say who Cosme is, critically or biographically. Rather, it would express its pride in her, even if it does finally interpret her, as the paragraph makes clear. By the mid-1930s, in other words, the journal had recognized that commentaries on Cosme—particularly from a "public at large," which encodes, I suggest, a *white* public—had settled on a conceit: the projection on Cosme, through cultural criticism, of any manner of national fantasies, including that of an imagined "*nacionalismo integrativo*." *Adelante*'s own variation on the conceit appears after the paragraph's transition, "For us she is something more," which proposes a different public: an Afro-Cuban one, in the print-culture space of the journal. What that "something more" turns out to be is both familiar—"emotion," "voice," "rhythm," "laughter"—and surprising: the attribution of such elements as "*negros*," which counters Ortiz's *mulata* refrain in the "Presentación." The implication is clear. As an organization "careful to note that [it] did not promote 'racial campaigns,'"[65] *Adelante* nevertheless insisted in "Eusebia Cosme" on the Cuban blackness of Cosme's performance, and perhaps even of Cosme herself, suggesting a "campaign" of black Cuban *feeling*—as "pride," as "black emotion," as "natural, infectious laughter"—that negotiated other uses of *negro*, particularly those in the discourses of Cuban racism: *negro* as a signifier of poor or working-class Afro-Cuban origins and thus a term particularly objectionable to middle-class and elite Afro-Cubans, as a racist term comparable to *nigger*, and as a belittling "endearment." Such a use of black feeling also invokes the violent histories of the plantation ("whipping pain," "tragic tempestuous cry"). And, finally, the essay claims Cosme in a conceit of collectivity (the "for us") in which Afro-Cubans feel themselves, together, as *negras/os*—a "something more" that, historically, has remained in tension with a "*nacionalismo integrativo*."

Adelante is also a crucial text for the way it juxtaposed two accounts of Cosme's 1938 arrival in the United States in the Latino and African American press, a juxtaposition representing an island Afro-Cuban framing (and translating) of the two U.S. cultures Cosme negotiated as an Afro-Latina over the next twenty-five years. "La triunfal *tournée* de Eusebia Cosme" (The Triumphant *Tournée* of Eusebia Cosme) appeared in *Adelante* in October 1938, a few months after her arrival in New York City. It begins with a reflection on Cosme's recent travels in Venezuela before turning to her trip north (and the possible reasons behind it):

> We have received an echo of the resounding triumphs obtained by the brilliant performer of black verse [*verso negro*], the amazing Eusebia Cosme, who recently left Cuban shores behind to captivate the Central and South American publics first, the New York [*neoy-orquino*] public later . . . .
>
> But to conquer Spanish-speaking [*de habla española*] countries wouldn't suffice a restless soul, ambitious of triumph, like that of the great black *declamadora* [in original]; thus her unswerving decision to conquer the great public of that populous city that someone rightly named the heart of the world. We are referring to New York.[66]

Adelante's celebratory account of Cosme's travels culminates with her arrival in New York City, presenting the magazine with a complication regarding the representation of her departure not only from Cuba but from Latin America. This involves the crucial question of an Afro-Cuban literature and performance relocated to the United States: to be in and belong to the United States suggests an Afro-Cuban desire asserted against the "best interests" of a postracial, *mestizo*, or even *negro* Cuban nation—indeed, against the "best interests" of Afro-Cubans themselves. Living in an Anglophone United States (implied by the "*habla española*" of Latin America) also implies the linguistic promiscuity of *barrio afrolatino* spaces, suggesting not only the possible "loss" of Spanish among Afro-Latinas/os but the emergence of bilingual Afro-Latino identities, cultures, and politics shaped by contacts, however fleeting or enduring, with African Americans. Significantly, *Adelante*'s figure for Cosme's U.S. desire, "a restless, ambitious soul," indexes feeling—here disquiet and ambition—as a professional condition: a soul ambitious of "triumph," which implicates the U.S. trip in professional questions and, hence, the problem of securing a performance career on the island for Afro-Cuban women in the early twentieth century.

Further, *Adelante*'s "Triunfal *tournée*" is an exemplary transamerican text in its quoting and translating the accounts of Cosme's arrival in the Latino and African American press—specifically, accounts in *La Prensa* and in the *Pittsburgh Courier*. "Let us allow that country's press to give us its impressions of the arrival in those parts of the celebrated artist," *Adelante* begins, before quoting in full from an article in *La Prensa*, "Eusebia Cosme decidida a averiguar 'si Nueva York tiene sentimiento'" (Eusebia Cosme Determined to Find Out "If New York Has Feelings"), published on September 2, 1938. In the article, Cosme responds to a question ("What if you discover that this mass of steel has no spirit?") by using metaphors of immateriality—feelings, souls—to reflect a history of African diaspora in the United States for the Latinas/os of *La Prensa* and the Cubans of *Adelante*: "I have always suspected that behind all this appearance of materialism, harshness, and 'mechanization' [in the United States] beats the rhythm of deep feeling [that] manifests itself, for example, in the passion, always voluptuous, for dance and for song— sometimes lilting, sometimes roughed up—in North American popular music [*música popular norteamericana*], based, like much Hispanic American national music [*música criolla hispanoamericana*], on the inspiration brought from Africa by the slave in former times."[67]

This passage reveals Cosme thinking about her own *poesía negra* practice. It also reveals her thinking about African diaspora through her own migrant condition in the United States. Even as she sets modernity, identified with (an Anglo-white) "materialism," "harshness," and "mechanization," against tradition, identified with an African-diasporic "feeling" and "passion," Cosme collapses the opposition, identifying such feeling and passion for dance and song with popularity: that is, with collective, modern practices of the people that involve an aesthetics of the sonic and body movements—of music—together with a hint of its reproduction and spread through recording technologies. Cosme confirms the collapse later in her appreciation of the "former times" of slavery and their relation to the present cultures she describes, a gesture appreciative of historicity (and belatedness) characteristic of the African-diaspora modernity she invokes. For the transamerican readers of *Adelante*, meanwhile, such an encoding of African diaspora in the *Prensa* reprint would have called forth the tensions between a *nacionalismo integrativo* and what *Adelante* had earlier acknowledged, in its own representation of Cosme, as the island's *negro* history and identity.

Immediately after *Adelante* quoted this article from *La Prensa*, which it called the "the only newspaper published in Spanish in the city of skyscrapers," it then quoted sections of two pieces on Cosme from the *Pittsburgh Courier*, which it recognized as the "great black newspaper" (*gran periódico negro*): "Patrons Have Paid $6 a Seat to Hear Eusebia Cosme, Who Is Cuba's Greatest Actress," written by Edgar T. Rouzeau, a key figure in the history of African American journalism, and "Harlem's Spanish Section Raves about Cuba's Premier Dramatic Artist, Eusebia Cosme," a long caption appearing under three photographs of Cosme in poses, likely also written by Rouzeau. Both appeared on September 10, 1938. *Adelante*'s translation of these *Pittsburgh Courier* pieces reveals Cosme to its island-Cuban readers as a figure of African American culture. I quote in full "Harlem's Spanish Section Raves about Cuba's Premier Dramatic Artist, Eusebia Cosme," as it appeared in the English original in the *Courier*, following it with *Adelante*'s Spanish version:

> Harlem's Spanish-speaking colony is playing host this week to Cuba's premier dramatic artist, Eusebia Cosme (pronounced You-say-bia Cos-may), who is visiting America for the first time. Although known to but few Americans, she is always ranked above the Ethel Barrymores, the Norma Shearers, Ginger Rogers, the Mae Wests and the Greta Garbos, when her name is billed by the leading theatres in Puerto Rico, San Domingo, and in certain South American countries, in addition to her own native land. Patrons in those countries have paid as high as $6 a seat to see her. Miss Cosme specializes in interpretive recitals in costume, featuring the work of Negro poets. Although still on this side of 30, critics are carried away by her work and claim that she runs the full gamut of human emotions and is equally proficient in all. Her one regret right now is that she is unable to digest enough English overnight so as to enjoy the works of Claude McKay, Langston Hughes, Zora Neale Hurston, Paul Laurence Dunbar, Countee Cullen and others. Someday she hopes to recite in English from their works. Very recently Miss Cosme appeared in a private recital in Haiti before President Stenio Vincent and members of his cabinet. She is shown here in various poses. While in Harlem she will reside at 408 Convent Avenue.[68]

> La Colonia de habla española de Harlem está rindiendo homenaje esta semana a la primera artista dramática cubana, Eusebia Cosme, que visita a Estados Unidos por primera vez. Aunque conocida por pocos norteamericanos, es siempre comparada con Ethel Barrymore, Norma Shears, Ginger Rogers, Mae West y Greta Garbo, cada vez que su nombre aparece en un programa de los principales

teatros de Puerto Rico, Santo Domingo y otros muchos países americanos, en adición de su propia patria. La afición en los mencionados países ha pagado hasta seis pesos por asiento para oír a la Cosme, la cual se especializa en recitales interpretativos de costumbres, propagando los trabajos de los poetas negros. Aunque es relativamente joven, los críticos se encuentran sorprendidos por su trabajo y aseguran que recorre todas las gamas de las emociones humanas y que es igualmente eficiente en cada una de ellas; su único pesar del momento consiste en no conocer el idioma inglés lo suficientemente para interpretar los trabajos de Claude McKay, Langston Hughes, Zora Neale Hurston, Paul Laurence Dunbar, Countee Cullen y otros. Ella espera algún día recitar sus obras en inglés. Recientemente Eusebia Cosme ofreció un recital privado en Haití para el Presidente Stenio Vincent y los miembros de su gabinete.[69]

The *Courier*'s interest in Cosme again affirms how, "from its beginnings, the African-American press was international in distribution and in its concerns."[70] *Adelante*'s translation and reprinting of "Harlem's Spanish Section Raves" extends the idea: the *Courier* functions in a network of African-diaspora print culture in which, in the particular case of *Adelante*'s "Triunfal *tournée*," the Afro-Cuban magazine's leadership used the *Courier*'s content not only to apprise Afro-Cubans of an African American perspective on Cosme but to translate the language of the African American press to reimagine her as an Afro-Latina in contact with African Americans. A sign of such a transamerican print-culture practice is the *Courier*'s guide regarding the pronunciation of Cosme's name—"pronounced You-say-bia Cos-may"—along with *Adelante*'s decision to cut it from its translation. The excision of "pronounced You-say-bia Cos-may" in *Adelante* denies the Cuban journal's readership an opportunity to reflect on such an admission of language difference as constitutive of African-diasporic collaboration, along with its particular effects on Cosme: the way in which Anglophone, African American voices would say Cosme's name aloud, Englishing (and African Americanizing) it (and her), thereby referencing the possible social transformations articulated in Eusebia/You-say-bia, Cosme/Cos-may, including the movement between Cosme's "*mulata*," "*negra*," and now "Negro" identities as an Afro-Latina performer in the United States. The figure of "Harlem's Spanish-speaking colony / la Colonia de habla española de Harlem" offers a kind of consolation—there is in New York City a space for the "proper" Hispanophone pronunciation of "Eusebia Cosme"—even as it implies "Harlem's English-speaking colony / la Colonia de habla inglesa de Harlem," where You-say-bia Cos-may is spoken, sounding African American. (The specific location of Harlem's English-speaking colony for Cosme was the Convent Avenue/Sugar Hill address where she stayed, the reference to which in the *Courier* article, as I discuss in note 71, *Adelante* moved to another section of its reprint/translation.)

The issue takes another turn in the *Courier*'s report of Cosme's interest in English and in "the works of Claude McKay, Langston Hughes, Zora Neale Hurston, Paul Laurence Dunbar, Countee Cullen and others." Here, it is the voice of Cosme herself that *Adelante*'s readers would imagine as Anglophone, sounding the works of an early twentieth-century, African American canon. Indeed, a challenge in the movement between the *Courier*'s English original and *Adelante*'s Spanish is occasioned by the *Courier*'s claim that Cosme is known for "featuring the work of Negro poets," which, in *Adelante*, appears as *"propagando los trabajos de los poetas negros"* (propagating the works of black poets). There is an "error" here that the *Courier* commits and *Adelante*'s translation lets pass. Up until that time, Cosme's repertoire was composed mainly of works by white Spanish and Latin American poets—by *poetas blancos*—with the most renowned of Cuban "Negro" poets, Guillén, often identifying himself as a *mulato*. The "error," to be sure, admits to an incommensurability: what Cosme is "actually" known for—in English, it would have been phrased as "featuring the works of white and Negro poets"—the *Courier* ignores, lest its African American readership associate the white-Cuban authorship of an Afro-Cuban literary voice with the minstrel tradition. It is an error that *Adelante*'s translation extends, thus circulating the possible meanings of such an African-diasporic incommensurability: among them, the sense that, with Cosme's migration to the United States, not only has she been "blackened" by her contacts with African Americans, but her repertoire has as well, the *poesía negra* she recites and its respective (mostly *blanco*) authors. The *Courier* thus imagines (and *Adelante* "mistranslates," as a desire perhaps for "something more" in African diaspora) a "U.S. Negro/Cuban *negro*" literary tradition in tension with the cultures of a Cuban *nacionalismo integrativo*. For an Afro-Cuban feminist critique such as Morejón's, however, the erasure here of the *poetas blancos* is the least of it, for the appellation "Negro poets/*poetas negros*" only serves to recall the absence of Afro-Cuban women writers—*"poetas negras"*—during the period.[71]

Adelante's other translation from the *Courier* in "Triunfal *tournée*"—two paragraphs from Rouzeau's "Patrons Have Paid $6 a Seat to Hear Eusebia Cosme, Who Is Cuba's Greatest Actress"—represents Cosme's experience of theater-career politics as a problem in a transamerican, African-diasporic print culture. The two *Courier* paragraphs, the second and third from Rouzeau's original five-paragraph article, appear here, followed by *Adelante*'s translation:

> In short, Eusebia Cosme, chocolate-complexioned and with great big eyes and a contagious smile, is Cuba's premier dramatic actress. But inasmuch as Cuban drama is still in an embryonic stage, she has had to fall back repeatedly on her great ability as a dramatic reader, and it is in this characterization that she is best known to audiences in Cuba, Porto Rico [*sic*], the Republic of San Domingo and in certain South American countries which she has included in her tours.
>
> She has been featured repeatedly at the Pro-Arte Musical in Havana, a place comparable to New York's Carnegie Hall, the Comedie Francaise [*sic*] in Paris or the Teatro Scala in Milan. It is the highest cultural center to which any Cuban actress or recitalist can aspire. She broke the house record at the Teatro Municipal in Puerto Rico, and she was called back for a return performance at the Teatro Nacional in Caracas, Republic of Venezuela. In Haiti, she gave a private recital for President Stenio Vincent and members of his cabinet.[72]

> En fin, Eusebia Cosme, con su complexión achocolatada, grandes ojos y sonrisa contagiosa, es la primera actriz dramática de Cuba; sin embargo, como que el drama cubano está todavía en estado embrionario, ella ha tenido que regresar repetídamente en sus grandes habilidades como lectora dramática, y es en estas caracterizaciones donde es mejor conocida por las audiencias de Cuba, Puerto Rico, Santo Domingo y otros países.
>
> Ha sido presentada repetidas veces por Pro-Arte Musical en la Habana, lugar comparable a la Carnegie Hall de Nueva York y a la Comedia Francaise de París o al Teatro Escala de Milán. Es el más alto centro cultural a que todo artista o recitador cubano puede aspirar. Ha roto el record de entrada en el Teatro Municipal de Puerto Rico y fue contratada para una nueva presentación en el Teatro Principal de Caracas.

Mientras permanezca en Nueva York la señorita Cosme residará en el 408 de Convent Avenue.[73]

The *Courier* and *Adelante* collaborate in a tacit critique of Cosme's professional chances: while her achievements in *recitación* are remarkable indeed, they signify in relation to the difficulty of a stage (or film) career for Afro-Cuban women during the period. The translation discrepancy in the earlier section of "Triunfal *tournée*"—in the *Courier*, Cosme is "ranked above" Anglo-white actresses such as "the Ethel Barrymores, the Norma Shearers, Ginger Rogers, the Mae Wests and the Greta Garbos," while in *Adelante*, she is *"comparada con"* (compared with) them—shows the problem of theatrical-career politics as a tension between African American and Afro-Cuban representations of Cosme's professional standing, with the *Courier* perhaps overstating her popularity "in Puerto Rico, San Domingo, and in certain South American countries, in addition to her own native land," while *Adelante* offers a corrective of sorts. The tension admits that the use of comparison and contrast to articulate the careers of Cosme and the Barrymores et al. fails, for what links them, in fact, is their incommensurability. What is more, the Anglo-white actresses suggest a "list" of possible *white-Cuban* actresses with whom the question of being "ranked" or *"comparada"* with, for Cosme, is also moot: she and such white-Cuban actresses, in the context of Cuban white supremacy, occupied different, asymmetrical professional fields. Still another implied cohort is that of African American actresses, those with whom comparisons or contrasts with Cosme would indeed obtain, suggesting a shared experience of race and gender in the context of performance careers in the United States and Cuba. The passage, in short, accounts for the impossibility of a "list" of Afro-Cuban women actresses, since it describes Cosme as "Cuba's premier dramatic actress / *la primera actriz dramática de Cuba*," only to show how an "embryonic" "Cuban drama" has required her to "fall back" on another professional opportunity: the performance of *poesía negra* at "$6 a seat." The *Courier/Adelante*'s foregrounding of Cosme's racial identity is important in this respect. Configured to racial and gender ideologies of the appetitive, consumption, and skin-tone hierarchies, the figure of a "chocolate-complexioned / *complexión achocolatada*" Cosme discloses an Afro-Cuban identity inseparable from the paradox of her professional one: that of a woman who is—and is not—an actress.[74]

Armstrong High and Guillén Again

Cosme's Carnegie Hall recital on December 4, 1938, is the starting point for surveying her personal and professional trajectory through 1952, when she returned to Cuba for the first time. The event was billed as "Eusebia Cosme: Only New York Recital of Afro-Antillian [sic] Poems." The program announced Cosme as the "Creator of a New Art" and "The Soul of the Tropics," and it listed the titles (in Spanish) of the seventeen poems, summarized in English, of her three-part performance, which was introduced by "Dr. Jorge Mañach, Professor of Spanish Literature at Columbia University," a major Cuban intellectual.[75] The Afro-Cuban Melba Alvarado, the great figure of twentieth-century Afro-Cuban social and cultural life in Harlem and the Bronx through her work with the important Club Cubano Inter-Americano, attended the performance with her family. "Everyone went," Alvarado said, and she recounted how Cosme received "a big ovation." (Cosme signed Alvarado's autograph book on October 1, 1939: "Para Melba, con mucha simpatía [For Melba, with much affection]. Eusebia Cosme, New York.")[76] The *Pittsburgh Courier* announced receipts of $6,000 and cited Cosme among Roland Hayes and Marian Anderson as the "only race artists to pack Carnegie Hall."[77]

Two months later, Cosme made her first appearance in Washington, DC, at the Armstrong High School Auditorium, in a performance organized by the Spanish Club of Howard University. A decade earlier, Armstrong had shifted from its original Washingtonian focus in vocational training, instituting an academic curriculum, while recently, in 1936 and 1937, its auditorium hosted performances by Marian Anderson. Indeed, in early 1939, around the time of Cosme's performance, the auditorium was again a key space in Anderson's career: it was considered a possible venue for her that spring after the Daughters of the American Revolution, adhering to a racist policy, had denied her the use of its Constitution Hall—an act involved in determining Anderson's eventual concert at the Lincoln Memorial and National Mall on Easter Sunday 1939.[78] V. D. Johnston, the Howard University treasurer who organized and did activist work with Anderson's performance that winter, was a sponsor of Cosme's Armstrong event, along with others in a remarkable list that included Carter G. Woodson, Edward Chalmer Hayes, and Mordecai Johnson. Announced as a "Spanish Recital of Afro-Antillean Poems," the performance nearly reproduced the program of the Carnegie Hall show.[79] In a review, the *Washington Afro-American* wrote that "Miss Eusebia Cosme, native Cuban girl," received "the thunderous applause of the many hundreds of Spanish-speaking spectators present," thus offering a glimpse of Cosme's DC Afro/Latino audience—and, very likely, Hispanophone African American audience, too.[80] Around the time of the Armstrong event, Cosme also appeared at the Unión Panamericana, the precursor to the Organization of American States. The Unión's headquarters was literally across the street—as it is today—from the DAR Constitution Hall, both of which are near the National Mall. Here, DC street-grid geographies suggest the social proximity and distance between Cosme and Anderson: the former's "*mulata*," "*negra*," and "Negro" identities did not prevent her from appearing in a primary U.S. space of the white Latin American nation-state elite—the space of an ideological Latin American inter*nacionalismo integrativo*—whereas the latter's "Negro" identity did indeed determine her absence from the DAR Constitution Hall and her later appearance, half a mile away, at the Lincoln Memorial.[81]

Beginning in early 1940 and through the end of World War II, Cosme extended *poesía negra*—in period, geographic, and ideological terms— beyond its island-Cuban flourishing, during a stretch of her U.S. career that rivaled anything she had achieved in Cuba and the Caribbean during the mid-1930s. I demonstrate this in what follows by focusing on the representation of Cosme in a *Chicago Defender* narrative written by the Afro-Cuban American Joaquín "Jack" Pelayo; an extant sound recording of her, originally created around the time of an appearance at Northwestern University; the scripts of her radio show on CBS's Cadena de las Américas (Network of the Americas); and the lyrics of her original music composition, "Fue en el África" (It Happened in Africa). Before discussing these crucial sites in the Cosme text, however, I offer a brief account of her personal and career itinerary in the United States during these important years.

Cosme appeared at Northwestern University in January 1940, under the auspices of the University College and the Instituto de las Españas en los Estados Unidos (Institute of the Spains in the United States). Shortly thereafter, she went to Mexico, where she performed at the Palacio de Bellas Artes in Mexico City and the Universidad Michoacana in Morelia. She returned to the United States in January 1941, around which time her address was 428 West 154th Street in Sugar Hill. It was during this time that Cosme wrote and published "Fue en el África." While she seems to have remained in New York City through the end of 1941, at some point during this time, Cosme returned to Mexico, for she reentered the United States through Laredo in October 1942, when, again, under "Race," the state identified her as "African black."[82]

Cosme went on to perform again at Carnegie Hall and Town Hall (1942, 1943), the latter of which was sponsored by the Ateneo Cubano, a social club in Manhattan with a history of discriminating against Afro-Cubans.[83] Around 1943, she began appearing on CBS's Cadena de las Américas, in what became the *Eusebia Cosme Show*, a fifteen-minute, shortwave broadcast to Latin America that appeared until 1945, during the period of Good Neighbor hegemony. She returned to Howard in 1944 and 1946.[84] In June 1945, in a Town Hall event commemorating the centenary of Antonio Maceo, Cosme recited poetry in a program that included Alberto Socarrás and Jesús Colón.[85] She performed at another Cuban event on February 24, 1947, in New York City in honor of Martí and Maceo on the anniversary of the Grito de Baire, which launched the 1895 Cuban revolution, sponsored by the Club Cubano Inter-Americano.[86] Cosme was involved in other activities of the Club Cubano during the period, although her role was largely limited to that of an invited guest; as Melba Alvarado put it, with regard to the ethics of inviting someone of Cosme's talent to the club, she never "took advantage [of Cosme] like that."[87] In May 1946, Cosme took part with Langston Hughes in Katherine Dunham's "Cuban Evening: The Poems and Songs of Nicolás Guillén," and in a further collaboration with African Americans, she appeared with Hughes, Carruthers, and Arna Bontemps at the Schomburg library in early 1949, where she performed in a program that included a celebration of *Cuba Libre*, the Carruthers and Hughes translation of Guillén. Carruthers, Cosme, and Hughes appear in a photograph at the library taken by the Fiftieth Street studio of Osvaldo Salas, who became a major photographer of the Cuban revolution. Hughes signed Cosme's copy of *Cuba Libre*—"Inscribed especially for Eusebia Cosme, foremost interpreter of Guillén's poetry, with admiration"—as did Guillén himself, who visited the city later that spring: "Para Eusebia, con el firme cariño de [with the firm affection of] Nicolás Guillén, New York, abril 1°, 1949."[88]

During this period, Cosme emerged as a sought-after figure for Cubans visiting New York City. In Rosendo Rosell's travels there in the late 1940s to dub English-language films into Spanish, for example, he would visit with members of New York City's Cuban American show-business world, including Cosme, whom he called of "high standing" (*categoría y puesto*).[89] Nicolás Guillén's own visit to New York City in the spring of 1949 yielded yet another representation of Cosme at this stage in her career, one framed by his "Camino de Harlem" spatial complexes. Guillén admits, "[I desired to] view 'with my own eyes' a half million people separated from the rest of the population, as if they suffered from a terrible, contagious illness. How often had I heard mention of Lenox Avenue and 145th Street!" His visit to a "small restaurant" in the "*barrio latino*" (Latin *barrio*)—presumably Latino Harlem—leads to another reflection: "The atmosphere was the same as in any bar in Havana, especially those in the old city: blacks with guitars, white men with black men and 'everyone' with black women and *mulatas . . . [negros con guitarras, blancos con negros y 'todos' con negras y mulatas*; ellipsis in original]."[90] Here, Guillén encounters a mid-twentieth-century Cuban American iteration of Latino New York City, and, while it is difficult to discern the attitude of his representation of the erotic in the scene of Afro-Cuban American women serving (in the absence of white Cuban American women) the multiracial bonding practices of Cuban American men, it is clear that Guillén has trouble recognizing the scene as *Latino*: he renders it "the same as" Havana, in other words, since to figure it as a space of Cuban diaspora would be to understand the "*barrio latino*" in terms of a possible *barrio afrolatino*, where diaspora as both blackness and *latinidad* may collapse the spatial (and other) boundaries between an African American Harlem, which Anglo white supremacy would signify as a zone of contagion, and a Latino Harlem, which Cuban white supremacy would cast as a heteronormative space of an "available," Afro-Cuban American feminine sexuality.

It is fitting, then, that when Guillén sets out to find Cosme in Latino New York City, he has trouble:

> But just as in this way I found many friends I wasn't expecting to come across, how difficult it was to find others I had intended to see! For example, I bumped into Eusebia Cosme nearly on the eve of my departure, and that was with the help of Bola de Nieve, who was over there in those days from piano to piano and triumph to triumph. The three of us would get together one memorable night at the home of the poet Langston Hughes. People who are friendly with Eusebia say the likeable *recitadora negra* [in original] has become very mysterious since she got married. I found her the same as always: the same age, the same pretty hands, the same Eastern-Cuban tone of voice—such as when students from Santiago say, "My father owns a coffee plantation"—the elusive, modest elegance that helped her come so far. She also told me she was preparing a return trip to Havana: She's only been doing that for ten years now.[91]

Guillén again resists the *latinidad* he encounters in New York City: now it is Cosme—through her body, voice, and career arc (she has "come so far")—whom he renders as a seemingly unchanging, *habanera* subject. To be sure, he intuits something new about Cosme, perhaps elements of her experience as an Afro-Latina in the United States over the past ten years, but he figures it as an effect of her marriage to Rafael Laviera: the "mysterious" thing about her. Unable to map Latino New York City, Guillén relies on another Afro-Cuban resident there, Ignacio "Bola de Nieve" Villa, to serve as his conduit to Cosme. His appeal to Hughes is even more significant in this regard: on March 29, 1949, Hughes wrote from Chicago to Cosme that Guillén was "in town" and "would love to see" her. Like Villa, Hughes mediated Cosme for Guillén, whose "Camino-de-Harlem" perspective disallowed the recognition of Cosme as an Afro-Latina in the city—an Afro-Latina who threatens Guillén by being "at home" in the United States, away from Cuba. Not surprisingly, Guillén would impose a nationalist ethics on Cosme, citing with chagrin her apparently promised, but, evidently, always postponed, return trip to Cuba, which suggests that the performative for Cosme extended to her sense of national belonging: she was always on the verge of going back to Cuba, announcing her intention to do so, yet she always ended up staying back in the United States.[92]

"The Linguistic Element Is Secondary"

Shortly after Cosme performed at Northwestern University in January 1940, an article appeared in the *Chicago Defender* written by Joaquín "Jack" Pelayo, an Afro-Cuban American resident in Chicago. Entitled "Cubans, Our Neighbors," Pelayo's piece is another example of "the African-American press [as] international in distribution and in its concerns," now in relation to its Afro-Latino contributors. In the context of a belated *poesía negra*, one migrating to the United States through her performances, the article represents Cosme's linguistic "unintelligibility" to African Americans as a condition of possibility for African diasporic connections—that African Americans need not understand what Cosme says during her performances, in other words, so long as her sound and, significantly, her body movements signify. The passage in question merits quoting at length:

AFRO-CUBAN RENAISSANCE

. . . About 1930, a group of young Negro poets under the leadership of Nicolas Guillen [*sic*], became interested in trying to preserve the traditions of [the] great Negroes [of Cuba] as well as the folklore of the common people, re-interpreting it through poetry and song of their own, as your own Langston Hughes, Countee Cullen, and Jean Toomer did in the days of the "New Negro Renaissance."

They wrote of Havana and Santiago's black girls who work all day and rhumba at night; of middle class mothers who objected to their daughters—school teachers—going to Havana's hot spots to do el son and rhumba; old Afro-Cuban lullabies and romances; laments of slave mothers; songs of revolt; and the gay songs of the people . . . .

EUSEBIA—"THE SOUL OF THE TROPICS"

Most folks don't like to read poetry. They do like to listen to it. So, to become known, poets have to recite their own works as did Paul Laurence Dunbar, James Weldon Johnson, and as does Langston Hughes—or someone else must recite it for them—someone with a fine voice and personality. Cuba has such a one—Eusebia Cosme, a brown girl with flashing eyes and a captivating smile, Santiago's "favorite daughter" and Cuba's ambassador of goodwill to North and South America. Eusebia was in Chicago this week at Northwestern University and the International House of the University of Chicago . . . .

Eusebia came to America to recite in Spanish. Would Americans like her? Of course, there was the opera where nobody understood the words anyhow. But would people come to hear a woman recite in a language they did not understand. Packed houses at Carnegie Hall and Town Hall in New York, and an impossible list of engagements on the eastern seaboard give the answer. A Howard University professor gives the reason.

". . . The artist's personality is so engaging, her mastery of pantomime so complete, and her sense of rhythm so refined that the linguistic element is secondary."

In other words, you just like to look at her and hear the sounds whether you know any Spanish or not. In fact, you actually get the ideas through the universal language of gesture inflection. She can be saucy or sad; heartbroken or gay; a slave mother crying for her daughter or a rhumba dancer, and you're bound to "catch on." This is the girl they call "The Soul of the Tropics"—Eusebia Cosme.[93]

Pelayo resituates in a critical way the texts "about 1930"—the belated texts of *poesía negra*—within the different parameters (temporal, geographic) of the Latino United States. The (majority) *mulato* and *blanco* poets of *poesía negra* and the movement's late 1920s/early 1930s apogee reemerge now as the "young Negro poets" of Cuba and the Afro-Cuban "renaissance," incorrect categories perhaps but also indicators of an urgency of articulation—because of their incommensurability—between such *mulato* and *blanco* Cuban poets and *poesía negra*, on the one hand, and the "Negro" writings (and identities) of Hughes, Cullen, and Toomer, on the other. Meanwhile, the high-culture texts of *poesía negra*, whose literary forms were often "popular" in theme, reemerge now as the popular-culture oral texts of an imagined audience of African American "most folks" who "don't like to read" but "like to listen." With such an invocation of a nonelite, non/literate, Anglophone African American audience, histories of plantation orality and a gendered, Afro-Cuban il/literacy reemerge now in terms of the devaluation of the Hispanophone words and literacies of *poesía negra*'s men poets, as well as the reestimation of the embodied visuality and vocalized sounds (outside of Hispanophone linguistic signification) of an Afro-Cuban American woman performer.[94]

In this regard, Pelayo turns to an authority on Cosme's linguistic un/intelligibility—the unnamed Howard University professor, who, it turns out, was the African American Valaurez Burwell Spratlin, a sponsor of Cosme's performance at the Armstrong Auditorium in Washington, DC, a year earlier. V. B. Spratlin was the head of the Romance Languages Department at Howard from 1927 to 1961. Over the course of his career, he supported "*declamación* contests" and "followed with interest the evolution of the art of Eusebia Cosme."[95] The full text from which Pelayo takes his quotation was handwritten by Spratlin in Washington, DC, on February 10, 1939:

> Students and the general public were so delighted with the incomparable art of Señorita Cosme that I am impelled to pass along the good news of her presence in the United States. The remarkable thing about the recital was the enthusiastic response of the audience, despite the fact that the great majority of those present did not understand Spanish. All are agreed that the artist's personality is so engaging, her mastery of pantomime so complete, and her sense of rhythm so refined that the linguistic element is secondary—or at least not essential to the enjoyment of her art.[96]

A publicity statement on her behalf, Spratlin's text, within Pelayo's *Defender* frame, vouches for Cosme before Anglophone African American audiences. It does so by figuring as "secondary" the linguistic differences of Cosme's performance, following its sonic and embodied (as

"rhythm" and "pantomime") elements. Spratlin thus invites an understanding of the way in which Cosme, in tension with the words and literacies of *poesía negra*'s men poets, occupies a hermeneutic *elsewhere* in
the histories of plantation orality and a gendered, Afro-Cuban il/literacy.
Here, her vocalized sounds (outside of Hispanophone linguistic signification) emerge as the meaningful elements of the Cosme text, those
open to interpretation. And, significantly, it is her Afro-Cuban American (in Pelayo) and African American (in Spratlin) collaborators who
have remarked on it and, just as importantly, spread the word within the
communities.

Cracks, Hisses, Pops

To listen to Cosme as someone who "did not understand Spanish" is
to align a particular historical Anglophone African American audition
of her with a feminist resistance to listening to the poetry of Guillén,
Palés Matos, and others as *the* experience of the Cosme text—indeed, in
the context of music, to align it with a feminist critique of the privileging
of words and writing in song over the vocality of women performers.[97]
As Farah Jasmine Griffin shows, "the singing New World black woman"
is crucial to such histories of feminine vocality: the "figure of the singing black woman is often similar to the uses of black women's bodies
as nurturing, healing, life and love giving for the majority culture. This
representation of the voice is in stark contrast to representations of that
voice in the service of disenfranchised black people, as a voice that poses
a challenge to the United States revealing its democratic pretense as a lie.
And, yet, this image contains both these possibilities."[98] Performances of
African-diasporic women's vocality in the Americas—as singing and, in
Cosme's case, the related *recitando* of lyric poetry—enact such possibilities: as endorsements and disruptions of *inter/nacionalismos integrativos*,
for example, and in African-diasporic collaborations through the un/
intelligibility of the Hispanophone vocal.

I propose such a listening of Cosme as represented in a sound recording of her voice produced around the time of her performance at Northwestern University on January 27, 1940—the Chicago visit that occasioned Pelayo's piece.[99] This listening would attend to Cosme's vocality
as "the articulation of the body, of the tongue, not that of meaning, of
language," even as such an embodied vocality is a signifier of sonic technology not only in its own right but in relation to its reproductions in
two phonograph discs, an audiotape, and a CD.[100] In Glissant's terms, the

Cosme sound text enacts the modality of African-diaspora "oral expression" as "organized in a discontinuous manner." It is hard to locate the time and place of the Cosme performance in question—not the event at Northwestern, in the auditorium at Thorne Hall on the Chicago campus, but the one before the device that produced the recording now at Indiana University's Archives of Traditional Music. The Indiana catalog admits that, while the performance was "recorded by an unknown collector during" the Northwestern event, it may have been created "on some other occasion (?)" as well. Cosme performed "La muerte de Taita Juan," by Arturo Clavijo Tisseur; "Sensemayá," by Guillén; "Coloquio," by Rafael Estenger; "Falsa canción de baquiné," by Palés Matos; "El bongocero," by Félix Caignet; and still another version of "Falsa canción de baquiné" before a device that recorded her voice onto two "acetate" discs—in fact, by this time, they were lacquered discs—from the inside out at 78 rpm.[101] It was a process paradigmatic of the way the phonograph's "recalibration of locality effected changes in its relation to other vicinities rather than erasing the local altogether."[102] Around 1963, the discs arrived at Indiana "with many other recordings" from the Northwestern ethnomusicology collection of Melville J. Herskovits.[103] While not entirely explaining the circumstances of the 1940 recording, the Herskovits provenance does identify the Cosme sound text as an object of modern anthropological knowledge on Africa and its diaspora. In 1988, the lacquer-disc recordings were transferred to an open-reel tape; in 2006, these analog-tape recordings were converted into digital form and transferred to a CD, with Cosme's performances appearing therein as six tracks totaling fifteen minutes.[104]

It is the two minutes and nineteen seconds of "Sensemayá" on this CD to which I listen in order to describe "the way in which (that is to say with what kind of voice and timbre)" Cosme speaks, recites, sings.[105] The recording begins with a member of the Indiana staff saying, "item number two, side B, strip one," while, in the background, a machine drones: the self-referential trace of recording technologies. This frame lasts for five seconds. The track then cracks, hisses, and pops, which the aural sense conveys as pastness. The cracks, hisses, and pops register the materiality of the recording's lacquer- and tape-based pretexts in a way that suggests a degradation that, here in CD form, is both halted and extended.

The cracks, hisses, and pops—its ambiance, in part—last for the remaining two minutes and thirteen seconds of the track. Cosme opens by speaking the following: "'Sensemayá: Canto negro para matar una culebra,' de Nicolás Guillén." She speaks timbre here in a way that suggests the performed "naturalness" of the elocutionist, stressing the first syllable of the first word, the first of the second, before moving in a brisk way to the end, pausing, nevertheless, after "Sensemayá" and "culebra." This becomes still another framing device, following the Indiana voice, the machine drone, and the cracks, hisses, and pops: Cosme's own introductory matter.

Then, for three seconds, the cracks, hisses, and pops sound alone, before Cosme sings: "Mayombe, bombe, mayombé." She sings slowly, producing a soft, low-pitched, three-tone phrase. She then repeats it in the same way, only now, in the middle of the singing, and for less than a second, the cracks, hisses, and pops intensify. She repeats it a third time in nearly the same way. The difference now is that she adds another tone: it is a higher-pitched sound, enlivening the mood with a feeling of anticipation, though just as soft as before.

After the third repetition, two seconds crack, hiss, and pop by, and Cosme returns, reciting for the first time: "La culebra tiene los ojos de vidrio." She recites timbre here as heavier than the spoken introduction. The mood shifts from anticipation to apprehension, while, toward the end, the cracks, hisses, and pops intensify again momentarily. "La culebra viene y se enreda en un palo," she then recites, uttering the first word loudly, scratching her throat. As she moves toward the end of "con sus ojos de vidrio en un palo, con sus ojos de vidrio," however, Cosme lowers the intensity once again—and the growing apprehension—a softness she extends through "la culebra camina sin patas." She then increases the intensity again momentarily, in the first word of "caminando se esconde en la yerba," thus heightening again the apprehension, only to soften it once more with "caminando sin patas," whose last word she utters almost inaudibly. The musical phrase now returns, and she sings it three times, using the same tonal shift as before: "Mayombe, bombe, mayombé."

Then, throughout the next seventeen seconds of the performance, Cosme recites timbre as rough. She performs "tú le das con el hacha y se muere. ¡Dale ya! ¡No le des con el pie que te muerde! No le des con el pie que se va" faster, louder, and at a high pitch. Then, even faster and louder, she recites "¡Sensemayá, la culebra! Sensemayá. ¡Sensemayá, con sus ojos! Sensemayá. ¡Sensemayá, con su lengua! Sensemayá. ¡Sensemayá, con su boca! Sensemayá," lowering the pitch toward the end. Among the sounds in this faster, louder episode are those of Cosme drawing in air and, just after the last word, clacking: perhaps jewelry banging against her body.

Throughout the next fifteen seconds, Cosme recites timbre as both elevated, particularly in her use of the alveolar trill, and rough, again by scratching her throat. She takes a sharp, deep breath. She recites loud and soft, high and low, mixing up the tempo: "La culebra muerta no puede comer. ¡La culebra muerta no puede silbar; no puede respirar; no puede morder! La culebra muerta no puede mirar. ¡La culebra muerta no puede beber; no puede caminar; no puede correr!" She ends on a slow, low note that leads to singing "mayombe, bombe, mayombé," after which, rather than repeating the phrase, she recites softly "Sensemayá" before uttering quickly, fast and rough, at a higher register, while clacking, "¡la culebra!" She sings again "mayombe, bombe, mayombé," and she recites "Sensemayá no se mueve, je," now more slowly, softly, and melodiously. "Mayombe, bombe, mayombé," she sings once more, then again recites "Sensemayá" softly, before quickly uttering again "¡la culebra!" at a higher register and in a fast, rough way, together with the clacking. Finally, she sings "Mayombe, bombe, mayombé" one last time and ends by reciting, as fast, rough, and loud, "¡Sensemayá se murió!" The last ten seconds crack, hiss, and pop, until the very end, when, with the stylus running off the engraved strip, the cracking and popping even out.

In such a listening of the Indiana track—a listening after an Anglophone, African American audition that, by suspending the poem's linguistic signification, privileges Cosme's embodied vocality—various sonic technologies converge: Cosme's variations in timbre and the hiss of the tape, for example. In this context, Cosme's own spoken self-introduction sounds natural only to the extent that it also cracks, hisses, and pops, which, more than just an introduction per se, renders it a *matter* of introduction: an act of framing that, in its layered, material pastness, foregrounds the history and significance of introductions throughout Cosme's career, from Ortiz's "presentación" at the Lyceum to the voice and machine drone of the Indiana archives, which situate Cosme in the institutional-archival spaces of "traditional music." Indeed, its song elements, together with its range of recitation sounds proper, are elements in the performance of another layered, material past, one that extends its own particular histories into the present of audition: that of Cosme's earlier singing career in the *cuplé* and, by extension, her experience of professional-career politics not only in general but in the theater in particular, with the sounds of her body in "pantomime"—its clacking gestures—suggestive of a dramatic performance staged audibly, yet invisibly, in Illinois, one that revises Ortiz's phobic metaphor of the phonograph in 1934: here, in the Cosme sound text, it is not a phonograph

hidden inside the hollow abdomen of a statue that haunts but the sound
of a body clacking inside the guts of a playback machine.[106]

The Eusebia Cosme Show

Another important Cosme text during the period is the *Eusebia
Cosme Show*, a shortwave radio program broadcast from New York City
to Latin America on CBS's Cadena de las Américas. Cosme performed
on it for three years, beginning in 1943. Unlike the sonic evidence of the
Indiana recording, the traces of the *Cosme Show* appear as photographs
and scripts in the Schomburg collection—which is to say, its evidence
derives from Eileen Charbo's Mexico City intervention.[107] The *Cosme
Show* was an instance of U.S. "Good Neighbor" ideology, which managed "the paradox between fraternity with neighboring republics and
domination over them" around World War II.[108] The program continued
Cosme's negotiations with *presentaciones*/introductions practices, while
her poetry selections for the show, now ten years on in her career, further
transformed the late category of *poesía negra*—all from a Latino New
York City location that, while apparently unacknowledged in the broadcasts themselves, was very much the determining space from which the
radio performances originated.

The weekly fifteen-minute show, broadcast at 7:45 p.m., featured an
announcer, the Colombian José Santos Quijano, and major musicians,
including the Argentine composer Terig Tucci, whose arrangements,
performed by the network's Orquesta Panamericana, provided the
theme—and often the backdrop—for Cosme's performances.[109] A review
of the scripts reveals that Cosme performed poems by Palés, Ballagas, and
Guillén but that she also moved beyond the familiar, choosing works by
Francisco Domínguez Charro and Franklin Mieses Burgos, two Dominicans, as well as works by the Venezuelan Manuel Rodríguez Cárdenas.
Cosme also included Spanish translations from Joseph S. Cotter, Sr.,
Paul Laurence Dunbar, James Weldon Johnson, and Langston Hughes,
thereby reversing the logic of her collaboration with African American
audiences up to that time: these African American authors would now
"speak" to Hispanophone Latin Americans "through" Cosme *because
of*, rather than despite, the way her performance conveyed a poem's
particular linguistic signification. Her "good-neighborhood" repertoire
also included a program devoted to Plácido (Gabriel de la Concepción
Valdés), the early nineteenth-century Afro-Cuban poet, and even a
selection from Elinor Wylie, the popular white writer from earlier in

FIGURE 5. Eusebia Cosme, c. 1943 (Eusebia Cosme
Photograph Collection, Photographs and Prints Divi-
sion, Schomburg Center for Research in Black Culture,
New York Public Library, Astor, Lenox and Tilden
Foundations)

the century. But the most significant change was Cosme's inclusion of
an Afro–Puerto Rican woman poet, Carmen María Colón Pellot, whose
own relation to the archive, in the words of one critic, resonates with
Cosme's: Colón Pellot suggests the "position that women of color have
occupied in history in general and in Puerto Rican history in particular,"
one in which "they have been simply absent—or, when they are present,
they are isolated points of reference usually cited out of context . . . and,
once again, fleetingly."[110]

The episodes of the *Cosme Show* arranged Cosme's performances around a variety of *presentación*/introduction practices. "Columbia Broadcasting System, La Cadena de las Américas, introduces [*presenta*] Eusebia Cosme," one script begins, followed by Cosme, "over music," speaking her own introduction: "We go into the future with an outstretched hand, a caravan shaded by our green jungles; the sorrow of a thousand birds shakes down upon the road the music sleeping in the boughs of *América* [in original]." This intro, which served also as Cosme's outro, appears indented and in quotation marks in the script, unlike any of the words spoken by the announcers, suggesting that these very framing words of Cosme's—and their idea of good-neighborly pan-Americanism as exoticist futurity—are themselves in a frame. With the theme song now playing, Santos Quijano, who would lead listeners into and out of Cosme's performances, followed: "Eusebia Cosme, performer [*intérprete*] of a poetry that found in her an ideal medium of expression, returns to you courtesy of La Cadena de las Américas to bring you the word of the poets of her race [*poetas de su raza*], fresh and beating with life like the moment it was born." Santos Quijano's *poesía negra* rhetoric refashions the problem of Pelayo's "young Negro poets of Cuba": the "poets of her race"—the phrase "*su raza*" intends *negro/a*, I believe—are few and far between, in contrast to the numbers of white poets in Ballagas, Caignet, and Palés Matos, for example, thus suggesting the show's interest in maintaining a fiction of prevailing *negro* writers, against *poesía negra*'s ideological multiracial authorship. "*Su raza*," of course, in the United States, signifies also Cosme's *mulata* and Negro identities and thus her connection with the "*mulato* Guillén," the "Negro Hughes." Such *raza* complexities constitute the *Eusebia Cosme Show*'s transnational "good *barrio*hood," multiply situated as it was in its U.S. Latino and Latin American broadcast origins and destinations.[111]

One of the Hughes poems that Cosme used in the show was "Aunt Sue's Stories." Translated by a certain Enrique Portes as "Cuentos de la tía Susie," the poem takes the *Cosme Show* back to the earliest of Hughes's writings in the 1920s, to a poem that, in "the flow of old Aunt Sue's voice," who "never got her stories out of any book at all," offers a symbol of il/literate performance that mirrors the cultural work of Cosme herself, who nevertheless *did* derive her "stories" from printed sources. The listening figure in the poem is "a brown-faced child" whom Aunt Sue "cuddles ... to her bosom" and "tells ... stories" to, a "dark-faced child, listening," a "dark-faced child [who] is quiet."[112] In the Portes translation, and therefore in the words that Cosme performed, each of these child images, "brown-faced" and "dark-faced," appears as *"niño negro"* (black boy).[113] The choice of *"negro"* over more "accurate" Spanish-language alternatives (*mulato* or *trigueño* for brown, for example; *oscuro* for dark) raises the possibility that the *Eusebia Cosme Show*, from its U.S. location, was "blackening" Hughes's "brown-faced child" for the benefit of its Latin American audiences, generating a sign for the way in which Afro-Cubans, for instance, as migrants in the United States, may experience a similar such racialization. Consider, in contrast, a translation of "Aunt Sue's Stories" published in 1931 in the Afro-Cuban Lino D'Ou's "Marcha de una raza" page in the Havana daily *El Mundo*, where Hughes's "brown-faced," "dark-faced" child appears as *"pardito,"* or "little *pardo*," a modern/colonial category of mixed-race identity whose use in this example more "accurately" reflected the meaning of Hughes's "brown."[114] By choosing *"negro"* over a term such as *"pardito,"* I think, the *Eusebia Cosme Show* allegorized the kind of racial reception that Afro–Latin Americans might expect to receive upon arrival in the United States: their identification as Negro, as "African black."[115]

The *presentación*/introduction complexities of the *Cosme Show* were in further evidence in an August 25, 1944, episode. Here, Cosme's intro and outro changed in ways that continued the transamerican use of Hughes. The announcer opened by saying that the network "introduces Eusebia Cosme, performer of the poetry of both *Américas* [*intérprete de la poesía de ambas Américas*]." Then, with the theme song as an undercurrent, Cosme spoke; this time, her words appear on the page unindented, unquoted: "This is Eusebia Cosme speaking. I bring you my old poems and many others that I have found along the way. My art is to perform them and convey the emotion I feel. [HAPPY] For as the poet has said . . . I, too, am *América* [in original], I am the black brother [*hermano negro*]." She then performed poems by Domínguez Charro, Wylie, and the Cuban Vicente Gómez Kemp, after which the announcer, over music, reminded listeners, "Next week, at the same time, Eusebia Cosme will be with you again." With the theme song now playing underneath her words, Cosme finished off the farewell: "To bring you another message from the brother, whose singing is the muscle below the skin of the soul, whose word comes damp from the jungles . . . [HAPPY] the black brother [*hermano negro*] who, too, is *América* [in original]."[116]

The richness of this script is first a matter of textual scholarship. Cosme's lines contain penciled-in edits, presumably in Cosme's own hand, that offer a glimpse of her agency in the show's production. Among the edits was a change to the phrase *"Pues como ha dicho el poeta"* (For as the poet has said): the original opening conjunction was *"y"* (and)—*"Y como ha dicho el poeta"* (And as the poet has said). *Pues* produces a relation of consequence between Cosme's self-presentation ("This is Eusebia Cosme speaking"), her professional self-affirmation (what she does is "bring poems to you"), and her invocation of Hughes's "I, too," also from *The Weary Blues*. Cosme uses the screen of a *"poeta de su raza"* by drawing on Hughes in such a way that her own *"yo/I"*—absent in the third-person "Eusebia Cosme," implied in *"traigo"* (I bring), and, finally, explicit in *"yo siento"* (I feel)—articulates (with) Hughes's *"yo también"* (I, too), elaborating a cross-gender connection with African American subjectivity, inscribed as Hughes's masculine brotherhood, and African American U.S. belonging, inscribed as Hughes's "being America." Through the flow of effects proper to *pues*, in other words, Cosme emerges as an *hermana negra* in *América* whose revision of "I, Too's" original "darker brother" as an *"hermano negro"* (instead of the more "correct" *"hermano más oscuro"*) yet again emphasizes to her Latin American listeners the blackness of a key figure in the Hughes oeuvre.[117] This episode of the *Cosme Show* thus challenges the geoontology of Hughes's "to be America" by marking the geographic keyword with an accent mark: *"América."* This *"América"* represents an alternative to both the hegemonic good neighborhood of the announcer's *"ambas Américas"* (both Américas), which isolates *latinidad* to a "foreign," Latin American location, and Hughes's own construction of an accentless "America," which connotes a U.S site of exclusive African American/Anglo-white relations. The *Cosme Show's* *"soy América,"* broadcast from its state-sponsored CBS studios, imagines instead a being situated in the Afro-Latino United States.

Dolor y Sufrir: "Fue en el África"

In 1941, the head of RCA Victor recording in Cuba wrote to Cosme in New York City, asking her whether she was the composer of the lyrics or the music (or both) of a song called "Fue en el África" (It Was in Africa). Ernesto Roca was representing the major Havana firm of Humara y Lastra, which was interested in recording the song. Cosme was indeed its composer—of the lyrics and music—as a contract later that year attested.[118] "Fue en el África" is an *afro son*, a musical "style . . . popular" at the time that "put themes about the African and slave past at the center of tunes and incorporated . . . rhythms from Cuba's African-derived Creole religions."[119] Cosme's lyrics in "Fue en el África" are an important element of the Cosme text, particularly in relation to constructions of *"América"* as an Afro-Latino space. I turn to these lyrics as *her own* words, aware of the weight they carry in restorative terms in relation to the words of *poesía negra*'s men poets and the histories of a gendered, Afro-Cuban il/literacy. Yet I recognize how the words are also *fragments arrachés*, both in terms of considering them apart from the music and in relation to the Cosme archive: I have had no access to the original, but rather a series of others' renditions, of "Fue en el África," ranging from the sheet-music arrangement of a white Cuban musician that includes as its primary words an English version by an Anglo-white woman to recorded performances by the Orquesta Casino de la Playa, Xavier Cugat and His Waldorf-Astoria Orchestra, and Xiomara Alfaro.

The sheet music in question is entitled "In Africa (Fué [*sic*] en el Africa [*sic*]): Afro Son." The arrangement is credited to Anselmo Sacasas, a pianist who had performed with the Orquesta Casino de la Playa, while the English lyric is attributed to Marion Sunshine. At the top of the sheet text, one reads, "Spanish words and music by Eusebia Cosme." The music was copyrighted in 1945 by the Antobal Music Company of New York City. Throughout, Cosme's "Spanish words" run below Sunshine's English rendition.[120] Using this text, and drawing on the aforementioned recordings, I arrive at the following version of Cosme's words in "Fue en el África," with my English translation included:

Fue en el África lejana
donde conocí el amor,
y en América, mi negro,
donde conocí el dolor.
Yo quiero ir al África lejana.
Yo quiero ver de nuevo sus palmeras
y al son de antiguos tambores
volver a ver nuestro sol.
En África gocé
y en América sufrí.
Yo quiero ver nuestro sol
al son de antiguos tambores.
Yo quiero ver sus palmeras
cubriendo nuestros amores.
En África gocé
y en América sufrí.

It was in distant Africa
where I knew love,

and in *América*, my black man [*mi negro*],
where I knew sorrow.
I want to go to distant Africa.
I want to see its palm trees again
and to the sound of ancient drums
once again see our sun.
I enjoyed myself in Africa
and in *América* I suffered.
I want to see our sun
to the sound of ancient drums.
I want to see its palm trees
covering our loves.
I enjoyed myself in Africa
and in *América* I suffered.

Cosme's "*América*" is a space in which the voice produces "memories" of and desires for Africa. It is also a space of present and historical sorrow and suffering (and physical pain, which is there in *dolor*, too). She thus adds to the meaning of the toponym in her work: *América* signifies here an African-diaspora space of slavery and postslavery experiences of (and reflections on) violence. The mode of the *afro-son* scaffolds such a representation of *América*, associating the vision of time, space, and feeling with sentimentality. Yet Cosme's lyrics—specifically around "*América*"—are still an intervention, the evidence for which I find in the way others have needed to alter them in their own versions of the song, a sign of unease over the critique conveyed by *dolor* and *sufrir*. In the Afro-Cuban Xiomara Alfaro's version, she sings "*en África goce y al salir de allí sufrí*" (I enjoyed myself in Africa, and on leaving there I suffered). Alfaro strikingly emphasizes the Middle Passage— the moment of an enslaved transit from Africa—yet this comes at the expense of *América*, which is nowhere in the song. Meanwhile, the white Cuban Miguelito Valdés, fronting Xavier Cugat's orchestra, sings "*en África goce y en América también*" (I enjoyed myself in Africa and in *América*, too). Valdés's version keeps *América* in the lyrics, obviously, but removes the *dolor* and *sufrir*, replacing these with *gozar* (enjoy), a gesture that seems less a way to claim a critically alternative experience of African diaspora in the hemisphere (an experience of pleasure) than a retreat from the challenge posed by Cosme's lyrics: that *América*, in fact because of its very production of *dolor* and *sufrir*, encourages expressions in African-diaspora music and literature that are irreducible to—yet still able to engage—slavery and postslavery feelings of sorrow, pain, and suffering.[121] As an instance of her own writing, the lyrics of "Fue en el África" invoke Cosme's "slipperiness, elsewhereness," here in the way her *América*, already an archival fragment, moves in and out of the multiple versions of her song.

The Child Corpse and the Return of the *Negrito*

Cosme's return to Cuba in 1952 and her life in New York City, Mexico City, and Miami from the mid-1950s through 1976 orient a discussion of her film roles in *The Pawnbroker*, *El derecho de nacer*, and *Mamá Dolores*, roles that involved the ongoing reorganization of Cosme's professional identity, with her *recitadora* career, in a major development, shifting now toward acting. After the highlights of the performance with Hughes at Katherine Dunham's School of Theater and Dance on Forty-Third Street, near Broadway, and a show at Town Hall commemorating the fiftieth anniversary of the Cuban republic, Cosme returned to Cuba in the spring of 1952.[122] It had been fourteen years since her departure. She arrived in Havana with Felo, her husband, and she stayed at least through the first half of the following year, when the country celebrated the centenary of José Martí and experienced the early stages of the Cuban revolution: the attack on the Moncada barracks. The visit was marked by professional disappointments, despite occasional signs of success; Cosme's first and only appearance in Havana, for example, did not occur until May 1953 at the Pro-Arte Musical's Auditorium.[123] Indeed, by that time, it was evident that something "had been done to" Cosme by those in the Cuban performance world that "has no name," and, "if it does have one, it's very ugly." While "cheap imitators of her inimitable art . . . offer recitals, with poems of Ballagas, Guillén, Palés Matos, and others," Cosme "watches the days pass slowly, with bitterness, in her homeland [*patria*]."[124] Among the sleights was that people in positions of authority refused "to include her incomparable art in the official celebrations" on behalf of Martí.[125]

By the mid-1950s, Cosme was back at her apartment on Forty-Seventh Street in New York City. A widow now, she attended shows in the evenings, went out to dinner often, and spent time with her friends.[126] Meanwhile, in letters, Langston Hughes told Cosme he wanted to give her a Spanish translation of his play *Mulatto* and a "good mailing list," two indications of his interest in her career prospects.[127] In September 1955, they took a major turn: Cosme "finally" appeared in her first acting role, as Mamá Dolores in a staging of Félix Caignet's *El derecho de nacer* at the Teatro Santurce on 116th Street and Fifth Avenue; the Santurce, of course, was the former Mt. Morris Theater/Teatro Campoamor/Teatro Cervantes/Teatro Hispano, where twenty years earlier Alberto O'Farrill had performed as the *negrito* to the music of Alberto Socarrás. A year later, she appeared in what was to be her last major poetry performance ever in the United States, in a "Recital de Poesía Afro-Antillana" at the Town Hall, sponsored by the New York chapter of the Puerto Rican Society of Journalists and Writers. The performance, her first "in many years," featured a significant debut text—Afro-Cuban *"refranes"* (sayings) collected by Lydia Cabrera—and it was accompanied by the publication of a memorial book in which appeared quotations from many of the countless reviews written about Cosme over the years, all of which lent the performance an air of valediction.[128]

The 1960s were the most transformative time in Cosme's career since the years between her first Lyceum performance and her broadcasts on CBS. Now in her fifties, she began a film and stage career. Leading up to it, Cosme had already begun exploring other creative pursuits, most significantly, painting: she had "traded the art of saying poems for the aesthetics of color," noted one critic in 1962.[129] The photographs of her at the Washington Square Outdoor Art Exhibit during the period show her work in abstract art.[130] In 1964, Cosme made her film debut in Sidney Lumet's *The Pawnbroker*, appearing alongside Rod Steiger, Juano Hernández, Brock Peters, and Jaime Sánchez. By 1966, she had relocated to Mexico City, where she was living in rooms at the Hotel Insurgentes; she became a recognizable figure in Mexican popular culture, appearing in *telenovelas*, plays, and several feature films through 1973, most famously in the role of Mamá Dolores in *El derecho de nacer* (1966).[131]

Cosme's performances in U.S. and Mexican film reveal the contradictions of her late professional success. Her upward mobility is compromised by the films themselves, which use her to represent Afro-Cuban characters in aged domestic-labor roles whose "service" on behalf of birth and miscegenation plots invokes ideologies of African-diasporic surrogate (and, on occasion, "natural") motherhood. The result of these plots is often a dead (or having nearly died) Afro/Latino child under the care of Cosme's motherhood, which thus figures a focus in the films on futurity: on futures to desire, futures to dread, here involving Afro-Latinas/os and Afro–Latin Americans.[132]

Lumet's *The Pawnbroker*, based on a novel by Edward Lewis Wallant, premiered in April 1965. Its eponymous protagonist, a Holocaust survivor named Nazerman (Rod Steiger), owns a pawnshop in the Puerto

FIGURE 6. Melba Alvarado, Francisco Álvarez Monteagudo
(Cuban Consul), and Eusebia Cosme at the Club Cubano
Inter-Americano, New York City, c. 1950 (Eusebia Cosme
Photograph Collection, Photographs and Prints Division,
Schomburg Center for Research in Black Culture, New
York Public Library, Astor, Lenox and Tilden Foundations)

Rican neighborhood around 116th Street and Park Avenue. He works
there with his assistant, Jesús Ortiz (Jaime Sánchez). Cosme plays Jesús's
single mother, Mrs. Ortiz. The plot builds to a scene in which Jesús takes
a bullet for Nazerman during a robbery attempt at the shop, thus cul-
tivating the irony of the cynical, traumatized Nazerman's redemption
through the sacrifice of Jesús. Echoes of the Latino-Jewish contact zones
of 1920s Harlem fill *The Pawnbroker*. Cosme appears in four scenes,

including one at the end, when, upon learning of Jesús's murder, she flees their apartment, screaming his name.

From the violence of Jesús's death, one can look back to his birth and recognize another kind of violence—the history of plantation sexual violence, which implicates Cosme's Mrs. Ortiz. In the novel, the point about Jesús's origins is made clear: his mother is a "husband-deserted . . . scrubwoman" who works "in a downtown office building." There is a photograph of her in the apartment: "a dark-skinned woman with pronounced Negroid features who smiled self-consciously, as though shy at the proximity to her husband in the twin frame," a man who, "long absent from their lives, . . . looked almost white, a thin-nosed, narrowlipped man with large, sensuous, slightly goiterous eyes like those of an ancient Spanish grandee."[133] The "twin frames" suggest nothing so much as the *cuadros de castas* (caste paintings) that emerged in New Spain and Peru to represent coloniality's racial hierarchies. In the words of José Buscaglia-Salgado, these paintings depicted "a terrible discourse of violence that speaks of the creole's desire to possess the human geography of the country 'forcibly by force.'"[134] The "ancient Spanish grandee," whose "almost whiteness" would "improve the race" through a possibly violent sexual encounter with Mrs. Ortiz, suggests here a fantasy of an earlier English and later U.S. imperialism in which Spanish coloniality is made to look inferior (as dissolute, for example, and absent, which the passage makes clear) in order to undermine its power as a rival for supremacy (white and otherwise) in the Americas.[135] It is not surprising, then, that the novel describes Jesús as a "brown-skinned youth," the subject of mixed-race fantasies, or that both the film and the novel match him with an African American girlfriend. Jesús's violent death, inseparable from the violence of his "almost-white" origin, thus indicates a Latino futurity that, configured to "brown" (and, with the African American girlfriend, possibly *negro*/black) identities, the film both imagines and thwarts. Mrs. Ortiz's bereaved motherhood, wailing on the street, stands as a sign for such loss, one that occurs in the narrative on the eve, ironically enough, of the Latino-movement era, central to which were youth like Jesús.[136]

Cosme's film career continued to display such motherhood scenarios in *El derecho de nacer* (1966), a Mexican production with a rich Cuban and Latino Harlem prehistory that includes a current of Cuban blackface.[137] Indeed, for the producers, the drama's blackface connections influenced their casting decision: Mamá Dolores "needs to be a black woman, an authentic black woman [*una negra, una negra auténtica*] and not a white woman smeared in black [*una mujer blanca embadurnada de negro*] like Lupe Suárez."[138] The melodramatic plot begins when a young woman from the white elite of Santiago becomes pregnant after a forbidden love affair. She gives birth to a boy whose life is threatened by his disgraced grandfather—a white boy rescued by Mamá Dolores, an Afro-Cuban servant woman, and raised by her into adulthood, at which time he redeems his mother, now a nun, as well as his father and grandfather.

Cosme's Dolores, like her Mrs. Ortiz, uses her position in Afro-Cuban domestic labor and surrogate motherhood to manage the film's investment in futurity. This involves at first, most obviously, the thread of reproductive heterosexuality in the plot, not just in the very person of the rescued boy but in his eventual vocation, too: under the care of Dolores, he becomes an obstetrician who counsels women against abortion. Yet, given the difficulty of representing the boy's origins—the result, after all, of forbidden sex—what the film offers instead as an origin scene is a queer union between the fallen, soon-to-be-cloistered white woman and her Afro-Cuban servant, Dolores. Just after childbirth, when the plot calls for the flight of the "true" mother and the arrival of the surrogate, the postpartum mother tells Dolores that, despite her impending flight, the child, thanks to the actions of Dolores, will in fact have two mothers, "you and I." The film thus troubles the white patriarchy of the Cuban republic with the suggestion of a multiracial, multigenerational lesbian coparenthood, one that echoes in the plot as the heterosexuality-in-abeyance of the "true" mother's church-imposed celibate body and as the posthetero-sexuality of Dolores's surrogate, geriatric motherhood, a characterization that likens her with the U.S. mammy in many respects, even as Cosme's small body allows her a contrast with the defining element of the Hollywood stereotype, the mammy's "large," "round" corporeality.[139]

One recognizes these themes in the film *Rosas blancas para mi hermana negra* (White Roses for My Black Sister; 1969), in which Cosme starred with the Argentine Libertad Lamarque. There, countering the title's claim to sorority, another feminine, multiracial queer union is imagined: Cosme's character's Afro–Latin American daughter, who was hit by a motorist and left "brain dead," becomes a heart donor for Lamarque's white Latin American daughter, who lives on as a result of the transplant. The relevant dialogue involves Lamarque's character telling Cosme's, in consolation, that the young white woman will be "our daughter, yours and mine," another form of queer coparenthood that, in this instance, extends a trope of miscegenation: the black woman's heart inside the white woman's chest. The death of the Afro–Latin American daughter resonates with the death of Jesús Ortiz in *The Pawnbroker*, which is to say that the Afro–Latin American body disappears in these film imaginings of the future, a disappearance that invokes a discourse of violent, future-oriented, reproductive "whitening" in the colonial and postcolonial Americas. Indeed, the prevalence of the Afro–Latin American child corpse in Cosme's Mexican film narratives is striking: in addition to the daughter of *Rosas blancas*, played by the Afro-Peruvian Robertha, *El derecho de nacer* includes a scene in which Dolores herself recalls her own dead infant son, while in *El derecho de los pobres* (The Right of the Poor; 1973), a Mexican-Ecuadorean production set in Guayaquil that consciously departs the elite world of *Nacer*, Cosme plays the grandmother of "el negro Tito" (Tito the black boy), the only Afro–Latin American character in a group of poor, soccer-enthusiast boys at the center of the story—and the only to die in the film's climactic confrontation.[140]

Mamá Dolores (1971), less a sequel to *Derecho* than a spin-off, exhausts this moment in Cosme's career, rendering the themes of the films parodic. It criminalizes, for example, Dolores's surrogate motherhood: rather than depict her as a rescuer and nurturer of the white boy, the plot of *Dolores* incorporates the police in order to frame her as his kidnapper, which produces a sensationalist women's prison narrative. But the most important moment in the film, one in which the *bufo* undercurrents of Cosme's Dolores finally surface, occurs when they are still on the run. Dolores and the boy are in Veracruz, and she intends to board a boat that will make "*la travesía de las antillas*" (the Caribbean crossing). In order to effect the plan, Dolores has taken a key step: she has put the boy in blackface. And not just his face. His arms and legs are painted black, too. Dolores then makes a proclamation: "Cuando lleguemos allá, mi niño dejará de ser negrito" (When we arrive over there, my boy will stop being black). The scene reimagines the prerogative of Afro-Cuban surrogate motherhood: it is now the Afro-Cuban surrogate mother who is the author—rather than object—of racial performance, seizing blackface and applying it on her white charge. She turns him both into a "little black boy," a generic *negrito*, and into a child version of the famous *bufo* type: the *negrito* we saw in O'Farrill. Because the plot puts Dolores in jail before she can board the boat, the film thwarts the promise of this blackface moment. Specifically, the anomalous future of an Afro-Cuban woman blackface impresario who has bequeathed the legacy of Lupe Sánchez on her white "son" never does in fact "arrive" "over there," in a Caribbean transregional zone that may include Havana, Miami, and New York City, territories whose publics are thus denied the opportunity to witness Dolores's great act of ironic redress on behalf of the corpses of her Afro–Latin American (and "brown" Latino) children: namely, her staging a new "*negrito.*"[141]

A Hialeah Tribute

After Cosme's stroke, it was she herself, of course, who arrived in Miami. The Cuban singer and actress Orquídea Pino, who lived in Mexico City, was instrumental in organizing and funding Cosme's arrival in Miami in 1974. Two years later, upon Cosme's death, Pino did the same with the funeral.[142] At the Miami Convalescent Home, Cosme received visitors from Cuban Miami's literary and entertainment worlds.[143] An element of this moving and significant Miami sojourn is the possibility that, in fact, had it not been for the stroke, Cosme would have gone back to New York City upon the conclusion of her Mexican period, rather than making a new start of it in Miami. "Whether I stay in Mexico or return to New York depends on the public's reception of [*Mamá Dolores*]," Cosme said in 1970.[144]

I want to conclude, however, not in Miami but in Hialeah, that other city of Cuban diaspora, northwest of Miami. On November 26, 1975, a performance space named the Teatro Lecuona was inaugurated at 1094 East Fourth Avenue. The city was already familiar then, as it was to be for most of the late twentieth century, for its many apartment buildings and factories, sites of Hialeah's working-class, Cuban American cultures. (Several blocks to the west of the Hialeah Park Race Track is Seminola, the city's still-segregated African American neighborhood.) At the Lecuona that night, a tribute was held on behalf of the theater's namesake. There was also an awards show. The honorees included remarkable figures in Cuban and Cuban American performance history such as Mimí Cal, Hortensia Coalla, and Aníbal de Mar.[145] Also among the honorees was Cosme herself. Her encounter that night with her fellow performers found its way into the record: the "Cuban luminaries at the theater covered her with hugs and kisses, making her cry with joy."[146]

3 / Supplementary Careers, Boricua Identifications

Among the modern Afro-Cuban American performance identities and archival sites of the first part of the book, there was always a mainland-boricua presence: the Puerto Rican in the United States. O'Farrill appeared at the Teatro Apolo and Teatro Campoamor before boricua audiences, while his *Gráfico* work brought him into contact, however tense, with Bernardo Vega. Cosme's midcentury watershed performance at the Teatro Santurce (formerly the Campoamor) put her before boricua publics, too. Prior to that, she had had many encounters with boricua writers, journalists, and intellectuals, both in New York City and in Puerto Rico in the mid-1930s.

In this chapter, I follow how such a connection to mainland Puerto Rican cultures is heightened in instances of a *boricua identification* among Afro-Cuban American writers and intellectuals: an identification with (and often as) mainland Puerto Ricans in which island and U.S. *cubanidad*, as identity and object of professional interest, yields to boricua alternatives, turning the Afro-Cuban American toward (and into) the mainland Afro-boricua, with concomitant risks and rewards.[1] Another Afro-Latino orientation away from island *afro/cubanidad*, such a mainland-boricua identification is a key sign in the cultures of Afro-Cuban America, one which I consider in a range of texts situated before and after the Latino-movement era by Rómulo Lachatañeré and Piri Thomas. Lachatañeré's early 1950s photographs of island and mainland Puerto Ricans, along with his untimely death in an iconic airplane crash off San Juan harbor, represent aspects of his boricua identification.

Meanwhile, Thomas's depiction of his Afro-Cuban American father as a mainland Afro–Puerto Rican in *Down These Mean Streets* (1967) configures a boricua identification to literary form. In a coda, I turn to Lourdes Casal to chart a seeming challenge to boricua identifications among Afro-Cuban Americans during the period: after more than a decade in the United States, Casal's brief 1973 return to Cuba, the first of several, confirmed the primacy of a "Cuba interest" in her life, one that lasted until her own untimely death.

Boricua identifications in Lachatañeré and Thomas emerge as elements of a *supplementary career*. I use the term to describe the "added" work done on other literary- and intellectual-career occasions by these figures, in contrast to the work in their more recognized, major texts and disciplines; included, too, in the term is the matter of reputation—their status as "major figures"—and the way in which such majority estimations are themselves in tension with extra, not necessarily canonical views of their work and career. A Derridean supplementarity is at play in the notion of a supplementary career: such other careers are "excessive" to, yet constitutive of, the recognized, established forms of a writer or intellectual's professional life.[2] Relevant here are ideas regarding the politics of an intellectual career in post/modernity. In the opening pages of *Minima Moralia: Reflections from Damaged Life*, Theodor Adorno posits that an "occupation with things of the mind" seems to have "become 'practical,' a business with strict division of labour, departments and restricted entry."[3] Later inquiries on intellectuals and professionalism have sought to determine (rather than to disavow) the viability of such intellectual work enmeshed in the rationalizations of capital, particularly with regard to a possible oppositionality. In many respects, the question toward the end of the twentieth century becomes one of critically engaging the political opacity of such "careerist" work in critique during an era of neoliberalism, specifically at a primary site of intellectual reproduction: the university.[4] In the context of such discourses on the "occupation of thought," a supplementary career among Afro-Cuban American writers and intellectuals appears as an occasion for "extra" work: work that may bring in a little more money and open a window, however small, for aesthetic experimentation, perhaps even new social commitments, to occur. A boricua identification, I am suggesting, is a consequence of such work.

The points of contact between mainland Puerto Rico and forms of the supplementary career in Lachatañeré and Thomas are multiple. Lachatañeré (1909–1952) is mainly remembered in Cuban Studies for two

1940s ethnographies of *regla de ocha*, the Yoruba-based Afro-Cuban religion familiar as *santería*, and for an earlier literary work, *¡¡Oh, mío, Yemayá!!* (1938), a narrative of the myths of the *orishas*, *santería*'s deities. Because Lachatañeré was just ten years younger than O'Farrill and nearly the same age as Cosme, an argument can be made for his inclusion in the first part of the book, both in period terms and with respect to the unevenness of his place in Cuban and Latino intellectual and literary histories, where his works, recognizable in the former, are candidates for recovery in the latter. I consider Lachatañeré's career supplementarity in his 1940s U.S. print-culture accounts of Latinas/os in New York City—a series of essays that, informed by, yet going beyond, ethnography, show in Lachatañeré the thinking of an Afro-Latino cultural critic. I extend this observation to his canonical ethnographic writings, "El sistema religioso de los lucumís y otras influencias africanas en Cuba" (The Religious System of the Lucumís and Other African Influences in Cuba; 1941) and *Manual de santería* (Santería Manual; 1942), both of which, while producing knowledge about Afro-Cuban religion on the island, were finished and published while Lachatañeré was living in New York City, a fact imbuing both texts with the author's *afrolatinidad*. My discussion leads to Lachatañeré's boricua identification in his photography, collected at the Schomburg Center, which offers a poignant evocation, in its images of solidarity with poor and working-class island and mainland Puerto Ricans, of his death in the waters off San Juan during the year of a crucial event in Puerto Rico's history: the confirmation of its "Estado Libre Asociado" (Free Associated State) or "commonwealth" status. Such a boricua identification in the photographic image becomes, in Thomas's *Down These Mean Streets*, a literary consolidation in the "passing" of the author's Afro-Cuban American father as a mainland Afro–Puerto Rican. I reflect on the novel's characterization of the father to discern in Thomas (recognized, of course, as a major mainland boricua writer) a supplementary literary career: that of a movement-period *Afro-Cuban American* writer whose novel, in its purchase on the historical, ranges from the high era of the Teatro Apolo (Thomas's 1928 birth in Harlem) to the moment of Lachatañeré's death (Thomas's 1955 release from prison). In the coda, Lourdes Casal (1938–1981) appears to unravel a supplementary career and boricua identification in the "excess" of her professional affiliations (poet, short-story writer, psychologist, sociologist, literary critic, activist, journal editor, faculty member) and the emergence, in view of her identity as an Afro-Latina, of a powerful interest in (returning to) Cuba.

Portorros, Cubiches

Mainland Puerto Rican experiences of U.S. colonial domination in the aftermath of the Jones Act (1917) and the establishment of the Estado Libre Asociado/Commonwealth (1952) frame a mid-twentieth-century boricua identification among Afro-Cuban Americans.[5] In particular, as we shall see, a boricua identification allows Afro-Cuban Americans to assume two of the constitutive dis/advantages specific to mainland Puerto Ricans: a "conferred" U.S. citizenship and an experience of "black" racialization in the United States. A way to understand the intra-Latino politics of a boricua identification is to consider the discourse of a mutual friendliness and ill will among Latinas/os of Cuban and Puerto Rican descent, a discourse I recognize through the categories of the "*portorro*" and "*cubiche*," colloquial terms for "Puerto Rican" and "Cuban" that invoke the shifting dispositions of amity and enmity characteristic of relations (and relationships) between the two communities. An example of the terms' use appears in an autobiographical narrative by the contemporary Cuban saxophonist Paquito D'Rivera. D'Rivera begins by listing the number of famous Cuban songs whose composers are not Cuban at all but are Puerto Rican. He then quotes famous Cuban and Puerto Rican musicians regarding relations between the two communities, beginning with Daniel Santos:

> "Cubans made me who I am," said Daniel Santos in his biography. And . . . "Listen, *mulato* [in original], to what I'm about to say," remarked that unforgettable character who was Frank Grillo (Machito), shortly after my arrival in the city of skyscrapers in 1980, "Cuban music was kept alive here in New York all these years thanks to the *boricuas* [in original]. Otherwise!"
>
> And I had much proof of that love and respect of the "*portorro*" [in original] toward our music from people like the brothers Jerry and Andy González, Bobby Capó, Tito Puente, . . . and many others! I personally have learned many things I didn't know about my own culture from them, especially from the musicologist René López, who knows more about that than the majority of *cubiches* [in original] I know.
>
> Who was going to tell us in the 1950s that soon it would be Puerto Ricans in New York and on the island itself who would most help our people when we had to leave in flight from the communist dictatorship that made life impossible in our very homes. There

isn't a single Cuban exile or his family who doesn't owe a *boricua* [in original] brother a favor or kind gesture during these long years of exile. We of the land of Maceo have not known a home as warm, a wife as sweet, or a friendship as loyal and disinterested as the compatriots of Betances have offered, and let's hope someday on returning to the homeland we can give back as much hospitality and sincere affection to these good people.[6]

The image of the boricua as both a specialist in things Cuban beyond the knowledge of even D'Rivera himself and as a steward of Cuba's music (what became "salsa") in the United States pivots on the intensities of amity. Yet there is a surplus meaning here, one D'Rivera holds off, and it involves this idea of the mainland boricua as a steward: specifically, the possibility that Cuban culture (and Cubans themselves), having come to the United States, are not only hosted by but are redone as the mainland boricua in ways that produce what I am calling a boricua identification. A related gesture involves race. Machito's *"mulato"* attribution to D'Rivera, situated in the recollected past of the autobiography, reasserts now, in the present event of its reading, D'Rivera's mixed-race identity: his Afro-Cubanness in the United States. Indeed, such *mulatez* as a sign of the Afro-Cuban American situation echoes in the reference to the *mulatos* Maceo and Betances, the significance of which is weirdly affirmed, through its excision, in the English-language translation of D'Rivera's narrative, which, in an act of textual whitening, replaces Maceo and Betances with José Martí and Eugenio María de Hostos.[7]

D'Rivera's use of *portorro* and *cubiche* indicates the mixing currents of friendliness and ill will that flow through relations between Cuban Americans and mainland Puerto Ricans. Among Cubans, *cubiche* connotes a close, often humorous, in-group recognition; it can also, however, enfold an insult, with the Cuban rendered abject. Fernando Ortiz begins a discussion of such meanings in his definition of *cubichería*, which he calls the "condition or thing proper to *cubiches* [in original]," a "pejorative form of address [*apelativo despectivo*]," and "not simply humorously [*no sólo festivamente*]," that "we Cubans give ourselves."[8] Such a name "we give ourselves" is also a name "others give us." Thus, another residue in D'Rivera's passage is how his *cubiche* serves too as a word that island and mainland Puerto Ricans, with all their amity, are able to "give us"— to use, in fact, with the edge of its other meaning, *cubiche* pejoratively. D'Rivera's *portorro* admits even more. A word that island and mainland Puerto Ricans "give themselves," with its own dialectics of the *festivo* and *despectivo, portorro* is used by others, too—in this instance, in fact, by D'Rivera himself, who, despite offering it humorously and with amity, suggests the word's *despectivo* associations through his application of quotation marks, which would guard against any such meanings of contempt. The strain within (and among) *portorro(s)* and *cubiche(s)* is apparent in D'Rivera's hope for a post-Castro opportunity to offer Puerto Ricans a Cuban "homeland" and "hospitality." What such a desire for a post-Castro Cuba forgets, of course, is the possibility of a future postcolonial Puerto Rico, one that brings with it the possibility of "ungrateful" Puerto Ricans who may have little need for (or reason to believe in the efficacy of) a post-Castro Cuban hospitality.

Such *portorro-cubiche* relations appear in an anecdote that Arturo Schomburg shared in a 1938 letter to the Cuban intellectual and historian Emilio Roig de Leuchsenring. Schomburg recalls how he and another mainland Afro–Puerto Rican with connections to the New York City–based Cuban/Puerto Rican independence movement of the late nineteenth century, Rosendo Rodríguez, had "saved the life of [José] Martí" from a Spanish assassination attempt in the city.[9] Schomburg's account of a Martí delivered crosses a terrain of Cuban mythography in a way that discomfits the Cuban/Puerto Rican collaborative amity at the heart of the story: it was two mainland Afro–Puerto Ricans who once saved the apostle of the Cuban nation. Without Schomburg and Rodríguez, in other words, there was no Martí, however ill fated his career in Cuban independence turned out to be.[10] Frances Negrón-Muntaner relates such a move to queerness, masculinity, and the U.S. colonial discourses on Puerto Rico between 1898 and 1917. The island's "new colonial administrators," she writes, "dismissed not only the elites but also all of the Islanders as unmanly and hence not fit for U.S. citizenship."

> Congressman Henry Teller, a champion of (at least nominal) sovereignty for Cuba, explicitly rejected the proposition that Puerto Ricans become citizens by casting *boricuas* as "queer" Cubans: "I don't like the Puerto Rican; they are not fighters like the Cubans; they were subjugated to Spanish tyranny for hundreds of years without being men enough to oppose it. Such a race is unworthy of American citizenship." In comparing the Puerto Ricans with the Cubans, the American colonial administrators and policy makers—like the Spaniards before them—again found *boricuas* "lacking," reinforcing the larger island's role as one of several fun house mirrors to see Puerto Rican ethno-national identity as queer

in the sense of both odd (nonnormative) and effeminate (weak, cowardly).[11]

Schomburg's narrative of a Martí delivered reverses such U.S. colonial representations of Cubans as "fighters" and Puerto Ricans as not "being men enough." Mainland Afro–Puerto Rican men, it turns out, were fighters, even as Cubans, it seems, were not men enough themselves, here in the protection not just of one of their own but of their most important national figure. In recounting the anecdote more than three decades after the event in question—long after, in other words, such an ideology of Cuban superiority/Puerto Rican inferiority has served in a primary way U.S. interests in dividing and conquering the Caribbean—Schomburg hails Roig de Leuchsenring as a *cubiche*: as a Cuban intimate he can prod with the story about Martí.

Another moment in the twentieth-century history of mainland Puerto Rican/Cuban American musical collaboration, years before D'Rivera's U.S. arrival, offers a literal staging of *portorro-cubiche* relations. I am referring to the battle of the bands on Easter Sunday 1936, at the Teatro Park Palace in Harlem: "Puerto Rico en guerra con Cuba" (Puerto Rico at War with Cuba).[12] The Afro–Puerto Rican Augusto Coen and his "Boricuas" played opposite the Afro-Cuban Alberto Socarrás and his Orquesta Campoamor—the house band, of course, for the theater where Alberto O'Farrill performed in blackface in the mid-1930s. "War" admits enmity between Cuban Americans and mainland Puerto Ricans, both figured here as "fighters." Yet, as Max Salazar reminds us, it was a well-managed conceit, one in which amity and, very likely, the *festivo* had settled: the members of the Socarrás band were mostly Puerto Ricans and Dominicans, Coen's Cubans and Panamanians.[13]

A different, though not unrelated, articulation of the *portorro*, the *cubiche*, and war appears in the Puerto Rican patriot and poet Lola Rodríguez de Tió's 1893 poem "A Cuba" (To Cuba) and its later transformations in twentieth-century popular and critical culture. The poem's famous lines, "Cuba y Puerto Rico son / de un pájaro las dos alas, / reciben flores o balas / sobre un mismo corazón . . ." (Cuba and Puerto Rico are / Two wings of the same bird, / They receive flowers or bullets / Upon the same heart . . .),[14] represent a Caribbean anticolonial unity that, hinging on a Cuban–Puerto Rican amity, rattles the U.S. distinction between "fighters" and those not "men enough": not only are both Cubans and Puerto Ricans taking a bullet here; they do so in a kind of singularity. Yet, as José Buscaglia-Salgado notes, the lines are often subject, in a kind of *portorro-cubiche* performance of the *despectivo*, to a Cuban appropriation and erasure: Cubans "are always anxious to recite [the lines] with genuine feelings of love for the Puerto Rican people," he writes, "always invariably pointing out with certain authority and intense pride that the poem was written by José Martí."[15] The Afro-Cuban Pablo Milanés's musical interpretation of the poem in his *nueva trova* song "Son de Cuba a Puerto Rico" (*Son* from Cuba to Puerto Rico) represents the tension well. "Puerto Rico, ala que cayó al mar, que no pudo volar, yo te invito a mi vuelo y buscamos juntos el mismo cielo" (Puerto Rico, wing that fell to the sea, that couldn't fly, I invite you on my flight and together we'll look for the same sky).[16] An expression emerging from 1970s revolutionary Cuba in support of Puerto Rican decolonization, the lyrics bear a striking resemblance, thematically if not politically, to D'Rivera's hope for a "someday" during which a Cuban hospitality toward boricuas might obtain. Like D'Rivera's thought, "Son de Cuba a Puerto Rico" runs a particular risk: in its case, the presumption of its liberation motive, which suggests the opposition between a liberated, post-1959 Cuba (captured in "mi vuelo") and a subjugated, post-1952 Puerto Rico ("que no pudo volar"), oppositions that, despite it all, recall the colonial assignments of Negrón-Muntaner's congressman: Cuban men are good, Puerto Rican bad. Another counterpossibility in the song, resonating with great poignancy in the history of Lachatañeré, is that Cubans have been known to fall to the sea themselves, literally so, too, both among and as boricuas. It is to these twists and turns of Rodríguez de Tió's intertexts that Lawrence La Fountain-Stokes contributes in his essay "De Un Pájaro Las Dos Alas: Travel Notes of a Queer Puerto Rican in Havana." A personal-critical narrative of a visit to Special-Period Cuba, "De Un Pájaro" considers not a *mismo cielo* that we, *portorros* and *cubiches*, *buscamos juntos* but a *mismo suelo*: the ground, floor, soil on which we tread. La Fountain-Stokes says as much in describing his personal-narrative persona as someone "thinking sardonically that Cuba and Puerto Rico are the sad flip-flop sandals of a myth that rots between the fungus-infected toes of a sickly, tired foot," thereby bringing us down to the level of the *chancleta* (flip-flop), that important material object and trope for the "poor," everyday people and cultures of Cuba, on the island and in the diaspora, around whose condition of "vulgar" ambulation and aurality—the "cheap" rubber *chancleta* slapping loudly against heel and sidewalk—cohere historical feelings and reflections often rendered abject (and simultaneously feminized) by elites on both sides of the Florida Straits, a reaction La Fountain-Stokes is clearly keen to counter, through reappropriation, with his metaphor.[17] Central to "De Un Pájaro" is its acknowledgment and use of the *despectivo* in the intertextual keyword *pájaro*, a pejorative term for a homosexual man that connects the amity-enmity/*festivo-despectivo* meanings of *portorro-cubiche* exchanges to relations of (and relationships in) gay sexuality, close to which are the figures of Rodríguez de Tió and Milanés themselves.[18]

Portorro-cubiche relations texture the two primary sites of a mainland boricua identification among Afro-Cuban Americans, migrant and U.S. born: a conferred U.S. citizenship and an experience of black racialization. That Puerto Ricans, represented in the U.S. colonial imaginary as "a race . . . unworthy of American citizenship," would nevertheless receive it suggests the vexed nature of their rights and privileges; theirs, in other words, would be a "distinctly subordinate U.S. citizenship," one characterized early on, for example, by the way in which "the Jones Act predictably secured voting rights in the hands of only the wealthiest and the 'whitest' Puerto Ricans," an instance of U.S. colonial domination that, as "race," "emerged as the determining factor in shaping policies that were ultimately not limited to Puerto Ricans living on the Island, but extended to migrants to the U.S. mainland and subsequent generations as well."[19] Between 1917 and 1959, Nancy Mirabal reminds us, "among Cubans already residing in New York and looking for work and housing, it was a common practice to identify themselves as Puerto Rican and therefore citizens of the United States," a practice of boricua identification, I am suggesting, in which Afro-Cuban Americans, as *cubiches*, perform the mainland Afro–Puerto Rican, as *portorros*, to benefit from, and run the risks of, "subordinate citizenship."[20] It is an act that "takes advantage" of a Puerto Rican colonial condition, to be sure, but also of a U.S. imperialism for which Cubans "will do" just as well as Puerto Ricans; meanwhile, such a boricua identification reveals Afro-Cubans, in their migration to the United States, as again moving "against" their own interests, to the frustration of the Cuban nation, whose republic they eschew, in favor of a colonial boricua citizenship.

In Ramón Grosfoguel's critique of mainstream sociology in relation to Puerto Rican migration to the mainland United States in the 1950s and 1960s, he demonstrates how the discipline's purchase on "poverty" depended on ideas of "Puerto Ricans and African-Americans [as] an example of negative social capital because of their 'inferior' cultural practices," in contrast, soon after 1959, to the (largely white, middle-class and elite) Cuban migrants from the revolution, who served U.S.

empire as "a positive version of social capital because of their 'superior' cultural practices." Such a Cold War narrative suggests that a boricua identification, already linked to forms of subordinate citizenship, signifies now as "black": here, Afro-Cuban Americans, as mainland Afro–Puerto Ricans, perhaps recoil from, perhaps manipulate the condition of "minority disadvantage" particular to mainland Puerto Ricans, who appear, with African Americans, in "the Euro-American imaginary" as "dangerous, lazy, and criminal or simply opportunistic people that take advantage of welfare programs," despite the fact that they "face discrimination in the spaces of everyday life in banks, stores, housing, and so on that white Americans take for granted."[21] Grosfoguel recognizes that "to be confused with Puerto Ricans or African-Americans could be useful for illegal immigrants who want to take provisional cover under the U.S. citizenship guaranteed to Puerto Ricans and African-Americans," yet he understands, too, the "strategy of disentanglement": that otherwise "illegal" others would "avoid the racialized and stereotypical construction of the 'colonial/racial subjects' of the U.S. empire."[22]

Boricua identifications in Lachatañeré and Thomas are cultural signs of these relations in coloniality and *latinidad*—the collaborations and disputes, both evanescent and enduring, among *portorros* and *cubiches* in the United States. They take shape around careers in their supplementary dimensions: the specific instances of Afro-Cuban American writers and intellectuals doing "side-work," the specific moments in which dominant explications of their standing in Cuban and Latino Studies (as Afro-Cuban ethnographer, as mainland Puerto Rican novelist) are "added on" to other, countervailing critical evaluations. The texts of an Afro-Cuban American boricua identification edge Cuban American literary history. To show how, I turn first to Rómulo Lachatañeré.

Lachatañeré in the Midcentury

During Nicolás Guillén's visit to New York City in the spring of 1949, he also met with Rómulo Lachatañeré, whom he had known in Havana a decade earlier; Lachatañeré had been in New York since 1939. Guillén's recollection of the meeting, like his account of Cosme during the same visit, reflects, in however inadvertent or resistant a way, Lachatañeré's *afrolatinidad* and, indeed, the elements in his life of a supplementary career. "In New York, we spent a pleasant, memorable day together," wrote Guillén, "accompanied by Eusebia Cosme. We had lunch in Harlem, and I remember it was there that he helped me buy a pair of shoes, which I still have. 'Shoes for a refined black man [*negro fino*],' as he told me then, in a very amusing way. Around that time, he was deep into his photography '*hobby*' [in English in original] and thus up to his old tricks with Eusebia and me. That night I had dinner at his house with his daughter and wife. . . . It was a Cuban [*criolla*] evening, full of memories and evocations of the beloved, far-off Island."[23]

The "Cuban evening" at the Lachatañerés, in its very occasion as a time and place for a recollected Cuba, is also something other than that: it is an "Afro-Cuban American evening," one in which Afro-Cuban Americans, migrant and U.S. born, enacted with Guillén an Afro-Latino practice (their hospitality, for example) that enabled the islandcentric "memories" and "evocations" Guillén references to occur in the first place. Such an *afrolatinidad*, of course, belongs also to Cosme, as we saw in chapter 2, and it is now Lachatañeré's, in terms of their respective identities and careers in the United States; the two figures, indeed, appear as such— as implied, if not openly acknowledged, Afro-Cuban Americans—in a document of the Sociedad de Estudios Afrocubanos, which lists them as the institution's only two "contributing members" in New York City.[24] The supplementary career is active here, too. Lachatañeré's photography is tellingly framed by Guillén as an amusement; that he uses English in order to arrive at that meaning only further estranges the photography. It is obvious that what Lachatañeré does—his "real" career and its supplementary manifestations—causes anxiety. A particular description captures this well in its profusion of terms to manage the excess (of social, economic, and cultural values) related to what Lachatañeré does: he was a "pharmacist by profession, writer and anthropologist by vocation and learning, photographer by emotion."[25]

The evening at the Lachatañerés is significant for another reason, and it involves the two other people present that night: Sara Lachatañeré (née Carranza), his wife, and Diana, his daughter. Sara suggests the passage's kernel of a boricua identification; born in Havana, she had come to the United States in 1938, using the papers of a Puerto Rican woman.[26] Diana, of course, is Diana Lachatanere, curator of the Manuscripts, Archives and Rare Books Division at the Schomburg Center. Lachatanere was three years old the night her family hosted Guillén. Her story stands on its own, yet it also intervenes in her father's, particularly as it relates to her personal and professional contributions to African American and Afro-Latino studies, which Guillén's narrative, read proleptically, suggests: Lachatanere's career at the New York Public Library on 135th Street picks up on—and, in a sense, revises, as its "successful," professional culmination—Rómulo's own experience, sometimes precarious, as an "unaffiliated" patron at that institution's Forty-Second Street location, where he researched in the 1940s, often with the assistance of Sara; further, his Harlem and Puerto Rico photographs reside today at the Schomburg Center's Photographs and Prints Division, with a compelling acquisition history that, as one might expect, involves Diana Lachatanere herself.[27] In all this, Guillén's narrative invokes Rómulo Lachatañeré's *afrolatinidad*, the defining element in much of his otherwise island-identified life and work.

Scholars of that work have rightly led, in a variety of ways, with Lachatañeré's African-diasporic identity, even if the question of his *afrolatinidad* remains unexplored. "Probably the most prominent African diasporic ethnographers were Rómulo Lachatañeré . . . , a pharmacist and photo-journalist who worked closely with Ortiz, and [the Afro-Brazilian] Édison Carneiro," writes Faye V. Harrison. Robin Moore notes that, "with the exception of Lachatañeré, the study of Afro-Cuban culture remained in the hands of white Cubans."[28] Lachatañeré's initial major publications were four ethnographic-fictional narratives in *Adelante* between February 1936 and August 1938.[29] The *Adelante* publications, which hinge on translations between Afro-Cuban practices of Yoruba orality and spirituality and Afro-Cuban working-class and "literary" Spanish, intervene, like Cosme's performances, as modern Afro-Cuban-authored expressions in a field of Cuban racial imagining marked by the *teatro bufo* and *negrismo*. In this regard, the *Adelante* texts anticipate Lachatañeré's first book, *¡¡Oh, mío, Yemayá!!* (1938), counted among the "most important narrative texts of Yoruba mythology in Cuba."[30] In a revealing statement, Lachatañeré explained his hope for *¡¡Oh, mío, Yemayá!!*: "to encourage others, with more discipline and capacity for work than me, to incorporate the black [*lo negro*]—which is very much in my flesh—into national culture."[31] Two major works would follow *¡¡Oh, mío, Yemayá!!*: the scholarly essay "El sistema religioso de los lucumí y otras influencias africanas en Cuba" (The Religious System of the *Lucumí* and Other African Influences in Cuba; 1941) and *Manual de santería* (Santería Handbook; 1942), both of which, together with essays of note published in U.S. Spanish-language magazines, I discuss later.

Lachatañeré was born in Santiago de Cuba in 1909. On his mother's side, he was a grandson of Flor Crombet, an Afro-Cuban general in the Liberation Army. His father, a veteran of the Liberation Army, was murdered when Lachatañeré was a year old. Among his ancestors were migrants from Haiti during the revolution. The last name, particularly in its morphology, bespeaks Haitian-Cuban-U.S. migrations: from the French La Châtaigneraie/Lachataignerais to the Spanish Lachatañeré, which, with Diana, becomes the "English" Lachatanere, with her removal of the *tilde* and *acento*. In 1929, after a three-year program, Lachatañeré graduated with a degree in pharmacy from the University of Havana. He found a job with the Institute for Venereal Diseases in the capital. In 1934, after a Fulgencio Batista–led coup, Lachatañeré was arrested and imprisoned at the Castillo del Príncipe.[32] It was the eve of his publishing in *Adelante*, with whose other contributors he participated "in socialist and communist organizations."[33] Under these circumstances, with his release, Lachatañeré returned to Santiago, and soon he left the country. On October 7, 1938, a little over a month after Eusebia Cosme's own arrival, Lachatañeré disembarked from the *Oriente* in New York City—his initial visit to the United States. His contact was his soon-to-be wife, Sara, who went by her Puerto Rican name, Carmen Martínez, and lived on 117th Street and Eighth Avenue. Like O'Farrill and Cosme before him, Lachatañeré was subject to the official migrant discourses of race in the United States: under "Race or People" on the "List or Manifest of Alien Passengers," "African" was typed, then struck, with "Cuban" written over it by hand.[34] Shortly after his arrival, with an introduction from Guillén, Lachatañeré wrote Langston Hughes, hoping to arrange a meeting.[35] By September of the following year, he had returned to New York City from Cuba, this time for good. His contact again was Sara, now his wife, named "Carmen Lachataignerais," and his "Race or People" was "Cuban," the word typed on the form.[36] Again he contacted Hughes, this time inquiring whether he had received a copy of *¡¡Oh, mío, Yemayá!!*: "a collection of black stories [*cuentos negros*] I collected during my stay in Cuba." Lachatañeré asked Hughes, "Could [you] translate a story or two—those you consider the best—and send them to me."[37] The overarching period of Lachatañeré's arrival and residence in New York City, from 1940 to 1960, saw a major increase in the city's Puerto Rican population, a result of the mass migration of workers in the context of U.S. colonial policy.[38] The first few years in New York City, it seems, were difficult for Lachatañeré, given his admission of "self-employment" from 1939 to 1943, during which he likely worked on translations "of articles, letters, or documents."[39] And then he joined the army. Among the many compelling things lost with Lachatañeré's early death was a possible account of his time in the service, from April 1943 to November 1944, a time spent in part aboard the hospital ship *Acadia* (berthed in Charleston, South Carolina), for Lachatañeré, in a segregated military, was inducted not into its "colored ranks" but into the "regular," which is to say "all-white," army. On his discharge papers, he was a U.S. citizen, and his "Race" was marked "White," suggesting how Afro-Cuban American articulations of *afrolatinidad* may register a dominant official identity alongside the "African" and "Cuban."[40] Lachatañeré spent a month in Medical Basic Training, six months working as a "Hospital Orderly," and three months as a "Medical Laboratory Technician." For a few days in February and again in March 1944, he sailed on the *Acadia* to North Africa, where the ship picked up wounded.[41] After the war, Lachatañeré continued to work as a medical technician, including jobs at Bellevue and Columbia Presbyterian Hospitals. In September 1945, he was among the founders of the important Club Cubano Inter-Americano, the Afro-Cuban American social club.

"El sistema religioso de los lucumí y otras influencias africanas en Cuba" (The Religious System of the *Lucumí* and Other African Influences in Cuba), published in *Estudios Afrocubanos* in the fall of 1941, is a major text of Cuban studies. In it, Lachatañeré marks a historical break in the national racist knowledge on Afro-Cubans. He looks back on the early work of Fernando Ortiz—the Lombrosian Ortiz of *Los negros brujos: Apuntes para un estudio de etnología criminal* (The Black Sorcerers: Notes toward a Study of Criminal Ethnology; 1906)—identifies in it the discourse of Afro-Cuban criminality, and challenges it, seizing, in particular, on the term *brujería* (witchcraft). It is with such a move that Lachatañeré stressed the parameters of a modern anthropology on the African diaspora, enacting, indeed, a counterdiscourse, one invested in critique. Lachatañeré was careful to note that the epistemic convergence of anthropology and criminology "dragged down professor Fernando Ortiz, who has the indisputable merit of having discovered the existence of Afro-Cuban religious forms." Despite Ortiz's *brujería* problem, Lachatañeré went on, it was his "contribution [that] opened the door to new research in this field," which was "carried on almost exclusively by him, since the Cuban-educated class still looks down on this kind of study or follows it with reservations."[42] Still, Lachatañeré made his challenge plain: "In the discussion presented by Fernando Ortiz, the term *brujería* [in original] is acknowledged as designating the beliefs of Afro-Cubans [*los afrocubanos*], just as the term *brujo* [in original] is applied to the cults' priests, words that have been put into practice not only by him but by other students of the presence of black religions [*religiones negras*] among the Afro-Americans of the New World [*los afroamericanos del Nuevo Mundo*], [students] to whom we should also refer in refuting the use of this designation, which, in frankness, we will call discriminatory [*discriminativa*]."[43]

What is unacknowledged about Lachatañeré's renowned *brujería* intervention in "El sistema" is its *afrolatinidad*: the way in which the essay, in its conditions of production, encodes Lachatañeré's Afro-Latino experience. A note accompanying "El sistema" opens the way, locating the work, if only in terms of its provenance, in the United States: the delay in publishing the "1939" issue allowed *Estudios Afrocubanos* "to include in it the very important study in Afro-Cuban ethnography that . . . Mr. Rómulo Lachatañeré has sent . . . from New York."[44] New York City, of course, is more than a simple origin. It signifies here Lachatañeré's Afro-Latino situation in the geopolitics of knowledge, the details of which are to be found in his correspondence with Ortiz over a year before the publication of "El sistema," in which he revealed how his work was proceeding; how he had submitted his manuscript to Melville Herskovits and William Bascom for review, thus putting himself into contact with the dominant social-institutional force of anthropology on the African diaspora; and how he planned to apply for graduate study with Ruth Benedict at Columbia University under a Rosenwald grant, which linked him to a "Negro" identity and brought out into the open his interest in *afrolatinidad*.[45]

In August 1940, Lachatañeré wrote Ortiz about the studies he was carrying out: "regarding the problems of my people [*mi gente*]." He said, "[I am in] this city's central library, trying to find 'the family tree of my ancestors,' a difficult task, that, but I push forward: I'm on the *lucumís* [in original], who you say came into Cuba as the Yoruba, and I accept your judgment."[46] The disclosure of a social commitment in the research and writing of "El sistema" is striking, as is Lachatañeré's identification with "*mi gente*," Afro-Cuban people; the personal here reveals itself as a source of the critique of a *brujería* "*discriminativa*." The scene for this, the New York Public Library, is thick with the significance of Diana Lachatanere's future career; it is the library, indeed, that allows for a representation of the conditions under which Lachatañeré worked. Lachatañeré cites library spaces time and again in his letters to Ortiz—he writes, "It's been nearly a year since I've been studying in the libraries of this city the influences of African religious beliefs poured into Cuba during slavery,"[47] thus dating the composition of "El sistema" at least to his arrival in New York City in the fall of 1939—and it is the library that prompts in him a confession to Ortiz: "Sometimes in my studies at the Library, I use the name of the Sociedad de Estudios Afrocubanos [in original]; I should have asked you for permission; I forgot to do so; forgive me this offense and accept that I used this institution's name in my research. It's a question of sometimes needing to obtain photostatic copies of maps or documents, and I sign as if my studies were backed by the Afrocubana. That isn't too serious, right?"[48] Lachatañeré enacts the situation of the scholar "without prestigious institutional affiliations or academic security."[49] In another way, his "unofficial" use of the society's name speaks to a lack of other income, professional or otherwise, such as Ortiz derived from his law practice or Lydia Cabrera from patronage.[50] Only a few weeks later, Ortiz sent along a note, written on Sociedad de Estudios Afrocubanos letterhead, stating, "[Lachatañeré] is a member of this Society and . . . has been named United States correspondent of our journal, *Estudios Afrocubanos.*" It was a "credential [that allowed Lachatañeré], on behalf of the Society, to carry out studies in his speciality, in Libraries as well as Archives of the United States."[51] Ortiz, in other words, occupied a familiar position in the narrative: through the form of the transamerican credential, he is the older mentor, a figure whose very social standing (in island-Cuban professional and racial terms) shapes, even as it alleviates, Lachatañeré's migrant Afro-Cuban American academic institutional-affiliation in/securities.[52]

In the year leading up to the publication of "El sistema," Lachatañeré was also in contact with Melville Herskovits and William Bascom, sending the former at Evanston his manuscript in hopes of receiving feedback.[53] Another aspect of the *afrolatinidad* of his *brujería* critique is thus evident. "El sistema," while published in Havana, was peer reviewed in the United States. Its geopolitics—indeed, the geopolitics of the peer review—reveal Lachatañeré's negotiation with modern anthropology on the African diaspora.[54] Lachatañeré's institutional in/security is most apparent in Herskovits's and Bascom's ex cathedra management of his *brujería* critique and, by extension, his relationship with Fernando Ortiz himself. In early 1941, Lachatañeré heard back from Herskovits. Herskovits had given the manuscript to Bascom for review. A recent Ph.D. with research experience in Nigeria on modern Yoruba cultures, Bascom was a few years younger than Lachatañeré. In agreement with his protégé's review, Herskovits touched on some of its points: that Lachatañeré be more specific about the Cuban geographic locations of his sources, for example, and that he credit Ortiz on syncretism. In fact, Herskovits wondered, was Lachatañeré familiar with the work of Ortiz?[55] (Later that winter, Ortiz made plain to others his mentorship role, writing in support of Lachatañeré to Herskovits, Franz Boas, and Ruth Benedict.)[56]

Bascom's review was encouraging, yet he urged revision. He was critical of Lachatañeré's choice and use of secondary sources on historical Yoruba cultures, sources, Bascom felt, that had clouded Lachatañeré's assessment of what was African and what was African diasporic.[57] Here, the vector of authenticity in an anthropology on the African diaspora appears in Bascom's review, hinting (and ignoring) the spaces, the libraries in New York City, which Lachatañeré had accessed with credentials sent from Cuba, spaces in which he had assembled not just an archive of primary and secondary sources, however dubious (to Bascom), but, in terms of the *brujería* response, an archive of critique.

Soon, it became clear to Herskovits that Lachatañeré did indeed know Ortiz's work. In a series of exchanges between Lachatañeré and Herskovits over the winter and spring of 1941, Lachatañeré expressed gratitude for the review. He also reemphasized the *brujería* concept as "*discriminativo*," an assessment, he explained, that did not take away from his appreciation of Ortiz. If Lachatañeré were to make that point in print, Herskovits suggested, it should be done within scholarly protocol.[58] Such an attention to the propriety with which Lachatañeré engaged Ortiz again speaks to the geopolitics of the peer review of "El sistema," allegorizing Herskovits's management of the professional prestige of Ortiz (and of anthropology on the African diaspora) in the face of Lachatañeré's critique from the edges, all of which transpired even as Herskovits and his Cuban colleague continued to mentor Lachatañeré toward the discipline's interior. It was an attention to propriety that only intensified after Herskovits received Ortiz's letter of recommendation for Lachatañeré—another sign, this recommendation, together with the other instances of the hidden, bureaucratic genres of the academy (the credential and the review) of the material, discursive conditions of professional in/security constitutive of Lachatañeré's project. That Ortiz wrote the recommendation showed the worthiness of his character, Herskovits argued, and left no doubt that Ortiz's "work [should be] treated with the respect it deserves."[59] With such a moral command hanging over the critique, Lachatañeré returned a revised version of the manuscript to Herskovits, though not without broaching the possibility, reminiscent of his earlier contact with Hughes, of publishing the material in an English translation—a task, suggestive of an *afrolatinidad* in its Anglophone desire, with which Lachatañeré asked Herskovits for help.[60] Meanwhile, the Herskovits *brujería* exchange affected Lachatañeré's show of deference vis-à-vis Ortiz in a particular way: writing to Ortiz, Lachatañeré admitted the critique's possible impropriety, couching it as a susceptibility to feelings ill befitting a scholar. "If

I have acted passionately [*apasionadamente*]," he wrote, it was because of a "desire to clear up some problems for the benefit of the Afro-Cuban studies [*los estudios afrocubanos*] initiated by you."[61] Ortiz wrote back to Lachatañeré and reassured him: "I am 'delighted' [*encantado*], as we say in our land [*por nuestra tierra*]," with the manuscript. Ortiz said it would be published "in the next number of the journal *Estudios Afrocubanos* that we are preparing for press." "El sistema," in other words, would see the light of day in Cuba—and in Spanish—with Ortiz acknowledging Lachatañeré's critique.[62] Yet no trace of the essay's Afro-Latino origins (Lachatañeré's research at the Forty-Second Street library, his exchange with Herskovits and Bascom) appeared in the journal, save for the reference to Lachatañeré's New York location.

In fact, it was Ruth Benedict who encouraged Lachatañeré to publish "El sistema" in Spanish rather than in an English translation.[63] Their relationship during the summer of 1941, centered on his (ultimately unsuccessful) application for a Rosenwald Fellowship to pursue an M.A. in anthropology under her direction at Columbia, reveals how, with "El sistema" pushed toward publication, Lachatañeré was exploring an interest in an "Afro-Latino studies," one in which the contours of a mainland boricua identification were visible, and which was premised on the financial support of an institution, in the Rosenwald, that guided Lachatañeré, just a few years from military induction as "white," toward appearing in paperwork as a "Cuban Negro": an English-language term for the Afro-Latino in which the signs of an already-racialized Latin American national identity (the "Cuban") and an Anglo-U.S. blackness (the "Negro") converge. Benedict wrote Edwin R. Embree, the Rosenwald's director, that she was "much interested in a Cuban Negro, Romulo Lachatanere [*sic*]," who had proposed to do "anthropological work in Harlem, 'Spanish Town.'" Benedict wanted to know if Lachatañeré should wait until his U.S. citizenship application was approved before he pursued the fellowship. In one way, Benedict's was a technical question: would a "non-citizen" meet the application requirements? In another, it was a specific inquiry into the conditions of the African diaspora in the United States: what was the place of an Afro-Latino vis-à-vis philanthropy toward the "Negro," as exemplified in the Rosenwald's history of supporting such figures as Hurston, Du Bois, and Ellison?[64] The place, Embree's reply suggests, was that of exceptionality: "While it is customary for these awards to be made to American Negroes," Embree wrote, "the Fellowship Committee is willing to consider exceptional cases on their merits."[65] In other words, an Afro-Cuban American, in a fellowship application, may be counted as a

"Negro"; upon his immigrant arrival to the United States, an "African"; and upon his enlistment in the army, a "white."

Accompanying the challenge for the Rosenwald of categorizing Lachatañeré's Afro-Latino identity was, for the applicant Lachatañeré himself, a comparable challenge regarding his inchoate Afro-Latino object of study, represented in his fellowship proposal, the "Plan of Work." In its English-language use and emerging boricua identification, the proposal (another hidden, minor genre of the academy) is exemplary of the Lachatañeré supplementary text, here as an expression of a modern Afro-Latino studies:

> I propose to make an ethnological study of the important Spanish-speaking community in New York's Harlem. This community is concentrated in the area extending from the north end of Central Park to 125th and from Morningside Park to the East River, and lives under conditions which allow it few possibilities of amalgamation with the native population . . . .
>
> Most of the "Hispanos" who live in this area are Portoricans and "Antillanos" from Cuba and Santo Domingo, though they hail also from South America and Mexico. As the Portoricans and "Antillanos" constitute the bulk of the population, this study will primarily concern these latter groups.
>
> Most of the Portoricans and "Antillanos" are Negroes and even when for their "protection" they stress instead their Spanish admixture, they are exposed to the difficulties faced by any Negro group in the United States. They [sic] cultural heritage also is in great part Negro. This is true not only in their cultural expressions such as religions and the arts, but also in the influence upon them of a history of Negro slavery. In addition they have been deeply influenced by Spanish culture of the colonial period. The proposed investigation therefore would have to consider this group as inheritors of both Negro and Spanish culture who are now plunged in the American environment of Harlem.
>
> It is proposed to center the investigation upon the religion of this group. This religion is highly mediumistic. The professional medium, in intercourse with the spirit, acts as diviner, as leechcraft doctor or as sorcerer (*brujo* and *bruja*) . . . .
>
> I intend to register at Columbia University for an MA degree in Anthropology. My life interest is in further study of Negro problems.[66]

The proposal is striking for the reemergence, seemingly unscathed, of the *bruja/o* concept, which I understand in the context of the challenge faced by a would-be graduate student before the professionalizing exigencies of a fellowship application. *Brujería*'s seeming sureness of usage, despite it all, was convenient, contrasting with the multiple, shifting terms Lachatañeré possessed to introduce his Afro-Latino object of study: the geolinguistic "Spanish-speaking community in New York's Harlem"; the identity-based "'Hispanos,'" which includes "Portoricans," "'Antillanos,'" and others "from South America and Mexico"; and, of course, the "'Antillanos'" itself, indicating those "from Cuba and Santo Domingo." Thus informed by a Hispanophone Caribbean-diaspora focus on mainland Puerto Ricans, Cuban Americans, and Dominican Americans, Lachatañeré envisions a modern Afro-Latino studies with remarkable clarity. As was done to him by Benedict, he relies on "Negro" to articulate an *afrolatinidad*, and he recognizes its political and historical immediacies: the (possibly violent) exposure of a "Negro" identification in the United States; the unreliable amelioration (perhaps even whitening) of a Spanish-language-oriented, Latin American–derived U.S. "ethnic" identity; the presence of African-diasporic cultural practices; and the referent of slavery. Indeed, however much a product of Rosenwald exigencies, his concluding expression of an intellectual commitment to "Negro problems" indicates that in this, his first, U.S.-based project, Lachatañeré was very much imagining an Afro-Latino inquiry.[67]

Manual de santería, a text lauded for its positive representations of *regla de ocha* practices on the island, is an unrecognized source for Lachatañeré's New York City "Antillano" representation. Its authorial stamp, "New York, 1941," hints at such a possibility, dating the book's composition (or, at the very least, completion) concurrently with the revisions of "El sistema."[68] Lachatañeré understood the book as "putting the Afro-Cuban himself [*al propio afrocubano*] on the stage and allowing him to act for himself and arrive at a theory to explain the only thing he may not know, the violent treatment he receives."[69] Just as significant as such a cultural politics, I argue, is the narrative's Latino location in the following passage, one that displaces an islandcentric fieldwork imaginary in Lachatañeré (located between Havana, Matanzas, Santiago, and Guantánamo) with a "Spanish Town" other.

> The *hair washing* [*lavarase la cabeza*] ceremony is another elevated technique recommended by the oracle, whose powers to straighten out a person's life are infallible.

A friend of ours, resident in Manhattan, N.Y., and who keeps alive a reminder of her *santos* [in original], burning a light to the Caridad del Cobre [in original] she brought with her, doing *mudanzas interiores* [in original] when her luck ran out, and *cleaning* the apartment with herbs bought at the "botanicalsgardens" [*sic*; in original] of "Spansih [*sic*] Town" [in original], which are places where they sell all kinds of herbs coming from across the Antilles, and who, furthermore, corresponds with her *santero* [in original] in Havana, upon leaving the former to come live in Nueva York [in original], not only brought her virgin and *oil lamps but*, among other precautions taken, had a *hair washing* done. The priest required the following ingredients: a chicken, a new white plate, cacao lard, and a coconut. At nightfall, said officiant appeared at the house and handled the ceremony, beginning by decapitating the chicken. Stepping on the head, the feet held together, he twisted, and pulling with violence, the head remained underfoot, cut off as if by a knife. The warm blood was spilled on the young woman's head, whose face had previously been smeared with *cascarilla* [in original] (the shell of an egg, ground up and turned into a fine powder). The bare bust was marked with four lines, a white chalk being used. A cross was done on the back with the same chalk. During the bloodshed, the *santero* [in original] pronounced a spell [in original]. This operation complete, he took a piece of coconut and a portion of cacao lard; *el santero* [in original] put both ingredients in his mouth and after a laborious chewing placed them on the new plate. Pronouncing another *encantamiento* [in original; spell], he smeared them on the young woman's hair, pressed together by the clots of chicken blood.

Later, tying a scarf around the head, he brought the operation to an end. The young woman slept that night with the ingredients placed like that and observed celibacy.

The plate with the rest of the coconut was to be left next to the railroad tracks. After fulfilling this last requirement, Cusita would acquire a formidable power to fight against the adversities in the complicated city of Nueva York [in original].

This *hair washing* was done in the name of Our Lady of Mercy and the priest officiated under the powers of Yemayá [in original].

The stipulated payment was three dollars [*pesos*].[70]

This remarkable narrative of a modern Afro-Cuban departure from Havana and arrival in New York City foregrounds the ethnographic representation of ritual in Cuba, yet, for all that, the "young woman's" life in "Spanish Town"—and, therefore, her implied *afrolatinidad*—interrupts island-Cuban ritual practices and their representation. The fact of an Afro-Latino experience in Manhattan, if not fully examined, in other words, is irrepressible in the book. Lacing Lachatañeré's invocation of an *afrolatinidad* here are the Anglophony and "errors" of the passage, all of which (like "New York, 1941") are signs, finally, of the writer-ethnographer's own Afro-Latino location: the "misspelled" "Spansih Town" and "botanicalsgardens" (the "fault," perhaps, of Lachatañeré himself or his island-based publisher), and especially the English-language word "spell."

A powerful expression of an Afro-Latino condition and inquiry in Lachatañeré—along with the Rosenwald proposal, the *Manual* passage, and his own experience in the geopolitics of the peer review—are several texts that appeared in the early 1940s in two U.S.-based, Latin American–oriented periodicals: *La Nueva Democracia* and *Norte, Revista Continental*.[71] These publications, as supplementary texts, include reviews of the film version of *Tobacco Road* and the Orson Welles–Canada Lee staging of *Native Son*, as well pieces on *afrocubanismo* and the culture industry and summaries of the research on Afro-Cuban religion.

Two works stand out in particular for their attention to an *afrolatinidad*. In "Coney Island: El centro de diversiones mayor del mundo" (Coney Island: The World's Greatest Amusement Park), Lachatañeré revises two of José Martí's chronicles, "El puente de Brooklyn" and "Coney Island," in particular the former, which, in a famous passage, draws on imaginaries of the racial and ethnic type to describe a crowd crossing the bridge, including "showy blacks [*negros lujosos*], Russians with burning eyes, redheaded Norwegians, elegant Japanese, lean and indifferent Chinese."[72] Nearly sixty years later, Lachatañeré refocused Brooklyn as a space of ethno-racial display to include Latinas/os and Afro-Latinas/os: among the "Irish from Chelsea; Jews from Germany, Poland, Czechoslovakia, Manhattan, North Africa," he saw "blacks from Alabama, Cuba, Puerto Rico, Abyssinia; '*hispanos*' [in original] from Harlem and 'Cherry Street.'"[73] Lachatañeré locates Afro-Latinas/os in a cartography of the African diaspora. Configuring their *afrolatinidad* to a modern logic of where one's U.S. black identity is *from* in the Americas, Lachatañeré suggests that Afro-Cuban Americans and mainland Afro–Puerto Ricans share with southern African Americans "the difficulties faced by any Negro group in the United States" (and, with the Abyssinia reference, "by any Negro group" in post/colonial Africa as well). It is

a striking, if oblique, affirmation of the way in which blackness determines the Afro-Latino social, an affirmation even more striking for the
way in which Lachatañeré's *lista martiana* separates Afro-Cuban Americans and mainland Afro–Puerto Ricans from "*hispanos.*" With such a
separation, one that implies the absence of a U.S. "*afrohispano*" category,
Lachatañeré hints at a Latino whiteness—and white Latino separation—
among the *hispanas/os* of New York City.

Another *Norte* article, "El barrio latino de Harlem" (The Latin Barrio of
Harlem), continues the Afro-Latino inquiry, now as a critique that shades
into a historicizing reflection on Latino Harlem's Apolo and Campoamor
eras.[74] Lachatañeré again works a cartography of the African diaspora
involving Afro-Latinas/os. He writes that it is "certain that the Barrio
Latino [in original] is a section of black [*negro*] Harlem," which includes
"'West Indians' [in original]," signifying here people from the "English
possessions and Haiti." (He is careful to note that Latino Harlem's majority
are "*portorriqueños.*") Then, in a critique in the spirit of his *brujería* observation, made now on behalf of African Americans, Lachatañeré character-
izes rote accounts of African American criminality in Harlem as a strategy
to "conceal the real consequences of poverty and the uprooted life led in
the black city of New York [*la ciudad negra de Nueva York*]." He extends
the critique in telling fashion to dominant representations of *latinidad* in
the term "Spanish Town," which, of course, he himself used as a graduate-
school aspirant in the Rosenwald proposal and "in error" in the *Manual*.
Unlike "Barrio Latino," a term used by "the very people" who live in the
area, "Spanish Town" is a term used by outsiders: by the "*neoyorkinos*" who
"know it as a section of Harlem, wrapped in a bad reputation." In a gesture
toward the temporal and spatial depth of such a "Barrio Latino," Lachatañeré turns his attention to Lenox Avenue. The street was the center of the
"Spanish-speaking population [*población de habla española*]" until "a few
years ago [*unos cuantos años atrás*]," he writes, invoking the Lenox Avenue
of the office of *Gráfico* during the height of Alberto O'Farrill's tenure, of the
early years of Simón Jou's bakery, La Moderna, and of Alberto Socarrás's
arrival in Harlem on the IRT in 1927. Now it is "the black American population [*la población negra-americana*]" who lives there, and Lachatañeré
imagines their sharing the street with the traces of such an Afro/Latino
past, figured as echoes of African-diasporic percussion: "Lenox Avenue
merely keeps the memory of the beating of Afro-Cuban drums [*atabales
afrocubanos*] during the summer."[75]

On April 11, 1952, a decade after these print-culture works, Lachatañeré boarded a New York City–bound Pan American DC-4 in San Juan,

Puerto Rico. Eleven minutes after takeoff, its engines failed, and the airplane crashed into the sea, five miles off the Spanish-colonial Morro castle. The majority of the passengers were Puerto Rican. Fifty-two died; seventeen survived. Lachatañeré's body was never recovered. He had been on the island since March, and among his activities there, as we know, was photography.[76] Posthumous accounts offer multiple reasons for Lachatañeré's trip to the island. He was interested in documenting the labor conditions; he wanted to gather information for a study of Puerto Rico's African-diasporic religions; he was on a vacation and would eventually make his way to Cuba for a family visit. Indeed, Sara, his wife, did not expect him on the flight.[77] That it was to Puerto Rico that he traveled (significantly, right around the same time that Eusebia Cosme finally returned to Cuba) suggests a narrative in which Lachatañeré responded to a boricua diaspora experience in New York City by choosing to go in search of its island "origins": "Having grown fond of the Puerto Ricans in New York, he wanted to become familiar with the origins of their problems in the land of Puerto Rico itself."[78]

To die in such a way as an Afro-Cuban American among Puerto Ricans, transiting with them the homeland-diaspora divide, suggests a boricua identification of great poignancy. The attribution to Lachatañeré of a fondness toward mainland Puerto Ricans makes sense in relation to *portorro-cubiche* relations. It speaks to a desire for amity. I also see the transitive quality of affection: what a feeling for mainland Puerto Ricans may have *done* to Lachatañeré. In this instance, it may have effected his participation, however inadvertent, in what was the "first mass airway migration in world history," on the eve of the Estado Libre Asociado.[79] A boricua identification through such a death involves notions of passing. As Lachatañeré passes away, he passes as a boricua, identified with the signal boricua historical form of the "airway migration" and its particular violent iteration on April 11, 1952. The date is important for the cultural point: Lachatañeré passed also into a signal boricua cultural form. Specifically, April 11, 1952, was Good Friday. Alberto Sandoval Sánchez, in his meditation on the crash, shows how, among other reasons, its coincidence with the Christian day of deathly commemoration ensured that the crash's "particular symbolism survived total cultural amnesia."[80] Linked to this, Sandoval Sánchez demonstrates, was the crash's representation in "Tragedia de Viernes Santo" (Tragedy of Good Friday), a song written that very year by Rafael Hernández, the great Afro–Puerto Rican musician with a connection to New York City, and later performed by the Trío Vegabajeño. Lachatañeré, in other words, passed into the particular signal cultural form of the "Tragedia" and its lyrics, which turn on figures of Puerto Rican national and U.S./Spanish colonial significance:

> Cae en las aguas bravías y frente al vigía del Morro en San Juan.
> Viendo a su patria querida, llenitos de vida, cayeron al mar.
> ¡Qué triste fue el Viernes Santo!
> ¡Qué horas de angustia y dolor, ay,
> sufrieron nuestros hermanos que volaban a New York!

> [The airplane] falls into the fierce waters
> in front of the sentinel of the Morro in San Juan.
> So full of life, they fell to the sea, seeing their beloved homeland.
> What a sad Good Friday!
> What hours of anguish and pain, oh,
> suffered our brothers who were flying to New York![81]

"Tragedia de Viernes Santo" is an important text of a boricua identification for the way in which it enfolds the death of the Afro-Cuban American Rómulo Lachatañeré. Lachatañeré is among the passengers whose final sight is the "beloved homeland" of Puerto Rico, a territory they see here in the act, interrupted, of becoming its mainland diaspora. The Morro's "sentinel" underscores the coloniality of *seeing* in the song. As "one of the most recurrent symbols of Puerto Rico," the sentinel represents a colonial surveillance, past and present, that comes from (and is directed back toward) the island—an architectural element that, because of its isolation on the fortress wall, also offered the people stationed there the anticolonial possibility of "desertion and escape."[82] Framed by the Morro castle, Lachatañeré's disappearing body, identified with a *patria* boricua, thus articulates other historical disappearances in the Caribbean: the runaway slave's into the jungle, the shipboard slave's into the sea.

The photographs Lachatañeré took of Puerto Rico did not fall into the sea with him but survived, even if, for most of the second half of the twentieth century, they went unrecovered. Their supplementary-career significance is inseparable from such an uneven survival, representing the unnerving afterlife of Lachatañeré's "hobby." How the photographs survived, and by whose hand, is crucial to the account. At the forefront here, returning us to the institutional sites and geopolitics of research, peer review, and publication—to the library and the archive as fraught locations in the life of Lachatañeré—is his daughter, Diana Lachatanere. One day in 1988, Lachatanere was at work when the telephone rang.

Her then-colleague Deborah Willis, the photographer and historian of African American photography, answered. Calling was the Bronx-born Puerto Rican photographer Tony Vélez. He had been cleaning out the studio of Jack Lessinger, the photographer and teacher who had recently died. Organizing Lessinger's possessions for his widow, Vélez had come across photographs and film attributed to Lachatañeré. He wanted to know if the Schomburg Center was interested. Willis immediately turned to Lachatanere and handed her the telephone. It turned out that Lachatañeré, while in Puerto Rico, had mailed his film to Sara, his wife, in New York City, and that she had eventually passed the material along to Lessinger. Along with the images from the Puerto Rico trip, Lessinger had held on to photographs Lachatañeré had taken earlier in Harlem. It is these images that were to compose the Rómulo Lachatañeré Photograph Collection at the Schomburg Center.[83]

Multiple histories converge on the recovery of Lachatañeré's photographs. Diana Lachatanere brought them to the Schomburg Center, an act of archival-cultural production I consider to be related to her work, less than ten years earlier, on what became the Cosme Collection. Lachatanere's role here in a post-1970s re/collection of the Afro-Cuban American literary and cultural past stands as a major contribution to Latino Studies during the period of its academic consolidation, not the least, as I have argued, because her professional location at the premier repository for African American culture reflects on her father's earlier, marginal relation to the New York Public Library itself.[84] Meanwhile, the other figure in the recovery of the photographs, Tony Vélez, knew Jack Lessinger from the Photographer's Forum, an organization that kept alive the spirit of the Photo League. A veteran of the Vietnam War, Vélez confers still another value on the recovery, that of a movement-era mainland boricua working-class cultural politics.[85] Related are the commemorations and exhibits that occurred in the immediate aftermath of Lachatañeré's death. An encounter between midcentury left politics (including African American radicalism) and the multiple times and places of a Latino Harlem popular culture occurred on May 13, 1952, when the New York Council of the Arts, Sciences, and Professions (ASP) paid homage to Lachatañeré with presentations on his life and an exhibition of the photographs at the Park Palace theater on 110th Street and Fifth Avenue: the very venue where, a quarter of a century earlier, Gráfico had held its "festival," which included an O'Farrill bufo, and, in the 1930s, Socarrás would go to play Cuban music after jazz sessions at the Savoy.[86] Around the time of the homage, the Park Palace "was the most popular dance hall in El Barrio."[87] Finally, that June, the Photography Workshop of the ASP organized "Puerto Rico Today," a showing of Lachatañeré's photographs at the Forty-Fourth Street Gallery, the space where, a year earlier, the African American photographer Roy DeCarava had had his first solo exhibition.[88]

The Lachatañeré photographs number over two hundred. The Harlem ones, many marked "East Harlem" on the back, include portraits of men, women, and children; scenes of individuals and crowds on the streets and in Central Park; and interiors, of people in apartment buildings and commercial centers. Its subjects are poor and working-class white Latinas/os, Afro-Latinas/os, and African Americans circa 1950. In the Puerto Rico photographs, Lachatañeré focused on both urban and rural zones: the sugarcane fields and sugar mills near the southern coast, settlements in the Cordillera Central (Central Mountain Range), and the new developments on the margin of cities such as Ponce and San Juan. Like the people in the Harlem photographs, those in the Puerto Rico images, figured both in portraiture and scenes of domestic routine and wage labor, are poor and working class.[89] The collection also includes two images of importance for representations of the Lachatañeré family: Lachatañeré's self-portrait, taken in the family's living room, and a portrait of Sara, taken outdoors (see figs. 7 and 8). Lachatañeré's photographs are intertwined with a history of the photographic documentation of race in the United States, which includes a generation of African American photographers emerging around the time of the 1935 Harlem uprising whose work challenged the association between the documentary image, race, and white supremacy.[90] For Lachatañeré, Latino Harlem as a boricua-dominant space and Puerto Rico itself were the settings for his Afro-Latino engagement with image and documentation. What is more, as final works, the photographs are exemplary of a boricua identification, here island and mainland, configured to visuality and the supplementary career, representing an Afro-Cuban American way of seeing and a developing métier cut short, all in (the) view of Puerto Ricans.

Of the collection's many remarkable photographs, two conclude my discussion of Lachatañeré, both of which appeared in print: one in the 1950s, the other in the 2000s. On May 16, 1952, the *Daily Compass*, a short-lived successor to the left New York City newspapers *PM* and the *New York Star*, carried a banner headline: "Dramatic Photos of Puerto Rico, 2 Pages of Pictures That Survived Artist's Death in April Plane Crash." Inside, in a two-page spread accompanied by an article entitled "These Pictures Lived On . . . After Puerto Rico Crash," five of Lachatañeré's

FIGURE 7. Rómulo Lachatañeré, self-portrait, c. 1950
(Courtesy of Diana Lachatanere; Rómulo Lachata-
ñeré Portrait Collection, Photographs and Prints
Division, Schomburg Center for Research in Black
Culture, New York Public Library, Astor, Lenox and
Tilden Foundations)

photographs were reproduced.[91] The first, which is my focus, shows a
man, a woman, and three girls in a room with unpainted slat-board
walls and a wooden floor. The man is sitting down. His hands are draped
around the shoulders and across the chest of a girl who stands between
his legs. The woman is sitting next to him. On her lap is another girl, eating from a bowl. The third girl sits on the floor, and she eats from a bowl,
too. It is a portrait of the *jíbaro* (white "peasant") family. In the seemingly absent looks of the adults and in the girls' act of eating, Lachatañeré
suggests economic oppression in the midcentury colony: its alienation
and scant resources. The gaze of the girl who stands, however, says something more: holding it as she does on the photographer and viewer, the

FIGURE 8. Portrait of Sara Lachatañeré by Rómulo Lach-
atañeré, c. 1950 (Courtesy of Diana Lachatanere; Rómulo
Lachatañeré Photograph Collection, Photographs and
Prints Division, Schomburg Center for Research in Black
Culture, New York Public Library, Astor, Lenox and
Tilden Foundations)

girl represents a self-awareness, both in Lachatañeré's depiction of "rural
poverty" and among its subjects, located here in a space of domestic
interiority significant for the precarious way its material construction
(as flimsy) seals off the rural outside. This photograph was cropped in
its appearance in the *Compass*, and it takes the print at the Schomburg
Center to reveal what haunts it: a fourth girl, also sitting on the floor, eating, and, on the wall above the adults, a pocket watch nailed to the wall,
next to which are the monthly sheets of a calendar and the commercial

FIGURE 9. Family in rural Puerto Rico, photographed by Rómulo Lachatañeré, c. 1952 (Courtesy of Diana Lachatanere; Rómulo Lachatañeré Photograph Collection, Photographs and Prints Division, Schomburg Center for Research in Black Culture, New York Public Library, Astor, Lenox and Tilden Foundations)

images of two feminine figures, one of which holds a child (see fig. 9). The latter image stands as an ideal of bourgeois maternity that doubles, and distances itself from, the woman holding the girl in the room, a seeming distance already imagined in spatial terms with the slat-board room, seemingly far away from the modernity of the metropolitan center, and in temporal terms with the time-measuring objects on display, suggesting a lag between "development" and "underdevelopment."[92]

If, in the pages of the *Daily Compass*, Lachatañeré's photograph of the Puerto Rican rural family is anticipatory of a Puerto Rican diaspora in its representation of those rural, "unskilled" men and women who would soon air-migrate to New York City in great numbers after the establishment of the Estado Libre Asociado, the photograph appearing on the cover of Juan Flores's edited collection *Puerto Rican Arrival in New York:*

Narratives of the Migration, 1920–1950 (2005) is retrospective[93] (see fig. 10). The presence on the stoop of the men, women, and children, both white and of African descent, suggests on the book cover a public, long-standing boricua presence in the United States, the recollection of which animates Flores's Latino Studies effort. It is fitting that the people in the photograph, with their air of anxious waiting, should come to stand for a literary history of boricua arrival. Their embodiment, arms folded, bodies leaning against the wall, shows a condition of migrant expectation: the act of attending, not without anxiety, a supposed better future in the United States.

"Supposed to Be a Puerto Rican"

At the moment the film *Every Child Is Born a Poet: The Life and Work of Piri Thomas* (2003) turns to its subject's adolescence, a succession of nine still images showing boys in a variety of city scenes appears on screen.[94] The images belong to the Harlem photographs of Lachatañeré. Their use in this part documentary, part narrative of Piri Thomas achieves an effect of archival temporality: the photographs, as surviving, institutional objects, materialize a past-in-the-present that suits the film's view of its author's established, yet timely, literary reputation. The use of the photographs also bridges fortuitously the different forms of emergence of a boricua identification between Lachatañeré and Thomas. The details of Piri Thomas's emergent boricua identification—his assumption in imaginative and professional ways of a mainland Puerto Rican, over a Cuban American, identity, in contrast with Lachatañeré's more contingent relations with the boricua—involve the biographical, the textual, and the literary-historical. Thomas's father, Juan Tomás, was born in Oriente province, Cuba, in 1907, came to the United States through Puerto Rico in the mid-1920s, and took on the identity of a mainland Afro–Puerto Rican.[95] The father's personal history challenges Thomas's *Down These Mean Streets* with its extratextual volatility, troubling the narrative's elision of an Afro-Cuban American identity (the character of the father is "fully" mainland Afro–Puerto Rican) in ways that the text's own articulation of the autobiographical and the fictional solicits. Finally, the mainland-boricua/Latino canonicity of *Down These Mean Streets* links such an Afro-Cuban American subtext to pedagogy, research, and the corporate "ethnic-literature" book market, where the contours of a supplementary career, for the book and for Thomas, become visible: the narrative as unacknowledged work of Afro-Cuban American

FIGURE 10. Street scene, Harlem, photographed by Rómulo Lachatañeré, c. 1950 (Courtesy of Diana Lachatanere; Rómulo Lachatañeré Photograph Collection, Photographs and Prints Division, Schomburg Center for Research in Black Culture, New York Public Library, Astor, Lenox and Tilden Foundations)

literature, the author as unacknowledged writer of Afro-Cuban American descent, here at a time, in the 1960s, when a post-1959, white-exile, Cuban American writing was soon to appear dominant, marking both a period and racial divide between itself and earlier literary-cultural practices among Afro-Cuban Americans in the twentieth century, represented in this book by the work of O'Farrill, Cosme, and Lachatañeré.[96] In this, *Down These Mean Streets* invokes the specific dis/advantages of a boricua identification among Afro-Cuban Americans—the gains of "subordinate citizenship," the losses of "black" racialization.

A boricua identification in *Down These Mean Streets* engages the text's thematic, genre, and period complexities. Lisa Sánchez González and Antonio Viego offer two defining perspectives on its theme: how the text parses an Afro-Latino identity formation ("the predicament of being marked Puerto Rican as well as Black in the United States") and how, at the same time, it brackets its protagonist's constitutive psychic distress ("Piri's profound alienation as a human speaking subject").[97] Close by is the text's aesthetic dilemma—its articulation of the auto-biographical and the fictional, whose formal irresolvability, often going by the name "novel" among critics, the recent corporate book market manages by emphasizing the authentic(ating) life story of the author, as the tags for Vintage's "Thirtieth-Anniversary Edition" demonstrate, categorizing the text as "Memoir" and, fantastically, as "Latin American Studies," an attribution, one presumes, that would signal to potential buyers the book's value as a sociological resource on Latinas/os, even as it rehearses a Cold War Latin American Studies institutional misrecognition of Latino histories, knowledges, and practices as "Latin American."[98] The "Thirtieth-Anniversary Edition" also raises the question of the text's 1967 publication in relation to its "historicalness," which further implicates genre. William Luis, for example, recognizes that *Streets* "narrates the same period of the Great Depression that *Memoirs of Bernardo Vega* and [Jesús Colón's] *A Puerto Rican in New York and Other Sketches* depict."[99] One can add that, with 1928 Harlem, the time and place of Thomas's birth, the narrative suggests an origin in the Apolo era; that its development of character and plot intensifies around 1941, with Cosme settling into a life in New York City and Lachatañeré producing "El sistema"; and that, in 1955, with Thomas's parole, it concludes the same year as Cosme's debut in *El derecho de nacer* at the Teatro Santurce, a debut just a few years removed from the showing of Lachatañeré's photographs at the Park Palace. The late 1960s mainland boricua-liberation significance of *Streets* (its insistence on "Boricua cultural citizenship as an organic—and organically resistant—North American formation")[100] is thus, in part, an effect of the text's investment in a twentieth-century Latino historical process prior to the movement era, the fictionalizing of which tempts readers and critics alike with the ideological accessibility and determinative force of past times: the desire that, in literary representation, "we should re-experience the social and human motives which led men to think, feel, and act just as they did in historical reality."[101]

These complexities hinge especially on Thomas's representation of his father, a man of the generation of O'Farrill, Cosme, and Lachatañeré who, as Thomas writes, came to the United States and "passed for Puerto Rican for the rest of his days."[102] Critics have recognized the thematic importance of the father—the way in which he stands for a supposed self-hating Afro-Latino, loathe to be mistaken for an African American—yet the matter of a boricua identification in the text has gone unexplored, no doubt because "Thomas's Cuban descent fails to come to light" in the text, either in the characterization of the father or in the self-representation of the narrator, Piri "himself."[103] Juan Tomás, the father, sailed from Cuba to Puerto Rico in 1923 when he was sixteen years old. After a year in Puerto Rico, during which he worked as a cutter in the cane fields (and on his Puerto Rican accent), Tomás sailed to the United States from San Juan aboard the *Marine Tiger*, the vessel famous for transporting migrants after the Jones Act. Upon arrival, Tomás made his way to Harlem, where his first job was bussing tables. Thomas has recalled that his father was a good athlete and played semiprofessional baseball in New York City with the Black Puerto Rican Stars.[104] And he jokes, "At the joy [of] my having been the first born—my father forgot he was supposed to be a Puerto Rican—and told the truth," that is, admitted his Cuban origins in writing on his son's birth certificate, but "nobody noticed—so he wasn't ever deported."[105] The birth certificate lists Thomas's name as "John Tomas [*sic*], Jr." Thomas surmises that it was his father who was responsible for the way it was "translated into its Yankee Doodle version"—Juan into John, presumably, and perhaps later "Tomas [*sic*]" into Thomas. Yet there was also the way in which English, as spoken language, was something to avoid, lest it produce an unwanted African Americanization: Thomas remembers how his father would "speak English with a pronounced Spanish accent" so as to signify "something more than an American Black."[106]

Piri Thomas's Harlem Hospital birth certificate, together with a selection of reviews from the 1967 publication of *Streets* in the Thomas Papers at the Schomburg Center, reveals a "confusion" regarding the father's racial identity that, as an effect of Juan Tomás's *afrolatinidad*, involves a boricua identification, too. The birth certificate defamiliarizes Thomas and his family in a way that resounds with Rómulo Lachatañeré's military record: under "color," the document identifies the mother, father, and son as "white," another sign in the official-record imaginary that promises Afro-Latinas/os a social advantage over African Americans; such a "white" designation lodges in the archival past of Thomas's personal history, adding to the meanings of whiteness in *Streets*, here as a memory of the novel protagonist's/autobiographical subject's assigned birth "color."[107] The 1967 review clippings further "confuse" matters by linking the father's African-diasporic identity to the marketing practices of the fiction industry. Thomas is the "son of Puerto Rican parents—one dark, one white"; his "own skin was dark like his father's"; he is the "dark son of a dark Puerto Rican father and a light Puerto Rican mother"; he is the son "of Puerto Rican parents, the father very dark and the mother white"; he is the "black son of a white mother from Puerto Rico and a Negro father"; he was the "blackest kid in a family where [the] father hid behind fictitious Indianship"; "though both his parents were Puerto Rican, his own skin was dark like his father's, while his mother and all his brothers and sisters were white"; and, finally, he is the "son of light-skinned Puerto Rican parents." The inside cover of the first edition of *Streets* echoes the reviews (Thomas is the son "of Puerto Rican parents—one white, one black"), while the cover page of the Thirtieth-Anniversary Edition, seeming to offer a resolution at last, in fact begs the question of the "memoir's" boricua identification, noting that Thomas "was born of Puerto Rican and Cuban parents in New York City's Spanish Harlem in 1928."[108]

The father's initial appearance in *Streets* occurs in the epigraph to the book's opening section, "Harlem": *"Pops, how come me and you is always on the outs? Is it something we don't know nothing about? I wonder if it's something I done, or something I am."*[109] Taken from the narrator's internal monologue in a later chapter, the epigraph identifies perhaps the defining quality of the relationship between father and son in the narrative to come: enmity. The plot will go on to suggest that the cause of the ill will, the reason behind the "something we don't know nothing about," is the father's negative attitude toward his own (and his son's) *afrolatini-dad*. Yet, to the extent that the text posits such an *afrolatinidad* as patri-lineal, the "something" which Piri and his father "don't know nothing about"—and which, in a different way, the "we" of the text's readership ignores, too—is the father's boricua identification, which implicates as well, as I have argued, the narrative itself ("something I done") and its author ("something I am"), determined as they are by that "something" extra, the thing supplementary to both the text and its author's career in mainland Puerto Rican literary history: an Afro-Cuban American-ness. It is the complex of an Afro-Cuban American father, narrative, and author/narrator, displaced on the boricua, that shapes the enmity of *Streets*—the way "me and you is always on the outs."

It is thus significant that in a chapter titled "Puerto Rican Paradise," the mother delivers a critical, nostalgic reflection on her Puerto Rican past that is interrupted by the father himself: "The door opened and put an end to the kitchen yak. It was Poppa coming home from work. He came into the kitchen and brought all the cold with him" (10). The mother's feminized domestic narrative, which spatializes the Harlem home with a boricua-diaspora history and feeling, yields to the arrival of the father, who trails a masculine public that, with his WPA assignment, signifies state "relief," the fact of which frustrates him, influencing his own talk in the chapter, a monologue, overheard and recounted by Piri, that expresses the family's deplorable material conditions: "My father kept talking to the walls. Some of the words came out loud, others stayed inside. I caught the inside ones—the damn WPA, the damn depression, the damn home relief, the damn poorness, the damn cold, the damn crummy apartments, the damn look on his damn kids, living so damn damned and his not being able to do a damn thing about it" (11). An attention to the here-and-now, in contrast to the mother's seemingly past-centered reflection, marks the masculinity of the father's monologue. Yet the monologue signals a narrative difficulty, too: the way it shuts down the "kitchen yak," which is to say, the mother's boricua-diaspora memory, suggests the "impossibility" of the father's own imagining and delivering a narrative of his own homeland past, one that would offer a reminiscence regarding his own past island(s), Cuba/Puerto Rico. "Puerto Rican Paradise" ends, appropriately enough, with a temporary reconciliation between the maternal boricua narrative and its paternal silencing, one occasioned by mass culture and indexed as historical: the family finally comes together to produce their own version of "Major Bowes' Amateur Hour," everyone is happy again, and then the "next day the Japanese bombed Pearl Harbor" (10–13).

The way in which violence circulates in relation to sexuality and the abject bears on a boricua identification in *Streets*.[110] A particular episode, the father's most extensive characterization in the book, is relevant: his "confession" of his *afrolatinidad*, offered on the eve of Piri's voyage to the U.S. South and the Caribbean. Two scenes leading up to it, both turning on violence, sexuality, and the abject, converge to shape the confession. The first is an episode of public sex set in the late 1940s, possibly early 1950s, involving Piri and an Anglo-white woman inside a crowded New York City subway car. *Streets* is careful to suggest the act's inadvertence, consensuality, and, finally, mutual pleasure, yet there is a menacing undercurrent, expressed in Piri's epithets for the woman, her "damn-liberal smile," her "liberal breasts" (136). Piri implicates the woman in the failures of a reformist democracy through the epithets' very figuration of a dismembered, feminine body, here suggestive of histories of rape and, in a related way, of African-diasporic men wrongfully accused of sexual violence toward white women—histories which the scene's other major participant, a "Chinaman" in the subway car standing next to Piri and the woman during the sex act, displaces and multiplies through his "unassimilable" ethnicity and "unthreatening" masculinity (136). Piri's conclusion regarding such a threesome is not unexpected: upon reaching the station, he says, "the opened door [of the subway car] shitted people out, releasing the pressure" (137).

Such abjection then follows Piri home to the suburbs of Long Island and, not insignificantly, the bathroom of his house, where, in the second scene leading up to the father's confession, Piri has just finished taking a shower, during which he fantasized about the white woman's description of the subway encounter with the "black boy," the "colored boy," to her friends (141). Piri allows his brother to come into the bathroom to urinate, teasing him over whether he would enjoy the taste of his own urine. Piri sees his brother's penis and thinks, *"Even his peter's white. . . . Only ones got black peters is Poppa and me"* (142). The conversation soon turns to the slave trade and the African diaspora in Puerto Rico, with Piri making a signal observation to his brother: that Piri himself and their father, and thus the family, are of African descent. The brother rejects the observation, appealing instead to ideologies of the nation and indigeneity: "We're Puerto Ricans, and that makes us different from black people" (144); "Poppa's the same as you . . . , Indian" (145). When the brother tells Piri, "I've busted my ass . . . trying to explain to people how come you so dark and how come your hair is so curly," Piri feels a "burning [come] up out of [him]": he hits his brother; the brother hits back (146). The two make visible the implied violence and sexuality of the subway scene, including the ejection (in literal and figurative terms) of bodily matter: the "bathroom door flew open and me, naked and wet with angry sweat, and José, his mouth bleedin', crashed out of the bathroom and rolled into the living room" (146).

These overlapping expressions of violence, sexuality, and the abject converge in the father's confession the following morning, demonstrating the way in which his boricua identification—that to which the confession gives form—is of a disturbing, unavowed significance in the text. Piri leads up to it, presenting his father with the charge that he privileges his other children over him. The father responds:

"I—I got pride in you, *hijo*," he said slowly. "Maybe I—I mean, maybe it looked like I did, or maybe deep down I have. I don't know. Maybe." Poppa's eyes were on his hands, and one fingernail was trying to peel the broken fingernail from another finger. "I ain't got one colored friend," he added, "at least no one American Negro friend. Only dark ones I got are Puerto Ricans or Cubans. I'm not a stupid man. I saw the look of white people on me when I was a young man, when I walked into a place where a dark skin wasn't supposed to be. I noticed how a cold rejection turned into an indifferent acceptance when they heard my exaggerated accent. I can remember the time when I made my accent heavier, to make me more of a Puerto Rican than the most Puerto Rican there ever was. I wanted a value on me, son. But I never changed my name. It was always John Thomas. Sometimes I was asked how come if I was Puerto Rican, I had John Thomas for a name."

"What'd you say, Poppa?"

Poppa's one fingernail finally peeled the broken fingernail off the other finger. In a voice like crying, he said, "I'd say, 'My father was so proud to be an American, that he named all his children fine American names.' God, I felt like a *puta* every time. A damn nothing." Poppa started looking for another broken fingernail.

I believed everything Poppa said 'cause I'd never heard his voice cry before. I didn't know what to say. I felt ashamed, but I didn't know who for. I had a going-away pain of wanting to be some place else.

"—even said I had Indian blood in me," Poppa mumbled.

That's what José had said. I backed away from Poppa's bed. "Bye, Poppa," I said. It didn't sound gentle enough. "Bye, Poppa," I said again, more gently.

Poppa didn't answer. He was way back when he was a young man and running into his own kinds of walls. I walked back into the kitchen. "I'm going," I said. I hugged Momma and Sis. I put up my hand for a good-bye to my brothers and thought I saw James do the same. José winked and maybe even smiled. I made it out the door." (153–54)

Even in confessing it, the father is conflicted, even evasive, regarding his own *afrolatinidad*, mentioning "dark" Cubans and Puerto Ricans; "colored" African Americans; and, himself in a synecdoche, "a dark skin" in public. The reference to Cubans is particularly striking. It leads to the further admission of a linguistic self-fashioning—the racialization of Afro-Latino voices—that renders the father "more of a Puerto Rican than the most Puerto Rican there ever was." His boricua identification is an open secret here: being mainland Puerto Rican is a matter of performance in the white-supremacist United States, and it is an Afro-Cuban American who does it "more" than anyone else. Piri's response is telling. He affirms a belief in the father's confession, even as, in a diffusion of shame, words fail him and a hurt from "some place else" grows—all of which indicate, I suggest, the text's boricua identification: its ineffability, its emotional and geographic difficulty. Relatedly, the confession relocates the abject, for, in the odd digression on his name (in the extraliterary birth certificate, the father's name is Juan Tomás), the father admits that the Anglophony of "John Thomas" would coerce expressions of "American" pride, the feigning of which provokes in the father a misogynist invocation of sex work—he likens himself to a "*puta*" (whore)—that surfaces anew the sexuality of the subway and bathroom scenes. Indeed, in figuring the father, at the end, as someone lost in thoughts "way back when he was a young man," the confession scene relocates, too, the impossibility of a paternal reminiscence in the text. Once again, we are tempted with a Cuban/Puerto Rican past in the father that *Streets* can only fail to represent.

Following upon the confession, Piri travels to the U.S. South and the "West Indies," an itinerary from which he returns bearing a *bufo* performance legacy that, in its violent, paternal effects, indicates again the text's (and his father's) boricua identification. In a parodic undoing of the father's own linguistic performance of a Puerto Rican identity, Piri returns north "speaking" in a representation of a regional African American vernacular that, presumably picked up in the U.S. South, begs the question of a possible Caribbean transregional vernacular—an Afro-Cuban, for example, or Afro–Puerto Rican way of speaking—similarly picked up, if unvoiced, by Piri. "Stop that goddamn way of talking," the father demands of him. "'Why sho', Pops,' I said, 'if y'all doan' like the way Ah's speakin', I reckon Ah could cut it out.'" The response provokes the father, who "grabbed [Piri] with both arms and lifted [him] off [his] feet." "'Is [a cotton field] where you came from, Pops?' I teased him. 'Ain't that what bugs you? Ain't that what bugs the hell out of you, Mistuh Blanco in natural black-face. Let me go, Pops, or I'll put my knee in your phony white balls'" (198–99).

To be sure, "natural black-face" describes Piri's portrayal of an "exaggerated" African American "accent," an Afro-Latino performance of the African American that traces to O'Farrill's *negro*-on-*negro bufo*: the Afro-Latino *negro* on the African American Negro. Piri's performance, in this last of the extended scenes in *Streets* involving the father, again links enmity, now unresolved by any familial Amateur Hour, with the problem of "where [the father] came from": if not a cotton field in the U.S. South, a sugarcane field in Cuba, Puerto Rico. Lacing the charge of a "Mistuh Blanco" and of "phony white balls," in other words, is the constitutive, alarming "phoniness" of a boricua identification, disciplined through enmity and violence in the text. To see a blackface Piri in this passage, recalling, as he does, O'Farrill's Apolo and Campoamor *bufos*, is to shade with new meaning the question posed to Piri by his mother earlier in the text: "Why does it hurt you so to be *un Negrito*?" (148).

Coda: Casal

In 1975, Piri Thomas traveled to Cuba. During the first half of the 1970s, the island had witnessed economic setbacks and political repression, exemplified in the failure of the planned ten-million-ton sugar harvest and the arrest of the poet Heberto Padilla. Thomas's view of Cuba reflected this: "What I felt was that the revolution had been won, but what good is that if now the minds of the people are in chains? You belong to the state, which is a mistake."[111] Just two years earlier, another Afro-Cuban American literary and intellectual figure had traveled to the island. For Lourdes Casal, that voyage was a return, her first since leaving Cuba twelve years earlier. If, through the 1960s and early 1970s, Casal's writings and actions had challenged the Cuban revolution along the lines of Thomas's comment, her 1973 return proved a turning point: from that moment on, until her death in 1981—like Lachatañeré, she died during her forty-third year—Casal set down a path of a Cuban, rather than a boricua, identification, committing herself to the Cuban revolution from geographic and print locations in the United States and, ultimately, Cuba itself.[112] I conclude this chapter with a brief reflection on how Casal's "Cuban identification," in its contrast with the boricua of Lachatañeré and Thomas, reveals the persistence in Afro-Cuban American literary history of supplementary-career logics and (as we saw with Lachatañeré and Thomas) an uncanny whiteness.

Casal arrived in New York City in 1961, and, over the course of the next twenty years, in the words of her former colleague María Cristina Herrera, "the totality of this woman [resisted] categorization."[113] Indeed, Casal's "excessive" work and career experiences are constitutive of her recognized place as "the first Cuban writer of the immigration to consider the conflict of an identity split between the culture of origin and that of the new country (in this case, the United States)."[114] Her editing and writing contributed significantly to the formation of post-1959 Cuban American print cultures with *Nueva Generación* and, later, *Areíto*, which she founded in 1974. Comparable to this was her institution building, particularly with the Grupo Areíto, whose intellectual production and activism, keeping close to the Cuban-state line, countered the Miami-exile right. Casal was a key figure in contacts with the Cuban government, which led to return voyages during the late 1970s among young, left-identified Cuban exiles through the Antonio Maceo Brigade. She defended her dissertation in psychology at the New School for Social Research in 1975, which suggests a graduate-student context for much of this work on Cuba and its diaspora; meanwhile, her dissertation itself, "Images of Cuban Society among Pre- and Post-Revolutionary Novelists," stresses disciplinary parameters, suggesting a cultural studies approach in its primary combination of sociology and literary criticism, with the psychological in view, too. It was as a graduate student that Casal taught at Brooklyn College, and she went on to teach as an A.B.D. in the Psychology Department at Rutgers University–Newark. Among communities in Latino Studies, she is best known for her poem "Para Ana Veltford" (For Ana Veltford), first published in *Areíto* in 1976. This text of a Cuban-diasporic identity stands next in importance to her sociological work on Cuban Americans and, in particular, Afro-Cuban Americans: "Cubans in the U.S.," *The Cuban Minority in the U.S.*, and "Black Cubans in the United States," all of which admirably attend to race in the description of post-1959 Cuban-diaspora societies across the U.S. North and South.[115] Casal even gave a talk on Antonio Maceo at the Club Cubano Inter-Americano—a seemingly isolated event that nevertheless linked her to the pre-1959 Afro-Cuban American cultures of Cosme and Lachatañeré.[116] In all this, finally, there was Casal's body and identity: her lesbian sexuality, her illness and disability, and her racial identity, as a subject of the "mulatto middle class [*clase media mulata*]," as a "*negra*," as a descendant of Chinese immigrants.[117]

In Casal's 1978 English-language essay "Memories of a Black Cuban Childhood," she engages her own Afro-Cuban/Afro-Cuban American identity in a direct manner, doing so in a publication, the magazine *Nuestro*, whose mainstream circulation renders it anomalous in Casal's oeuvre.[118] In "Memories," Casal counters the expectations raised by her title, for more than just casting the question of her African-diasporic identity into the past, into the figure of the child, she moves across the multiple periods of her experiences in race. Casal narrates the paradigmatic experience of an Afro-Cuban arrival in the United States: "In the U.S. during the 60s, I was forced to look at my Blackness with different eyes. I had become accustomed to considering myself *una mulata* in a mulatto country, in a quintessentially mulatto culture. The U.S. was a shock. Here I had to learn to assert my Blackness somehow—even or particularly as a Hispanic Black—in a country where Black and white were defined in opposition to one another and where any attempt to avoid the dichotomy seemed to be some kind of betrayal." She remembers her childhood initiation into *santería*. And, in the end, she recounts a visit to Africa she had taken years earlier, in 1962. Casal describes an event that occurred at a market in Lagos, Nigeria—"a jolting experience," in her words. A group of children "started shouting something," "laughing and pointing" at Casal and her guide: "screaming a word which I could not distinguish with clarity and which I did not understand." The guide explains it to Casal: "You know . . . the children back there, at the school . . . they were calling you white." Like Lachatañeré and Thomas, Casal is attributed a whiteness, only with her, it is evident less as an archival trace of U.S. apprehensions of Afro-Latinas/os than it is as a personal experience of the differences in African diaspora. "Something had snapped open inside," Casal wrote. "It took me years to process all the experiences of that African pilgrimage, including the children's innocent joke." The conclusion to which Casal arrived announces a Cuban identification: "I confirmed that home, for better or worse, was not in Nigeria, or anywhere else, but in Cuba."[119]

4 / Around 1979: Mariel, McDuffie, and the Afterlives of Antonio

I turn now to the cultures of two 1979 Miami murders, seeing in them still other signs of the circulation of race in Cuban America. In March of that year, a white Cuban American was found dead on SW Eighth Street, killed as a consequence of his work in the illegal-drug economy. No one was ever charged in the murder. This was Antonio López, my father. In December, an African American was murdered on North Miami Avenue, with a white Cuban American police officer, among others, implicated. No one was ever convicted in the murder. This was Arthur McDuffie. The figure of a murdered Cuban American drug dealer appeared in the lyrics of the many African American rappers who intertextualized the 1980 Mariel boatlift-migrant protagonist of the 1983 film *Scarface*. The violence represented in the *Scarface* metatext, which includes the 1930 pulp novel, the original 1932 film and its remake, and the rap revisions, was both state and market sponsored. The killing of Arthur McDuffie and the 1980 African American uprising in Miami after the acquittal of everyone charged in the murder and its cover-up are still other manifestations of such violence. The story of Antonio López, needless to say, is personal to me. So, too, in a different way, is that of Arthur McDuffie, through a remarkable, print-culture coincidence, as I show. The two encourage me to consider the cultural and historical alignment of those two signal Miami Cuban American and African American events of 1980: boatlift and uprising.

In April 1980, a driver rammed his bus through the gates of the Peruvian embassy in Havana. Over 10,000 people eventually sought asylum on its grounds. By the end of the month, the Cuban government had declared the town of Mariel, just west of Havana, an open port. Starting in April of that year, over 120,000 people crossed the Florida Straits to the United States, making the Mariel boatlift the third wave of postrevolutionary Cuban migration, following the initial departures after 1959 and the U.S.-sponsored Freedom Flights between 1965 and 1973. *Marielito*, whose diminutive ending, like the *-ito* in *negrito*, combines affection and disdain, came to signify the 1980 migrants. So did another word, heard at the port of Mariel and on the streets of Hialeah and Miami, a word now stripped of any pretense toward the affectionate: *escoria*—dregs, dross, scum.[1]

Escoria was a manifestation in popular speech of the idea of a lumpenproletariat, criminal, disabled Mariel migrant, after accounts of how the Cuban government had used the episode to depopulate its prisons and mental hospitals. In *Areíto*, for example, Lourdes Casal wrote that the migrants were "overrepresented" by "marginal elements, delinquents, [and] lumpen" who, lacking the education necessary for incorporation into the Cuban revolution, lived off "the black market and theft"; they were "undesirables" with "prison records."[2] *El Sol de Hialeah*, a local newspaper with a perspective in obvious contrast to *Areíto*'s, echoed Casal, only it recognized in the "undesirables" a Castro plot: the "Tyrant infiltrated a great number of delinquents, the depraved, and even the insane," thus "infesting the Cuban colony with those dangerous species and provoking the protest and rejection of the native citizenry."[3] Meanwhile, the literary journal *Mariel*, among whose directors was the boatlift migrant Reinaldo Arenas, editorialized that the aim of media representations of the "undesirables" was to "deform the social as well as the political content of the exodus" through a focus, at the expense of regular refugees, on "those who had been driven to crime and insanity by the very government that was expelling them irresponsibly."[4] Loathed as a timeless infestation, suffered as a historical deformation, the *escoria* appeared across all manner of Cuban American discourses on Mariel.

Such undesirability, in more or less tacit ways, also involved the sexuality of the Mariel migrants. Important here were the experiences of gay men in managing the institutions of Cuban departure and Cuban American arrival.[5] The place of sexuality in imaginings of a Mariel undesirability is contiguous with that of race: in particular, the Afro-Cuban identity of the migrants, who arrived in a predominantly white Cuban America. The front page of *El Expreso de Miami*, another local newspaper, exhibited the peculiarity of Cuban American admissions regarding the racial identity of the migrants, who, as it stated, hailed from "all classes": "Elderly women, children, young women, whites and blacks," all fleeing "the terrible communism."[6] The admission of whites among the arrivals is too obvious, given the historical white exile: of course, white Cubans have once again come to the United States. I view the reference to whites, instead, as an assurance—an urgent one, to judge from the uncommon disclosure of whiteness in the Cuban American public— against that other racial category of Mariel migrant to which it is linked, the blacks. *Blancos*/whites makes it acceptable to say *negros*/blacks, to remark on those whose arrival confirms that, this time around, indeed "all classes," even Afro-Cubans, are coming. The "blackening" of Cuban America through Mariel is well recognized. Many Cuban Americans "were amazed at how dark [*lo oscuro*] these new Cubans were."[7] If, at the beginning of the 1970s, less than 3 percent of Cuban Americans were of African descent, the estimates of a 20 to 50 percent Afro-Cuban Mariel population signaled a major change indeed.[8] The role of the U.S. government in the ongoing racialization of the Mariel migrants was crucial. By 1980, the Cold War Cuban Refugee Program had ended; therefore, as Ramón Grosfoguel and Chloe Georas demonstrate, the "migrants could not access state assistance and in turn were not cushioned against racial discrimination." They "were 'Puerto Ricanized' in New York City and 'African Americanized' in Miami," which is to say, they experienced "a social process similar to the U.S. empire's colonial/racial subjects."[9]

The undesirability as criminality of the Mariel migrant was inseparable—in part, as its projection—from the violence of Miami during the period. In 1979, over 350 homicides were reported in Dade County, the greatest number ever at the time.[10] A context was the drug economy. The film *Cocaine Cowboys*, a documentary compromised by the white Anglocentricity of its expert and witness testimonies regarding the hemispheric powder-cocaine trade during the 1970s and 1980s, may stand as a text of such overlapping criminalities, particularly in an instance of racist representation, when a "fearless Marielito," an Afro-Cuban implicated in the drug business, is described by an interviewee as a "nigger," a disturbing sign of race and *latinidad* in a film that traffics in many.[11] Overlapping with such Anglo-white representations of Mariel criminality and race are Cuban American ones. In the example of white Cuban American *santeros*, such representations retreated from (or perhaps had never even arrived at) the Lachatañeré-Ortiz debate on *brujería*, attributing, as they did, the apparent rise of witchcraft in Miami not only to the "thriving drug trade" but to "the advent of the 'antisocial scum from the black barrios of Havana' in the course of the so-called Mariel exodus of 1980."[12] Furthermore, Miami/Mariel 1979/1980 criminalities included the state murder of Arthur McDuffie, a historical event whose Cuban American dimension, in the person of Alex Marrero, the Cuban American policeman charged with second-degree murder, is too often unrecognized. The white Cuban American rapper Pitbull demonstrates the perils of ignoring that dimension in the outro to his album *El Mariel*, in which he cites "Arthur McDuffie . . . being beat to death by four white cops."[13] The crux, ignored by Pitbull, is that it was a white Latino, Marerro, along with three Anglo whites, who was charged in the murder of McDuffie; that Marrero's Cuban American whiteness was aligned with the Anglo whiteness of his fellow officers in a physical expression of state-sponsored, white-supremacist violence; and that, over and over in the historical record, this Anglo-Latino alignment is elided, reappearing simply as "white." It is also, of course, a matter of Cuban American implication: that a Cuban American man was responsible for the death of McDuffie and that, in a more general way, pre-1980 Cuban Americans benefited from the unjust conditions of African Americans in Miami, given that, during the Cold War, Cuban Americans had received "the lion's share of public dollars," while, after McDuffie's murder, as business owners in the affected area, Cuban Americans, along with Anglo whites, were among those to receive "most of the federal money to deal with the riot."[14] Merely to cite "four white cops" in the greater narrative of Miami around 1979 is to waste the specific, troubling, Cuban American value of that time and place.

In this chapter, I begin with African American literary and popular representations of Arthur McDuffie's murder to reflect on the way in which Cuban American whiteness and shame converge in the production of his corpse. The dead, African American man's body of McDuffie, mourned in African American writing and song, disgraces Cuban American history and culture, where its memory is "deformed," as Pitbull's "Outro" demonstrates. The corpse, if not of McDuffie, then not entirely disassociated from him, recurs in Cuban American invocations of race around 1979. In particular, I argue that public Cuban American responses to the gangster corpses of the *Scarface* metatext—the corpses of Tony Guarino in the 1930 novel, Antonio Camonte in the 1932 film, and Antonio Montana in the 1983 film—articulate an anxiety regarding the "blackening" of Cuban America after Mariel, with its concomitant compromising of a pre-1980 Cuban American whiteness seemingly, shamefully consolidated in the murder of McDuffie. Rap music references to

Scarface after 1983 extend the racializing, Cuban American logic of the Antonio corpses, locating them in narratives of African American masculinity, criminality, and upward mobility that appear to reflect, but in fact challenge, capitalist drug-war pathologies. Central, in this regard, is *Scarface* minstrelsy: the way in which the Austro-Hungarian-born Jewish actor Meshilem Meier Weisenfreund, also known as Paul Muni, wore "Italianface" in the 1932 film, and the Italian American actor Al Pacino wore "Cubanface" in the 1983 film, instances both of a performance of ethnic whiteness (and, indeed, of trajectories "out of" ethnicity, toward whiteness, in the United States) that are not unrelated to the affirmation of Cuban American whiteness in the civic effort to manage (and, finally, to shut down) the Miami production of *Scarface* in 1982, the relative success of which suggested a crisis in ethnic whiteness (here as Cuban American) averted, only to be restaged later in the rap-lyric donning (and critique) of the prerogative of ethnic whiteness by African Americans, for whom Pacino's Cubanface afforded an opportunity of aesthetic and economic transformation. In short, I understand the African American use of *Scarface* (in the aftermath of its white Cuban American rejection in Miami) as a collaboration with the film's Anglo-U.S. "spicsploitation" meanings, here associated with the screenwriting of Oliver Stone and the directing of Brian De Palma, and its Latino meanings, which, to keep a focus on its production, point to the film's renowned Mexican American cinematographer, John Alonzo, and its two iconic Latino actors, the Cuban American Rocky Echeverría/Steven Bauer and the Puerto Rican Miriam Colón. I conclude the chapter with a discussion of the short fiction of Esteban Luis Cárdenas, an Afro-Cuban who arrived in the United States in January 1980. Cárdenas's text resituates Mariel undesirability, while in his body, as a disabled survivor of two instances of motorist, carcentric violence, he revises the primacy of the corpse. But, before that, I address still another corpse, that of Antonio López, El Viejo, by looking at the presence of his dead body in a 1979 edition of the *Miami Herald* and in the autopsy report of the Dade County Medical Examiner's Office. I texture here as personal the story of Cuban American race and criminality around 1979, and, in doing so, I draw on an autobiographical approach which colleagues in Latino Studies have used in recent years in ways that invoke the historical and theoretical.[15] I mourn El Viejo. Jacques Derrida guides me in appreciating mourning's attraction to the remains, so long as they remain—as long they stay *there*, on the other side, leaving us, regarding the question of who really rests there, with some confusion, this being preferable over the certainty, often intolerable, of knowing.[16] I turn now to tell of the remains of El Viejo.

El Viejo y La Vieja, McDuffie and Migue

Pilar Díaz, La Vieja, my mother, used to take me to the pond at Comstock Park on NW Twenty-Eighth Street and Seventeenth Avenue in the Allapattah neighborhood of Miami to catch tadpoles with a strainer. This was in the mid-1970s, just before I started kindergarten at the nearby Comstock Elementary School, when Allapattah was mostly Cuban and African American—and, by then, in contrast with Little Havana to the south, known as a preferred place to live by migrant Afro-Cubans. La Vieja was in her midthirties. She had grown up in Havana, in a large family that moved between poverty and the working class. She gained a second-grade education during the republic, and, eventually, with the revolution, she expressed her dissatisfaction by coming to the United States in 1967 aboard one of the Freedom Flights. She found herself living in an apartment near Journal Square in Jersey City, where she worked in factories and people's houses. Years later, during her citizenship ceremony in Miami Beach, I saw her Cuban passport for the first and last time. Under "Skin Color," it said, "*trigueña*," a historical category of Cuban "color" with the literal meaning "wheat colored." During our time in Allapattah, El Viejo, her boyfriend, was incarcerated at the U.S. Penitentiary, Terre Haute.

Terre Haute was not El Viejo's first time in prison. In Cuba, he was jailed for street-level political violence during the first Batista presidency (1940–1944), though on which side he was a participant is unclear. El Viejo was born in 1921 in the town of Aguada de Pasajeros, in the former province of Santa Clara. His father, Antonio López Queipo, originally from Asturias, was a stowaway on one of the Cuban voyages of the *Valbanera*, the Spanish steamship lost off Key West during the 1919 hurricane. El Viejo's mother, Maria Olarriaga Leal, was Cuban; her mother, my great-grandmother, Felipa, was a *mambisa*—a Cuban woman independence fighter against Spanish colonialism. Olarriaga Leal died young, leading López Queipo to move with his son to Marianao, just west of Havana. López Queipo was a merchant: he sold coal from the *carbonería* on Fourth Street and First Avenue in Marianao with two Afro-Cuban employees, and he ran a country store in Bahía Honda, Pinar del Río. El Viejo grew up in Marianao. He was a student at the technical school for boys in nearby Rancho Boyeros, and he did deliveries for the Farmacia Taquechel in La Habana Vieja. He was not in jail for long in the 1940s. With the help of the warden, he escaped to Mexico. He eventually returned to Cuba, and, in 1946, he migrated to Miami, where his cousin María had been living. El Viejo was a *primitivo*, a word that post-1959 Cuban migrants in Miami use to identify those whose arrival had predated the revolution. In 1967, El Viejo was arrested for drug trafficking in Chicago; it was around this time that he met La Vieja. At one point, he was held at the U.S. Penitentiary in Atlanta, where he earned a High School Equivalency Diploma. In 1987, the Atlanta Penitentiary witnessed Mariel-era prisoners and other Cuban-born inmates rising up after word of a U.S. plan to repatriate them circulated.

The state released El Viejo from Terre Haute on October 9, 1974. He was fifty-three years old. By then, La Vieja and I were in Allapattah. The occasion of my first encounter with El Viejo was a party. I knew that this man I had never seen before was supposed to be my father. El Viejo moved in with us, and it went poorly. He began having an affair with the building manager, a woman called La Presidenta. La Vieja found out, and one night, she locked him out. He tried to break in through the glass-louvered kitchen door, but she had barricaded it with the refrigerator. He punched the glass and tried to push the refrigerator out of the way, but his hand, now bloodied, could not manage it. In time, he came back into our lives, and we left Allapattah, the three of us moving into someone's furnished house in a middle-class Miami neighborhood. It was clear the arrangement was temporary. Where had the owners gone? The real family had a child, and, for a few weeks, I lived in his room. We moved again, this time to an apartment on SW Twelfth Street and Second Avenue, just south of the Miami River, east of I-95. This is where, in 1978, my brother, Migue, was born. I rode in the back of El Viejo's blue and white Cadillac Coupe de Ville while he and his friend, a man named Gorrita, got stoned in the front. One day, I learned El Viejo was going on a trip to New York. I asked him if I could come, and he agreed. He got dressed and packed, and so did I. When he opened the door to leave, I hesitated. He looked at me and turned away. "Lo sabía. No ibas a venir": "I knew it. You weren't coming." It was the last time I saw El Viejo.

Soon thereafter, La Vieja told me I would stay with our neighbors across the hallway for a few days. I was seven years old. When she came back to pick me up, La Vieja looked tired and worried. She had left Migue somewhere. As I played in the street, she stood by, looking in my direction. She finally walked up. My friends were all around. "Tu papá se murió. Le chocaron el carro": "Your father died. It was a car crash." I was ashamed, that others were learning of this at the same time I did, and I was angry, that La Vieja, with such a public announcement, had spoiled a secret that, by all rights, was mine to share with them. I stood still, worried that everyone was looking at me. I wailed. And then I stopped. "Mentira," I told La Vieja. "Ya yo lo sabía": "Just kidding. I already knew about it." I laughed and ran down the street.

Two years later, I found El Viejo's death certificate in La Vieja's dresser drawer. It said the cause of death was a gunshot wound to the head. I wondered how to explain it to Migue, a three-year-old at the time. I wanted him to know the truth, to know it from me—but when? Two decades later, researching for the first time the topic that became this chapter, I found the newspaper reports of the murder. "Woman Leads Police to Body of Boyfriend," wrote the *Miami Herald* on March 10, 1979, page 3B, identifying El Viejo as "a Latin in his late 40s." La Vieja had been driving around the city in search of him. She finally located his Cadillac in a parking lot: "West Miami Police Officer Dori Palant was about to eat lunch at Lum's Restaurant, 6355 S.W. 8th Street, when a woman told her that there might be a body in a car outside. Police refused to identify the woman. The man she lived with for eight years, she said, had been missing since Saturday." The next day, "Body Found in Trunk Is Identified" appeared in the *Herald*, page 6B. It identified El Viejo as "Antonio Perez [*sic*], 57," La Vieja as "his common-law wife, the mother of his two small children"; she had "opened the driver's door, smelled a foul odor and notified a West Miami policewoman." The day after that, the last report appeared, now in the *Miami News*, page 5A. It identified El Viejo as "Antonio Lopez [*sic*] Olarriaga of 191 S.W. 12th St.," La Vieja as "a woman friend of Olarriaga." Thirty years later, while writing this book, I requested the medical examiner's report from Miami-Dade County. It identified El Viejo as a "57 year-old Caucasian male." He was five feet, six inches tall, 151 pounds. There were two gunshot wounds to the head. One was a contact wound. The gun had been pressed an inch and a half behind the left ear. The bullet had stopped just below the right eye. The other bullet entered an inch and a half above the left ear and had lodged in the back of the head. There was much blood, and the brain, covered with bone fragments, had liquefied. They weighed the organs: the heart 320 grams, the lungs 810, the brain 1,180. They summarized the findings: two gunshot wounds to the head, a markedly decomposed body. The medical examiner sent El Viejo's corpse to the Caballero Funeral Home on Calle Ocho, the one where, less than three years earlier, the remains of Eusebia Cosme had lain. Over the years, people have told me that El Viejo was murdered by his employers in the Cuban-Colombian drug industry for misplacing his product: marijuana, cocaine, I have never been sure. His partner betrayed him, it seems, and El Viejo suffered the consequences. I came home from college for Christmas one year. An older cousin—he had been in the Florida State Prison for drug trafficking himself—visited us for *nochebuena*. He took me aside and said the men responsible for El Viejo's murder were still alive—old they were, but alive. If I wanted to know more, we could meet somewhere and talk. I thanked him. When the time comes, I said, we would.

The day after La Vieja broke the news to me, we left the apartment at 191 SW Twelfth Street without packing: she, Migue, and I, at last the family we were to become, alone. We went to an aunt's apartment. At night, my cousins arrived with brand-new shotguns and a hacksaw. They sawed off half the barrel of the first one, then the second, then the rest. Soon everyone held a sawed-off shotgun. They turned off the lights and looked out the window.

The next morning, I was riding in the back of a car with Migue and La Vieja. Leo, a cousin of mine, was driving, and next to him was his girlfriend, Tina. With us in the back were their children, Umbi and Tita. Leo was a *mulato*, the out-of-wedlock son of one of La Vieja's brothers. La Vieja had helped raise Leo in Havana, and when Leo came to the United States as a teenager, she continued supporting him, off and on. Tina was a redheaded Anglo-white woman whom Leo had met in Tennessee during his time as a long-haul trucker. We were going to Chicago, where Leo's father, my uncle Mingo, lived with his wife, Amelia, and their five children: Martica, Moraima, Nelson, Aldo, and Ariel.

Chicago was wondrous. The fourteen of us lived in the apartment, everyone sharing beds, someone always coming and going. My cousin Nelson took to me right away—and I to him. He was appearing in his high school's production of *Bye Bye Birdie*. He sang and rehearsed his lines in our room. Nelson showed me downtown. He stood me on the sidewalk and pointed out how the Sears Tower disappeared into the clouds. We went to Lincoln Park and the Museum of Science and Industry. My uncle Mingo worked in a jewelry store. His workbench, off in a corner of the kitchen, was covered with soldering torches, magnifying glasses, and the metal and stone materials that he worked: the latter coming in all colors and secured in tiny envelopes that he spilled across the table for me to see. My cousin Aldo, just a few years older than I, let me ride on the handlebar of his bicycle after school. He introduced me to the alleys, fire escapes, and rooftops of the city, and, in these places, I met his friends, girlfriends, enemies—and, for the first time, in the Mexican American kids, Latinas/os other than who we were. And then, one day, it ended. I was standing on the sidewalk in front of the building with my aunt Amelia, waiting for La Vieja to come. I expected us to go to the store. Instead, La Vieja drove up in a car with two people I had last seen in Miami: my aunt Veneranda and my cousin Efrén. La Vieja stepped out and said we were leaving Chicago that instant. I cried. I told her I did not want to go back to Miami. "No nos vamos para Miami," La Vieja said. "Nos vamos para Hialeah": "We're not going to Miami. We're going to Hialeah." With that, she put me in the car. I looked out the window for Amelia, hoping she would do something. She was gone. The drive from Chicago to Hialeah has always been a blank.

Our first home was a motel on Okeechobee Road, across from the Miami Canal. I became friends with a boricua family there—still others among the Latinas/os I had never met before. Veneranda took care of us while La Vieja looked for a place to live. One day, she thought she found one. We drove down Okeechobee into Miami, to Liberty City, and met a social worker at the entrance to a block of attached, single-family housing units: a project in that historic, African American neighborhood. I realized we were the only Cubans there—at least the only people who were not black. Everyone looked at us as the social worker showed us the available unit. I liked it because it had a little yard and a bedroom for Migue and me. But then I heard La Vieja in the kitchen complaining to the social worker. There was fire damage, it turned out, and the county had not repaired it—the discolored walls, the odor. La Vieja rejected the unit and took us back to the motel. She was hoping for something to happen, and it did: our Section Eight application was approved, which meant the state would help us pay the rent—this in addition to the welfare, food stamps, and Medicaid we received. We finally left Okeechobee Road when La Vieja rented an apartment for us in a building at 151 East Fifth Street in Hialeah. It was the summer of 1979. The apartment was where we lived when Arthur McDuffie was murdered.

On December 24, 1979, the reporter Edna Buchanan published "Cops' Role in Death Probed" on the front page of the *Herald* local section, page 1B. This was the first article to notice a problem with the police account of McDuffie's death: the possible murder and cover-up. I knew nothing of the article at the time. In the mid-1990s, sitting at a microfilm machine in the library at Florida International University, I discovered the article while researching El Viejo and McDuffie. I scrolled through the December dates of the *Herald*. The film moved from the bottom of the screen to the top. I saw "Cops' Role in Death" scroll by, then a photograph of McDuffie: his smiling face, a happy-looking man. I prepared to read the Buchanan report, when an image just beneath the article caught my eye. I scrolled up a little bit more, and I froze. It was a photograph of Migue, my brother. I could not believe what I was seeing. I zoomed in on the image and focused it, and there was no mistaking it. It was my little brother's face, looking as he did over fifteen years before. He was held in the arms of his *madrina*. I read the caption: "Olga Hernandez [*sic*] is thrilled with godson Miguel Lopez' [*sic*] gift, but Miguel, 2, is waiting until the wrapping comes off before he ventures a smile. Some 3,000 were served candy, fruit and soft drinks, treated to disco music and given Christmas presents at the U.S. Marine Corps Reserve's annual Toys for Tots party at Bayfront Auditorium." I have always taken the remarkable coincidence of the photographs of Miguel López and Arthur McDuffie in the *Miami Herald* as a sign of narrative encouragement: that the story of the injustice done to McDuffie might again be told, in a new way, through the story of my family, with the hope of creating a further interest in McDuffie and the struggle toward justice for African Americans. It is a coincidence in irony, too. Not only was McDuffie himself a Marine. He appears in the article as the victim, however implied, of a white-supremacist violence enacted by the state; meanwhile, my brother enjoyed the beneficence of the state, joined here with private individuals, in the Christmas present the Marines gave him. (Another coincidence involves Battle Vaughn, the photographer of Migue and Olga; Vaughn was among the first *Herald* employees on the scene of the uprising.)[17] I was at that Toys for Tots event with Migue on December 23, 1979. I stood in line at a table marked "Boys, 8–12." When I got to the front, a Marine gave me a gift-wrapped box and wished me a Merry Christmas. I wondered what the present was, of course, but, more than that, I recognized that these men had no idea who I was, that no one had chosen this gift especially for me, yet there it was, mine all the same. I can say today that the impersonality of the gift is what enamored me of it that day—that no one cared who I was, aside from how I fit a profile, which was enough for the gift to be bestowed. It was such an impersonality, such a profiling that, earlier that week, in a different encounter with the state, helped to kill McDuffie.

Number 151 was where La Vieja bought a .45-caliber revolver. She hid it in the cupboard. I took it out often, felt the heft, cupped the bullets in my hand. It was New Year's Eve 1979, and I knew what La Vieja was going to do. I begged her not to: I was terrified of the noise. She did it anyway. Just before midnight, she stepped onto the balcony. When the clock struck twelve, she pointed the gun at the sky and fired all six rounds. She reloaded and did it again. La Vieja was saying goodbye to 1979. She was also saying something else: Don't fuck with us. And no one ever did.

"How They Beat You and How They Lied"

In the early hours of December 17, 1979, a group of police officers, six to twelve of them, beat Arthur McDuffie to death at the intersection of Thirty-Eighth Street and North Miami Avenue, after stopping him on his motorcycle for a traffic violation. Officers Ira Diggs, Michael Watts, William Hanlon, and Alex Marrero were charged with manslaughter and evidence tampering, with Marrero's charge later upgraded to second-degree murder. Another officer, Herbert Evans, Jr., was charged with tampering and the cover-up.[18] An all-white jury in Tampa, Florida, where the trial had been moved, found the officers not guilty on May 17, 1980— the afternoon of which witnessed the start of the Miami uprising. The officers punched McDuffie that night. They hit him with nightsticks and Kel-Lites, a heavy flashlight that doubled as a weapon. They fractured his skull, which, according to the medical examiner, occurred as McDuffie lay on the ground, face down.[19] Alex Marrero's charges were upgraded because some of the other officers, turned state's witness, testified that he delivered the death blow, straddling McDuffie, raising his nightstick or Kel-Lite above his head, and bringing it down on McDuffie's head, splattering blood several feet away.[20] Recognizing Marrero's role is important, as I have suggested, for an account of the Cuban American significance of the murder—a significance, as Pitbull's "Outro" demonstrates, which is too often ignored. The journalist and crime writer Edna Buchanan, who broke the story in the *Herald* on December 24, exhibits a characteristic reluctance, if not resistance, to call Marrero a Cuban American in print. In a follow-up report at the time of the murder, she enfolds Marrero, as Pitbull does, into Anglo whiteness, describing him as one of "four white Metro officers" charged in the death; a few years later, she acknowledged Marrero's difference, albeit in generic—and, indeed, anonymous—ethnic terms: "The prisoner was helpless on the pavement when a Latin officer swung back over his head with both arms, to smash down a two-handed blow with his big metal flashlight. It connected right between the eyes of Arthur McDuffie."[21] The "white" and "Latin" identities of Marrero signify, in their historical "inaccuracy," his Cuban American whiteness, just as El

Viejo's own "Caucasian" and "Latin" identities, in the medical examiner and *Herald* texts, did with regard to him. The sorry Cuban American element of Marrero in the McDuffie narrative included a prehistory: an earlier accusation against him of police violence toward African Americans.[22] It included a mockery of minority-rights discourses in the insistence of his friends and family, who had raised money and printed fliers on his behalf, that Marrero was a victim of anti-Latino discrimination as the only officer to receive upgraded charges.[23] And it included a posthistory: Marrero's arrest a decade later on charges of conspiring to commit bribery and distribute cocaine.[24]

The Miami uprising left eighteen people dead. In "The Fire This Time," a 1980 essay on the event, Manning Marable remarked that, "historically, the Miami rebellion has only been surpassed in its manifestations of social unrest in this century by the bloody Chicago race riot of 1919, and perhaps by the Watts and Detroit Rebellions of the 1960s." Recognizing the uprising's deep determination in history, Marable also pointed to its relation to recent U.S. imperial maneuvers across the Caribbean transregion of Miami, Cuba, and Haiti: "An influx of black refugees from the pro-U.S., puppet dictatorship of Jean Claude Duvalier could not be tolerated," he writes, referring to the thousands of Haitians who had been turned away from Miami around the time, whereas "the arrival of mostly white, politically reactionary (or at least anti-Communist) Cubans fleeing from a nearby socialist state" was welcomed, since it "would undermine the legitimacy of Castro in the light of Third World and international diplomacy."[25] June Jordan, writing shortly after the event, called it "the massive Black peoples' uprising of Miami, 1980," and focused on its violence as one among her themes—a violence that involved "attacking and killing white people," as commentators observed.[26]

> And then the good news of Miami burst upon America. It was such good news. A whole lot of silence had ended, at last! Misbegotten courtesies of behavior were put aside. There were no leaders. There was no organization and no spokesman. There was no agenda. There were no meetings, no negotiations. A violated people reacted with violence. An extremity of want, an extremity of neglect, and extremity of racist oppression had been met, at last, with an appropriate, extreme reaction: an outcry and a reaching for vengeance, a wreaking of havoc in return for wrecked lives, a mutilation of passers-by in return for generations mutilated by contempt and by the immutable mutilations of poverty.[27]

Jordan saw the violence as "an ending of self-hatred" through an "expression of hatred for your enemies," and she argued for its transformation as love: "Miami was an act of love: love for Arthur McDuffie and love for every jeopardized Black life."[28] In a later writing, after Rodney King, Jordan revisited the uprising, concluding that the apparent "good news of Miami . . . was politically indefensible as such because it did not lead to something big, new, humane, and irreversible." She added, "We must take care not to become like our enemies: I do not accept that we should fall upon a stranger, outnumber him or her, and beat and possibly kill our 'prey.'" It is necessary to "distinguish between our enemies and our allies," she concluded, "and not confuse them or forget the difference between a maniac and a potential comrade."[29]

Jordan's rich survey of her thinking on enemies and allies helps me further explore the uprising's Cuban American layers, which involve not just the actions of Alex Marrero, as I said earlier, but the foreign and domestic U.S. policies that favored (white) Cuban Americans over African Americans in Miami between 1959 and 1980. One such layer appears in "Allapattah Latins Play Dominoes on Front Lines," a *Herald* text published just two days after the start of the uprising. "Allapattah Latins" interviewed a white Cuban American who claimed he had "already shot and wounded a black man he accused of looting" his furniture store. "'You had better speak Spanish or show the Cuban flag,' [the man] yelled at a car passing the corner of N.W. 34th Street and 17th Avenue"—an area a few blocks north of Comstock Park.[30] Here, one notices the point of Anglophone/Hispanophone language use among Afro-Latinas/os: speaking Spanish affords Afro-Latinas/os a social advantage as African-diasporic subjects in the United States over their African American counterparts, with the implication that such a performance of Hispanophone ability, in Allapattah during the uprising, is a matter of life and death. Of course, such a Hispanophone injunction courts the possibility of racial performance—that African Americans, for example, will "put on" Cuban American Spanish, will unfurl the Cuban flag, so as to navigate the white Cuban American threat of violence. Indeed, the racial performance of Cuban American Spanish among African Americans, as I will show in the following section, became a staple of Scarface minstrelsy in rap music: a cultural sign of the post-Mariel, post-McDuffie "blackening" of Cuban America unwanted by the old-guard exile.

The representation of Arthur McDuffie's murder appears in a range of texts that mark the period around 1979. One is "The Ballad of Arthur McDuffie," a "contemporary gospel" song performed by the Miamian

Ella Washington and a twenty-two-person choir. Significantly, part of the idea for the song came from a nineteen-year-old Dade County employee, which suggests a hopeful, creative role, one other than violence and its failed redress, for those who were associated with the state in its relations with McDuffie.[31] Washington sings of McDuffie as "a kind and gentle man, the kind his mother wanted him to be," a man who "served his country with such pride." She ascribes culpability to the police: "They beat him till he died. Arthur McDuffie, they put you in the ground." Indeed, Washington's "they" is powerful for the way it attributes the murder to the police while allowing them anonymity—a concession to the historical reality of the verdict, which implied that "no one" killed McDuffie. The power of that rhetorical move is at least matched by Washington's direct address to McDuffie—her "Arthur McDuffie, you"—an address which the song's call-and-response intensifies: the chorus repeats "forgive and not forget," while Washington sings, "how they beat you and how they lied." "The Ballad" also visits June Jordan's vision of the uprising's transformation into love: "Arthur McDuffie, now all your troubles ceased. We love you, brother. Try to rest in peace." And it spatializes the murder, doing so in its invocation of McDuffie's corpse and its final resting place, again in a direct address: "Arthur McDuffie, they put you in the ground." It also does so with the murder scene itself, with Washington singing, "They couldn't have done it if you had your friends around," "They chased you to an empty place," "They caught you all by yourself."[32] The "empty place" where no one was "around," where the police seized McDuffie "all by [him]self," is, of course, Thirty-Eighth Street and North Miami Avenue. Washington re-creates the intersection, implying that its street, sidewalk, and streetlamps—the stuff of its "empty place"—have somehow figured into the murder. "The Ballad," in short, suggests an indictment of the city's form, Miami's built environment, in the production of this racialized killing.

Two other McDuffie texts extend Washington's work on his culpable-yet-anonymous murderers and the city space in which they acted. The poem "Who Killed McDuffie (A Definitive Question)," written in 1980 by Hakim Al-Jamil (Harold Lee Rush), speaks to the former concern. Rush wrote the poem while a prisoner at the U.S. Penitentiary, Leavenworth, where he was serving a sentence for his involvement in a gunfight with the FBI.[33] It opens by invoking McDuffie's corpse:

His brain was bashed
cranium crushed

skull fracture/broken
all the way around
but they say those who beat him
didn't kill him
so who killed mc duffie?
maybe it was the same ones
who didn't kill
clifford glover/randy heath/jay parker
claude reese/bonita carter/eula love
elizabeth magnum/arthur muller &
countless others
when they musta tripped or
their fingers slipped
maybe it was the same ones who didn't kill
jose torres/zayd shakur/fred & carl hampton
jonathan & george/joe dell
twyman myers/spurgeon winters & a few
thousand more[34]

As the title suggests, and as these lines show, the poem enacts in literary terms the legal fantasy of police inculpability in the murder of McDuffie. Whereas Washington's critique turns on a culpable *they* that *did,* Al-Jamil's turns on an inculpable *who* that "*didn't.*" The ironic force of the poem is greater for the way in which it links McDuffie to the list—in fact, only the fragment of a list—of the many African American men, women, and children (and, in the case of José Campos Torres, a Mexican American) killed by the police: activists, revolutionaries, and everyday people all.

Ella Washington's singing on the matter of space in McDuffie draws us to a group of texts inscribed into the built environment itself at and around Thirty-Eighth Street and North Miami Avenue. The weekend of the uprising, someone spray-painted "McDuffie" in large, plain letters—as large as a one-story building—on the side of Joe's Market on NW Forty-Sixth Street and Twenty-Second Avenue in Liberty City, just north of Allapattah.[35] Like much unofficial street art, this example, facing the Twenty-Second Avenue side of the building, transformed a possible "empty place" of violence into a space of aesthetic and social signification. The spray-painted "McDuffie" stands for the value of personal expression among responses to the murder, even as it harbors a public meaning, too: that, far from "empty places," the spaces in Miami marked

"McDuffie" contain memories, contain histories, and these matter, too, in their conceptuality, as we look to ward off the enemy's attack, the enemy's forgetting, when, as Washington sings, we find ourselves without our "friends around." Such is the case, in an official way, with the renaming of a twenty-block stretch of NW Seventeenth Avenue around NW Fifty-Fourth Street as Arthur Lee McDuffie Avenue in 2003.[36] Again, the state intervenes in the life of McDuffie, though now in a positive way, adding something of its discursive impersonality to the narrative of the murder it helped produce—namely, the green street sign, which resembles every other street sign in the city, its metal form promising to endure, in contrast to the paint of the unofficial graffiti, which proved so vulnerable to erasure. And there is one final, significantly unintentional, text of McDuffie in the built environment—this one at Thirty-Eighth and North Miami itself. Edna Buchanan conjures an automobile-centric environment when she writes that McDuffie was killed "near the shadows of an expressway ramp, a ramp that would have led to almost certain escape had he used it."[37] The ramp in question leads to I-195, an eastbound highway that spurs off I-95 to cross a causeway over Biscayne Bay toward Miami Beach. The meaning of McDuffie's murder off I-95 is great. The construction of the interstate highway through Overtown (earlier known as Colored Town) destroyed the integrity of that historic Miami African American neighborhood, demolishing its houses and businesses, displacing its people in the thousands.[38] Today, the street intersection of the murder reveals even more about the geographic economy of Miami, situated as it is on the edge of Wynwood, a neighborhood identified with the mid-twentieth-century migration of Puerto Ricans to the city and, more recently, with its transformation into a gentrified Design District. If you stand at the intersection and face northwest, you will see a mural stretching across the front of the low-slung building on the corner. The building is for sale, and, in one respect, its corner location is an illusion. There is no way to enter the building from the sidewalk, on foot, which articulates the automobile-centricity of the streetscape: no one is supposed to walk here, as the absence of crosswalks and the threat of motorists speeding onto the highway testify. It is a logic, of course, that, producing Washington's violent "empty place," is also apt for the placement of a mural: all those blank walls and false entrances along the sidewalk. Titled *Reina del Sur* (Queen of the South), the mural was created in 2007 for Art Basel Miami. Its artists, El Mac, Retna, and Reyes, worked in acrylic and spray paint. Retna (Marquis Lewis), born in 1979 of African American and Salvadoran descent, was unaware of the location's significance. Art Basel encouraged the artists to use the site, given its proximity to the Design District and I-195.[39] At the center of the mural appears the face of a young woman, looking over her right shoulder. Her skin is tinged blue, the mural's dominant color. Her long black hair falls across a part of her face, and she looks down, with a distant, though not unsympathetic, expression. Around her head is a golden-hued calligraphic composition in the shape of a halo; a calligraphic pattern, in shades of blue, also forms the mural's background. The woman's face dominates the corner of the building. Wrapped around the corner are her wings. The wing to her left is a modernist abstraction, with shapes that include a striking turquoise pattern; the one to her right is representational, its feathers suggesting the eyed plumes of a peacock. The mural's angelic beholding of the murder scene puts *Reina del Sur* in a particular relation to the spray-painted McDuffie of 1979 and the street-sign McDuffie of 2003: *Reina* looks over the injustice, offering the murder scene a grace, even if it never meant to.

Scarface Minstrelsy

My mourning of El Viejo's corpse in this chapter and the mourning of McDuffie's in literature, song, and space guide us toward those other mourning texts around 1979: the rapping of the corpse of the *Scarface* Antonio. Cuban American Studies has not gone very far in its recognition of the connection between *Scarface* and Cuban America. Scholars have noted that the film "used the Cuban diaspora to update an old American story of power and corruption," and they have recognized its protagonist, Antonio Montana, as "a dusky-skinned *Marielito*."[40] When not an "update" of the 1932 film, *Scarface* 1983 is remembered as a "remake," one "in which the mobster made famous by James Cagney [*sic*] became a *marielito* cocaine king, played by Al Pacino," whose performance was based on "stereotypes" of Mariel migrants.[41]

More than a sequel with a Cuban American setting, *Scarface* 1983 shapes and responds to the Cuban American experience of race after Mariel. The "duskiness" of Pacino's character and the "stereotypes" of his performance indicate a compulsory "brownface" Hollywood spicsploitative characterization in which white Cuban America sees a threatening representation of itself—the compromising of its Cuban American whiteness—which African American rappers go on to amplify in their embrace of Montana. I see in such an African American use (even, at times, erasure) of this "Latino" character a circulation of the metatext's minstrel logic in a way that redirects how racist white-Latino and Anglo-white blackface performances have historically shut out, but also established market spaces for, African-diasporic performers in the Americas, however limited such spaces may be. In this way, I depart somewhat from the view of a critic such as Raquel Rivera, who sees in rap's use of *Scarface* 1983 an example of the music's "somewhat detached and abstract . . . glamorization of and identification with Latino outlaws." The rap moments of the *Scarface* metatext, at least in their most compelling variations, represent as well an involved reflection on the specificity of Pacino's racial performance. Rivera further notes, and I agree, that such connections involve still "another level of identification, . . . one rooted in lived experiences and Afro-diasporic identities reinforced through mass media images."[42] At a slightly earlier critical moment, Todd Boyd offers another insight regarding *Scarface* 1983, writing that the film marks yet another historic "shift away from the ethnic gangster to the racialized gangster," now in a post-Soul setting, where the Italian American of 1932 yields to the "racialized Cuban" of 1983, with his "broken accent, penchant for garishness, and overall ruthless approach to wealth and human life"—an observation regarding the character's racialization that I prefer to frame more as a constant rearticulation of, rather than as a series of shifts from, Jewish American, Italian American, Cuban American, and African American identifications across the *Scarface* metatext.[43] Antonio Montana "starts from the bottom, with no hope of making it and no skills for making it besides a willingness to put his life on the line for the deal," as one writer puts it in her search for an answer to the question regarding African American masculinity and *Scarface*: "Why does a 1983 movie starring an Italian American man playing a Cuban criminal speak so loudly to so many Black men?"[44] An answer, I am proposing, is that rappers appreciate (and, in their rhymes, reproduce) the way in which an Italian American *plays* a Cuban American, regardless of what that particular community—the Cuban Americans, fearing themselves *played*, which is to say "blackened," in the United States—may think.

The movements between ethnicity and race, the characterization of Antonio, and professional acting practices in the *Scarface* metatext are fascinating. Al Capone offers a point of origin—he of the scar across his left cheek, the "whiteness" of which was "whiter by contrast to his darkish jowls," a contrast he attempted to remedy by applying "talcum powder to the rest of his face." Capone, misnamed "Tony" by the press early in his career, thus establishes a relation in the metatext between "disfigurement," skin tone, and artifice: the use of makeup to dissimulate a violent incorrection of color.[45] In 1930, the popular writer Armitage Trail (Maurice Coons) transformed Capone into Tony Guarino, a character whose "fierce, clan-love of the Latin" was intended to signify Italian Americanness.[46] Trail's novel is the basis for the 1932 film produced by Howard Hughes and directed by Howard Hawks—and starring Paul Muni, who was born Meshilem Meier Weisenfreund in Lemberg, Austria-Hungary (today Lvov, Ukraine). Muni immigrated to the United States in 1902, and he first appeared on the Yiddish stage in Cleveland six years later. He wanted to "revolutionize the whole art of makeup"—indeed, to "completely cover" his face with putty—and in *Seven Faces* (1929), he did so, in the roles of Napoleon and Schubert, for example. He also played a boxer named Joe Gans in the film, which required him to appear in blackface. Further, Muni used language and accent to signify ethnicity to his advantage in both public and professional settings—the former during his citizenship ceremony, during which he fooled the presiding judge by speaking at the beginning in "a halting and heavy *mittel-Europa* accent," only to end the ceremony with "impeccable English," thereby parodying his Jewish-immigrant assimilation to Anglophony and "American whiteness."[47] In his professional preparation for the role of Antonio Camonte in *Scarface*, the matter of language and accent in the performance of Italian Americanness was foremost:

> [Muni] tried a variety of accents. When they rehearsed the opening lines, Hawks said, "It's too Latin, too Italian. Cut it down. In half." "There won't be enough," Muni said, "but I'll try." He read a few more lines. "Cut it in half again," Hawks directed. "Howard, this isn't right," Muni protested. "Look," Hawks said, "we just want the *suggestion* you're Italian. It's more in the inflection than in the accent. Besides, we want to understand you." Muni smiled. "That makes sense." Hawks reports that Muni found a rhythm and a subtle oily lilt which "worked beautifully through the whole picture."[48]

The spirit of such performed voicings of Italian Americanness on the *Scarface* set and of Jewish assimilation in the citizenship ceremony—both of which determine Muni's purchase on Anglo whiteness—carries over into the late twentieth-century *Scarface* metatext, where, in Pacino's work and, to a greater degree, in rap music, the staging of a U.S. belonging (as citizenship, as culture) hinges not only on one's ability to modulate an accented Cuban American voice but on the flaunting, through performance, of that very linguistic ability. For Muni's Antonio Camonte, appearing in "one of the most highly censored films in

Hollywood history"[49] due to the Hays Code and Production Code Administration, the "oily lilt" of immigrant-ethnic vocal performance is silenced by the police officers who shoot Camonte in the street outside his Chicago rowhouse, his corpse lying next to the rails of a streetcar line—the signs, these, of a nineteenth-century urban-dwelling and transportation modernity on the wane. The state kills the gangster in the 1932 film, as the market, represented by the now-famous advertisement located high above the street—"The World Is Yours, Cooks Tours"—looks on in ironic judgment. It is a public tableau that, as we will see, *Scarface* 1983 renders private.

Al Pacino's performance of Antonio Montana in that film is an example of brownface: the practice of non-Latino, Anglo-white actors in Hollywood playing characters whose "white-Latino" or "mixed-raced" identity signifies "brown," a category of Latino identity that has animated both Latino resistance practices (forms of the Chicano movement, for example) and their containment (U.S. state and culture-industry privilegings of a "brown" Latino, with divide-and-conquer implications akin to ideological Latin American *mestizaje* practices), with the Afro-Latino always located in a precarious relation to (and, more often, outside) such "brownings," as we saw with O'Farrill and Cosme, the sometime "Africans." Frances Negrón-Muntaner explains brownface as "a way to get outside of 'white' skin—although not too far—and into the skin of another without risk."[50] Off the *Scarface* metatext, I extend the concept to suggest that Pacino's performance of Montana is as much about allowing the "ethnic-white" Italian American a chance to exit his own "white" skin as it is about invoking the different modernist minstrel object that was the Italian American skin (through Muni) of Antonio Camonte, which, like that of Montana's Mariel migrant, represented the "skin of another," the invocation of which involves a "risk" for ethnic-white Italian Americans not unlike the risk perceived by white Cuban Americans in Montana: a troubling of their claim to whiteness in the United States. Pacino was familiar with the 1932 film; he wanted to "imitate Paul Muni" after watching it.[51] Pacino's grandfather, who helped raise him after his father left the family, sparks another connection to modernism and "Latin" identity: the grandfather lived in East Harlem in the early twentieth century and would talk to his grandson about that time of overlapping Latino, African American, Jewish American, and Italian American spaces, which we saw in chapter 1. Indeed, Pacino's own sense of identity includes the early twentieth-century "Latin": "Coming from the South Bronx, being, in a sense, Latin myself, I have a certain connection to the Latin feeling," he has said.[52]

During production, Pacino's costar, the Cuban American Steven Bauer, known earlier in his career as Rocky Echeverría, instructed Pacino on Cuban Spanish and Cuban American English: "We worked together closely, especially in our off-hours," Pacino recalls. "Being Cuban, he helped me with the language; he taped things for me, he told me things I wouldn't have known."[53] The influence of Echeverría/Bauer on Pacino's brownface speech exemplifies a Latino Studies reorientation of the Hawks-Muni collaboration on the "oily lilt." Before appearing in the film, Echeverría/Bauer was cast in the classic Cuban American situation comedy ¿Qué pasa, U.S.A.?, another key text around 1979. Brownface speech in Scarface is connected through Echeverría/Bauer's professional past to Cuban Miami's geopolitical emergence in relation to U.S. government funding: specifically, ¿Qué pasa? was developed through a grant by the U.S. Department of Health, Education, and Welfare, secured by two Miami-Dade Community College faculty to produce the show, provided they made it bilingual.[54] (Another connection to Cuban American culture is that the idea of a "Cuban Scarface" originated with Sydney Lumet, who, of course, offered Eusebia Cosme her first cinematic role.)[55] Pacino admits thwarting expectations of realism in his performance of Cuban Spanish and Cuban American English. He describes his speech in the film as a rejection of the authentic, choosing instead to "heighten" Montana's "accent."[56] And, indeed, the film highlights the apparent oddity of Montana (the man, the surname) as a Cuban subject through the very question of the character's English-language ability. During the immigration interview that opens the film, Montana says that his father was born in the United States and that it was from him, in addition to the movies and school, that he learned to speak English. The confession, whether true or not, is useful. On the one hand, the state hears that the Cuban migrant has arrived on U.S. soil because the United States was there, in Cuba, to begin with; on the other, the audience has a reason to suspend its disbelief regarding why Montana and his friend Manolo, the Echeverría/Bauer character, will spend almost the entire film speaking English, not Spanish.

That Cuban Americans in Miami would engage the "negative publicity" of Scarface by founding the Pynchonian FACE—Facts About Cuban Exiles—in 1982 suggests something of a choteo (mocking humor with an edge of critique) sensibility in their response to the film. They created an organization that cut the Scar out of Scarface and saved face, as it were, by putting the remaining word in all capitals, an act of linguistic cosmetic surgery that corrected the mark of violence otherwise marking the visages of Capone, Guarino, Camonte, and Montana. A Miami city commissioner named Demetrio Pérez, who had come from Cuba in the early 1960s, supported an effort to shut down the production of *Scarface*. Even though he failed to convince the Commission, by September 1982, after only a few weeks, the production moved to Los Angeles, where *Scarface* was mostly filmed, returning to South Florida later that winter only for location shots.[57] "I consider the withdrawal of the film producers a victory for the people of Miami," said Pérez at the time.[58]

The attitude toward *Scarface* 1983 on the part of rappers such as Scarface, Nas, and Raekwon is one of cultural reappropriation, in contrast to the political misappropriation of Demetrio Pérez. The appearance of *Scarface* in rap music coincides with the origins of gangsta in Los Angeles in the late 1980s—the genre associated with the group N.W.A. and, in particular, two of its members, Dr. Dre and Ice Cube. Gangsta's social and aesthetic significance is well-known. Its narratives, rhymed by MCs with a "speech-effusive" flow, derive from the "badman" tales of the nineteenth century, the blues, and signifying. Expressive at times of misogyny and homophobia, masculine gangsta personae represent certain particulars of a ghetto reality: the exploits of post-civil-rights, postindustrial African American workers in the economies of crack cocaine, shadowed by the state as welfare and the prison; the violence of gangs and police in the community, the representation of which reflects on the criminalizing of young African American men; and the post-"urban-renewal" disappearance of public space, as its physical destruction or privatization.[59] Eithne Quinn explains how an important attribute of gangsta is its unabashed embrace of (its own) cultural commodification, resignified by the music form as a kind of ghetto "realness": that "gangsta constructs itself as a hustle, that it continually reflects on its own commercial properties," Quinn writes, speaks in general to "the reduction of culture to a hustle" under capitalism, the gangsta awareness of which "itself stands as a grim ghetto truth."[60] Rap turns to *Scarface* in part because of the film's unrelenting thematizing of the "hustle" through Antonio Montana, despite (in fact, because of) his hustle's ultimate failure, ending as it does in a death that, in the liberal imaginary, reads too seductively as a cautionary tale.[61] More to the point here, rap reproductions of the *Scarface* "hustle" suggest an understanding that, from Hawks and Muni to DePalma and Pacino, the hustle involves the ability of artists to invest themselves (and to attract the investment of others) in the ethnicized, racialized performance, often as accent, of the metatext's Antonios.

It comes as no surprise that a ska song—Prince Buster's 1965 "Al Capone"—is a precursor to rap uses of *Scarface*, given ska's importance to the development of rap. After an opening that samples gunfire, Buster repeats Capone's name (and, indeed, spells it out), suggesting the kind of self-reflexivity regarding gangster personae that will mark many rap uses of the film. "Don't call me Scarface," Prince Buster intones. "My name is Capone. C-A-P-O-N-E. Capone. Al Capone. My name is Capone. Al Capone."[62] The disavowal of the nickname, in favor of the proper name, is itself of ironic significance to rap, which will use "Scarface" at least as often as "Tony Montana" to name the film's protagonist, despite the fact that *Scarface* 1983 itself only names him as such once and, even then, in Spanish—namely, the phrase "*cara de cicatriz,*" uttered by the "Colombian" wielding the chainsaw during the infamous dismemberment scene, which marks the nickname and, in this instance, the Spanish language and "Latin America" as beyond the pale, a charge familiar in the U.S. imperial repertoire.

A discussion of the rapper Nas, from the Queensbridge housing projects, leads into a selection of *Scarface* rap uses—one that focuses on the major figures in the "renaissance of East Coast hip-hop"[63] as gangsta around the mid-1990s, a focus that, while suggesting a particular geographic and period parameter for rap interests in the film, is by no means exclusive, as the example of the rapper Scarface demonstrates shortly. Thirty years after Buster's "Al Capone," Nas's "N.Y. State of Mind," off the album *Illmatic*, offers a Scarface persona with an even clearer nod toward the discursive: "I'm like Scarface, sniffing cocaine, holding an M-16. See? With the pen, I'm extreme."[64] For the Notorious B.I.G., *Scarface* affords a point of reference for his own past as a worker in crack. "Respect," from 1994's *Ready to Die*, makes the reference poignant by representing a mother's failure to best the film in its influence over her son, a poignancy B.I.G. complements with a strategic ambiguity: "Mom said that I should grow up and check myself before I wreck myself, disrespect myself. Put the drugs on the shelf? Nah, couldn't see it. Scarface, King of New York, I wanna be it."[65] That it is possible to take "Scarface" (like "King of New York") as a reference to both the film's character and the film itself ("*Scarface*") is one of B.I.G.'s implications: in particular, a desire to be both the subject and creator of a gangsta narrative, which, of course, is what the autobiographical B.I.G. does over the course of *Ready to Die*. Raekwon's *Only Built 4 Cuban Linx* (1995) offers still another example of the flexibility of rap's *Scarface*: "Incarcerated Scarfaces," in its very title, slides the meaning of the word back toward the character;

"Criminology" samples dialogue from the film; and "Ice Water" features Ghostface Killah calling out to "all my Al Capone, Al Pacino niggas."[66] And then there are the many samples of the film's soundtrack: in the 1990s, Mobb Deep's "G.O.D. Pt. III" (*Hell on Earth*) and "It's Mine" (*Murda Muzik*) and, more recently, Rick Ross's "Push It" (*Port of Miami*).

One rapper whose use of *Scarface* predates such East Coast cuts and relocates the film to South Park in Houston's Fifth Ward is Brad Jordan, otherwise known as Scarface (and, earlier, Akshen). In three songs with the Geto Boys and solo from 1989 to 1993—"Scarface," "Mr. Scarface," and "Mr. Scarface, Part III: The Final Chapter"—Scarface seizes on racial performance and accent in the *Scarface* metatext as a creative possibility, one that belies the straightforward logic of his identification with the character: that "this cat was just like me."[67] "Scarface" first appeared in 1989 and was remixed a year later in the Geto Boys' self-titled album on Def American, whose distributor, Geffen Records, refused the album for its "violent, sexist, racist, and indecent" content.[68] "Scarface" is a first-person account of a day in the life of the song's eponymous persona. After Scarface introduces himself as a drug dealer, he unfolds in detail two scenes in which he plays a role in retribution killings involving rival drug gangs and the police. At the end of the rap, he claims to leave the drug economy behind: "I had to leave everything I've ever worked for," we hear, over a sample of James Brown's "Blues and Pants." "But best believe I won't get sentenced for a drug war. But maybe one day, in the future, I can come back. But until then I'm going home, where I'm from, black. Nobody knows my name. They'll only know this face. And ask my posse. They say, 'We call him Scarface.'"[69]

"We call him Scarface," the final words of the rap proper, bookends the song's opening use of *Scarface*, a sample that includes Antonio Montana's famous line, "all I have in this world is my balls and my word," which "Scarface" cuts into repetitions of "all I have in," "this world," and "balls": "All I have in, all I have in, all I have in, all I have in. This world. Balls, balls, balls, balls." The sample establishes, even as it risks repeating to absurdity, the character's masculinist premise, emphasized at the expense of Montana's "word." But, even more than this, the sample subjects to repetition—and hence to defamiliarization—the sound of Montana's accent, which is to say, the sound of Pacino's brownface dialogue. The possibility that "Scarface" is drawing attention to the sound of Montana's "Cuban-American English" in more than a casual way is suggested by the rap's opening lines after the sample: "I started small, on the dope game, cocaine. Pushing rocks on the block, I'm never broke, *meng.*" I write "*meng*" in order to capture Scarface's sonic re-creation of the popular Cuban American pronunciation of *man*, where the ending sound is nasalized, signaled here by *-ng*. In pronouncing "*meng*," Scarface shows his care as a listener of the *Scarface* metatext, for one of the ways in which the 1983 film signified Montana's Cuban Americanness was through the character's frequent use of *meng*, which, learned from Echeverría/Bauer or not, was a way in which Pacino guaranteed the script's Latino "oily lilt," so crucial to the *Scarface* metatext. In using *meng* here and in one more instance in the rap proper—"Nobody crosses me, especially in this dope game. So raise up off me. I show them I don't joke, *meng*"—Scarface takes part in (while taking apart) the *Scarface* performance of accent as the province of the ethnic-white subject: here, an African American sounds like a white Cuban American, as voiced by a brownface Italian American. What distresses white Cuban America, its possible black racialization in the Anglo United States after Mariel, becomes "reality" in the "realness" of Scarface's *meng*.

The sense that Scarface is aware of the performance of accent in the *Scarface* metatext is only intensified at the end of the rap proper of "Scarface," in what amounts to the song's outro, when Scarface speaks the following lines in a full Montana accent, over the "all I have in / this world / balls" sample:

> Hey, coño, *meng*. Listen to me, *meng*. Now that we got Texas fiending, *meng*, it's time to make the whole fucking world start geeking. We expand across the whole motherfucking world, *meng*. And we get the dope out there, *meng*, we fuck them up! You motherfuckers thought I wasn't going to make a comeback, *meng*. I'm here to tell you something, *meng*. I'm coming back, *meng*. Geto Boy, 1990. And if you ain't down with the Geto program, fuck you, *meng*.

All these many *mengs* in the midst of all the other words uttered in "Montana brownface"—and over Montana himself, cut in the sample— suggest Scarface is in on it: that Montana/Pacino "is just like" him as much in terms of a fictional rise and fall as of a performance in accent.[70] Scarface uses *meng* in subsequent revisions of the song in two solo albums, though arguably to lesser effect. Again sampling "all I have in this world," "Mr. Scarface," off *Mr. Scarface Is Back* (1991), offers a metacritical observation on the increasing references to *Scarface* in rap: "I bet there's a lot of wannabe Scarfaces. I've heard the name in ninety-nine different places. I'm here to squash it all. Original will speak. Scarface on your ass from the streets."[71] And by the time "Mr. Scarface, Part III: The

Final Chapter" appears on *The World Is Yours* (*Face II Face*) (1993), yet
again sampling "all I have in this world," Scarface's self-reflexivity seems
perfunctory: he breaks character in the midst of the familiar day-in-the-
life narrative to admit he is "just freestyling in the studio, though."[72]

A decade after Scarface's three-rap cycle, another rapper worked the
matter of accent into his performance of *Scarface*, though now with an
Afro-Latino twist: Cuban Link, the Afro-Cuban rapper with a tattoo of
the white-suited Antonio Montana on his right arm who identifies as a
"*puro cubano del ochenta*" (pure 1980 Cuban), a Mariel migrant himself.[73] Cuban Link configures the fraught situation of the Spanish-speaking, Spanish-accented Latino rapper to the language politics of the *Scarface* metatext. I am referring to the unwelcome response often received
by Latino rappers through the 1990s for using Spanish in their music.
Raquel Rivera elaborates: "Puerto Rican and other Latino rap artists had
to be careful about the amount of Spanish words" used in their lyrics, lest
they "be accused of corrupting the hip hop musical aesthetic and defect-
ing to the 'Latin hip hop' artistic ghetto." However, "once African American rap artists incorporated Spanish phrases" in "the latter half of the
1990s," the Latino use of Spanish "became much more palatable within
the mainstream rap market."[74] I suggest that an element in such a genealogy is the articulation of accent—the "oily lilt"—and racial performance
in rap expressions of the *Scarface* metatext: the way in which Latino rappers invoke hip-hop credibility and Latino authenticity by participating
in the performance of a brownface Pacino and African American *meng*.

With Cuban Link, we see an example in his collaboration on "As the
World Turns" with Terror Squad, from *Terror Squad, the Album* (1999).[75]
Cuban Link opens the rap:

> Yo, no lies.
> When I was five,
> I arrived in America.
> Made it alive, survived a hell of a trip,
> kid, I'm telling ya.
> Sailing to Freedomtown
> to put my feet on the ground.
> See what's around,
> then lock shit down like Nino Brown.
> I'm bound by honor and down for drama
> like Tony *Montana*.
> You clowns don't want to fuck around, *pana*.[76]

The reality of Cuban Link's Mariel arrival—"no lies"—depends on the intertextual: first, the reference to *New Jack City* (1991), directed by Mario Van Peebles, which surfaces that film's own African American revision of Pacino brownface.[77] And, of course, there is the mention of Montana. I italicize his name to show that Cuban Link pronounces it in Spanish on the track, which he resolves with the Puerto Rican–identified *pana*—a significant choice for "friend," since it "Puerto Ricanizes" Cuban Link, signifying his Bronx boricua associations in a way that a Cuban equivalent (say, *asere*) would not. Cuban link's *Montana*, in this micronarrative of an Afro-Cuban American arrival to the United States, confirms the film's significance in the metatext's production of accent: it is Montana that provokes the rapper into sounding Spanish.

Cuban Link's reference to "Freedomtown" intertextualizes his Mariel migration in another way. Freedomtown was the name *Scarface* 1983 used to represent the government camp established in Miami for unsponsored Mariel migrants. It is the setting of an uprising during which Montana takes his first step toward upward mobility by contract-killing the former "communist" Emilio Rabenga, whom Cuban Link cites by name in a later song.[78] When he says he "sailed to Freedomtown," Cuban Link suggests biographical and creative arrivals: to the United States via Mariel, to the *Scarface* metatext through rap. The actual camp opened in July 1980, when 650 migrants who had been living at the Orange Bowl were relocated due to the upcoming football season. Another 200 soon arrived.[79] The camp was known as the Ciudad de las Carpas, Tent City, and it was located underneath I-95, near SW Fourth Street and SW Fourth Avenue, between Little Havana and downtown Miami, three miles from the I-395 ramp where Arthur McDuffie was murdered. Tent City was a space of gay Mariel culture.[80] It was also, of course, one of an Afro-Cuban Mariel experience, as the testimony of one Julio Méndez Laferté indicates: "In Cuba, they said dogs were set upon black people here, that this and that happened. . . . A lie is a lie. The best cars around here belong to black Americans [*negros americanos*]. For us, we were proud to see that with our own eyes. . . . But, yes, we were also in error, because they said this is the land of dreams, etc. No, everything happens with sacrifice and work. [Still, this] is a billion times better than Cuba."[81] Freedomtown/Tent City represents what the state and Cuban Americans enacted in the shadows of the Interstate Highway System in Miami around 1979: the murders committed, the shelters set up, the lives begun anew, like Méndez Laferté's, who expresses well both an identification with African

Americans and the Afro-Cuban difference of his arrival in the United
States, fashioned as it was by (island-Cuban narratives of) the threat of
Anglo white-supremacist violence. Freedomtown/Tent City maps, too,
the other Mariel camps of the period—at Fort Chaffee, Arkansas; Fort
Indiantown Gap, Pennsylvania; and Fort McCoy, Wisconsin, themselves scenes of Mariel undesirability and uprising.[82] Mapped, too,
is the "harder" camp that was the Krome Avenue Detention Center,
eighteen miles west of Tent City, on the edge of the Everglades, where
Mariel Cubans but also others—in particular, the Haitians migrating
from the Duvalier regime—experienced the juridico-political exceptionality of the camp: its suspension of the law as state of being.[83] And
in the Freedomtown uprising (set in Miami, filmed in Los Angeles)
that offers Montana his big chance, there is an echo of the uprising of
McDuffie, otherwise ignored in the film, an element here that transforms the minstrelsy of the *Scarface* metatext into a kind of blackface
geography, where *place* instead of *face* signals racial performance: the
L.A.-produced Freedomtown uprising of *Scarface* 1983 acting out the
Liberty City uprising of McDuffie.

Coda: Cárdenas

Gangsters and police, corpses and cocaine all converge in the work of
an Afro-Cuban American writer around 1979: Esteban Luis Cárdenas.
Cárdenas belongs to a generation of Mariel writers whose major figures
are Carlos Victoria, Guillermo Rosales, and, of course, Reinaldo Arenas. In a critical essay, Iván de la Nuez ascribes Mariel writers a particular U.S. literary identity. These writers "did not dedicate themselves to
'dreaming in Cuban,'" writes de la Nuez, "but, rather, to having Miami
nightmares." The reference, of course, is to the novelist Cristina García, who represents a post-1980s Cuban American literature that, to de
la Nuez, exhibits a "cloying sublimation of Cuban culture" beholden to
"multicultural prescriptions."[84] De la Nuez is too reductive—in all likelihood, too polemical. Yet the distinction he makes is worth improving
on. To imagine Cárdenas as an Afro-Cuban American literary interlocu-
tor with the McDuffie and *Scarface* texts is to acknowledge the marginality of his *latinidad* in relation to the more recognizable creators of Cuban
American literature, a marginality that, as this book argues, is about race
but involves also aesthetic and market relations (in the case of Cárdenas,
his Spanish-language production and small-press publication). It is also
a matter of embodiment: illness and disability.

Cárdenas was born in Ciego de Ávila in 1945. He attended the University of Havana, from which he was expelled for political reasons. In 1975, a collection of short stories earned him mention as a finalist for the national award of the Union of Cuban Writers and Artists. Over the years, he was arrested multiple times, again for political nonconformity. In 1978, Cárdenas attempted to enter the Argentine embassy, but the government of that country expelled him. He went to prison. On January 10, 1980, Cárdenas arrived in the United States—a fact that places him on the margin of an already marginalized Mariel experience, identified as he is with the migration yet not a part of it.[85] In the summer of 2008, I met Cárdenas at his assisted-living facility off Palm Avenue in Hialeah.[86] We spoke there and at a Cuban restaurant on Forty-Ninth Street. He remembered Mariel: "¡Cómo venían miles de amigos míos!" (How my friends came, in the thousands!). Two weeks after his arrival in the United States, Cárdenas was in a car crash that left him in a coma. In the early 1990s, he suffered another violent episode: a drunken motorist struck him on Flagler Street in Little Havana. Cárdenas lost his sense of smell, a vocal cord, and much of the movement in his right hand. His vision was impaired, his ability to walk diminished. Yet he continued writing. Poems appeared in the inaugural issue of *Mariel* and subsequent numbers, and several poetry collections followed.

The title story of the collection *Un café exquisito* (A Delicious Coffee) shows how Cárdenas imagines an aspect of gangster violence at times intimated in the *Scarface* metatext: its mundanity. The narrator, "Esteban," invites us, like Scarface and Cuban Link, to associate his story with the autobiographical and, in particular, to see in the act of drinking Cuban coffee a gustatory, addictive signifier of the body and, indeed, (exiled) nation: sugar on the tongue, caffeine in the bloodstream.[87] In fact, it is a craving for *café cubano* that starts the story. Esteban drives on Seventeenth Avenue, just north of Flagler Street in Little Havana, when he decides to visit his friend, Peter "el *gangster* [in original]," who lives near the Orange Bowl, in hopes of sharing in some of his wife's excellent coffee.[88] At Peter's, Esteban finds a young man tied up in a corner, "pale as a corpse." His "blue eyes expressed fear and helplessness" (47). Esteban halfheartedly intervenes on the young man's behalf with Peter, who refuses to spare him. Esteban enjoys the aroma in the kitchen as Peter's wife brews the coffee; he chats with her. And then he ventures out into the backyard, where he sees "the blond man again," now a cadaver, his face bruised, apparently having been "hung with the very rope used to tie up his hands" (50). Peter's brother-in-law is in the backyard, too.

Cross-eyed, he strikes the rope against a tree, letting loose each time with a "lunatic laugh" (51). Esteban soon ends the visit with small talk before he drives off into the dusk, leaving behind a white Latino corpse that, for Cárdenas, appears a tedious plot necessity: an ironic underplaying of white *latinidad* in Cuban American literature. The places of the body in "Un café exquisito"—the corpse of the *rubio*, the disabled body of the brother-in-law, the caffeinated body of Esteban—involve also an extraliterary dimension, for stamped at the end of the story is a sign of the time and place of Cárdenas's own body as he wrote: The Pointe, North Gables, ACLF, Miami, 2000. This is the assisted-living facility that was the home of Cárdenas, located on Calle Ocho—just down the street, in fact, from where, twenty-one years earlier, La Vieja discovered the corpse of El Viejo.

5 / _Cosa de Blancos_: Cuban American Whiteness and the Afro-Cuban-Occupied House

During the 1990s, a narrative flashpoint appeared repeatedly in the works of Cuban American writers, particularly among those with origins in the first postrevolutionary migration (1959–1962): that of a return trip to Cuba. As even a brief selection shows, Cuban American return narratives of the 1990s signify in multiple ways. Pablo Medina's autobiography _Exiled Memories: A Cuban Childhood_ recounts a "visit to the island after an absence of thirty-eight years," confirming ideas in the Cuban American imaginary of a static, ruined island in its representation of a Havana that "has not evolved" but "merely crumbled."[1] Alina Troyano's queer performance piece _Milk of Amnesia_ imagines a return to the homeland that, as "the place that suckled" its character Camelita Topicana "as a newborn babe," may heal her wounded, migrant memory.[2] And there are others: return as the need to vindicate a feminine family history in Cristina García's novel _The Agüero Sisters_ (1997), as a link between words and images in Tony Mendoza's personal photo-narrative _Cuba: Going Back_ (1999), and as a step toward discovering a Cuban-Jewish identity in Achy Obejas's novel _Days of Awe_ (2001).[3]

The discourses of Cuban return in the 1990s engage issues of "repressed and abandoned memories" and conceptions of "home" and "history,"[4] and they hinge on metaphors of political economy, with the revolution's early nationalization of private property playing an especially important role. As Ricardo Ortiz has observed, when it comes to returning to Cuba, the political and affective discourses of the old-guard Cuban exile are often marked by a powerful resentment over island property long lost to the revolution. This, according to Ortiz, is one of the paradoxes of exile, for in certain Cuban Americans' "stubborn, compulsive refusal to surrender their claim to lost property and lost capital," what they "may persist in delaying, if not preventing, is precisely . . . their own still-possible return home."[5] First-wave, 1990s Cuban American return narratives thus critically engage, if not fully enact, this ideal of an open-ended "surrender." As such, they articulate the literary cultures of the Cuban diaspora in the United States with "Cuba's Special Period—roughly, the decade of the 1990s, immediately following the country's loss of Soviet trade and support." During this time, Cubans experienced intense material want, with the Cuban state itself "surrendering" to capitalist reforms, including a dollarization that, toward the end of the decade, had eased the hardship for some and "expanded the arenas for public expression," even as the Castro regime reconsolidated its power.[6] In this context, "thanks to both a limited relaxation of the embargo and Cuba's promotion of tourism, pursued as a means to attract foreign currency,"[7] Cuban Americans would go back to Cuba in an unprecedented way. Return narratives of the 1990s thus reimagine, with their own, related interests in "lost property and capital," two historic projects of the Cuban state. One was the Special Period "incorporation into the nation of the much-vilified exiled community, . . . now refashioned as a 'diaspora.'"[8] Another was the state's early redefinition of *vivienda* (housing) from an object of capitalist exchange to a "*servicio social*" with the 1960 Law of Urban Reform, which banned evictions and cut rents by terminating private property— a revolutionary project that itself experienced transformations during the 1990s.[9]

I am interested in how 1990s return narratives enfold into issues of transnational memory and un/relinquished capital an underdiscussed dimension of contemporary Cuban American culture: the dimension of Cuban American *whiteness*. This chapter analyzes iterations of 1990s return in Cuban American autobiography as aspects of the *blanco criollo* (white creole) condition of Cubans in the United States—a white-Latino condition shaped by Cuban nationalism and Spanish coloniality, and in tension with ideologies of U.S. Anglo whiteness, which often cast such Latino whiteness as "off-white."[10] In this way, I conclude this book's discussion of the twentieth-century literary and performance cultures of Afro-Cubans in the United States with a reflection on representations of Cuban whiteness as a crucial element of Cuban race in the United States, a whiteness otherwise taken for granted. This chapter harks back to earlier figurations of Cuban whiteness in the United States that I only touched on in my discussion of Afro-Cuban American writers and performers, and it builds on the previous chapter, in which I demonstrated how the Miami exile's attempt to reconsolidate a distressed Cuban American whiteness in response to the *afrocubanidad* of the Mariel boatlift stood in contrast with the many texts of a *Scarface* minstrelsy.

I am particularly interested in how the "white logic" of 1990s return narratives—linked to the overwhelming demographic whiteness of Cubans in the United States—involves an encounter between white Cuban Americans and island Afro-Cubans through what I term the *Afro-Cuban-occupied house*: a trope in which Cuban houses, once lived in by first-wave, exiled white families (and therefore the object of the voyage back), are now inhabited by Afro-Cubans, most often women— and just as often the family's former servants—whose residence results from either official revolutionary policy or the informal scenario of having remained "in place" for decades after the white family fled.[11] I analyze the Afro-Cuban-occupied house in autobiographical texts by Gustavo Pérez Firmat, Román de la Campa, and Ruth Behar. Each of these figures has produced a personal narrative from different experiences of white, middle-class migration as a young person from Cuba to the United States in the early 1960s. Pérez Firmat's *Next Year in Cuba: A Cubano's Coming-of-Age in America* (1995) most approximates, even as it wrinkles, the idea of a "stubborn, compulsive refusal," while de la Campa's 1990s return in *Cuba on My Mind: Journeys to a Severed Nation* (2000) happens after a long, vexed history of earlier returns, beginning with the Antonio Maceo Brigade in late 1977. The return in Behar's film *Adio Kerida/Goodbye Dear Love* (2002), meanwhile, is also related to prior trips back—in her case, to returns in the late 1970s and in the early 1990s itself.[12] I argue that encounters in these texts with the house and its Afro-Cuban inhabitants mediate Cuban American whiteness's constitutive element, its social privilege, related to the authors' tenured academic positions. The narrative of a return to the Afro-Cuban-occupied house reproduces, even as it opens to critique, Cuban American whiteness's historical claims to superior culture and associations with social and economic dominance. The trope signals, too, a hallmark of post-1959 Cuban American whiteness: its constitution *at a distance* from the majority of island Afro-Cubans, yet *in close*, segregated, often conflictive proximity to African Americans in the United States, especially in Miami. With Cuban and U.S. African-diasporic subjects at once near and far, the Afro-Cuban-occupied house stages the "fundamental paradox of whiteness: the persistent need of nonwhiteness to give it form and expression."[13] In this way, beyond simply reimagining familiar Cuban postracial and *mestizaje* identity practices transnationally, the Afro-Cuban-occupied house represents Cuban American whiteness simultaneously as an unhyphenated "majority" white-Cuban identity on the island and as a hyphenated, "minority," white-Latino identity in the Anglo-white United States. The trope is thus neither exclusively racist nor antiracist. Rather, in the texts of Pérez Firmat, de la Campa, and Behar, it is a signifier of the white Cuban American condition, one in which Afro-Cuban former servant women on the island figure centrally, underscoring how imaginings of race and gender together constitute the diaspora aesthetics of 1990s Cuban American return. Toward the end of the chapter, I consider two *Afro-Cuban* texts of return and the occupied house that steer the argument in still other directions: Pam Sporn's documentary film *Cuban Roots/Bronx Stories* (2000), which features a first-wave, 1990s *Afro-Cuban American* voyage back, one that imagines forms of island Afro-Cubanness in languages other than Spanish and "at home" in (memories of) nations other than Cuba, and María de los Reyes Castillo Bueno's testimonial narrative *Reyita, sencillamente: Testimonio de una negra cubana nonagenaria* (Simply Reyita: The Testimony of a Nonagenarian Black Cuban Woman; 1996), an island Afro-Cuban text that offers a different understanding of Afro-Cuban women's relations to the houses of the nation.

This chapter invites a conversation on whiteness and power in the Cuban transnational literary and cultural studies contexts. In particular, my interpretation of the Afro-Cuban-occupied house engages conversations in critical Anglo-whiteness studies, a multidiscipline with origins dating back at least a century among African American writers and intellectuals but cohering in the academy around the early 1990s in many excellent works that, nevertheless, locate themselves "almost exclusively within North American [read: Anglo U.S.] terms."[14] As a contribution to a critical "*Latino* whiteness studies," one that considers such whiteness from its origins in early-modern Spain and post/colonial Latin America to the modern and postmodern Latino United States, my work here inquires not only into Latino self-interpellations as Latin American or Spanish colonial-derived whites but into white-Anglo and white-Latino struggles over hemispheric hegemony: what Silvio Torres-Saillant has called the "white supremacist legacy that the [Latino] community inherits from its tributary cultures on both sides of the Rio Grande."[15]

In the context of a critical Latino whiteness studies, a discussion of the Afro-Cuban-occupied house challenges the view that Afro-Cuban figures in white Cuban and Cuban American literary texts signify primarily as allegories of Afro-Cuban trans/national identity—a critical tendency that rightfully challenges postracial "silences" on Afro-Cubanness,[16] even as it influences, by its tacit approach to *lo blanco criollo*, how Cuban/Cuban American whiteness, in the words of Nancy Mirabal, is "normalized and erased" in public discourse.[17] With the Afro-Cuban-occupied house, I recognize another significance of the Afro-Cuban figure in the white Cuban American text: that of revealing Cuban American whiteness in its conditions of privilege.[18] I call this mode of representing Afro-Cuban figures in white Cuban American texts a *cosa de blancos*, a concept I devise by drawing on the Afro-Cuban American critic Enrique Patterson's provocative idea that the general Cuban "discourse on identity [*discurso sobre la identidad*] has always been a white discourse [*un discurso blanco*]," whereas for Afro-Cubans, what has mattered most is not so much "the ontological problem as the juridical one [*el problema ontológico como el jurídico*]: to put in black and white the laws and rules of the game."[19] I see the possibility here of revising the familiar Cuban expression *cosa de negros* (a black thing). While depending on tone and context, *cosa de negros* typically ascribes inferiority to, and thus dismisses, all manner of Afro-Cuban life, from affective concerns and cultural practices to social institutions. The phrase, in short, would effect oppression through embarrassment. Its intention is to belittle, and hence to hamper, Afro-Cubans. Playing off Patterson, I suggest that representations of Afro-Cuban identity in white Cuban American culture are, among other things, a *cosa de blancos* (a white thing): a displacement, through Afro-Cuban figures, of the way Cuban American whiteness, as an articulation of privilege, might shame and hamper its very own subjects, white Cuban Americans. Of course, *cosa de blancos* fails to enact the violent, binary logic of Cuban racism. It cannot say and do, in the social, as *cosa de negros* does. Yet the phrase thrives within the formal logic of its racist relative, particularly the rhythm, syntax, and feel of *cosa de negros*. The Afro-Cuban-occupied house in Pérez Firmat, de la Campa, and Behar is just such a *cosa de blancos*: a display of Cuban American whiteness that would otherwise pass as literary Afro-Cubanness.

Morrison and Miami

Cuban American autobiography in the 1990s is "an important document reflecting the history of the Cuban American community within the United States,"[20] a history, as I have suggested, significant for its reproduction of Cuban whiteness beyond the island. Cuban American autobiographical narratives link—but also trouble the connections between—subjectivity, whiteness, nation, and diaspora as "whole, seamless, and 'true,'" as "capacious, current, and accessible."[21] Like return narratives in certain kinds of contemporary African diasporic writing, they tend also "to undercut the concept of return altogether."[22] Such genre matters, in the Afro-Cuban-occupied house, involve what Toni Morrison calls "American Africanism," her concept for a mode in white U.S. literary production in which a "black presence" "makes it possible to say and not say, to inscribe and erase, to escape and engage, to act out and act on, to historicize and render timeless" the conflicts and contradictions of race in the United States.[23]

I am interested in shifting Morrison's concept in the direction of Cuban American literary whiteness to enact the kinds challenging, productive, cross-spheres practices of method in Americas whiteness work that a critical Latino whiteness studies emblematizes: challenging because Cuban American whiteness differs conceptually and historically from the Anglo-U.S. whiteness that Morrison reflects on, productive because the articulation of different Cuban and U.S. concepts and histories of white supremacy and the plantation system, here in a Morrison-inflected Latino Studies, may encourage critiques of Cuban American whiteness beyond the parameters of the Cuban postracial and *mestizaje*. In this way, I propose a genealogy of Cuban American literary whiteness through Morrison's signal observation that "what Africanism became for, and how it functioned in, the literary imagination is of paramount interest because it may be possible to discover, through a close look at literary 'blackness,' the nature—even the cause—of literary 'whiteness.'"[24]

Such an African American–influenced analysis of Cuban American literary whiteness invites a critique of the symbolic (and, at times, actual) center of Cuban whiteness in the United States: Cuban Miami. While the Afro-Cuban-occupied house in Pérez Firmat, de la Campa, and Behar is not necessarily of a particularly Miami-Cuban derivation, neither is it disconnected from Miami histories of African American/white Cuban American relations, histories whose role in shaping the discourses and practices of Cuban American whiteness is significant.

The early post-1959 migration of white Cuban privilege to Miami reflects historical ideas on the whitening of Cuba. "The [Cuban] upper and middle classes, displaced by Castro's rule," writes Enrique Patterson, "settled in Miami. Given the fact that the majority of the members of these classes was white, and that the black exiled middle class settled, in large part, in the north, the illusion or the dream come true of the [nineteenth-century] Cuban sugar-plantation ruling class was created: [all] Cubans were white."[25] The issue also involves the particular history of the early Cuban exile's connection to African Americans in Miami, whose own oppression under U.S. white-supremacist institutions the Cubans generally ignored or, at worst, went on to benefit from and exacerbate.[26] Indeed, as people who "were 'white' in the context of their homeland" yet often "perceived to be nonwhite"[27]—or off-white—in the United States, white Cuban Americans in Miami "reclaimed" whiteness in part as a benefit of U.S. state intervention, which positioned them against African American Miamians, sparing them, in the process, what Ramón Grosfoguel calls "Puerto Ricanization": racialization as nonwhite Latinas/os. As Grosfoguel shows, Cuban exiles "received more than one billion dollars from the U.S. government's Cuban Refugee Program," a form of "privileged treatment [that] can be accounted for by the geopolitical symbolic strategies of the cold war" and that, further, emphasized Cuban whiteness by marking the Cuban migrant experience as "different," particularly in contrast to the longstanding "racialization of Puerto Ricans as inferior 'Others' . . . entangled with the racialization of African Americans." In the particular case of the Small Business Administration in Miami, for example, Cubans received "66 percent of its total loans between 1968 and 1979, compared to a mere 8 percent of loans given to African Americans during that same period." All in all, U.S. state intervention encouraged "'whitening' the perception of [the Cuban American] difference in the imaginary of 'White' America."[28] As Marvin Dunn, a historian of African American Miami, explains, not only did Cuban exiles succeed "in diverting attention from Miami blacks during the crucial integration period," but, because "of their greater social acceptability and entrepreneurial skills," they received "the lion's share of public dollars."[29]

"Social acceptability" and "entrepreneurial skills" call forth historical white Cuban, now Cuban American, privilege. It is such privilege, emerging historically in a Cuban Miami in tension with post-civil-rights African Americans, that *Next Year in Cuba*, *Cuba on My Mind*, and *Adio Kerida* reimagine in the trope of Afro-Cubans living in the long-lost family house. To unpack the trope, I turn now to Pérez-Firmat.

Pérez Firmat's Plantation Patio

Gustavo Pérez Firmat's *Next Year in Cuba*, in its depiction of a return to the Afro-Cuban-occupied house, is a key text of Cuban American whiteness. Pérez Firmat's publications in literary criticism, poetry, and fiction date from the early 1980s, with his *Life on the Hyphen: The Cuban-American Way* standing out as "a very influential and somewhat controversial study" that "went quite directly against the political grain of much U.S. Latino studies at the time (and perhaps still today)."[30] *Next Year in Cuba*, which appeared a year later and was nominated for a Pulitzer Prize in nonfiction, features a particular return to the island—an imagined return, as we shall see, rather than an "actual" one—many years after its subject's exile to the United States in 1960. At first, however, in keeping with the futurity of the title, return is a proposition to hold off: "Much as I would like to think otherwise," Pérez Firmat says, "deep down I fear that I belong with those for whom there is no going back: *no tengo regreso*." For him, "returning to Cuba would be tantamount to going into exile a *second* time."[31] The rejection of return is an affective issue, too, marked by "lost property and lost capital": "I have refused to go back not just because I don't want to help Fidel out with my dollars, but primarily because I'd find it intolerable to visit places that belonged to us, that were taken from my parents and my family. For me, this amounts to acquiescence and even complicity in the theft" (36).

Yet return does occur in *Next Year in Cuba*: as a "memory exercise" that would forestall the overwhelming politics and emotions associated with an actual return itself and its object, the lost, nationalized, Pérez Firmat house in the once middle- and upper-middle-class Havana neighborhood of Kohly, across the Almendares River in west Havana. Pérez Firmat writes of what he intends to do through his "memory exercise": "to describe our house in Havana," "to walk myself through the house I have not seen, and not thought about much, since the morning we" left Cuba, "to walk through our house not the way it looks now, practically a shambles, but the way it was the last time I saw it" (38). By intimating what the house may possibly look like "now, practically a shambles," but, preferring, in the end, to describe it "the way it was the last time" he saw it, the text would seem to elide the present, and everything leading up to it, in favor of the past—with the "shambles" of the present, of course, serving as a signifier for the island's Special Period conditions.

And yet the insistence on separating 1960 ("the way it was") from 1995 ("now") does not so much erase as transfigure history and temporality in the text: how is going back to the house "the way it was the last time" inseparable from (imagining) going back to the house "now, practically a shambles"? Further, how is "a shambles" racialized, a matter of white Cuban Americans engaging a "ruined," Afro-Cuban island? How, in other words, might the Pérez Firmat abode shelter an Afro-Cuban-occupied house? A place to begin is a passage that opens the door, in more ways than one, to the house itself, which, significantly, was "exactly [Pérez Firmat's] age," "a one-story masonry structure with a vaguely modernist or Art Deco look" built in 1949 (38–39):

> I begin my imaginary visit by walking up from the sidewalk onto the wide granite stairs, which taper at the top. My hand slides along the top of the low stone wall where I sit in the morning waiting for the school bus. Behind the wall lies a large patch of greenery—*arecas*. The front door has a dark iron grating and thick milky glass; I don't remember the pattern of the grating, but I imagine it similar to those I have often seen in Miami—flamingos or palm trees or some other leafy, vegetable design. When I ring the doorbell, our manservant ("butler" is too formal a word for Vargas) lets me in. On the wall next to the door is a shiny gadget, a set of golden cylinders of varying lengths shaped like a pan flute: the doorbell. A long hallway runs down the middle of the house, with the rooms opening out on either side. The terrazzo tiles, joined together by thin copper strips, are always cool, and in the summers my brother Pepe and I like to take our shirts off and lie with our bellies to the floor. (39)

Caught in all the sensory detail of the passage is a sentence invoking an odd register of character and action: "When I ring the doorbell, our manservant ('butler' is too formal a word for Vargas) lets me in." Ringing the doorbell, rather than simply walking in the door, troubles the premise of traveling back in Cuban-time to the days of preexpropriated property, for ringing implies asking permission to come inside and hence the possibility that the house one is entering is no longer one's own. Further, if the autobiographical narrator needs permission, someone needs the agency to grant it. And that someone is a subject both specifically identified and not, both attributed and denied a motive, put at the center of a flowingly descriptive passage yet himself embodying a disruption of that very descriptive flow. The character in question, in the syntax of the sentence, is bracketed, his name deferred until the end: "manservant," then, in parentheses and quotation marks, "butler," and finally a name—not a given name, but a last name—"Vargas." Indeed, that it is "a word for

Vargas" that one finally gets, rather than Vargas himself, only accentuates the discursive maneuvers necessary to introduce, and manage, the man behind the name. The distress evident in writing ("a word for") Vargas indicates the fraught nature of the text's (imagined) return to Cuba, where a "memory exercise" connects Pérez Firmat with a stand-in, in Vargas, for contemporary island Cubans. What are these Cubans doing back home? How are they occupying it? An answer appears in the name, and subject, of Vargas, who does the "letting" in the sentence, to be sure, but who is also separated from the verb by parentheses. The right to do, in other words, even the compromised form of doing that "letting" represents, is both close to Vargas—something he can approximate—and also beyond him, an active role instead granted, grammatically at least, to the "manservant": to an *occupation*.

Vargas's sentence exhibits what Morrison calls "disjointed" and "repetitive" language, here indicative of "a loss of control in the text" often "attributed to the objects of its attention rather than to the text's own dynamics." The locus of such textual distress is an "Africanist persona," one whose presence enables a "reflexive" and "extraordinary meditation on the self" that mediates "the fears and desires . . . in the [white] writerly conscious."[32] Vargas is such a figure, only it is not until later in the scene, shortly after the "disjointed," "repetitive" sentence, that the text finally admits his Afro-Cubanness, setting up the reader to assume, if only so Pérez Firmat himself can confirm, that another word for "manservant" might in fact be *negro*: "On this particular afternoon," says Pérez Firmat, "I'm going to help Vargas polish the silverware inside the vitrines and cabinets, and in return he's going to play catch with me. A black man in his early twenties, Vargas once played first base for a semipro team, and in my eyes he's as good as Rocky Nelson, the American first baseman on Almendares, my favorite Cuban baseball team. As we rub the pleasant smelling gray paste into the forks and knives, the radio in the kitchen is playing the hit song of the day, a *cha-cha-chá* about a merchant who dances in his *bodega*. Tapping on a silver tray as if it were a conga drum, Vargas does a few steps of his own, which I try to imitate" (Pérez Firmat, *Next Year in Cuba*, 39).

The Afro-Cuban-occupied house turns here on Vargas. Consider how the autobiographical narrator's agreement to play at domestic work now, in exchange for the servant's agreement to work at child's play later, would blur the lines between master and servant, wage labor and friendship, Afro-Cuban and white Cuban—in short, between dimensions of disadvantage and privilege—thus asserting ideals of class and postracial harmony that would "normalize and erase" Cuban American whiteness. Yet off Vargas, Pérez Firmat references his fondness for a white-U.S. baseball player in the Cuban leagues, while thanks to Vargas's work near the kitchen, Pérez Firmat hears a song about a *bodeguero*—a song, that is, about a middle-class occupation, the grocery-store merchant, historically restricted almost exclusively to Spanish immigrants and their descendants in early twentieth-century Cuba. In other words, as an Afro-Cuban servant figure "alive with the turbulent significance of moves and countermoves,"[33] Vargas occasions a disclosure of the text's investment in two symbols of hegemonic whiteness in the Americas: one in the baseball player, representing a "visiting" Anglo-U.S. white identity on the island, the other in the *bodeguero*, representing the island's longstanding, Spanish-derived whiteness. In characteristic *cosa de blancos* fashion, the text would dissemble such markers of whiteness in the Americas through the figure of Vargas by staging, to the tune of a *cha-cha-chá*, an "imitation" of Vargas's Afro-Cuban dance moves. The white-U.S. baseball player and the white-Cuban *bodeguero* are apt figures in other ways. The former suggests the uneven manner in which nineteenth- and twentieth-century transamerican baseball cultures codified whether "individuals of 'Spanish extraction' . . . were racially eligible to enter organized baseball."[34] In the latter, meanwhile, dancing to a song about a dancing *bodeguero* becomes a metacommentary, since the *cha-cha-chá* is itself a mid-twentieth-century form devised in part to help middle-class (and often white) Cubans move their bodies to a rhythm only marginally suggestive, it was hoped, of Afro-Cuban working-class identity. Knowingly or not, the text offers up Cuban American whiteness on a silver platter that plays the part of a conga drum. In the carefully arranged move from a "disjointed," "repetitive" "word for Vargas," to the dancing, working, and friendly embodied Vargas himself, *Next Year in Cuba* evinces Cuban American whiteness.[35]

But what of the "fears and desires" that Morrison says lie behind the kind of figure for which Vargas stands? The intimacy with Vargas offers a clue, particularly with regard to gender, sexuality, and the violent legacies of the plantation. As Iraida López suggests, *Next Year in Cuba*'s otherwise keen autobiographical self-reflexivity fails to extend to masculinity.[36] The intimacy with Vargas reinscribes early twentieth-century ideologies of Cuban *mestizaje* in which "men of European and of African ancestry rhetorically reconcile their differences" through representations of the *mulata*,[37] a discursive effect of postslavery sexual violence against Afro-Cuban women. In this context, to resolve the possible queer intimacy between white Cuban American and Afro-Cuban men, *Next Year in Cuba* pushes toward the Afro-Cuban-occupied house's gendered, racialized limit spaces, going outside, into the yard, near the "servants' quarters":

> In the middle of the patio, next to Vargas's room, stood a tall mango tree girded by a small stone bench. One day when I was nine or ten, one of the maids climbed up into the tree to pick some mangoes; sitting on the bench, I sneaked a look up her dress. Vargas caught me looking and called up to Aselia, "Hey, see what Junior is doing!" Aselia laughed and said, "*Déjalo que mire que eso es bueno*"—"Let him look, it's good for him"—and kept right on picking mangoes. I cannot say now exactly what, if anything, I saw. I suspect that my recollection of Aselia's white panties, with strands of curly black hair peeking out from under the elastic, has been embroidered with subsequent fantasies. A few years later, in Miami, many were the adolescent daydreams I spun around the general theme of "maid in mango tree." Proust had his madeleines; I have my mangoes. To this day I cannot bite into the pulp of this juicy fruit without thinking of Aselia's undies. This is one memory I did not repress. (Pérez Firmat, *Next Year in Cuba*, 43)

Like Vargas earlier, and, in fact, taking over his role now, the servant woman has a particular job to do, here in the liminal spaces of the house: to dismiss Vargas's mock shock and condone her own violation, thereby encouraging the autobiographical narrator's normative sexuality, thus marking the text with gendered, white Cuban American privilege. The very job of picking fruit, in other words, exposes the servant woman's body in the first place to Pérez Firmat's child-self's gaze, giving him an "unfair" advantage, while linking the logic of work to histories of rape. The servant woman also has the job of mediating her own racialization. Since the text itself fails to speak her racial identity, it puts her in the position of having to "work for it": to articulate, through embodied work, her place in the historical (here "post-") plantation system of gender, sexual, and racial exploitation, the logic of which is "condensed in the well-known saying 'the white woman for marriage, the mulatto woman for a good time, and the black woman for work.'"[38] A servant such as Aselia, constructed according to a field of gendered and racialized representation, provides a "good time" even as she is always ready for—indeed, always at—work. In short, she is the possible producer, through sexual violence, of *mulatas/os*: the mixed-race subjects of the

Caribbean transregion whose purported movement toward whiteness augurs also, in their very embodiment, the ironic dissolution of the white ideal: *mulataje*.[39] Return in *Next Year in Cuba* thus intensifies around a sublimation of whiteness that, as an element of fear, enfolds the possible, perhaps desired, "undoing" of whiteness. That Aselia's body is the "proper" figure for this is a predictable, significant element of the text and its troubling politics in the trope, which Pérez Firmat's concluding gesture—the geographic relocation (indeed, repossession, as property) of the patio scene to the United States—marks as a *cosa de blancos*, with the imagined boy's privileged white masculinity and heterosexuality now configured (if not "normalized and erased") to the uncertainty of a daydream, a literary allusion, a memory, all of which, needless to say, happens in Miami.[40]

No One's Servants: De la Campa's and Behar's Disoccupations

In contrast to Pérez Firmat's "memory exercise," it is prior personal experiences of going back to Cuba that shape Román de la Campa's representation of the Afro-Cuban-occupied house. The 1990s return in *Cuba on My Mind* occurs within memory of his important earlier trips to Cuba, from his first return in 1977 as part of the Antonio Maceo Brigade, associated with *Areíto*, to his "last" in 1982.[41] Another important difference is the circumstance of his white, middle-class departure from Cuba shortly after the revolution: de la Campa was an adolescent in the Peter Pan program, in which Cuban parents, fearful of state intervention into the family, drew on Catholic Church support to send thousands of Cuban boys and girls alone to the United States.[42]

"Back Again," the final chapter of *Cuba on My Mind*, describes de la Campa's reasons for the 1999 return in a way that links career issues (de la Campa is in Cuba for a conference) and an urge to "peek at Cuba's looming future before the new millennium" with a personal interest in seeing his "past once again."[43] Indeed, this personal interest structures de la Campa's encounter with Special Period Cuba: "It was an emotional trip—I walked around Havana as never before, incessantly, day and night, as if on a mission driven by the need to know, learn, remember, and engrave new and old memories" (21).

Because *Cuba on My Mind* layers critique and personal narrative,[44] it leans toward these kinds of critical reflections on the public and private dimensions of a return to Cuba—reflections that also shape the narrative's use of the Afro-Cuban-occupied house. In this regard, it is propitious, too, that there is no single, original house to which to return and cathect but rather one already understood as a surrogate, a dwelling resulting from an exchange that underscores again the importance of "lost property and lost capital" to the trope: the original family house was sold shortly after the revolution to acquire "dollars in preparation for a possible stay in the United States," leaving the family to move (and de la Campa, years later, to return) to "an older one owned by [his] grandmother" in the upper-class Vedado neighborhood of Havana (de la Campa, *Cuba on My Mind*, 28). The Vedado house was inhabited by a beloved aunt, and in the 1970s she arranged for "a friend to help her with the house and keep her company": "a black woman from Santiago de Cuba" named Ramona (168). Ramona and the aunt, eventually living together, "became very good friends—family" (168). De la Campa recalls staying in the house during his trips to Cuba between 1977 and 1982. When his aunt died, Ramona remained and was later joined by her sister, Hortensia. By 1999, in the absence of relatives, de la Campa can say, "The house is now theirs" and "They and the house, in turn, are what remains of my immediate family in Cuba" (168).

The Afro-Cuban-occupied house here counters elements of what I would call the Cuban *transnational romance*: a Latino inflection of Latin American national-romance archetypes that interpellates, through the erotic, Cuban island and diasporic subjects.[45] In the absence of men, for example, the passage supplants heterosexuality with an unreproductive, if not queer, feminine intimacy: the aunt and her friend, the two sisters. The house unsettles romance conventions less so in the case of race, implying (and thus silencing) the whiteness of the aunt, in contrast to the announced Afro-Cubanness of Ramona, especially as it relates to the historically more Afro-Cuban regions to the east of Havana (Santiago). In tension with feminine intimacy, meanwhile, is the crucial romance element of the family, offered as a sisterly connection (real and figurative) between Ramona, Hortensia, and the aunt, and also as a bond that the autobiographical narrator, in the absence of de la Campa family "blood," now imagines between himself and the Afro-Cuban women. Indeed, as if to affirm that there are no Aselias here, de la Campa historicizes Ramona and Hortensia: far from the "dear old servants" of yesteryear who "never quite crossed the lines of class and race hierarchies, much less in terms of property ownership," the sisters are "educated by the revolution" and are "no one's servants." They have "good state jobs" and "own a home in one of Havana's best neighborhoods" (de la Campa, *Cuba on My Mind*, 169).

In the context of a Latino transnational romance, *Cuba on My Mind* would "surrender" the class and property relations of the past, and, even more, it would reimagine island Afro-Cuban femininity against the historical grain of the plantation. But what of the claim to Cuban American whiteness? A passage I quote at length offers a glimpse. Significantly, it is preceded by de la Campa's interpretation of the Special Period sex industry, with a particular emphasis on Afro-Cuban prostitutes, whose apparent overrepresentation de la Campa is "inclined to believe . . . has to do with the higher percentage of Blacks in Cuba now, as well as the extraordinary migration wave of poor Cubans from the countryside to Havana in the 1990s," all of which makes Havana "now a city where Blacks are a majority, and unlike before the revolution, they live everywhere, including the most prestigious neighborhoods of yesteryear" (166–67). The very next paragraph then extends the point: "My aunt Rosa's house is in one of those neighborhoods—the once-elegant Vedado section of Havana" (167). *Cuba on My Mind* locates the Afro-Cuban-occupied house in relations of intraisland migration and Afro-Cuban women's sex work, figured here as outside the house, on the street—apart from Ramona and Hortensia's Afro-Cuban femininity yet still nearby. De la Campa's observation suggests such sex work is a risky Special Period iteration (because violent in its conditions and challenging in its feminine rearrangements of dollar-production gender orders) of the transnational romance, here with the erotic figured as sex tourism. The text then leads to the passage in question, *Cuba on My Mind*'s most charged instance of the trope, a representation of a kind of Afro-Cuban women's "domestic work" on behalf of the white returnee:

The minute I got to Havana, I walked over to Mina's house [the deceased aunt Rosa was known as Mina]. I sat in the same living-room rocking chairs I have sat in since I was a child. Yet this visit felt different, since it was the first time I had ever been there in my aunt's absence. I soon sensed that Ramona and Hortensia see themselves as an extension of my family. It is not just because they live in that house but, rather, because of the memories that go with it, which they have effortlessly integrated into their own affective makeup. They keep in touch with my mother in Miami by phone. They know my son's and daughter's name, as well as my sisters' and their children's. They keep track of where everyone lives; indeed, they have a firm command of all the details of our family's history that my aunt passed along to Ramona, and she in turn to her sister.

They keep the family pictures sitting on the dressers and walls
next to their own family pictures. They rock in the same chairs we
always did, when my father, my grandmother and my aunt were
still alive, and they recall the same stories we used to recite over
and over again. (168)

The invocation of the child shows the closeness between de la Campa
and Pérez Firmat in their uses of the Afro-Cuban-occupied house, even
as the child's dismissal ("Yet this visit felt different") demonstrates their
distance. The autobiography links the sisters to a particular kind of
immaterial "labor" that, "in return" for occupying the house, they seem
willing to *perform*: inheriting and reproducing, in language and even
in feeling, the de la Campa family past and present. Seeing the sisters
as new, Special Period "servants" to the white returnee—different from
the servants of "yesteryear"—requires that one recognize their performativity *at work*, particularly in terms of an important difficulty in the
passage, one that weighs specifically on the question of their relation to
Cuban American whiteness as privilege: the repeated insistence that the
sisters are reproducing "memories," "names," "where everyone lives,"
"details," and "stories."

Such a repeated insistence implies advantages enjoyed by the de la
Campas *above* the usual. It also represents a generative, perhaps inten-
tional, "loss of control in the text" over how Afro-Cuban women "serve"
the de la Campa family through memory. The passage, in other words,
stands as *Cuba on My Mind*'s *cosa de blancos* moment. The sisters seem
to remember everything, rendering what is remembered *excessive*, thus
suggesting an awareness of—and an unease with—privilege as that
which goes *beyond*. Moreover, the act of remembering "the same stories
we used to recite over and over again" is itself repetitive, another Morrison characteristic of formal crisis in the racializing texts of the Americas. Ramona and Hortensia's excessive, repetitive work of recollection is
a device through which the text expresses the "normalized and erased"
condition of the de la Campas' deep, specific history: its Cuban, and now
Cuban American, whiteness and white privilege. "Over and over again,"
and despite the text's insistence, the stories (of whiteness) are too much
for the sisters (not) to tell, particularly without any stock figures of *lo
blanco cubano* (outside of the *gallego* or the *guajiro*) to help them tell
it: no white Vargases to tap a figurative conga drum, no white Aselias
to climb a mango tree.[46] If Cuba is on the book's mind, in other words,
Cuban American whiteness is on the sisters', in the form of an excessive,

repetitive discourse on identity and privilege that Ramona and Hortensia perform.

The personal-critical works of Ruth Behar are a superb text for considering such forms of Cuban whiteness in transit between the island and the United States. Behar's returns to Cuba, over two dozen during the 1990s, with the first occurring in 1979, shape her writings and documentary film, *Adio Kerida*, which she created over a three-year period beginning in 1999 and released in 2002.[47] Her edited *Bridges to Cuba* is, of course, a key text of the 1990s; her recent volume, *The Portable Island: Cubans at Home in the World* (2008), coedited with Lucía M. Suárez, reflects on *Bridges*, moving with it—and beyond it—into a discussion of Cuban globality. In *Adio Kerida*, Behar documents the Jewish presence in Cuba and its diaspora by weaving its history with her own family's Jewish-Cuban story. The film is also a primary text of the Afro-Cuban-occupied house, drawing on her earlier autoethnographies to confront the whiteness of a Cuban American return. Indeed, Behar's Jewish identity, already of "mixed" Ashkenazi and Sephardic descent, shapes her critical attitude toward the *cosa de blancos* text, for Jewishness inflects not only Cuban whiteness but the Cuban postracial and *mestizaje* as well with the "Juban" difference, which signifies an "amalgam that is different from assimilation," premised in part on how the Jew is "not expected to have Spanish as a mother tongue, nor to be from Latin America."[48] After 1959, the Behar family's Juban condition travels to the United States in ironic fashion: whereas early twentieth-century U.S. racist immigration policy deemed Behar's grandparents "not 'white enough'" to enter the country, just "two generations later" she herself "arrives in the U.S. . . . with symbolic capital as a Cuban refugee from communism," only now to be considered "'too white' and 'too Jewish' to be authentically Latina."[49]

Behar's feminism is relevant, too, particularly in relation to her family's former servant and Behar's own former nanny, Caro, an Afro-Cuban woman on the island who is central to Behar's rendition of the trope. In several autoethnographic texts,[50] Behar not only writes about Caro, whom she visits on her return trips to Cuba; she adopts the first-person voice of Caro herself, a narrative decision premised, in part, on their "relationship of trust and intimacy," the result of having accepted each other as "kin." Behar hopes that "crafting the story" of their "shared present" will offer "an emancipatory twist to this re-encounter of black nanny and white girl-woman," even as she admits, "it is always I who am coming and going, and it is always Caro who stays behind."[51] In fact, as a self-professed "snatcher of stories of women less privileged than" herself, Behar imagines "accusations of appropriation, inauthenticity, ventriloquism," yet she remains committed to the project: "because I believe that the question of women 'serving' other women . . . is one of the most fundamental dilemmas of feminist thought."[52]

Caro appears in Behar's *Bridges* contribution, "Queer Times in Cuba," an essay in which a screening of the film *Fresa y chocolate* serves to organize Behar's impressions of a 1993 visit to the island. Behar describes Caro in that text this way: "the black woman who was nanny to my brother and me until we left Cuba in 1961 when I was four and a half years old."[53] The "return to the home she left behind" involves Caro specifically. It is to Caro that the family bequeathed their residence in Vedado before leaving Cuba, only it happened with a twist: not only was the house in fact a rented apartment; the government eventually denied Caro its lease. In place of Caro, another Afro-Cuban woman, Hilda, resided in the apartment and inherited the Behar family furniture, which she has "taken good care of" and maintained "exactly as they left."[54] Behar's source for the Afro-Cuban-occupied house thus reconfigures the trope around rental-property relations, with the commodification of dwelling assuming "absent" owners and the likelihood of multiple tenants. Indeed, centered on a rental apartment, the Afro-Cuban-occupied house plays against the conventions of "lost property and lost capital," connoting temporary possession, albeit in tension with the way the apartment's Afro-Cuban occupant seems to commemorate (even as she uses) its contents: the exiled family's former furniture.

My main figure of the Afro-Cuban-occupied house in Behar—the visual example in *Adio Kerida*—relies on these earlier, textual representations of return, the apartment, and Caro. Turning to that scene in the film now, the viewer sees Behar approaching the building in Vedado from the street and follows her going up the stairs. As she does so, the camera comes in and out of focus, a formal strategy that, along with the advent of "vintage" graininess, announces the significance of the space soon to appear on screen. These formal decisions also intensify the experience of temporality: the pasts and presents of Cuban time, which are matters to elide in Pérez Firmat's narrative, are in Behar's elements to emphasize, in keeping with her more critical use of the trope. And then a narrator speaks: "Hilda, the tenant who occupies our old apartment, always opens her door to me. She indulges my quest for memory and lets me wander through the dining room, living room, and bedrooms. From the balcony, I see the arch of the Patronato Synagogue, so close I feel I can almost touch it. The table and chairs, the sofa, the bed and dresser which my parents left behind nearly forty years ago, continue to be preserved and used."[55] In a gesture that turns Behar's "ventriloquism" of Caro back on itself, the narrator of these lines is not Behar but the white Cuban American actress Elizabeth Peña. It is the film's casting of Peña (and Peña's performance) as Behar's "I" that most powerfully transforms *Adio Kerida*'s representation of the Afro-Cuban-occupied house.[56] Peña played the role of Pilar in John Sayles's well-known film *Lone Star* (1996), a Chicana character who, as Rosa Linda Fregoso has argued, "embodies the borderlands and allegorizes hybridity, racial crossing and mixing across a new terrain in which white male access to the multicultural nation takes place through the body of a brown woman."[57] Perhaps less known is Peña's performance as the character of Aurelita in Orlando Jiménez-Leal and León Ichaso's *El súper* (1979), "the first Cuban exile fictional feature to be broadly distributed and exhibited in the United States and to win international awards." *El súper* is "solidly a film of exile longing and displacement"—an exile always verging on, when not coming into, a whiteness "naturalized and erased"—whose subplot concerns how Peña's teenage character's "increasingly visible Americanness," heterosexual activity, and possible pregnancy trouble her working-class parents.[58]

Peña's narrator-voice in *Adio Kerida* sounds off her other roles in *Lone Star* and *El súper*, putting in tension performances of white Cuban American and *mestiza*-Chicana femininity. Peña's ventriloquism, indeed, refracts the apartment encounter between Behar and Hilda (who is "in the place" of Caro) through two important (and often conflicting) experiences of whiteness among Latinas/os: one representing a Chicano experience as *mestizo* subjects beset by the whiteness of Anglo domination, the other representing a Cuban American experience as white Latinas/os invested in white Cuban American privilege. In the scene, in other words, Behar's representation of the Afro-Cuban-occupied house extends the *cosa de blancos* of the Caro passages: it is the voice of Peña's overdetermined Latina figure that we hear, guiding our gaze through the apartment, even as it is Behar's body doing the actual walking on screen. Again, as was the case with Caro, *someone else* (in addition to Hilda) is assisting Behar enact, however critically in relation to whiteness and its privileges, the returnee's paradigmatic visit. In this instance, it is the figure of Peña, whose other roles, dozens in addition to *Lone Star* and *El súper*, describe the vicissitudes of a Latina's professional experience in the entertainment industry, with roles in "positive," popular representations of *latinidad* such as the film *Crossover Dreams* (1984) and the television series *Resurrection Blvd.* (2000–2002) recalling, as their obverse, her earlier roles as an "illegal" Mexican domestic worker and Salvadoran nanny, roles that are thus reinscribed, too, in the *Kerida* voice-over, mapping the apartment as a space accessible through (a memory of) the imbricated, domestic labors of Afro-Cuban women on the island and Latinas in the United States.[59] Much beyond Pérez Firmat's narrative, and even beyond de la Campa's (with which it shares a politics), *Adio Kerida* draws critical attention to the white Cuban American condition.

Bajareques and *Casas Mías*

I begin the final section of this chapter with Pam Sporn's documentary video *Cuban Roots/Bronx Stories* (2000), which intervenes in my discussion of Cuban American whiteness in its depiction of an *Afro-Cuban American* return to the Afro-Cuban-occupied house. The video documents three generations of the Foster family, Afro-Cubans of Jamaican descent who migrated to the United States. Carlos Foster, the father who came in 1960, was born in Oriente in 1922, the son of Jamaican immigrants to Cuba who worked for the United Fruit Company; Foster himself worked at the United States Naval Base in Guantánamo Bay and later as a singer in Havana. Three of his children appear in the film: Pablo Foster, Rubén Foster, and Diana-Elena Matsoukas, all of whom migrated with their mother in 1962, eventually settling in the Bronx. The video's narrator is Pablo Foster's son, also named Pablo, and the director is Foster Sr.'s wife, Pam Sporn, a white documentary filmmaker and teacher. Sporn's role recalls Morrison's American Africanism, yet the video's politics, while seemingly in key with Morrison's concept, are different: *Cuban Roots* documents Afro-Cuban Americans as protagonists in a first-wave exile, 1990s return story that nearly always assumes a white Cuban American cast and context. The Afro-Cuban American difference is apparent in the testimonies of its subjects: the narrator, Foster Jr., announces, "This film is my family's reflection on cultural, political, and racial identity—what was left behind in Cuba, and what was discovered in the Bronx."[60] Rubén describes what happened when the family arrived in Miami in 1962: "the white Cubans went one way, the black Cubans went another." Diana-Elena, meanwhile, mentions how in the Bronx, when African Americans heard her speak Spanish, her "blackness" was called into question, which prompts her to ask, "If I'm not black, what am I?" In other words, *Cuban Roots* represents the

Afro-Cuban American difference as an experience of black racialization in the United States.

In 1995, again, in the midst of the Special Period, Pablo Foster, Sr., returns to Cuba for the first time since 1962. A return to the house for Foster is complicated by the existence of multiple former houses across the country, as well as the condition of apartment-rental relations. Consider the first encounter with a former residence—in this instance, in Havana. In the scene, Foster rides in a taxi with his daughter. As the driver comes to a building that, at first, the camera does not film, Foster says, "Aquí mismito es" (Here it is). He then says in English, "This is where I lived." Soon, in the hallway of the apartment building, Foster knocks on a door. Someone answers, and he says, in Spanish, "Hello, ma'am. I'm sorry to disturb you, but I lived here over thirty-three years ago, and I only wanted to show my daughter where I lived. My family lived here, and this is my wife filming here. This is the last apartment we lived in before leaving." As this is happening, an older white woman appears in the doorway. She invites Foster inside and gives them a tour of the apartment. "Ésto sí que me recuerdo" (I do remember this), says Foster as he walks past the bathroom, while the woman asks, "Y ella, ¿qué hace? ¿Retratando?" (And what is she doing? Filming?). Foster, in reply, says, "Sí, porque yo soy el único que ha regresado" (Yes, because I am the only one who has returned). The video then cuts to a scene showing Foster walking back out of the apartment building to the street.

What is significant about this counterversion of the trope is that, with a propertyless, Afro-Cuban returnee, and in the absence of Afro-Cuban "occupiers," the house signifies a routine return experience: it welcomes someone who, walking around in it, remarks, as Foster does, that everything seems smaller than it did when he was a child, which, of course, is true. Missing here, in Foster's offhand invocation of the child, are the kinds of child selves (and their ideological vectors) specific to Pérez Firmat's and Behar's stories. Missing, too, are overwrought servant figures (Pérez Firmat), the excess of memory (de la Campa), and negotiations of intimacy and surrogacy (Behar, but de la Campa and, very differently, Pérez Firmat, too), all of which have exemplified Morrison's "loss of control in the text," the condition of a *cosa de blancos*.

With this revision to the occupied house, *Cuban Roots* features a final—and most pivotal—use of the trope. Foster eventually travels to Guaro, a former hometown of his in the eastern Cuban province of Holguín, where his aunt, an eighty-eight-year-old named Elisa Beatriz Shand Coombs (nicknamed Cattá), still lives. Cattá was born in Colón,

Panamá, to Jamaican parents and later moved to Cuba with her mother when she was eleven years old. She once worked as a maid for the U.S. families of the United Fruit Company. She also helped raise the Foster children. At one point, the camera frames Cattá, then cuts back to a shot of the house in which she and the Foster family once lived. A caption describes the structure: "The wooden house where Pablo [Foster] lived with his aunt is no longer in livable condition." Foster tours the house with his aunt, and, at the end of the visit, as the camera captures him leaving it behind, Cattá sings, in a voice-over, a song in English about love and collapsed temporalities: "Tell [me] why all of sometime comes like one time when I am with you. Why should I need to hold you? Some hearts are always lonely, and if you know, dear, please tell me why." Cattá died three years after her nephew's return.[61]

This iteration of the Foster house counters the Pérez Firmat, de la Campa, and Behar houses/apartment in a crucial way. A structure in a small town hundreds of miles to the east of Havana, the house enjoys "no place" in the Cuban and Cuban American property-value imaginary. It could not be occupied and therefore "valued" by the material and affective labor of an Afro-Cuban woman former servant or servant figure on behalf of white Cuban American returnees, for the house "belonged" to just such a person in the first place, one whose domestic labor had already been expended elsewhere, in the family houses of the United. What the house does represent, I suggest, is the transnational Afro-Cuban *bajareque*: a space of paradox in Cuba (and in circuits of Afro-Cuban American return to the island) where African-diasporic histories, "no longer in livable condition," dwell still. The word *bajareque*, to someone versed in the late twentieth-century Cuban American vernacular spoken in a place such as Hialeah, Florida, connotes a very run-down house, apartment building, or apartment unit. A *bajareque* is just barely inhabitable, but that is the point: one manages to inhabit the uninhabitable space of the *bajareque* despite the risk of a roof possibly falling in on one's head or the presumed social embarrassment of being seen by others living nearly "unlivably." The term *bajareque*, as Fernando Ortiz imagined it, has a rich cultural-linguistic meaning in the discourses of Caribbean word origins. Ortiz holds that *bajareque* denotes the "frame/texture" (*tejido*) for the indigenous and later colonial/national Cuban thatched-roof dwelling that is the iconic *bohío*. He narrates, in fact, a history of how the term, in the context of its defining "Caribbeanness" (*antillanismo*), "has spread across the continent," from its origins in an "Arabic word, *albahareque*," which arrived with "Columbus's disembarking in Cuba for the first time," to the term's transformation, in the pronunciation of colonial Cuban subjects, into "the Cuban *bahareque*," a term that, in a form of reverse migration, reappears "over there in Spain" as "*bareque*."[62]

The Foster transnational Afro-Cuban *bajareque* links the word's cultural-linguistic "un/inhabitability"—its "*tejido*" of territorial displacement and violence across medieval and early-modern Islamo-Judeo-Christian Spain and the post/colonial Americas—to the figure of Aunt Cattá and her identity as a Panamanian woman of "West Indian" descent in Cuba. In the early twentieth century, West Indian migrant sugarcane workers on the island became a target of Cuban racism. Their presence, the state and civil society claimed, would result in an uncivilizing "blackening" of the island.[63] In Aunt Cattá's migrant history, and in the English language she uses to sing her song, she invokes the West Indianness of Cuba: the multilingual culture, the international black politics, the migrant labor of serving others and cutting cane, and, of course, an African-diasporic identity in tension with the Cuban postracial and *mestizaje*. It signifies a West Indian Cuba in a text of Afro/Cuban/American culture—a story explored by the Afro-Cuban filmmaker Gloria Rolando in *Los hijos de Baraguá/My Footsteps in Baraguá* (1996). To identify a West Indian Cubanness as one among a variety of histories and identities invoked in the transnational Afro-Cuban *bajareque* is thus to worry island and diasporic *cubanidad* with a Caribbean cultural politics, one in which the term *West Indian* represents less "the largely Anglophone African population of certain islands," an idea reflective of "the divisiveness imposed by the Euro-based fragmentation of the Caribbean,"[64] and more the Caribbean as a transregion constituted by national, linguistic, and racial difference.

Such a West Indian Cuba, in the context of early twentieth-century experiences of the Universal Negro Improvement Association on the island, plays into *Reyita, sencillamente: Testimonio de una negra cubana nonagenaria* (Simply Reyita: The Testimony of a Nonagenarian Black Cuban Woman; 1996), the *testimonio* narrative of María de los Reyes Castillo Bueno (1902–1997), as written by her daughter, Daisy Rubiera Castillo.[65] I conclude with a look at *Reyita*'s own counterexample of the Afro-Cuban-occupied house.

Reyita's revision of the trope draws on Castillo Bueno's lifetime experiences of never quite "owning" property and often being forced by familial conflict and economic exploitation to move from one poor *vivienda* to another. When Castillo Bueno was a girl, an aunt on her father's side gave her family "a little piece of land . . . where [her father] made a thatched house [*de yaguas y guano*]," but when her father abandons the family, her aunt took back "the little piece of land [*pedacito de tierra*]."[66] She laments how as a girl she had "to wander so much, from the house of one family member to another" (40). Such careful attention to the many displacements throughout her life demonstrates how a deep, detailed memory of multiple dwellings is not incompatible with conditions of propertylessness and repeated migration across eastern Cuba.

Reyita further resituates the trope in its associations with gender, domestic labor, and surrogate motherhood. Castillo Bueno mentions how "black girls [*niñas negras*], little black girls [*las negritas*], were put to work in the houses of white people [*los blancos*], where they would make them cut their hair so as 'not to see their "disheveled, bad hair" [*pasas revueltas*]'" (24). In one of the moves within Santiago, Castillo Bueno ends up living "on the frontier of the zone of tolerance" (68). There, she takes care of the children of prostitutes, which thus positively encodes Castillo Bueno's endeavors in "illegitimate" labor/reproduction—she is outside capital exchange with "legitimate" white employers; she raises children whose lineage is in dispute—thereby challenging the typical scenarios (literal and symbolic) of Afro-Cuban women's domestic labor/ surrogate motherhood (including its violence, as suggested in the hair cutting).

These earlier (prerevolutionary) signs of the houses of Castillo Bueno inform the text's exemplary use of the trope: a description of her "final" house, one "given" to her by the (now revolutionary) state, as described in a section titled "My House!" (¡Mi casa!) in the book's final chapter.

> I have lived in this development [*reparto*] for thirty-five years. It is relatively new; it was constructed after the triumph of the Revolution. They gave me the house for being the mother of a martyr. . . . It is called 30 de Noviembre after a historic event. Nearly all the houses look alike; they are spacious and have a big garden. It seems they made it just for me, since I am still enjoying gardening. I think the Virgencita [in original] had a lot to do with my having my own house, a house of my own.
>
> It was right here where I had to do something that has always weighed on me. You know that I had the picture of the Virgin on the wall facing the street, but when your niece María Elena gained membership into the Party, she came home one day—she lived with me—and said to me: "Grandmother, I would like you to remove that image from the living room. We don't believe in that and it

embarrasses me when my comrades come over and see it there. Why don't you put it in your bedroom?"

I have the same faith in the Virgin that I have always had. But times change. I understood my granddaughter and put it in my bedroom. In the position it's in it's visible from the living room. . . . I know it's not pretty and it's even quite faded. It's almost three-quarters of a century old! . . .

In this house I have had more happy moments than sad. Here I saw you graduate from the university; this has been the place where nearly all my granddaughters and some of my grandsons have chosen to get married; it was where we celebrated the return of my son Nené, my granddaughter Chabela, and other grandchildren from their internationalist missions in Africa, where they fulfilled a double duty, the duty of solidarity and the duty they indirectly had to the land of my grandmother [*la tierra de mi abuela*]. (149–50)

Located in Santiago/Oriente, *Reyita*'s Afro-Cuban-occupied house, like the *bajareque* in *Cuban Roots*, counters the Havana-centricity of the trope, even as it challenges the "uninhabitability" of the *bajareque* with its location in an early 1960s "*reparto*" whose purpose, in line with Urban Reform, was to correct conditions of poor, unaffordable, or absent *viviendas* on the island. As such a *reparto* dwelling—one named for the date of a 1956 anti-Batista uprising in Santiago—Castillo Bueno's house is outside the return itineraries of Cuban American whiteness. Instead, its origins in the revolutionary state suggest different relations between the house and *lo blanco criollo*: Castillo Bueno's *casa mía* was built during the moment of massive "white flight" from Cuba that was the first-wave exile, while her moving into the *casa* brought to an end years of itinerant habitation produced, in part, by the unhappy relationship with her white husband—a relationship symbolic of her negotiations with white supremacy. The house also traces the *blanco criollo* power of its "owner," the (socialist) Cuban nation-state, whose white elites in leadership, with their formative "Eurocentric values,"[67] used initiatives such as Urban Reform to challenge historical structures of inequality in class terms, even as they "normalized and erased," through their silence on the matter, the ways in which whiteness was constitutive of (the pasts, presents, and futures of) such inequality.

Yet, less a conclusion to Castillo Bueno's earlier moves and labors, the house in the *reparto* represents her reorganizing them under a new roof, one under which, indeed, she also resettles her identity in relation to grand/motherhood, "real" and surrogate, and the "homework" of Afro-Cuban femininity: the "domestic" labor of cleaning and cooking for others that she would do inside her own, but not inside someone else's, house. A sign of this reorganization and resettlement is her managing the aesthetics of the state-built house and *reparto*. She recognizes that the houses all "look alike" (*se parecen*), a critical statement indicative of her coming to terms with a signal fact of the built environment: its homogeneity. Also critical in its creativity is her gardening, which, indeed, tells the story of the hybrid forces, politically and economically, bearing on the construction of the house and *reparto*. Specifically, drawing on money from the still-existing National Lottery, the early-revolutionary centralizing state employed its own architects and laborers, but also still-existing private contractors and self-employed workers, to build *viviendas* in the form of "individual housing" that "responded to the value system of the petit bourgeoisie," an example of which, in fact, was the very "reparto 30 de Noviembre," with its "isolated dwelling [*vivienda aislada*], surrounded by a small garden and equipped with a garage."[68] The significance is that Castillo Bueno inhabits a house that in its early 1960s origins was residual of the "bourgeois" past in a way that her 1990s narrative, located in the Special Period, suggests its own relations to the "reemergence" of capital on the island, a relation that Elizabeth Dore captures well by explaining that "few books of any kind were published [during the Special Period] because of shortages of paper," making *Reyita*, a finalist for the Casa de las Américas Prize, an exception. Dore reminds us that the book "did not circulate widely, and was available only at 'dollar shops,'" which, in the context of dollar remittances reaching the island mainly from white Cuban Americans, suggests that "Afro-Cubans might have had even less access to *Reyita* than white Cubans."[69]

Under this roof, then, Castillo Bueno reorganizes her history in reproduction and grand/motherhood, which includes a memory of both the "illegitimate" children of the sex industry and her own dead son, whose martyrdom she cites as a reason for the state's granting her the house.[70] Here, too, are her living grandchildren, in whose careers Cuban internationalism in Africa and their maternal great-great-grandmother's African identity converge: a commingling of their respective "returns" to Africa. And there is Castillo Bueno's assertion that the Virgen de la Caridad del Cobre, Cuba's patron saint, also had "a lot to do" with her acquiring the house. The "*mulata*" Virgen, who is also the *orisha* Ochún in *regla de ocha/santería*, offers another explanation for her acquiring the house, one based on Castillo Bueno's lifelong devotional practices, and it is controversial, as the niece's request makes clear. Castillo Bueno moves the statue from its place on the living-room wall facing the street to her bedroom. Locating it there, she reassures us that it is still visible from the living room, thus enacting her particular transformation (indeed, occupation) of the house, connecting the privacy of the bedroom to the quasi-privacy of the living room and, from there, the public possibilities of the street.

Conclusion: "Write the Word *Black* Twice"

A few years ago, I discovered an article in a Spanish-language newspaper in Washington, DC, that, returning to it now, I realize connects to my work in a way I had failed to anticipate. It describes the lives of Latinas/os of African descent in the area, and it makes a striking claim: while "in some studies" they are known "as Afro-Latinos [*afrolatinos*] or Afro-Hispanics [*afrohispanos*]," in "our community" they "are called '*morenos*' [in original]."[1] I place my work among those "studies" that, as the article says, view Afro-Cuban Americans as "Afro-Latinos" (if not as "Afro-Hispanics," a term that, in any case, at least modifies the compromised "Hispanic" in the direction of an African-diasporic meaning). The acknowledgment of a category of "*afrolatinos*," and hence the tacit validation of an (academic) inquiry into *afrolatinidad*, comes with a catch: those who "mention *afrolatinos*" seem to stand for a "them," a gathering whose implied outsider status puts it (and its forms of knowledge) in contrast with those on the inside, a favored location from which the newspaper speaks as an "us." And that "us" is "our community" (*nuestra comunidad*), a pan-Latino grouping with its own way of "calling" Afro-Latinas/os: as "*morenos*."

I am a white Cuban American who lives in Adams Morgan and teaches in the English department at George Washington University, so I find myself in both places, an author of "some studies" (*algunos estudios*), a member of *nuestra comunidad*. I remark how a Latino print culture in the early twenty-first century surfaces the very same word for

Afro-Latinas/os in "our community" that *La Prensa* used in the 1920s to describe Alberto O'Farrill's *teatro bufo* at the Apolo, descriptions in which the word did the work of a double euphemism: *moreno* as a nicer *negro*, *moreno* as a nicer *negrito*. The DC newspaper displaces the *negro* in favor of the *moreno* in order to intimate that the proper subjects of a *negro* identification are others: African Americans. *Morenos*, in contrast, is the word "we" use for "our blacks," who are not (in their identity, in their social and cultural practices) related to African Americans. Such expressions of an unbecoming blackness in the Latino United States— here as an insinuation of a *moreno* superiority over the *negro*—is what the figures in this book, from Alberto O'Farrill and Eusebia Cosme to Cuban Link and Esteban Luis Cárdenas, have engaged, offering, if not a definitive example of what they would "call themselves," then an array of texts on the experiences of Afro-Latino racialization in the United States. The temporality of *moreno*—its past in *La Prensa* and present in an early twenty-first-century DC newspaper—confirms the (un)timeliness of my project: the way I have located the Afro- in Cuban America (and, along the way, the whiteness of Cuban America, too) in and beyond the archives of literature and performance.

A prime example of the past and the present of race and *latinidad* in Afro-Cuban American literature is *Black Cuban, Black American: A Memoir* (2000), by Evelio Grillo (1919–2008). *Black Cuban, Black American* recounts events in Grillo's life occurring largely from the 1920s to the 1940s—his youth and adolescence in Ybor City, Florida, and at Dunbar High School in DC, his army experiences in South Asia during World War II—a stretch that aligns Grillo with the major periods of O'Farrill and Cosme, even as the memoir's date of publication marks it as a text of contemporary Latino literature. Indeed, the question of the past and the present is very much at the heart of the publication history of *Black Cuban, Black American*. The book was published by the discipline-altering Arte Público Press as part of its Recovering the U.S. Hispanic Literary Heritage series, under a subimprint, Hispanic Civil Rights. The back of the book suggests more: "Arte Público Press's landmark 'Recovering the U.S. Hispanic Literary Heritage' series has traditionally been devoted to long-lost literary and historical works by Hispanics of many decades—even centuries—past. Publication of *Black Cuban, Black American: A Memoir* marks the first work by a living author in this series. The reason for this unprecedented honor can be seen in Evelio Grillo's path-breaking life."[2]

Grillo's relation to Latino recovery is anomalous: the work of an Afro-Cuban American "living author," his text was never lost to begin with.

Indeed, it was Grillo himself, through his agent, who submitted the manuscript to Arte Público for consideration—an act, as it were, of self-recovery.[3] I offer that such a recovery of *Black Cuban, Black American* compensates, in a sense, for the "irrecoverability" of its earlier-period Afro-Cuban American context (the 1920s through the 1940s of an Afro-Latino modernism) and its two representative figures, according to my version of an Afro-Cuban American cultural history: O'Farrill and Cosme. O'Farrill's and Cosme's irrecoverability is due, in part, to the ephemerality of their performance texts. Beyond that, as I have demonstrated, the fact of their *afrolatinidad* in the entertainment industries of the early twentieth-century Americas made finding work and, therefore, leaving a (recoverable) trace even more difficult. In *Black Cuban, Black American*, a "living author" articulates these dead ones; he offers his text in a way that recalls, even as it takes, their places.

A further connection to the *moreno* (as haunted by the *negro*) is the official "colored" identification of Grillo's island-born, Afro-Cuban parents, as marked on his Florida birth certificate, as well as Grillo's own "colored" identity as a member of the 823rd Engineer Aviator Battalion (Colored) during World War II.[4] His engagement with "African Americanization"—in fact, his "passing" as African American—structures *Black Cuban, Black American*, which includes accounts of the many African American mentors and institutions responsible for Grillo's upward mobility. Yet, even as he engaged in African Americanization practices, Grillo was conscious of the difference his *afrolatinidad* made. In a 2007 conversation that I had the pleasure of sharing with him in Oakland, Grillo remarked to me, apropos of his book title, "It pleases me that I have to write the word *black* twice," a self-reflective comment, as I understand it, channeling a special insight: that the multiple "blacks" of the title, neither interchangeable nor unrelated, hint at the social collaboration between Afro-Latinas/os and African Americans characterizing Grillo's life, a collaboration that finds expression in the artistic pleasure Grillo admits taking in the seemingly repetitive—but, in fact, different—act of writing the word(s) "twice."[5]

Shadowing *Black Cuban, Black American* are two Grillo archival sites whose contents escape the book's boundaries. It is these sites that offer tangible evidence of the Grillo text as a *fragment arraché*. The first is in Oakland, Grillo's longtime home, the place where he made his biggest impact in community work. There, at the house of his son, Judge Evelio Grillo, Jr., one finds boxes containing letters, manuscripts, clippings, and photos of Grillo's postwar work with "large populations of Negro and of Mexican-American residents," as well as his post-Tampa connection to Cuba—in particular, a mention of his translations on behalf of the National Council of Negro Women of the United States, which had organized a visit to Cuba in 1940 that involved other members of the Grillo family, including his sister Sylvia, mother Amparo, and brother Enrique ("Henry"), who, a year earlier, as we saw, had supported Cosme's Armstrong performance.[6] What lends even greater meaning to the Oakland materials is that the Schomburg Center for Research in Black Culture had declined to acquire them, thus marking them as uninstitutional in a way suggestive of what the Cosme Papers may have looked like before Eileen Charbo's intervention.[7] The other Grillo archival site is the Anacostia Community Museum of the Smithsonian Institution, located in the Anacostia neighborhood in southeast DC, a city that, like Oakland, has a powerful meaning in the life of Grillo. The origins of the small collection here are in a 2004 presentation that Grillo made at the museum, during which he deposited a manuscript copy of *Black Cuban, Black American* under its original title, "Tally Wop"—a term ("Italian without papers") among Tampa Anglo whites for Afro-Cubans that Grillo discarded with some reservation, for, as he put it, it was "a frank, open statement about who I am."[8] And there are the other archival traces of Grillo, such as those at the Moorland-Spingarn Research Center at Howard University. There, the Alain Locke Papers contain letters between the two in which Grillo describes himself working for Locke as an assistant during the Dunbar years and later, during the war, making port in Africa, where he "thought of [Locke] often . . . , remembering . . . how great [his] interest in that land is."[9]

Yet there is a another group of Grillo fragments, and these are the ones I want to end with: the nine issues of the online journal *Asili: The Journal of Multicultural Heartspeak*, which serialized the chapters of *Black Cuban, Black American* beginning in 1997. No mention of this earlier publication history appears in the Arte Público publication. With the first installment, the journal's editor, Joseph McNair, wrote, "This memoir is a work in progress. We are serializing this work and presenting it for public exposure because of the important insights it brings to the relationships of Americans and Cubans of African descent. As is his wont, Mr. Grillo may choose to revise any of these revelations, which may cause the final version to differ from what is seen here. We are grateful to our elder brother, our griot and scribe, that he has consented to release these papers to *Asili* for preliminary publication."[10] The *Asili* record, otherwise unrecognized, knits Grillo's experiences from the

1920s with early twenty-first-century Cuban Miami. McNair, who had known Grillo years earlier in Oakland activist circles, is on the faculty at Miami-Dade College (formerly Miami-Dade Community College), North Campus. Grillo was the one who reached out, contacting McNair about publishing the manuscript. A few years later, with *Black Cuban, Black American* already in print, McNair invited Grillo to Dade-North, and he accepted. Rightfully, it was a visit for which many Afro-Cuban Americans turned out—a Miami diaspora, doubled.[11]

Notes

Introduction

1. "Ideales" ran from 1928 to 1931. Urrutia also wrote "Armonías" (Harmonies), a column that well outlived the Sunday page, only ceasing with its author's death in 1958. Guillén, later known as Cuba's national poet, first published his influential poems "Motivos de son" (*Son* Motifs) in "Ideales" in 1930. Rafael Serra, with whom José Martí collaborated, founded La Liga in New York City in 1890, a society that offered night-school classes to people of African descent from the Hispanophone Caribbean.

2. José Ramón León, "La doctora Serra de González Veranes," *Adelante* 2.16 (September 1936): 20; "Takes Course While on 'Little Vacation,'" *New York Amsterdam News*, 7/25/1936: 6.

3. Nicolás Guillén, "Señorita Consuelo Serra," *Diario de la Marina*, 12/1/1929: sec. 4, p. 5. Unless otherwise noted, all translations are mine.

4. Ibid.

5. Work needs to be done on the full extent of Consuelo Serra's life and writing. She founded a residential school for girls (Escuela Hogar Consuelo Serra) and taught normal school in Havana. She later earned graduate degrees in pedagogy and philosophy. Her writing appeared in *El Diario de la Marina* and, during the mid-1930s, in the Afro-Cuban journal *Adelante*, for which she wrote a column on pedagogy. She returned to New York City for the first time in 1936. "Takes Course," 6. Education, of course, was primary in Rafael Serra's program for Afro-Cuban liberation.

6. Miguel Gualba, "Consuelo Serra y Heredia," *El Nuevo Criollo*, 6/18/1905, in Rafael Serra, *Para negros y para blancos: Ensayos políticos, sociales, y económicos, cuarte serie*, 120–22 (Havana: Imprenta "El Score," 1907), 121. *El Nuevo Criollo* was a newspaper founded and edited by Rafael Serra.

7. Guillén, "Señorita Consuelo Serra."

8. Brent Edwards, *The Practice of Diaspora: Literature, Translation, and the Rise of Black Internationalism* (Cambridge: Harvard University Press, 2003), 12–13. Edwards, "The Uses of Diaspora," *Social Text* 19.1 (2001): 45–73, is his account of the concept.

9. Brent Edwards, "Pebbles of Consonance: A Reply to Critics," *Small Axe* 9.1 (2005): 135.

10. Ricardo Ortiz, *Cultural Erotics in Cuban America* (Minneapolis: University of Minnesota Press, 2007), 2–8. The Clifford text is *Routes: Travel and Translation in the Late Twentieth Century* (Cambridge: Harvard University Press, 1997).

11. Ada Ferrer, *Insurgent Cuba: Race, Nation, and Revolution, 1868–1898* (Chapel Hill: University of North Carolina Press, 1999), discusses the nineteenth-century discourse of the postracial, in which a postindependence Cuban national identity renders unnecessary (and, indeed, unpatriotic and potentially treasonous) Afro-Cuban public self-identifications. Vera Kutzinski, *Sugar's Secrets: Race and the Erotics of Cuban Nationalism* (Charlottesville: University of Virginia Press, 1993), and Robin Moore, *Nationalizing Blackness: Afrocubanismo and Artistic Revolution in Havana, 1920–1940* (Pittsburgh: University of Pittsburgh Press, 1997), chart Cuban *mestizaje*, a highly eroticized and gendered ideology of the nation as a mixed-race construction developing in tension with the postracial over the twentieth century. Alejandro de la Fuente, *A Nation for All: Race, Inequality, and Politics in Twentieth-Century Cuba* (Chapel Hill: University of North Carolina Press, 2001), describes how Afro-Cubans from a variety of political and class backgrounds participated in twentieth-century republican and revolutionary Cuban state and civil society institutions to realize, against great odds and often unsuccessfully, the promise of a Cuban postracial/*mestizo* "nation for all."

12. De la Fuente, *A Nation for All*, includes a political history of Afro-Cuban civil society before 1959; Stephan Palmié, *Wizards and Scientists: Explorations in Afro-Cuban Modernity and Tradition* (Durham: Duke University Press, 2002), reads across Cuba's African-diasporic religious institutions and practices. See also Alejandra Bronfman, *Measures of Equality: Social Science, Citizenship, and Race in Cuba, 1902–1940* (Chapel Hill: University of North Carolina Press, 2004).

13. See Aline Helg, *Our Rightful Share: The Afro-Cuban Struggle for Equality, 1886–1912* (Chapel Hill: University of North Carolina Press, 1995), 162–226; Ruiz Suárez, *The Color Question in the Two Americas*, trans. John Crosby Gordon (New York: Hunt, 1922). A section of *Color Question* deals with 1912.

14. Even though I do not engage the rich theoretical work of Deleuze and Guattari and especially later feminist critics on "becoming" (*devenir*) that my use of the term in its negation implies, I nevertheless recognize their insights regarding the concept's always moving, multidirectional, recomposing force in accounts of an array of biosocial organisms. See Gilles Deleuze and Félix Guattari, *A Thousand Plateaus: Capitalism and Schizophrenia*, trans. Brian Massumi (Minneapolis: University of Minnesota Press, 1987); and Ian Buchanan and Claire Colebrook, eds., *Deleuze and Feminist Theory* (Edinburgh: Edinburgh University Press, 2000).

15. Suárez, *Color Question*, 22, 24, 26, 34. I have been unable to locate a Spanish-language original. Ruiz Suárez, a lawyer, published poetry in Cuba—*Vibraciones: Producciones poéticas* (Havana: Gutiérrez y Compañía, n.d.)—and later a booklet in the United States: *Maceo: Liberator of Cuba* (Tampa, FL: Tampa Bulletin, 1924). The latter (in English, with no indication of a translation from Spanish) was included in the library of the Unión Martí-Maceo, the important twentieth-century Afro-Cuban American club in Tampa, Florida; Shelf One, La Unión Martí-Maceo Collection, Special Collections, University of South Florida Library.

16. Jorge Ulla and Miñuca Villaverde, *Dos filmes de Mariel* (Madrid: Editorial Playor, 1986), 72.

17. On desire against "the good," fantasy, and enjoyment in nationalism, see Slavoj Žižek, *Tarrying with the Negative: Kant, Hegel, and the Critique of Ideology* (Durham: Duke University Press, 1993), 200–237, particularly the argument on the other as "thief" of national enjoyment in the supremacist imagination.

18. H. G. Carrillo, *Loosing My Espanish* (New York: Pantheon Books, 2004), 21.

19. José Piedra, "Literary Whiteness and the Afro-Hispanic Difference," *New Literary History* 18.2 (Winter 1987): 303–32, is a key critical account of the way in which the early-modern consolidation of Spanish—*castellano*—constituted Spanish-colonial (and later Latin American national) power, in particular by allowing its nonwhite subjects literacy (and "citizenship") through the language, so long as they avoided self-representations of racial difference, the very dictate Carrillo's narrator upends. See also Ana Margarita Cervantes-Rodríguez and Amy Lutz, "Coloniality of Power, Immigration, and the English-Spanish Asymmetry in the United States," *Nepantla: Views from South* 4.3 (2003): 523–60.

20. Michelle Ann Stephens, *Black Empire: The Masculine Global Imaginary of Caribbean Intellectuals in the United States, 1914–1962* (Durham: Duke University Press, 2005), 6.

21. Gustavo Urrutia, "Imperialismo afrocubano," *Diario de la Marina*, 3/1/1936: 2.

22. Schomburg to Urrutia, 2/6/1936, "Letters by Arthur Schomburg, 1914–1938," Box 9, Folder 21, Arthur A. Schomburg Papers, 1724–1895 (1904–1938), Schomburg Center for Research in Black Culture, New York Public Library.

23. For the volume in question, see Gustavo Urrutia, *Armonías, por Gustavo E. Urrutia*, Havana, 1931 (?), the Schomburg Center for Research in Black Culture, Jean Blackwell Hutson General Research and Reference Division, New York Public Library. The oversized volume contains selected broadsheets of "Ideales" over the course of the page's run; it also contains several broadsheet selections of "La Marcha de una Raza" (The March of a Race), a "successor" page to "Ideales" authored by the Afro-Cuban Lino D'Ou in the Havana daily *El Mundo*. On Schomburg as both an African American and mainland Afro–Puerto Rican figure, see Lisa Sánchez González, *Boricua Literature: A Literary History of the Puerto Rican Diaspora* (New York: NYU Press, 2001), 42–70.

24. W. A. Domingo, "Gift of the Black Tropics," in *The New Negro*, ed. Alain Locke (1925; repr., New York: Macmillan, 1992), 342.

25. Ira Reid, *The Negro Immigrant* (New York: Columbia University Press, 1939), 101.

26. Jairo Moreno, "Bauzá—Gillespie—Latin/Jazz: Difference, Modernity, and the Black Caribbean," *South Atlantic Quarterly* 103.1 (Winter 2004): 86, my italics. Moreno is discussing musicians in the passage. The Afro-Cuban Juan Mallea, a president of the Unión Martí-Maceo, recalled that, in early twentieth-century Tampa, "if you spoke Spanish you were considered black" and that "Spanish-speaking whites were considered black"; Enrique Cordero, *Preliminary Research Report, Part Two: The Afro-Cuban Community in Tampa, Florida*, 1984, 13, Special Collections, University of South Florida Library.

27. "Graciela Pérez, Interviewed in Her Home, 141 W. 73rd Street, by René López and Raúl Fernández," interview date 9/19/1998, Jazz Oral History Project, Collection

Number 808, Series 2, Box 33, Tape One, Side A, Oral History Program of the National Museum of American History, Smithsonian Institution.

28. "Interview of Bauzá by Anthony Brown, New York City, September 9, 1992," Jazz Oral History Project, Collection Number 808, Series 2, Box 4, Tape One, Side Two, Oral History Program of the National Museum of American History, Smithsonian Institution.

29. The literature in this area is voluminous. I have already mentioned the work of Helg, Moore, Ferrer, de la Fuente, Palmié, and Bronfman. See also Sujatha Fernandes, *Cuba Represent! Cuban Arts, State Power, and the Making of New Revolutionary Cultures* (Durham: Duke University Press), 2006. Tomás Fernández Robaina has made important island-based contributions—for example, *El negro en Cuba, 1902–1958: Apuntes para la historia de la lucha contra la discriminación racial* (Havana: Editorial de Ciencias Sociales, 1990).

30. A selection of Afro-Hispanist criticism appears in Miriam DeCosta, ed., *Blacks in Hispanic Literature: Critical Essays* (Port Washington, NY: Kennikat, 1977). Richard L. Jackson, *Black Writers in Latin America* (Albuquerque: University of New Mexico Press, 1979), is a text by one of its key figures. See also Roberto Márquez, "Raza, Racismo e Historia: 'Are All My Bones from There,'" *Latino(a) Research Review* 4.3 (2000): 8–22. Kutzinski, *Sugar's Secrets*, is, in many respects, a critique of Afro-Hispanism.

31. See, for example, Nancy Morejón, *Nación y mestizaje en Nicolás Guillén* (Havana: Unión de Escritores y Artistas de Cuba, 1982). A recent island-situated critique of race and Cuban literature by an Afro-Cuban intellectual is Roberto Zurbano, "El triángulo invisible del siglo XX cubano: Raza, literatura, y nación," *Temas* 46 (April–June 2006): 111–23.

32. See Lourdes Casal and Yolanda Prieto, "Black Cubans in the United States: Basic Demographic Information," in *Female Immigrants to the United States: Caribbean, Latin American, and African Experiences*, ed. Delores M. Mortimer and Roy S. Bryce-Laporte, 314–48 (Washington, DC: Research Institute on Immigration and Ethnic Studies, Smithsonian Institution, 1981), appearing posthumously, with Prieto's final writing and editing; Nancy Mirabal, "'Ser De Aquí': Beyond the Cuban Exile Model," *Latino Studies* 1.3 (November 2003): 366–82, and "Scripting Race, Finding Place: African Americans, Afro-Cubans, and the Diasporic Imaginary in the United States," in *Neither Enemies nor Friends: Latinos, Blacks, Afro-Latinos*, ed. Anani Dzidzienyo and Suzanne Oboler, 189–207 (New York: Palgrave, 2005); Susan Greenbaum, *More Than Black: Afro-Cubans in Tampa* (Gainesville: University Press of Florida, 2002); and Frank Guridy, *Forging Diaspora: Afro-Cubans and African Americans in a World of Empire and Jim Crow* (Chapel Hill: University of North Carolina Press, 2010), which offers a view not only of relations between Afro-Cubans and African Americans on the island but of Afro-Cuban migrant experiences in the United States (for example, as students in black colleges and universities).

33. The work on these topics is extensive. See Frances Aparicio, "The Blackness of Sugar: Celia Cruz and the Performance of (Trans)nationalism," *Cultural Studies* 13.2 (1999): 223–36; Raquel Rivera, *New York Ricans from the Hip Hop Zone* (New York: Palgrave Macmillan, 2003); Moreno, "Bauzá—Gillespie—Latin/Jazz"; and David García, *Arsenio Rodríguez and the Transnational Flows of Latin Popular Music* (Philadelphia: Temple University Press, 2006), for discussions of Afro-Cuban Americans, among other Afro-Latinas/os, in music from the Cuban *son* and Latin jazz to salsa

and rap. Adrián Burgos, *Playing America's Game: Baseball, Latinos, and the Color Line* (Berkeley: University of California Press, 2007), includes the participation of Afro-Cuban Americans.

34. Juan Flores, "Islands and Enclaves: Caribbean Latinos in Historical Perspective," in *Latinos Remaking America*, ed. Marcelo M. Suárez-Orozco and Mariela M. Páez (Berkeley: University of California Press, 2002), 68. Miriam Jiménez Román and Juan Flores, eds., *The Afro-Latin@ Reader: History and Culture in the United States* (Durham: Duke University Press, 2010). See also Flores, *From Bomba to Hip-Hop: Puerto Rican Culture and Latino Identity* (New York: Columbia University Press, 2000), and *The Diaspora Strikes Back: Caribeño Tales of Learning and Turning* (New York: Routledge, 2009). *The Afro-Latin@ Reader* contains a section on Schomburg, which reminds us of the important place of scholarship on him and other mainland Afro–Puerto Ricans such as Jesús Colón and Piri Thomas (who is also of Afro-Cuban descent) in these discussions. See, for example, William Luis, "Black Latinos Speak: The Politics of Race in Piri Thomas's *Down These Mean Streets*," *Indiana Journal of Hispanic Literatures* 12 (1998): 27–49. Another volume with an explicit commitment to Afro-Latino issues is Dzidzienyo and Oboler, eds., *Neither Enemies nor Friends: Latinos, Blacks, Afro-Latinos*, while the journal *Latino Studies*, since its inception, has proven itself a venue for afrolatinidad. See Anani Dzidzienyo, "Coming to Terms with the African Connection in Latino Studies," *Latino Studies* 1.1 (March 2003): 160–67; Tanya Katerí Hernández, "'Too Black to Be Latino/a': Blackness and Blacks as Foreigners in Latino Studies," *Latino Studies* 1.1 (March 2003): 152–59; and the special issue "Race and Blackness in the Latino/a Community," *Latino Studies* 8.2 (Summer 2010). The work of Silvio Torres-Saillant on blackness in the Dominican Republic and its diaspora also reflects an overt commitment to *afrolatinidad*. See "The Tribulations of Blackness: Stages in Dominican Racial Identity," *Callaloo* 23.3 (2000): 1086–1111, and "Afro-Latinas/os and the Racial Wall," in *A Companion to Latina/o Studies*, ed. Juan Flores and Renato Rosaldo, 363–75 (Oxford, UK: Blackwell, 2007).

35. Rodrigo Lazo, *Writing to Cuba: Filibustering and Cuban Exiles in the United States* (Chapel Hill: University of North Carolina Press, 2005); Ortiz, *Cultural Erotics*; Laura Lomas, *Translating Empire: José Martí, Migrant Latino Subjects, and American Modernities* (Durham: Duke University Press, 2008).

36. Édouard Glissant, *Poétique de la relation* (Paris: Gallimard, 1990), 83, translated by Betsy Wing as *Poetics of Relation* (Ann Arbor: University of Michigan Press, 1997), 69 (translation modified).

37. David Scott, "On the Archaeologies of Black Memory," *Small Axe* 26.12 (June 2008): vii.

1 / Alberto O'Farrill

1. Gustavo Urrutia, "El teatro cubano," *Diario de la Marina*, 4/21/1929: sec. 4, p. 11. Nicolás Guillén, "El camino de Harlem," *Diario de la Marina*, 4/21/1929: sec. 4, p. 11.

2. On other barrio categories in Chicano history and culture, see Raúl Homero Villa, *Barrio-Logos: Space and Place in Urban Chicano Literature and Culture* (Austin: University of Texas Press, 2000).

3. Bronfman, *Measures of Equality*, 137–38. On the cultures of *mestizaje* in relation to *afrocubanismo*—a major cultural movement of the 1920s and 1930s that produced

"stylized" versions of Afro-Cuban working-class culture—see Moore, *Nationalizing Blackness*.

4. *Raza de color*, a term with origins in the late nineteenth century that intended to unify *negras/os* and *mulatas/os* across class lines, by the first decades of the twentieth century came under increasing social stress. See de la Fuente, *A Nation for All*, 149–71.

5. Mirabal, "Scripting Race," 201–2.

6. Virginia E. Sánchez Korrol, *From Colonia to Community: The History of Puerto Ricans in New York City* (Berkeley: University of California Press, 1983), 55. Mirabal, "Scripting Race," 197–202, discusses Afro-Cuban migration to the United States during the period, while Greenbaum, *More Than Black*, 233–38, speaks to the particular 1930s migrations of white Cubans and Afro-Cubans from Tampa to New York City. Estimations are that, in 1930, nearly 19,000 Cubans were living in the United States (Mirabal, "Scripting Race," 200). Of these, according to the 1930 census, 2,362 were Cuban-born "Negroes." See Reid, *Negro Immigrant*, 237. After the Immigration Act of 1924, Cubans were nonquota immigrants, unlike, for example, Caribbean subjects of the British empire. Winston James cites estimations of Puerto Ricans in New York City of between 53,000 (minimalist) and 200,000 (maximalist) in 1930 and notes the difficulty of determining the number of Afro–Puerto Ricans among them, a cautious approach well suited also to estimations of Afro-Cubans in the United States, given the variables in how census takers might or might not have "counted" a Cuban as Afro-Cuban or how a Cuban might or might not have self-identified as Afro-Cuban. See James, *Holding Aloft the Banner of Ethiopia: Caribbean Radicalism in Early Twentieth-Century America* (New York: Routledge, 1999), 197. On the history of Puerto Migration to New York City in the early twentieth century, See Sánchez Korrol, *From Colonia to Community*. See also Irma Watkins-Owens, *Blood Relations: Caribbean Immigrants and the Harlem Community, 1900–1930* (Bloomington: Indiana University Press, 1996), on the history of Anglophone Caribbean migrations.

7. Also emerging around this time, of course, was African American Harlem, a key space of culture and politics in which developments such as "the 'New Negro' movement," with its "themes of cultural nationalism, civil rights protest, and uplift," represented "at the same time a 'new' black internationalism," which hinged on practices of translation among African and African-diasporic literary and political figures, including, but not limited to, their participation in institutions such as the Communist International, the Universal Negro Improvement Association, and the Pan-African Congress. Edwards, *Practice of Diaspora*, 2.

8. Ali Behdad, "*Une Pratique Sauvage*: Postcolonial Belatedness and Cultural Politics," in *The Pre-occupation of Postcolonial Studies*, ed. Fawzia Afzal-Khan and Kalpana Seshadri-Crooks, 71–85 (Durham: Duke University Press, 2000).

9. Ancestry.com, *Florida Passenger Lists, 1898–1951* (Provo, UT: Generations Network, 2006).

10. Mae M. Ngai, *Impossible Subjects: Illegal Aliens and the Making of Modern America* (Princeton: Princeton University Press, 2004), 37, 38, 41.

11. Ibid., 24. Reid, in *Negro Immigrant*, remarks that "'Africans, black' is the cover-all term employed by the Bureau of Immigration and Naturalization to cloak with racial identification all persons of Negro extraction admitted to or departing from the United States. It is a conjure-word that metamorphoses persons who, prior to

embarking for the United States, may have been known as 'coloured,' 'mulatto,' or 'black,' or, who had not been grouped by race or color" (24).

12. *Florida: Semenario Independiente*, 9/26/1925: 6. The San Carlos, dating to 1871, was central to the nineteenth-century independence movement, hosting organizing and fund-raising visits by Antonio Maceo and José Martí. See Gerald E. Poyo, *"With All, and for the Good of All": The Emergence of Popular Nationalism in the Cuban Communities of the United States, 1848–1898* (Durham: Duke University Press, 1989). Nicolás Kanellos locates the Arango-Moreno at the white-Cuban Círculo Cubano club in Tampa in the spring of 1925 and says the company included an "all-black cast," which was "unusual" at the time. The implication, although unclear, is that "all black" was "all Afro-Cuban"—which is to say, all Afro-Cuban actors (in blackface?) rather than white Cubans (in blackface). Kanellos, *A History of Hispanic Theatre in the United States: Origins to 1940* (Austin: University of Texas Press, 1990), 163.

13. Rosendo Rosell, *Vida y milagros de la farándula de Cuba* (Miami: Ediciones Universal, 1992), 19. The racial identity of Pous is a matter of uncertainty. Recognized as the most accomplished writer and performer of Cuban blackface in the early twentieth century, Pous, who died in 1926, is at times called "white" (he "was one of the few white actors capable of dancing various distinct forms of rumba" [Moore, *Nationalizing Blackness*, 48]), at times "black" ("Pous, who was black" [Kenya C. Dworkin y Méndez, "Cuban Theater, American Stage: Before Exile," in *The State of Latino Theater in the United States*, ed. Luis A. Ramos-García, 103–30 (New York: Routledge, 2002), 111]). In a tape-recorded interview, Alberto Socarrás, the major Afro-Cuban flutist, composer, and arranger, recalled working in Pous's orchestra in Cuba in the early 1920s. Speaking in English, Socarrás says that Pous "was not white, but he was not black neither," at which point his interviewer, the music historian and journalist Max Salazar, interrupts, saying, "mulato." Socarrás replies, "was a mulato." "Alberto Socarrás Oral History," interview by Max Salazar, New York, New York, January 16, 1983, Jazz Oral History Project, John Cotton Dana Library, Rutgers University, Newark, New Jersey. I discuss Socarrás later in this chapter. On the particulars of Pous's performance, see Moore, *Nationalizing Blackness*, 48.

14. Moore, *Nationalizing Blackness*, 45.

15. See Jill Lane, *Blackface Cuba, 1840–1895* (Philadelphia: University of Pennsylvania Press, 2005), for the relations between Cuban nationalism, independence, and nineteenth-century Cuban blackface.

16. Kanellos, *History of Hispanic Theatre*, 138; Nicolás Kanellos, *Hispanic Periodicals in the United States, Origins to 1960: A Brief History and Comprehensive Bibliography* (Houston: Arte Público, 2000), 54. Another scholar responsible for O'Farrill's appearance in Latino studies is Alejandra Balestra, who identified O'Farrill as the writer behind the pseudonyms of Domifá and Gavitofa in *Gráfico*. Balestra, "Alberto O'Farrill y Jesús Colón: Dos Cronistas en Nueva York," in *Recovering the U.S. Hispanic Literary Heritage*, vol. 4, ed. José F. Aranda, Jr., and Silvio Torres-Saillant, 133–44 (Houston: Arte Público, 2002).

17. Alberto O'Farrill, "Easy Jobs," in *Herencia: The Anthology of Hispanic Literature of the United States*, ed. Nicolás Kanellos (Oxford: Oxford University Press, 2002), 372–73.

18. Kanellos, *History of Hispanic Theatre*, 124–25; Kanellos, *Hispanic Periodicals*, 54–55.

19. I am referring to ideas of print culture and counterpublics in Michael Warner, *Publics and Counterpublics* (New York: Zone Books, 2002).

20. Moore, *Nationalizing Blackness*, 42. On white Cuban identity formation through the representation of "improper" Afro-Cuban speech in the *teatro bufo*, see Christina Civantos, "Race/Class/Language: 'El Negro' Speaks Cuban Whiteness in the Teatro Bufo," in *Latin American Theatre Review* 39.1 (2005): 49–69.

21. Lane, *Blackface Cuba*, 3, 237n. 1.

22. Ibid., 2–3. Minor characters included representations of a Chinese immigrant, an Afro-Cuban "witch" (*negra lucumí*), and a white Cuban peasant (*guarjiro*). Moore, *Nationalizing Blackness*, 42, 46. Others reference the character of a poor, white Cuban woman, the *blanca sucia* ("dirty white woman"). Bobby Collazo, *La última noche que pasé contigo* (Hato Rey, Puerto Rico: Editorial Cubanacán, 1987), 13, 167. Variations on the *negrito* included a pompous pseudo-professor (*catédratico*), an African-born slave (*bozal*), a conceited coachman (*calesero*), and others. Moore, *Nationalizing Blackness*, 46–47.

23. Lane, *Blackface Cuba*, x.

24. Moore, *Nationalizing Blackness*, 46.

25. Lane, *Blackface Cuba*, 3; Moore, *Nationalizing Blackness*, 44.

26. Collazo, *La última noche*, 96, 167. During the 1920s, the *negrito* also appeared in the Cuban *zarzuela* (light opera). Susan Thomas, *Cuban Zarzuela: Performing Race and Gender on Havana's Lyric Stage* (Urbana: University of Illinois Press, 2008), 81–108. Moore, *Nationalizing Blackness*, documents a *negrito* performance in Havana in the 1990s (151).

27. Eduardo Robreño, introduction to *Teatro Alhambra: Antología*, ed. Eduardo Robreño (Havana: Editorial Letras Cubanas, 1979), 17–18.

28. Emilio Ballagas, *Antología de poesía negra hispano americana* (Madrid: M. Aguilar, 1935), 19; Consuelo Serra, "El teatro y la preparación de festivales en la educación del pueblo cubano," *Adelante* 1.3 (August 1935): 16.

29. Lane, *Blackface Cuba*, 237n. 1. "Clean" versions of Alhambra performances would open at the Payret theater, whose audience included women and children.

30. Raymond Williams, *Marxism and Literature* (Oxford: Oxford University Press, 1977), 123.

31. Ruth Glasser, *My Music Is My Flag: Puerto Rican Musicians and Their New York Communities, 1917–1940* (Berkeley: University of California Press, 1995), 113–14; emphasis added. Another Latino *bufo* space during the period was Tampa. See Dworkin y Méndez, "Cuban Theater, American Stage."

32. Louis Chude-Sokei, *The Last "Darky": Bert Williams, Black-on-Black Minstrelsy, and the African Diaspora* (Durham: Duke University Press, 2006), 7, 26.

33. Eric Lott, *Love and Theft: Blackface Minstrelsy and the American Working Class* (New York: Oxford University Press, 1993), 39.

34. Rosell, *Vida y milagros*, 370–71.

35. Jill Lane, "ImpersoNation: Toward a Theory of Black-, Red-, and Yellowface in the Americas," *PMLA* 123.5 (October 2008): 1730.

36. My estimation of the number of plays in which O'Farrill appeared derives from my reading of the theater coverage in the New York City Spanish-language newspaper *La Prensa* during the years in question. The number is likely even greater. According to José Luis Perrier, in *Bibliografía dramática cubana* (New York: Phos,

1926), 71, O'Farrill worked on stage and in print in Cuba prior to his migration, directing *Proteo*, a Havana newspaper, and authoring two zarzuelas with likely *bufo* elements, *Un negro misterioso* and *Las pamplinas de Agapito*, both performed in 1921 in Havana's Teatro Esemeralda. Among the New York City *bufos* attributed to O'Farrill from 1926, Perrier cites *Los misterios de Changó* and *Un negro en Andalucía* (which he also calls zarzuelas), while *La Prensa* records *Un doctor accidental, El fantasma de la sopera*, and *Una viuda como no hay dos*. More often, however, the authorship of *bufo* plays was never attributed in the press (Kanellos, *History of Hispanic Theatre*, 137). In any event, New York City *bufo* works were loosely scripted affairs, heavy with ad-libbing, as the Puerto Rican signer, dancer, and actress Diosa Costello recalls; as a teenager in the early 1930s, Costello appeared with O'Farrill on the New York City stage, and she spoke highly of his ad-libbing ability. Diosa Costello, telephone interview, 4/24/2009.

37. Kanellos, *History of Hispanic Theatre*, 123. The Teatro Apolo in question was not the Apollo Theater of current renown (which, in the 1920s, was called the Hurtig and Seamon Theater). Rather, it was a venue located at 211 West 125th Street, on the same block as the Hurtig and Seamon but closer to Seventh Avenue. The Apolo "was a small but elegant 900-seat theatre with a huge stage, located in a space above the foyer of the Schiffman and Brecher's Harlem Opera House." Ted Fox, *Showtime at the Apollo* (New York: Holt, Rinehart, and Winston, 1983), 60. In 1929, the Apolo was renamed the Teatro Español (Kanellos, *History of Hispanic Theatre*, 126). Other theaters in which O'Farrill performed included the Jewell on 116th Street and Fifth Avenue; the Alhambra on Seventh Avenue between 125th and 126th Streets, just around the corner from the Apolo; the Park Palace on 110th Street, near the northeast corner of Central Park; and the Hurtig and Seamon itself.

38. Glasser, *My Music Is My Flag*, 112–13. Among the impresarios who contracted with the Harlem theater ownership during the transformation of 125th Street was an Afro-Cuban, José Antonio Miranda. As the Miranda Brothers, Miranda was instrumental in establishing the Apolo as a Latino venue. See *La Prensa*, 6/23/1926: 6; "Arte Hispano," *La Prensa*, 11/6/1926: 2; "El éxito de la empresa Miranda," *La Prensa*, 4/2/1927: 2; and "Teatro Hispano," *La Prensa*, 6/23/1928: 2. On the origins in general of Latino theater in New York City, see Kanellos, *History of Hispanic Theatre*, 104–21.

39. Kanellos, *Hispanic Periodicals*, 58.

40. "Arte Hispano," *La Prensa*, 8/10/1926: 4.

41. Silvio Torres-Saillant, "Tribulations of Blackness: Stages in Dominican Racial Identity," *Callaloo* 23.3 (2000): 1102.

42. Clara E. Rodríguez, *Changing Race: Latinos, the Census, and the History of Ethnicity in the United States* (New York: NYU Press, 2000), 123.

43. Martha Menchaca, *Recovering History, Constructing Race: The Indian, Black, and White Roots of Mexican Americans* (Austin: University of Texas Press, 2001), 166–67.

44. "Arte Hispano," *La Prensa*, 6/15/1926: 5.

45. "Arte Hispano," *La Prensa*, 7/15/1926: 4.

46. "Arte Hispano," *La Prensa*, 8/3/1926: 4.

47. "Arte Hispano," *La Prensa*, 8/10/1926: 4.

48. Another *La Prensa* term for *negrito* during the period—used, however, less often than *moreno*—was *mulato*.

49. José Buscaglia-Salgado, *Undoing Empire: Race and Nation in the Mulatto Caribbean* (Minneapolis: University of Minnesota Press, 2003), 51.

50. Esteban Pichardo, *Diccionario provincial casi razonado de vozes y frases cubanas* (Havana: Editorial de Ciencias Sociales, 1976), 433.

51. Ibid., 589.

52. "Teatro Hispano," *La Prensa*, 1/24/1928: 2.

53. *Gráfico*, 5/29/1927: 8.

54. "Arte Hispano," *La Prensa*, 10/19/1926: 6.

55. "Vida Teatral," *Gráfico*, 3/20/1927: 5.

56. "Vida Teatral," *Gráfico*, 4/17/1927: 5; "Chismes de la Farándula," *Gráfico*, 5/1/1927: 14.

57. "Vida Teatral," *Gráfico*, 3/6/1927: 3.

58. "En la brega," *Gráfico*, 2/27/1927: 2.

59. "Buzón Secreto," *Gráfico*, 4/3/1927: 13; "Liga Portorriqueña e Hispana," *Gráfico*, 4/3/1927: 13; "El viaje del Presidente Machado," *Gráfico*, 5/1/1927: 9. During *Gráfico*'s first period, its front page typically displayed drawings by O'Farrill of young white women in risqué poses. On these drawings and U.S. gender history, see Martha H. Patterson, introduction to part 8, in *The American New Woman Revisited: A Reader*, ed. Martha H. Patterson (New Brunswick: Rutgers University Press, 2008), 243–44. See also Kanellos, *Hispanic Periodicals*, 54–58.

60. "Los portorriqueños," *Gráfico*, 3/27/1927: 2; "Curvas y rectas," *Gráfico*, 4/17/1927: 3.

61. In this respect, one of *Gráfico*'s most representative texts was "Simonadas" (Simonisms), written by the Catalonian-born, Cuban-raised baker, chef, Cuban-drum technician, and overall wit Simón Jou. See, e.g., "Simonadas," *Gráfico*, 4/24/1927: 6. Jou learned bakery and *pâtisserie* on the island and in France. He moved to New York City in the early 1920s, taking a job at the Hotel McAlpin. Jou eventually opened the bakery La Moderna at 116th Street between Seventh and Eighth Avenues; it later moved to Lenox between 115th and 116th Streets, the Cuban center of early twentieth-century Latino Harlem, where it remained in business until the 1960s. La Moderna is a major space of Latino cultural history: in addition to selling wonderful desserts and cooked meals, Jou sold Cuban musical instruments, which his brother exported from Cuba. Luciano "Chano" Pozo, Graciela Pérez, Frank "Machito" Grillo, Miguelito Valdés, Al McKibbon, and Noro Morales were among the great Cuban, Puerto Rican, and African American musicians who frequented La Moderna. Simón Jou, Jr., interview, Miami, Florida, 6/6/2009; Graciela Pérez, telephone interview, 6/6/2009; Raúl Fernández, interview, Irvine, California, 11/4/2010; Max Salazar, "Alberto Socarrás: The Color of Music," *Latin Beat* (December–January 1993): 27–30; Max Salazar, *Mambo Kingdom: Latin Music in New York* (London: Music Sales Corporation, 2002), 2; Isabelle Leymarie, *Cuban Fire: The Story of Salsa and Latin Jazz* (New York: Continuum, 2003), 194. On the satirical as a sign of the newspaper's Latino working-class identity, see Sánchez Korrol, *From Colonia to Community*, 72.

62. It is important to note that Vega had purchased *Gráfico* on March 20, 1927, four months prior to going public as its editor and president. Rather than choose the former date as the start of *Gráfico*'s second period, I have selected July 24, 1927, in order to emphasize Vega's public acknowledgment of his position. See Bernardo Vega, *Memorias*, ed. César Andreu Iglesias (Río Piedras: Ediciones Huracán, 1984), 182.

63. Juan Flores, introduction to section on Vega, in *Puerto Rican Arrival in New York: Narratives of the Migration, 1920–1950*, ed. Juan Flores (Princeton, NJ: Markus Wiener, 2005), 33. Flores translated the *Memorias* into English: *Memoirs of Bernardo Vega*, ed. César Andreu Iglesias (New York: Monthly Review Press, 1984).

64. See Jesús Colón, *"Lo que el pueblo me dice . . ."* (Houston: Arte Público, 2001), 3–64, for the *Gráfico* writings.

65. "Palabras de aliento," *Gráfico*, 7/24/1927: 8.

66. Vega, *Memorias*, 182.

67. *Gráfico*, 9/11/1927: 2.

68. *Gráfico*, 8/7/1927: 3.

69. *Gráfico*, 8/21/1927: 10.

70. "Cosas que Ud. no verá," *Gráfico*, 9/4/1927: 15.

71. Editorial, *Gráfico*, 9/25/1927: 10.

72. *Gráfico*, 5/15/1927: 8–9; *Gráfico*, 6/11/1927: 8–9.

73. "Chismes de la farandula," *Gráfico*, 5/22/1927: 14.

74. "Ecos de la colonia," *Gráfico*, 6/5/1927: 7; "Lo cuento aunque no lo crean," *Gráfico*, 9/11/1927: 6; "Lo cuento aunque no lo crean," *Gráfico*, 9/18/1927: 9.

75. "Simonadas," *Gráfico*, 4/17/1927: 6.

76. *Gráfico*, 3/18/1928: 2.

77. *Gráfico*, 3/18/1928: 20; *Gráfico*, 3/25/1928: 20; *Gráfico*, 4/15/1928: 21.

78. *Gráfico*, 9/11/1927: 13. "Se dice que a mí no me importa" appeared in August and September of 1927.

79. *Gráfico*, 6/19/1927: 14.

80. I wish to thank Pedro Juan Hernández, Senior Archivist at the Center, for bringing this photograph to my attention.

81. The seeming insensibility of the *negrito* connects to the violent discourses and practices of lynching in the United States in the decades leading up to the Apolo era, during which white supremacy produced an "insensible" black body that suffered the terror of lynching. See Mark Michael Smith, *How Race Is Made: Slavery, Segregation, and the Senses* (Chapel Hill: University of North Carolina Press, 2006), 59.

82. See Edwards, *Practice of Diaspora*, 201–3.

83. Critics have identified the "Pegas" as Latino modernist *crónicas* (chronicles). See Edwin Karli Padilla Aponte, introducción to Colón, *"Lo que el pueblo me dice . . . ,"* xiii–xlix. On the *crónica* in Latin America, see Susana Rotker, *Fundación de una escritura: Las crónicas de José Martí* (Havana: Casa de las Américas, 1992).

84. Nicolás Kanellos, "Recovering and Re-constructing Early Twentieth-Century Hispanic Immigrant Print Culture in the U.S.," *American Literary History* 19.2 (Summer 2007): 446–47.

85. As with the other generally (as well as specifically Cuban) popular terms and phrases O'Farrill uses in "Pegas," I am indicating *chola*'s popular difference by bracketing its "standard" English version in the text, rather than by offering a translation of a comparable English popular term—"noggin," e.g.—a move that would risk smoothing over Latino-Anglo differences in popularity and language.

86. In Cuban popular culture, this phrase suggests the possible malicious effects of stepping outside and "catching" (*coger*) a treacherous puff of cool air or wind (*airecito*, or "little air"), which could give one pneumonia and leave a permanent "crooked neck" (*pescuezo jorobado*).

87. *Gráfico*, 7/10/1927: 12.

88. Chude-Sokei, *The Last "Darky,"* 83. Chude-Sokei is working from Houston Baker's arguments in *Modernism and the Harlem Renaissance* (Chicago: University of Chicago Press, 1987) on biological constructions and racial performance.

89. *Cholos* and *gauchos* in original.

90. *Gráfico*, 7/24/1927: 2; again, my translation. *Gráfico's* own side-by-side English version reads thus: "As a rule, the masses of the American people do believe that the countries South to the Río Grande are inhabited by Toltecs and Mayas, Cholos and Gauchos, living in savage conditions and incapable of civilized life."

91. *Gráfico*, 9/4/1927: 14

92. *Gráfico*, 6/11/1927: 12.

93. According to Michael Rogin, such Jewish American blackface performers signified a "Jewish/black alliance [that] worked better for American Jewish assimilation than did the Jewish/worker alliance for European Jewish cosmopolitanism." *Blackface, White Noise: Jewish Immigrants in the Hollywood Melting Pot* (Berkeley: University of California Press, 1998), 17, 68.

94. Jeffrey S. Gurock, *When Harlem Was Jewish, 1870–1930* (New York: Columbia University Press, 1979), 150.

95. "Trio Held as Police Block Harlem Riot," *New York Times*, 7/27/1926: 21.

96. Vega, *Memorias*, 175; Claude McKay, *Harlem: Negro Metropolis* (1940; repr., New York: Harcourt, Brace, Jovanovich, 1968), 137.

97. Salazar, *Mambo Kingdom*, 22, in reference to Gabriel Oller, the important Puerto Rican owner of a music store and a record label; Joaquín Colón López, *Pioneros puertorriqueños en Nueva York: 1917–1947* (Houston: Arte Público, 2002), 81.

98. Slavoj Žižek, *The Sublime Object of Ideology* (New York: Verso, 1989), 48.

99. Aviva Ben-Ur, *Sephardic Jews in America: A Diasporic History* (New York: NYU Press, 2009), 152.

100. Buscaglia-Salgado, *Undoing Empire*, 63.

101. "Arte Hispano," *Gráfico*, 8/10/1926: 4.

102. "Los teatros españoles" (Spanish Theaters), *Gráfico*, 7/3/1927: 9.

103. "Filosofía barata" (Cheap Philosophy), *Gráfico*, 7/17/1927: 2, italics in original.

104. *Gráfico*, 10/2/1927: 10, my italics.

105. Although the word "*indios*," as "Indians," appears in the English, it soon fades from the editorial, as was the case in the Spanish version, thus marginalizing in the text an already marginalized figure of "uncivilized" indigeneity.

106. Other representations of Latino-Jewish relations in *Gráfico* include Jesús Colón's. In the summer of 1928, Colón published two essays called "¿Quiénes son los judíos?" (Who are the Jews?), summarizing Jewish history with the aim of encouraging understanding between Jews and Latinas/os in Harlem. See Colón, *"Lo que el pueblo me dice . . . ,"* 53–56.

107. *La Prensa*, 3/21/1931: 5.

108. Rine Leal, *Breve historia del teatro cubano* (Havana: Editorial Letras Cubanas, 1980), 76. As Robin Moore shows, the *bufo* "stage rumba" "was a loose adaptation of traditional street rumba" that, in "melodies and lyrics," was "often taken directly from popular compositions, arranged with a harmonic accompaniment, and performed by orchestral instruments [the *timbal* or snare drum] rather than traditional Afrocuban percussion" (*Nationalizing Blackness*, 56).

109. Guthrie P. Ramsey, Jr., *Race Music: Black Cultures from Bebop to Hip-Hop* (Berkeley: University of California Press, 2003), 113.

110. Leonardo Acosta, *Cubano Be, Cubano Bop: One Hundred Years of Jazz in Cuba*, trans. Daniel S. Whitesell (Washington, DC: Smithsonian Books, 2003), 94.

111. Salazar, *Mambo Kingdom*, 7; Acosta, *Cubano Be, Cubano Bop*, 96.

112. New York City, *The Complete Report of Mayor LaGuardia's Commission on the Harlem Riot of March 19, 1935* (New York: Arno, 1969), 7. E. Franklin Frazier was the report's research director. On the suppression of the report during the period, see Janet L. Abu-Lughod, *Race, Space, and Riots in Chicago, New York, and Los Angeles* (New York: Oxford University Press, 2007), 143–44.

113. Eduardo Robreño, *Historia del teatro popular cubano* (Havana: Oficina del Historiador de la Ciudad de la Habana, 1961), 47–48.

114. There is evidence that O'Farrill spent some time in Puerto Rico in the early 1930s. An Alberto O'Farrell [*sic*] Gavito arrived in New York City from San Juan in the spring of 1933. Ancestry.com, *New York Passenger Lists, 1820–1957* (Provo, UT: Generations Network, 2006). In 1933, beginning in the summer and through the end of the year, O'Farrill's *negrito* was one of the featured characters at the Teatro Variedades (formerly the San José), where he appeared with another *negrito*, Carlos Pous, Arquímedes's nephew, and with the *gallego* Guillermo Moreno, who, of course, was half of the Arango-Moreno company that performed in Key West at the time of O'Farrill's arrival. In December of that year, O'Farrill appears to have traveled again: "With the intention of spending a few weeks on tour through various cities in Mexico, the recognized comic actor Alberto O'Farrill, who has performed such significant stage roles in Hispanic [*hispanos*] and American [*americanos*] theaters in this city (most recently as one of the attractions at the Teatro Variedades), left yesterday via automobile." In recognition of the trip, O'Farrill was honored at the Variedades by his fellow performers and others for having lived in New York City "for years" and for his representations of "New York life [*la vida neoyorquina*] in its different aspects" and, "above all," of "Harlem, which he knows so well." "Por los Teatros: Alberto O'Farrill Rumbo a Méjico," *La Prensa*, 12/9/1933: 5. Depression-era out-migration on the part of noncitizen Latino New York City performers was not uncommon (Glasser, *My Music Is My Flag*, 113).

115. Kanellos, *Hispanic Theatre*, 130. As the Mount Morris, the theater featured "a splendid program of Hispanic numbers [*numeros hispanos*] led by the Cuarteto Machín," whose leader, the Afro-Cuban Antonio Machín, was by then internationally known as the vocalist of the song "El manisero" (The Peanut Vendor). "Por los Teatros," *La Prensa*, 11/28/1933: 5.

116. Salazar, *Mambo Kingdom*, 4; Leymarie, *Cuban Fire*, 86. Kanellos, in *Hispanic Theatre*, 130, cites the Spanish poet Ramón de Campoamor as the theater's namesake, which is likely true of the Havana theater, too.

117. "Alberto Socarrás Oral History." The English is Socarrás's in the interview.

118. Diosa Costello, telephone interview, 4/24/2009.

119. Kanellos, *Hispanic Theatre*, 127–30; Glasser, *My Music Is My Flag*, 113–15.

120. "Para el día 14 ha fijado Fernando Luis la inauguración del Teatro Cervantes," *La Prensa*, 8/8/1936: 5.

121. Kanellos, *Hispanic Theatre*, 132.

122. "Alberto Socarrás Oral History."

123. Ibid. Again, the English is original to Socarrás.

124. Ibid.

125. Leymarie, *Cuban Fire*, 95. For Socarrás's career after 1935 (his work with the Anacaona, the gigs at the Glen Island Casino, and more), the Rutgers interview is an invaluable resource.

126. John Wise, director, *Música* (New York: Third World Newsreel, 1984).

127. Salazar, "Alberto Socarrás," 29.

128. "Alberto Socarrás Oral History." On the Campoamor and other upper-Manhattan music and dance venues as spaces of a Latino popular culture during the period, in contrast with the downtown, Anglicized, white Latino-identified hotel and club scene, see Cristóbal Díaz Ayala, *Música cubana: Del areyto al rap cubano* (San Juan, Puerto Rico: Fundación Musicalia, 2003), 354–55.

129. "Por los teatros," *La Prensa*, 6/1/1935; *La Prensa*, 6/15/1935: 5.

130. *La Prensa*, 10/26/1935: 5.

131. *La Prensa*, 11/14/1935: 5.

132. "Graves resultados de simple incidente," *La Prensa*, 3/21/1935: 1. The uprising that followed the Rivera episode had its origins in other popular responses to capitalist and white-supremacist oppression in Harlem. See Abu-Lughod, *Race, Space, and Riots*, 140.

133. Vega, *Memorias*, 214.

134. "Graves resultados de simple incidente," *La Prensa*, 3/21/1935: 1.

135. "False Report Held Cause of Harlem Race Riot," *Pittsburgh Courier*, 5/23/1935: 1.

136. "Harlem Stores Ask Soldier Guard," *New York Times*, 3/21/1935: 16.

137. Alain Locke, "Harlem: Dark Weather-Vane," *Survey Graphic* (August 1936): 457, 459.

138. "Police Still on Riot Duty," *Amsterdam News*, 3/30/1935: 1.

139. Emilio García Riera, *Historia documental del cine mexicano* (Guadalajara: Universidad de Guadalajara, 1992), 205. For more on Contreras Torres, see Gabriel Ramírez, *Miguel Contreras Torres, 1899–1981* (Guadalajara: Centro de Investigación y Enseñanza Cinematográficas, Universidad de Guadalajara, 1994).

140. García Riera, *Historia*, 205; Ramírez, *Miguel Contreras Torres*, 153.

141. In the discussion that follows, I am relying on both the script-continuity of *No matarás* located at the New York State Archives and a DVD of the film itself. Robert Dickson alerted me to the possibility of the script-continuity's location in New York, a suggestion essential to this chapter for which I express my gratitude. See *No matarás*, Motion Picture Division Case Files, 30056-403, 1, Series A1418, State of New York Education Department, Cultural Education Center, New York State Archives. Several scenes were censored and deleted from the final print shown in New York State, about which I have more to say later in this chapter. I obtained the DVD of the film thanks to José Díaz and Lucio Ortigoza of the Cinemas Lumiere in Mexico City; Mr. Díaz owns the rights to the film. I express my gratitude to them as well.

142. "Teatros," *La Prensa*, 6/1/1935: 5.

143. *La Prensa*, 6/1/1935: 5; *La Prensa*, 6/8/1935: 5; advertisement, *La Prensa*, 7/27/1935: 5.

144. Advertisement, *La Prensa*, 10/26/1935: 5; advertisement, *La Prensa*, 11/5/1935: 5.

145. "Teatros," *La Prensa*, 7/13/1935: 5.

146. Advertisement, *La Prensa*, 11/15/1935: 5. Robert Dickson and Juan Heinink, *Cita en Hollywood: Antología de las películas norteamericanas habladas en castellano*

(Bilbao, Spain: Mensajero, 1990), is a superb history of early twentieth-century Spanish-language film in the United States. Clara Rodríguez calls this period "very likely the most generous of times for Latinos in film; many Latinos appeared in these early films, and they appealed to a wide audience." Rodríguez, *Heroes, Lovers, and Others: The Story of Latinos in Hollywood* (New York: Oxford University Press, 2008), 2.

147. "The Screen: At the Campoamor," *New York Times*, 11/11/1935: 20.

148. "Reviews of the New Films," *Film Daily*, 11/12/1935: 7.

149. "Arte," *La Prensa*, 12/11/1926: 4.

150. Advertisement, *La Prensa*, 9/14/1935: 5; *La Prensa*, 11/8/1935: 5.

151. "La película *No matarás* es una feliz producción hispano-parlante," *La Prensa*, 11/11/1935: 5.

152. Letter, Motion Picture Division Case Files, 30056-403, Series A1418, State of New York Education Department, Cultural Education Center, New York State Archives.

153. Moore, *Nationalizing Blackness*, 56.

154. "Sociedades Hispanas," *La Prensa*, 11/23/1935: 7.

155. "Sociedades Hispanas," *La Prensa*, 11/26/1935: 7; "Homenaje de admiración y simpatía al gran actor hispano Alberto O'Farrill," Erasmo Vando Papers, Box 2, Folder 6, Archives of the Puerto Rican Diaspora at the Centro de Estudios Puertorriqueños/Center for Puerto Rican Studies, Hunter College, City University of New York.

156. Moore, *Nationalizing Blackness*, 248n. 8.

157. "Prado: Debut de 'The O'Farrill's Scandals,'" *Diario de la Marina*, 2/21/1936: 6.

158. *Diario de la Marina*, 2/26/1936: 6; *Diario de la Marina*, 3/14/1936: 6.

159. Ancestry.com, *New York Passengers Lists, 1820–1957* (Provo, UT: Generations Network, 2006). Upon his return to the United States and through early July 1936, O'Farrill continued performing at the Campoamor. The evidence of him on the New York City stage then begins to thin. A reference to him far afield, in Santiago de Chile, appears in 1938, where he was billed as the *"negro cubano Alberto O'Farrill"* (the black Cuban Alberto O'Farrill). *"A ningun pobre se le niega un alce y Sangre bajo un puente* hoy en populares del bataclánico Balmaceda," *El Mercurio*, 3/7/1938: 23. I thank Tomás Fernández Robaina for suggesting this Chilean connection. By 1939, in an article on the films at the Campoamor—by then called the Hispano—*La Prensa* imbued the name of O'Farrill with a bygone quality, reminiscing about *No matarás* and the "actors of our colony" who appeared in it, "such as the '*negrito*' O'Farrill." "Por los Teatros," *La Prensa*, 3/11/1939: 5. Diosa Costello lost track of O'Farrill in the 1930s, and Simón Jou, Jr., never recalled meeting him. Diosa Costello, telephone interview; Simón Jou, Jr., interview.

2 / Re/Citing Eusebia Cosme

1. "Eusebia Cosme decidida a averiguar 'si Nueva York tiene sentimiento,'" *La Prensa*, 9/2/1938: 3; advertisement, *La Prensa*, 11/26/1938, 5; Collazo, *La última noche*, 180; "Carnegie Hall Debut Success," *Pittsburgh Courier*, 12/17/1938: 13; Melba Alvarado, interview, New York City, 11/16/2007.

2. José Sariego, "Cuban Actress 'La Negrita' Cosme Buried in Simple Rites at Flagler," *Miami Herald*, 7/13/1976: 4B.

3. Ancestry.com, *New York Passenger Lists, 1820–1957* (Provo, UT: Generations

Network, 2006); Ancestry.com, *Border Crossings: From Mexico to the U.S., 1903–1957* (Provo, UT: Generations Network, 2006). Significantly, in the document of her January 14, 1941, Laredo reentry, under the category "Race," the words "African black" are handwritten over another word—likely "Cuban"—revealing a palimpsest in the official U.S. documentation of Cosme's racial identity.

4. Nancy Morejón, "Las poéticas de Nancy Morejón," *Afro-Hispanic Review* 15.1 (1996): 7.

5. Kutzinski, *Sugar's Secrets*, 16.

6. Carol Boyce Davies, *Black Women, Writing, and Identity: Migrations of the Subject* (New York: Routledge, 1994), 4, 36.

7. "Eusebia Cosme decidida a averiguar," 3.

8. Diana Lachatanere, interview, New York City, 3/8/2008.

9. Blackwell Hutson's tenure at the Schomburg stretched from 1948 to 1980, but her earliest professional experiences on 135th Street date to the 1930s, when she worked with Schomburg himself. See Glendora Johnson-Cooper, "African-American Historical Continuity: Jean Blackwell Hutson and the Schomburg Center for Research in Black Culture," in *Reclaiming the American Library Past: Writing the Women In*, ed. Suzanne Hildenbrand, 27–51 (Norwood, NJ: Ablex, 1996).

10. Diana Lachatanere, email correspondence, 12/16/2008.

11. Eileen Charbo to Jean Blackwell Hutson, 6/17/1975, Eusebia Cosme Accession File, Schomburg Center for Research in Black Culture, New York Public Library (hereafter ECAF).

12. Eileen Charbo to Jean Blackwell Hutson, 7/6/1975, ECAF.

13. Eileen Charbo, interview, Santa Fe, New Mexico, 12/2/2007.

14. A medical document from the Sociedad de Beneficiencia Española in Mexico City says Cosme was brought to the Hospital Español in Mexico City on May 31, 1973, with "episodes of speech impairment and mental confusion." Personal Papers, 1927, June 2 to 1973, June 29, Box One, Eusebia Cosme Papers, 1927 to 1973, Schomburg Center for Research in Black Culture, New York Public Library (hereafter ECP).

15. Cosme's husband was a white Puerto Rican car mechanic from New York named Rafael "Felo" Laviera who died in the 1950s. Nydia Sarabia, "La rosa canela," *Opus Habana* 5.3 (2001): 59; Enrique Río Prado, "Eusebia Cosme, una voz olvidada," *Signos* 53 (January–June 2006): 68.

16. Kutzinski, *Sugar's Secrets*, makes this argument about *poesía negra* and issues of gender, race, and the erotic. See Miguel Arnedo-Gómez, *Writing Rumba: The Afrocubanista Movement in Poetry* (Charlottesville: University of Virginia Press, 2006), for another view of *poesía negra*'s mediation of the Afro-Cuban social. Moore, in *Nationalizing Blackness*, weaves *poesía negra* into his musicological history of *afrocubanismo* around the time of the Machadato.

17. Other Cuban figures included José Antonio Portuondo, Marcelino Arozarena, and Vicente Gómez Kemp, all of whom (including Ballagas and Guillén) appeared in Ramón Guirao's key *poesía negra* anthology, *Órbita de la poesía afrocubana: 1928–1937 (antología)* (Havana: Ucar, García, y Cía., 1938). Guillén's relations with *poesía negra* as an Afro-Cuban writer (and as Cuba's "national poet") are complex, with his work between *Motivos de Son* (1930) and *West Indies, Ltd.* (1934) often identified with the phenomenon (especially through Cosme's performances), even as these works and his

later production (in addition to his critical writings) challenged *poesía negra*'s exoticist, sometimes racist representations.

18. Oscar Fernández de la Vega, "Medio siglo de poesía negrista," *Cubanacan* 1.1 (1974): 77n. 25; Emilio Ballagas, "Poesía afrocubana," *Revista de la biblioteca nacional* (October–December 1951): 7. For Fernández de la Vega, *poesía negra*'s belatedness is likely a matter of its appearance after *vanguardismo*'s mid-1920s highpoint. The Palés Matos poem in question is probably "Africa" or "Danza negra," and the year Ballagas has in mind is more likely 1926; see Kutzinski, *Sugar's Secrets*, 148, 242n. 46.

19. Hortensia Ruiz del Vizo, ed., *Poesía negra del caribe y otras áreas* (Miami: Ediciones Universal, 1972), offers a selection of characteristic poems. Consider, for example, the first sentence of Palés Matos's "Majestad negra": "Por la encendida calle antillana / va Tembandumba de la Qumbamba / —Rumba, macumba, candombe, bámbula— / entre dos filas de caras negras" (Down the flaming Caribbean street goes Tembandumba of the Qumbamba—Rumba, macumba, candombe, bámbula—between two rows of black faces; 118).

20. Ramón Lavandero, "Negrismo poético y Eusebia Cosme," *Revista bimestre cubana* 38 (1936): 43.

21. Luisa Quintero, "Eusebia Cosme: La poesía mulata hecha carne," *Ecos*, 4/20/1952: 18, Box One, Printed Material, Newspaper and Magazine Clippings, 1950–1959, ECP. The adjectival noun *cumbanchero* suggests the music and dance elements of a popular, rollicking party.

22. "Eusebia Cosme decidida a averiguar," 3.

23. Emilio Belaval, *Areyto* (San Juan, Puerto Rico: Biblioteca de Autores Puertorriqueños, 1948), 99–100.

24. Andrés Iduarte, "Eusebia Cosme," *Revista Hispánica Moderna: Boletín del Instituto de las Españas* 5 (1939): 85.

25. Roy-Féquière, *Women, Creole Identity, and Intellectual Life in Early Twentieth-Century Puerto Rico* (Philadelphia: Temple University Press, 2004), 226.

26. For a discussion of Latin American women writers that touches on the ways in which the twentieth-century cultures of *declamación* relate to a masculinist "equation of a woman's talent with her performative presence," see Vicky Unruh, *Performing Women and Modern Literary Culture in Latin America: Intervening Acts* (Austin: University of Texas Press, 2006), quote on 1. Among the major *recitadoras* of the time were the Cuban Dalia Íñiguez and the Russian-born, Argentine-raised Berta Singerman.

27. Collazo, *La última noche*, 75; diploma, Box One, Personal File, 1927–1973, ECP; Kathleen M. Vernon, "Theatricality, Melodrama, and Stardom in *El último cuplé*," in *Gender and Spanish Cinema*, ed. Steven Marsh and Parvati Nair, 183–200 (New York: Berg, 2004), 191.

28. Graziella Garbalosa, "Algo sobre el arte . . . ," n.d., n.p., Box One, Printed Material, Newspapers and Magazine Clippings, n.d., ECP. A program for an evening of *declamación* and music at the Municipal in February 1932 featured "poetry by Miss Eusebia Almanza." Box One, Printed Material, Programs (Concerts) 1930, May to 1958, May, n.d., ECP.

29. Fernando Ortiz, "Predisposición de lector," in Rómulo Lachatañeré, *¡Oh, mío, Yemayá!* (Manzanillo, Cuba: Editorial "El Arte," 1938), xii.

30. Emilio de Torre, "Hablando con Eusebia Cosme," *Ecos de Nueva York:*

Semanario del Mundo Hispano, 12/15/1946: 32, Box One, Printed Material, Newspaper and Magazine Clippings, 1943–1948, ECP.

31. Felipe Arana, "Eusebia Cosme, Emperatriz del verso negroide," *Ecos*, 5/25/1950: 9, Box One, Printed Material, Newspaper and Magazine Clippings, 1950–1959, ECP.

32. Eusebia Cosme to Langston Hughes, 8/15/1957, Series One, Personal Correspondence, Box 47, Folder 882, Cosme, Eusebia, 1944–1957, n.d., Langston Hughes Papers, James Weldon Johnson Collection, Beinecke Rare Book and Manuscript Library, Yale University (hereafter LHP).

33. Louis Pérez, Jr., *On Becoming Cuban: Identity, Nationality, Culture* (Chapel Hill: University of North Carolina Press, 1999), 236.

34. Sarabia, "La rosa canela," 58.

35. Garbalosa, "Algo sobre el arte."

36. Gustavo Urrutia, "Armonías: Eusebia," *Diario de la marina*, n.d., Box One, Printed Material, Newspaper and Magazine Clippings, n.d., ECP.

37. Don Galaor, "Eusebia Cosme," *Bohemia*, 7/29/1934: 38. For Cosme's account of José González Marín's mentorship, see Quintero, "Eusebia Cosme."

38. Garbalosa, "Algo sobre el arte."

39. Box One, Printed Material, Programs (Non-Concert), 1932–1972, n.d., ECP.

40. Gustavo Urrutia, "Armonías," *Diario de la Marina*, 5/3/1934: 2.

41. Belaval, *Areyto*, 99; Galaor, "Eusebia Cosme," 38.

42. Cosme opened the performance with Guillén's "Mujer nueva," which led to a two-part set. The first included Palés Matos's "Danza negra," Félix Pita Rodriguez's "Romance de la Reina Camándula," Arozarena's "Marcelina," Guillén's "Balada del güije," and Ballagas's "Lavandera con negrito." The second part included an unspecified selection from Eugenio Florit's *Trópico*, Ballagas's "María Belén Chacón," Guillén's "Sensemayá (canto negro para matar una culebra)," Regino Pedroso's "Una canción de vida bajo los astros," and José Antonio Portuondo's "Rumba de la negra Pancha." Significant among the *poesía negra* texts is the Spanish-born Florit's *Trópico*, which works off the *guajiro*-identified *décima* form and its associations with rural Cuban whiteness, an important element alongside the urban Afro-Cuban in constructions of Cubanness during the period.

43. Quintero, "Eusebia Cosme," 18.

44. Ramón Fajardo, *Rita Montaner: Testimonio de una época* (Havana: Fondo Editorial Casa de las Américas, 1997), 134–35. The *Hora Sensemayá* was broadcast on Tuesdays, Thursdays, and Saturdays from eight p.m. to nine p.m., and its director was the Afro-Cuban journalist Manuel Cuéllar Vizcaíno. See the undated clipping "Dos aspectos del acto inaugural de la Hora Sensemayá," Box One, Folder Two, Manuel Cuéllar Vizcaíno Collection, Amherst College Archives and Special Collections, which includes a photograph of Cosme with Cuéllar Vizcaíno.

45. Cintio Vitier, "La poesía de Emilio Ballagas," in Emilio Ballagas, *Obra poética de Emilio Ballagas* (1955; repr., Miami: Mnemosyne, 1969), xiv–xv.

46. Program, Casino Español, 1/16/1936, Cuban Heritage Collection, University of Miami. Cosme had also appeared at such other institutions of "prestige and privilege" (Pérez, *On Becoming Cuban*, 375) as the Miramar Yacht Club and the Casino Deportivo. "Eusebia Cosme," *El artista* 27, n.d., n.p., Box One, Printed Material, Newspaper and Magazine Clippings, n.d., ECP.

47. "Debut del 'Gallego Mendoza' en el Martí," *Diario de la Marina*, 2/21/1936: 6.

48. Cuarto Recital de la Poesía Negra, Teatro Municipal, San Juan, Puerto Rico, April 5, 1936, Box One, Printed Material, Programs (Non-Concert), 1932–1972, n.d., ECP.

49. Quintero, "Eusebia Cosme," 45; Despedida de Eusebia Cosme, Teatro Broadway, Ponce, Puerto Rico, June 5, 1936, Box One, Printed Material, Programs (Non-Concert), 1932–1972, n.d., ECP. See Ramón Lavandero, "Negrismo poético y Eusebia Cosme," *Revista bimestre cubana* 38 (1936): 39–45, for a representation of Cosme during this Puerto Rican sojourn.

50. Sarabia, "La rosa canela," 59; Tomás Hernández Franco, "La poesía negra: Presentación de Eusebia Cosme," in *Obras completas literarias* (Santo Domingo: Consejo Presidencial de Cultura, 2000), 509; "Harlem's Spanish Section Raves about Cuba's Premier Dramatic Artist, Eusebia Cosme," *Pittsburgh Courier*, 9/10/1938: 13.

51. Francisco Ichaso, "La reaparición de Eusebia Cosme," *Diario de la Marina*, 11/27/1936: 8.

52. Modesto Justiz Mozo, "Notas del interior: Sociales de Santiago de Cuba," *Adelante* 2.19 (December 1936): 17.

53. Tres Únicos Recitales por la Eminente Recitadora, Eusebia Cosme, Teatro Baralt, Maracaibo, Venezuela, April 18, 20, and 22, 1938, Box One, Printed Material, Programs (Concerts) 1930, May to 1958, May, n.d., ECP; photograph of Cosme with Blanco, Box One, Group Portraits, n.d., Eusebia Cosme Photograph Collection, Photographs and Prints Division, Schomburg Center for Research in Black Culture, New York Public Library, Astor, Lenox and Tilden Foundations (hereafter ECPC); Oscar Yanes, *Los anõs inolvidables: La historia venezolana desconocida: Política, intriga, farándula y el suceso pasional* (Caracas: Editorial Melvin, 1989), 135.

54. Quintero, "Eusebia Cosme," 18.

55. Ancestry.com, *New York Passenger Lists, 1820–1957.*

56. Arnedo-Gómez, *Writing Rumba*, 75. The *minoristas*, young intellectuals identified "with educational reform and university autonomy" during the 1920s, "denounced United States imperialism, called for labor and agrarian reform, and demanded an end to political corruption and electoral fraud." Louis A. Pérez, Jr., *Cuba: Between Reform and Revolution* (New York: Oxford University Press, 1988), 237.

57. Fernando Ortiz, "La poesía mulata: Presentación de Eusebia Cosme, la recitadora," *Revista Bimestre Cubana* 34 (September–December 1934): 213; subsequent references appear in the text.

58. Alexander G. Weheliye, *Phonographies: Grooves in Sonic Afro-Modernity* (Durham: Duke University Press, 2005), 31, 35, 36, 38, italics in original.

59. Ibid., 41, italics in original.

60. Glissant, *Poétique*, 82.

61. Cosme's appearance at the Lyceum that day in 1934 is not unrelated to the institution's complex engagement in social activism, particularly in night-school curricula for working-class people (including Afro-Cubans) and in women's prison reform. See K. Lynn Stoner, *From the House to the Streets: The Cuban Woman's Movement for Legal Reform, 1898–1940* (Durham: Duke University Press, 1991). See also the Lyceum materials at the Cuban Heritage Collection.

62. De la Fuente, *A Nation for All*, 202.

63. Bronfman, *Measures of Equality*, 165–68.

64. "Eusebia Cosme," *Adelante* 1.6 (November 1935): 13.

65. De la Fuente, *A Nation for All*, 202.

66. "La triunfal *tournée* de Eusebia Cosme," *Adelante* 4.41 (October 1938): 14, 20. I have found no evidence that Cosme toured through Central America.

67. "Eusebia Cosme decidida a averiguar."

68. "Harlem's Spanish Section Raves about Cuba's Premier Dramatic Artist, Eusebia Cosme," *Pittsburgh Courier*, 9/10/1938: 13.

69. "La triunfal *tournée* de Eusebia Cosme," *Adelante* 4.41 (October 1938): 14, 20.

70. Frances Smith Foster, "A Narrative of the Interesting Origins and (Somewhat) Surprising Developments of African-American Print Culture," *American Literary History* 17 (2005): 727.

71. The reference to Cosme's New York City address, 408 Convent Avenue, which would have denoted to the *Courier*'s readership (and perhaps to some of *Adelante*'s) a Sugar Hill—and, hence, a middle-class and elite African American—residence, was moved by *Adelante* to the very end of "Triunfal *tournée*," as the concluding sentence of its translation of the *Courier*'s "Patrons Have Paid $6."

72. Edgar T. Rouzeau, "Patrons Have Paid $6 a Seat to Hear Eusebia Cosme, Who Is Cuba's Greatest Actress," *Pittsburgh Courier*, 9/10/1938: 13.

73. "La triunfal *tournée* de Eusebia Cosme," 20.

74. See Buster Vodery, "Top Girl Dramatist Is Cuba's Ambassador of Good Will to America," *Washington Afro-American*, 9/17/1938: 9, which does in fact mention African American actresses/singers in relation to Cosme, linking her to Ethel Waters and Louise Beavers as performers known "to America." Vodery notes that the Cuban government had paid Cosme's "passport and passage fee" in return for her "ambassadorial" role in performing abroad, which suggests Cosme's manipulation of Cuban state expectations regarding her 1938 migration—and, eventually, settlement—in the United States. Luis Carbonell, the Afro-Cuban *recitador* renowned in his own right, cites the 1939 New York World's Fair (and Cosme's possible appearance therein) as a motive for the government's support of her trip. "Entrevista a Luis Carbonell," interview by Edmundo García, *La Noche Se Mueve*, WNMA 1210 AM, February 2008, http://lanochesemueve.us/Entrevista%20a%20Luis%20Carbonell.pdf (accessed 1/31/2009). I discuss the relationship between Carbonell and Cosme later in this chapter.

75. The Carnegie Hall poetry selections resembled those of Cosme's recent performances in Cuba and Puerto Rico, including works by Guillén ("Balada de Simón Caraballo," "Balada del güije," and "Sensemayá"); Palés Matos ("Falsa canción de baquiné" and "Danza negra"); and, by now, other standards by Caignet ("'Cotel' de son"), Camín ("Macorina"), and Ballagas ("Nombres negros en el son"). A recent addition seems to have been Andrés Eloy Blanco's "Píntame angelitos negros," which Cosme used to close the show. Programa, Carnegie Hall, December 4, 1937, Box One, Printed Material, Programs (Concerts), 1930, May to 1958, May, n.d., ECP.

76. Melba Alvarado, interview. Alvarado arrived in New York City in 1936 from the town of Mayarí in Oriente, and she lived at first in the Cuban neighborhood of Lenox Avenue, near the Teatro Campoamor/Teatro Cervantes/Teatro Hispano. See Mirabal, "Scripting Race," and "Melba Alvarado, El Club Cubano Inter-Americano, and the Creation of Afro-Cubanidades in New York City," in Jiménez Román and Juan Flores, *Afro-Latin@ Reader*, 120–26.

77. "Carnegie Hall Debut Success," *Pittsburgh Courier*, 12/17/1938: 13.

78. Allan Keiler, *Marian Anderson: A Singer's Journey* (Urbana-Champaign: University of Illinois Press, 2002), 189–217.

79. Also among the sponsors was Ben Frederic Carruthers, the Howard Spanish professor and translator who collaborated with Langston Hughes on *Cuba Libre* (1948), a translation of Guillén's poetry; V. B. Spratlin, the head of Howard's Romance Languages Department; and Enrique "Henry" Grillo, the older brother of the Afro-Cuban American Evelio Grillo, whom I discuss in the conclusion. Spanish Recital of Afro-Antillean Poems, February 7, 1939, Box One, Printed Material, Programs (Concerts), 1930, May to 1958, May, n.d., ECP.

80. "Cuban Girl in Recital," *Washington Afro-American*, 2/18/1939: 10.

81. "Eusebia Cosme en otro recital el domingo 28," *La Prensa*, 5/13/1939: 7, states that she had appeared before the "Cuerpo Diplomático Latino Americano" at the Unión Panamericana in Washington.

82. "Music News," *Chicago Defender*, 2/3/1940: 18; Ancestry.com, *Border Crossings*; Quintero, "Eusebia Cosme," 45, which says Cosme performed at the Bellas Artes six times; Program for the Universidad Michoacana, May 18, 1940, Box One, Programs (Concerts) 1930, May to 1958, May, n.d., ECP; Songwriters Contract, Box One, Personal File, ECP.

83. The Town Hall performance occurred on May 9, 1943. Melba Alvarado recalled that the Ateneo *"siempre ha sido de los blancos"* (has always been for the whites) and that, shortly after the fall of Fulgencio Batista, the Ateneo itself collapsed. Melba Alvarado, interview.

84. Postcard from Eusebia Cosme to Langston Hughes from Washington, DC, April 13, 1944. Cosme had written "Howard University" on it. Series One, Personal Correspondence, Box 47, Folder 882, Cosme, Eusebia, 1944–1957, n.d., LHP.

85. This Maceo event was the origin for the Club Cubano Inter-Americano, founded later on September 17, 1945. "Centenario del Natalicio del General Antonio Maceo," Box 5, Events, 1945–1946, 1953, 1957, n.d., Club Cubano Inter-Americano Papers, Schomburg Center for Research in Black Culture; Melba Alvarado, interview.

86. "Un homenaje a Martí y Maceo en N.Y.," *Carteles*, 3/16/1947: 32; Sarabia, "Rosa canela," 59.

87. Melba Alvarado, interview. A clipping from *La Prensa* circa 1950 shows Cosme at the Club Cubano with a large, majority Afro-Cuban/Afro-Latino group, which included Alvarado herself and Arsenio Rodríguez. Box One, Printed Material, Newspaper and Magazine Clippings, n.d., ECP. Another image, this one a photograph from 1957, shows Cosme with Celia Cruz and Melba Alvarado in what was likely another Club Cubano event. Box 9, Cuban Performers, "Cruz, Celia, 1957," Justo A. Martí Collection, Archives of the Puerto Rican Diaspora at the Centro de Estudios Puertorriqueños/Center for Puerto Rican Studies, Hunter College, City University of New York.

88. "Music Calendar," *Amsterdam News*, 1/8/1949: 4; photograph with Ben Frederic Carruthers and Langston Hughes, Folder One, ECPC; Guillén added a caricature of himself to his dedication. Guillén, *Cuba Libre*, trans. Ben Frederic Carruthers and Langston Hughes (Los Angeles: Ward Ritchie, 1948), Manuscripts, Archives and Rare Books, Schomburg Center for Research in Black Culture.

89. Rosendo Rosell, telephone interview, 7/28/2008. Luisa Amparo Quintero stated

that Cosme also worked in Spanish dubbing at the time, including, significantly, Hattie McDaniel's role in *Gone with the Wind*. Quintero, "Eusebia Cosme," 18.

90. Nicolás Guillén, "De Nueva York a Moscú, pasando por París," in *Prosa de prisa: 1929–1972, tomo II*, 23–44 (Havana: Editorial Arte y Literatura, 1975), 23–24, 26. The essay originally appeared in *Bohemia* in December 1949.

91. Ibid., 26–27.

92. Langston Hughes to Eusebia Cosme, 3/29/1949, Series One, Personal Correspondence, Box 47, Folder 882, Cosme, Eusebia, 1944–1957, n.d., LHP. During this period of the late 1940s, Cosme held court a the Horn and Hardart Automat on Forty-Seventh Street and Broadway. The renowned Cuban American theater figure René Buch was a part of this scene, too. He remembered the queer Cosme: "She was the godmother [*madrina*] of all the gay Latin men [*locas latinas*] of New York." René Buch, interview, New York City, 1/13/2010.

93. Joaquín Pelayo, "Cubans, Our Neighbors," *Chicago Defender*, 2/3/1940: 13.

94. Pelayo published several articles on Cuba and race in the *Defender* around this time. See (as Jacques Pelayo), "Real Strongholds of Democracy," *Chicago Defender*, 12/14/1940: 13, and ("as told to Jack Pelayo"), "Our Five Days in Havana," *Chicago Defender*, 8/14/1940: 13. "Cubans, Our Neighbors" describes Pelayo as an associate of Pedro Portundo Calá, the Afro-Cuban journalist.

95. José Ferrer Canales, "Valaurez Burwell Spratlin (1897–1961)," *Hispania* 45.3 (September 1962): 446–50.

96. Manuscript document by Spratlin, Box One, Poems and Essay, Folder Four, Written about Cosme, 1937–1952, n.d., ECP.

97. See Leslie C. Dunn and Nancy A. Jones, eds., *Embodied Voices: Representing Female Vocality in Western Culture* (New York: Cambridge University Press, 1994).

98. Farah Jasmine Griffin, "When Malindy Sings: A Meditation on Black Women's Vocality," in *Uptown Conversation: The New Jazz Studies*, ed. Robert G. O'Meally, Brent Hayes Edwards, and Farah Jasmine Griffin, 102–25 (New York: Columbia University Press, 2004), 104, 113.

99. "Eusebia Cosme in a Recital of Afro-Antillian Poems," Illinois, Evanston, 1/27/1940, 87-137-F, Archives of Traditional Music, Indiana University. The program was characteristic of Cosme's repertoire at the time: a three-part performance of Guillén, Palés Matos, Ballagas and others, it was the same set, for example, she had performed at the Armstrong Auditorium a year earlier.

100. Roland Barthes, *The Pleasure of the Text*, trans. Richard Miller (New York: Hill and Wang, 1975), 66–67.

101. "United States, Illinois, Evanston, Afro-Antilleans, 1940," sound recording, Archives of Traditional Music, Indiana University; Michael Casey, Associate Director for Recording Services, Archives of Traditional Music, Indiana University, email correspondence, 2/22/2010.

102. Weheliye, *Phonographies*, 21.

103. Marilyn Graf, Archivist, Archives of Traditional Music, Indiana University, email correspondence, 12/15/2009.

104. Michael Casey, email correspondence.

105. Joke Dame, "Theme and Variations: Feminist Musicology," in *Women's Studies and Culture: A Feminist Introduction*, ed. Rosemarie Buikema and Anneke Smelik, 106–16 (London: Zed Books, 1995), 113.

106. "Sensemayá" appeared in Guillén's 1934 volume *West Indies, Ltd.*; see Nicolás Guillén, *Obra poética: Tomo 1* (Havana: Editorial Letras Cubanas, 2002), 118–20. Both the poem's date of publication and, as Vera Kutzinski demonstrates, its formal and thematic ambitions distinguish it from an earlier (now exoticist) *poesía negra*; see Kutzinski, *Against the American Grain: Myth and History in William Carlos Williams, Jay Wright, and Nicolás Guillén* (Baltimore: Johns Hopkins University Press, 1987), 136–39. Cosme modifies the poem in the sound text, changing the order of a handful of lines; she also adds the word *negro*, otherwise absent, to its "subtitle": "Canto negro para matar una culebra." Mayombe is an area north of the Congo river basin, and *palo mayombe* is one of the *reglas de congo*, an Afro-Cuban religious tradition from central Africa.

107. Luisa Quintero gives three years as the duration of the program. Quintero, "Eusebia Cosme," 18. Cosme also appeared on NBC radio. Julia de Burgos, "Con Eusebia Cosme: Gran recitadora cubana," *Pueblos Hispanos*, 5/20/1944: 2.

108. Eric Paul Roorda, *The Dictator Next Door: The Good Neighbor Policy and the Trujillo Regime in the Dominican Republic, 1930–1945* (Durham: Duke University Press, 1998), 27. CBS began the Cadena de las Américas in 1942; by the end of the year, it was under the control of Nelson A. Rockefeller's Office of Inter-American Affairs.

109. Quintero, "Eusebia Cosme," 18. "Eusebia Cosme Program 24," Box Three, Scripts, Columbia Broadcasting System Eusebia Cosme Radio Show, ECP.

110. Gladys M. Jiménez-Muñoz, "Carmen María Colón Pellot: On 'Womanhood' and 'Race' in Puerto Rico during the Interwar Period," *New Centennial Review* 3.3 (Fall 2003): 76, ellipsis in original. The Colón Pellot poem Cosme included in the show was "Caridá."

111. "Eusebia Cosme Program 7," Box Three, Scripts, Columbia Broadcasting System Eusebia Cosme Radio Show, ECP.

112. Langston Hughes, *The Weary Blues* (New York: Knopf, 1926), 57.

113. Untitled script, Box Three, Scripts, Columbia Broadcasting System Eusebia Cosme Radio Show, ECP.

114. Langston Hughes, "Los cuentos de tía Susana," trans. Arturo González Dorticós, *El Mundo*, 7/12/1931: n.p., in Urrutia, *Armonías*.

115. Vera Kutzinski has shown how such instances of translating Hughes into Spanish during the period foreground differences that challenge assumptions of "cultural and political sameness" among African-diaspora groups in the Americas. See "'Yo también soy América': Langston Hughes Translated," *American Literary History* 18.3 (2006): 551.

116. Program Number Five, 8/25/1944, Box Three, Scripts, Columbia Broadcasting System Eusebia Cosme Radio Show, ECP, ellipses in original.

117. The *Cosme Show* thus extends what Kutzinski has identified as a longstanding Hispanophone (and, in particular, Cuban) translation difficulty regarding "I, Too." See "Yo también."

118. Ernesto Roca to Eusebia Cosme, 5/6/1941, and Songwriters Contract, 9/11/1941, Box One, Personal File, ECP.

119. Raúl A. Fernández, *From Afro-Cuban Rhythms to Latin Jazz* (Berkeley: University of California Press, 2006), 38.

120. Anselmo Sacasas (arranger), Marion Sunshine (English lyric), Eusebia Cosme (music and Spanish lyric), "In Africa (Fué en el Africa)," Antobal Music, University of North Texas Music Library.

121. Xiomara Alfaro, "Fue en el África," in *Xiomara Alfaro en Nueva York*, n.d., and Miguelito Valdés with Xavier Cugat and His Waldorf-Astoria Orchestra, "In Africa," 1941, both in the Díaz-Ayala Cuban and Latin-American Popular Music Collection, Florida International University.

122. "Katherine Dunham Stages a Cuban Evening," Box One, Printed Material, Programs (Concert) 1930–1958, n.d., ECP; "Eusebia Cosme en un recital de poemas afroantillanos," Town Hall, 4/13/1952, Box One, Printed Material, Programs (Concerts) 1930, May to 1958, May, n.d., ECP.

123. For accounts of Cosme's return, see Don Galaor, "¡Hasta qué vino Eusebia Cosme!," *Bohemia*, 6/8/1952: 32–33, 108–9; and Nicolás Guillén, "Regreso de Eusebia Cosme," in *Prosa de prisa: Crónicas*, 155–60 (Buenos Aires: Editorial Hernández, 1968), 156–57. Among the successes of Cosme's return to Cuba were performances in Bayamo, Holguín, and Santiago; an homage in Santiago; and her receiving the National Order of Merit Carlos Manuel de Céspedes. On the Pro-Arte shows, see "De la farandula," *Carteles*, 5/10/1953: 98, 102.

124. Carlos Peralta, "Señal: Eusebia Cosme, ausente ilustre," *Tiempo*, 4/3/1953: n.p., Box One, Printed Material, Newspaper and Magazine Clippings, 1950–1959, ECP.

125. "Eusebia Cosme," *Germinal: Revista de artes, letras, y ciencias* (June 1953): 16, Box One, Printed Material, Newspaper and Magazine Clippings, 1950–1959, ECP. Among the new generation of poetry performers was the Afro-Cuban Luis Carbonell, a major figure in twentieth-century Cuban culture in his own right. Cosme and Carbonell's relationship is complicated, going back at least to 1946, when Carbonell made his own trip to New York City and, depending on the source, was either rebuffed by Cosme or offered support by her. See the transcript of a Miami-area radio interview with Carbonell in February 2008, in which he offers an ungenerous recollection of Cosme's 1952 return: "She didn't attract attention. She had to return to the United States, and she died there some years later." "Entrevista a Luis Carbonell."

126. Gonzalo de Palacio, "Como viven los artistas cubanos en New York," *El mundo*, 9/23/1954: n.p., Box One, Printed Material, Newspaper and Magazine Clippings, 1950–1959, ECP. It is not clear when Cosme finally resettled in New York City. A program for a performance at the Lyceum in April 1954 suggests that Cosme was still in Cuba—or at the very least had returned there again—that year. Box One, Printed Material, Programs (Concerts) 1930, May to 1958, May, n.d., ECP.

127. Langston Hughes to Eusebia Cosme, 6/21/1954 and 11/17/1956, Series One, Personal Correspondence, Box 47, Folder 882, Cosme, Eusebia, 1944–1957, n.d., LHP. I have found no evidence that Cosme was ever in a Spanish-language production of *Mulatto*. However, Hughes did eventually send Cosme a copy of the Spanish translation of the play, done by the Argentine Julio Galer, as a penciled-in note at the bottom of a typed list of recipients demonstrates: "Sent to Eusebia Cosme—Xmas, 1955." Series 5, General Writings: *Mulatto*, Box 317, Folder 5193, LHP.

128. "Eusebia Cosme, en un Recital de Poesía Afro-Antillana," Town Hall, 12/9/1956, and memorial book, 12/9/1956, Box One, Printed Material, Programs (Concerts) 1930, May to 1958, May, n.d., ECP; Ángel Rigau, "Triunfa en recital auspiciado por la Sociedad de Periodistas Puertorriquenos," *La Prensa*, 12/11/1956: n.p., Box One, Printed Material, Newspaper and Magazine Clippings, 1950–1959, ECP.

129. Canales, "Valaurez Burwell Spratlin," 447.

130. Photograph, 50th Washington Square Outdoor Art Exhibit [1959], May Include Other Dates, ECPC.

131. Letters between 1968 and 1972 place Cosme at the Hotel Insurgentes. Box One, Correspondence, ECP.

132. For queer engagements with the future, see Lee Edelman, *No Future: Queer Theory and the Death Drive* (Durham: Duke University Press, 2004); and José Esteban Muñoz, *Cruising Utopia: The Then and There of Queer Futurity* (New York: NYU Press, 2009).

133. Edward Lewis Wallant, *The Pawnbroker* (New York: Harcourt, Brace, and World, 1961), 9, 70.

134. Buscaglia-Salgado, *Undoing Empire*, 173, 180.

135. See María DeGuzmán, *Spain's Long Shadow: The Black Legend, Off-Whiteness, and Anglo-American Empire* (Minneapolis: University of Minnesota Press, 2005).

136. *The Pawnbroker*, dir. Sidney Lumet, VHS (Los Angeles: Republic Pictures Home Video, 1965). Melba Alvarado surmised that Cosme's presence in the "performance world" around her neighborhood in the West Forties helped her land the role of Mrs. Ortiz. Alvarado, interview.

137. *Derecho* originated as an immensely popular Cuban radio drama written by Félix Caignet in 1948. Its Mamá Dolores was played by a white Cuban actress, Lupe Suárez, who went on to play the role in the story's first film version in 1952—in blackface (Rosell, *Vidas y milagros*, 190). Cosme's performance as Dolores in the 1955 Teatro Santurce (formerly Campoamor) stage play placed her alongside local Harlem actors such as Edelmiro Borras, who had performed the *negrito* years earlier on the New York City *bufo* stage (Kanellos, *Hispanic Theatre*, 134). Cosme would have known of the Santurce/Campoamor's *bufo* past from Alberto Socarrás himself, who was a personal friend. Socarrás stands next to Cosme in a photograph taken during a 1958 tribute to her at the Club Cubano Inter-Americano; photograph, Box 8, Folder 7, Club Cubano Inter-Americano Photograph Collection, Schomburg Center for Research in Black Culture, New York Public Library. On the Socarrás friendship, see also Alberto Alonso, "Rosas blancas para mi hermana negra sobre la tumba de Eusebia Cosme, voz de arte que la muerte acalló," *El Diario La Prensa*, 7/16/1976: 15.

138. Vicente Leñero, "El derecho de llorar," in *A ustedes les consta: Antología de la crónica en México*, ed. Carlos Monsiváis (México, DF: Ediciones Era, DF, 1980), 272, 276, 278.

139. Among the U.S. mammy characteristics shared by Dolores are a "calming" voice, self-deprecating sense of humor, and devotion to the white family. See Kimberly Wallace-Sanders, *Mammy: A Century of Race, Gender, and Southern Memory* (Ann Arbor: University of Michigan Press, 2008), 2.

140. *El derecho de nacer*, dir. Tito Davison, DVD (México: Llamento, S.L., 1966); *Rosas blancas para mi hermana negra*, dir. Abel Salazar, VHS (Los Angeles: Video Visa, 1969); *El derecho de los pobres*, dir. René Cardona, VHS (Madera, CA: Madera CineVideo, 1973). Cosme also appeared in *Vuelo 701* (1971), a thriller. She was scheduled to work in a film called *Negro es un bello color* (Black Is a Beautiful Color) prior to her stroke. Cima Films, S.A., to Cosme, 3/2/1973, Box One, Correspondence, ECP. She won the Mexican Onix film award for her performance in *Nacer*, and she appeared in three *telenovelas* during this period, including a version of *Nacer*. She also performed in several Mexican plays, always in the role of a servant, except for her appearance as

the *"bruja"* (witch) in the Mexican scholar and playwright Othón Arróniz's *Yanga* (1971), a play based on the historical slave uprising and *cimmarronaje* of Yanga in early colonial México. "Confirmado el Estreno Mundial de *Yanga*, el 30, en Córdoba," *Novedades*, 3/18/1971: n.p., Box One, Printed Material, Newspaper and Magazine Clippings, 1970–1972, ECP; program for *Yanga*, Box One, Printed Material, Programs (Non-Concert), 1932 September, to 1972 December, n.d., ECP.

141. *Mamá Dolores*, dir. Tito Davison, VHS (Madera, CA: Madera CineVideo, 1971).

142. René Buch, interview. Alonso, in "Rosas blancas," suggests that the Asociación Nacional de Actores (National Association of Actors) in Mexico eventually denied Cosme benefits, which led to Pino's intervention. Two decades earlier, Pino had participated in the early stages of the Cuban revolution.

143. Alonso, "Rosas blancas," 15.

144. Ángel Costa, "Reportaje Especial: Eusebia Cosme es una extraordinaria declamadora de poesía afro-antillana," *Procinemex*, 1970, Box One, Printed Material, Newspaper and Magazine Clippings, 1970–1972, ECP.

145. Evaristo R. Savón, "Inauguran este miércoles el Teatro Lecuona de Hialeah," *Diario las Américas*, 11/26/1975: 12+.

146. Evaristo R. Savón, "Gran asistencia de público al sepelio de Eusebia Cosme," *Diario de las Americas*, 7/13/1976: 20.

3 / Supplementary Careers, Boricua Identifications

1. My use of "identification," after José Esteban Muñoz, presumes within it the "dissing" performances of disidentificatory cultural practices: the (not quite) assuming another's identity among minority performers to contest (and manage one's exposure to) power. Muñoz, *Disidentifications: Queers of Color and the Performance of Politics* (Minneapolis: University of Minnesota Press, 1999).

2. See, for example, Derrida on supplementarity and Rousseau in *Of Grammatology*, trans. Gayatri Chakravorty Spivak (Baltimore: Johns Hopkins University Press, 1976).

3. Theodor Adorno, *Minima Moralia: Reflections from Damaged Life*, trans. E. F. N. Jephcott (London: New Left Books, 1974), 21.

4. Bruce Robbins, *Secular Vocations: Intellectuals, Professionalism, Culture* (New York: Verso, 1993).

5. The Jones Act granted Puerto Ricans U.S. citizenship. One of its consequences was the drafting of Puerto Ricans into World War I. The Estado Libre Asociado (ELA) was passed in a referendum and approved by Congress. The ELA "allowed the United States to relieve international pressure to 'decolonize' Puerto Rico while still retaining control over the Island. Even though Puerto Rico remains a colony, the ELA provided a higher standard of living for the working class, transferred control of key Island institutions to the local elites, and co-opted many pro-independence supporters to run them. The ELA also allowed the U.S. political elites to diffuse their own shame as colonial rulers internationally." Frances Negrón-Muntaner, *Boricua Pop: Puerto Ricans and the Latinization of American Culture* (New York: NYU Press, 2004), 6–7.

6. Paquito D'Rivera, *Mi vida sexual* (Barcelona: Seix Barral, 2000), 62, ellipses in first paragraph in original.

7. Paquito D'Rivera, *My Sax Life: A Memoir*, trans. Luis Tamargo (Evanston, IL: Northwestern University Press, 2005), 34.

8. Fernando Ortiz, *Nuevo catauro de cubanismos* (Havana: Editorial de Ciencias Sociales, 1985), 179.

9. Arturo Schomburg to Emilio Roig de Leuchsenring, 5/14/1938, "Letters by Arthur Schomburg, 1914–1938," Box 9, Folder 18, Arthur A. Schomburg Papers, 1724–1895 (1904–1938), Schomburg Center for Research in Black Culture, New York Public Library. Schomburg also related the anecdote in "General Antonio Maceo," *Crisis* (May 1931): 155–56, 174, 176.

10. The most well-known instance of the Afro-Latino deliverance of Martí involves an Afro-Latina: Paulina Pedroso, the Tampa Afro-Cuban American. See James, *Holding Aloft*, 245.

11. Negrón-Muntaner, *Boricua Pop*, 13.

12. Advertisement, *La Prensa*, 4/11/1936: 5.

13. Salazar, "Alberto Socarrás," 29.

14. Lola Rodríguez de Tió, "A Cuba," in *Mi libro de Cuba: Poesías* (Havana: Imprenta la Moderna, 1893), 5, ellipsis in original.

15. José Buscaglia-Salgado, "Leaving Us for Nowhere: The Cuban Pursuit of 'the American Dream,'" *CR: The New Centennial Review* 2.2 (2002): 292.

16. The song appears on the compilation album *Viva Puerto Rico Libre* (Paredon Records, 1978).

17. Lawrence La Fountain-Stokes, "De Un Pájaro Las Dos Alas: Travel Notes of a Queer Puerto Rican in Havana," *GLQ: A Journal of Lesbian and Gay Studies* 8.1–2 (2002): 10.

18. On Rodríguez de Tió as a lesbian, see ibid., 19. Robin Moore discusses how around 1966 the Cuban state accused Milanés "of being a homosexual and sentenced him to an UMAP (Unidades Militares para la Ayuda a la Producción) prison in Camagüey, where he remained for over a year." Robin Moore, *Music and Revolution: Cultural Change in Socialist Cuba* (Berkeley: University of California Press, 2006), 151–52. Still other *portorro-cubiche* occasions occur in Puerto Rico itself. See Jorge Duany, "Becoming Cuba-Rican," in *The Portable Island: Cubans at Home in the World*, ed. Ruth Behar and Lucía M. Suárez, 197–208 (New York: Palgrave, 2008).

19. Nicholas De Genova and Ana Y. Ramos-Zayas, *Latino Crossings: Mexicans, Puerto Ricans, and the Politics of Race and Citizenship* (New York: Routledge, 2003), 15.

20. Mirabal, "Scripting Race," 205n. 18.

21. Ramón Grosfoguel, *Colonial Subjects: Puerto Ricans in a Global Perspective* (Berkeley: University of California Press, 2003), 28, 33.

22. Ibid., 149. Raquel Rivera, *New York Ricans from the Hip Hop Zone* (New York: Palgrave, 2003), describes in great detail the cultures of rap, DJing, breakdancing, and graffiti produced by mainland Puerto Ricans and African Americans in New York City out of such close colonial/racial historical experiences.

23. Nicolás Guillén, "Rómulo Lachatañeré," in *Prosa de prisa (1929–1985)*, 100–103 (Havana: Ediciones Unión, 2002), 102–3. The date given in the collection, 1951, is incorrect; the actual date is 1952.

24. "Socios colaboradores," n.d., Colección de manuscritos Fernando Ortiz, Biblioteca Nacional José Martí, Carpeta 1, Revista de estudios afrocubanos (hereafter CMFO).

25. Andrés Iduarte, "Ha muerto Romulo Lachantanere [*sic*]," n.d., Rómulo Lachatañeré Papers, privately held (hereafter RLP).

26. Diana Lachatanere, telephone interview, 11/16/2007.

27. See chapter 2 for Diana Lachatanere's decisive role in the processing of the Eusebia Cosme Papers.

28. Faye V. Harrison, *Outsider Within: Reworking Anthropology in the Global Age* (Urbana: University of Illinois Press, 2008), 12. Moore, *Music and Revolution*, 172.

29. Rómulo Lachataignerais, "El milagro de Babaya-Ayé (Leyenda Afro-Cubana)," *Adelante* 1.9 (February 1936): 12; Lachataignerais, "El nacimiento de Changó," *Adelante* 1.11 (April 1936): 6; Lachataignerais, "La justicia de Olofi," *Adelante* 2.14 (July 1936): 10; Lachataignerais, "La caída del casto Orisaoco (cuento afrocubano)," *Adelante* 4.39 (August 1938): 10, 21.

30. Julia Cuervo Hewitt, "From Nigerian Oral Literature to Cuban Narrative," in *Voices from Under: Black Narrative in Latin America and the Caribbean*, ed. William Luis, 65–85 (Westport, CT: Greenwood, 1984), 67.

31. Rómulo Lachatañeré, "Notas de referencia," in *¡¡Oh, mío, Yemayá!!* (Manzanillo: Editorial "El Arte," 1938), xxxi. Jorge Castellanos states that the title refers to the phrase *omi o Yemayá*, or "water, you, *Yemayá*," a reference to the ocean associations of the *orisha* in question; Castellanos, *Pioneros de la etnografía afrocubana* (Miami: Ediciones Universal, 2003), 154n. 69.

32. Diana Lachatanere, email correspondence, 12/4/2010. A letter from Juan Marinello to Maria J. Vidaurreta de Marinello dated 5/24/1935, in Juan Marinello, *Cada tiempo trae una faena: Selección de correspondencia de Juan Marinello Vidaurreta, 1923–1940*, vol. 2 (Havana: Centro de Investigación y Desarrollo de la Cultura Cubana Juan Marinello, 2004), 491–92, places Lachatañeré at the prison. Some of my biographical information in this section draws on Isaac Barreal's "Prólogo," in Rómulo Lachatañeré, *El sistema religioso de los afrocubanos* (Havana: Editorial de Ciencias Sociales, 2004), vii–xxiv.

33. Bronfman, *Measures of Equality*, 166.

34. Ancestry.com, *New York Passenger Lists, 1820–1957*.

35. Rómulo Lachatañeré to Langston Hughes, 11/15/1938, Series I, Personal Correspondence, Box 100, Folder 1873, LHP. It is unclear if the meeting ever happened.

36. Lachatañeré rearrived on 9/5/1939 aboard the *Siboney*. Ancestry.com, *New York Passenger Lists, 1820–1957*.

37. Rómulo Lachatañeré to Langston Hughes, 1/10/1940, Series I, Personal Correspondence, Box 100, Folder 1873, LHP. There is no evidence that Hughes did the translations.

38. By 1960, there were 612,574 Puerto Ricans in New York City. The increase in Cubans during the period, while incomparable, was noticeable, from 23,124 in 1940 to 42,694 in 1960; García, *Arsenio Rodríguez*, 85.

39. "Army Separation Qualification Record," 11/13/1944, RLP.

40. "Report of Separation," n.d., RLP. Lachatañeré's World War II experience, however incomplete it comes down to us, thus serves as a counterpoint, in its Afro-Cuban American use of a U.S. whiteness, to Evelio Grillo's *Black Cuban, Black American*, a prime example of the Afro-Cuban American experience (and use) of the "colored" army during the war.

41. "Army Separation Qualification Record"; "Enlisted Record," n.d., RLP.

42. Rómulo Lachatañeré, "El sistema religioso de los lucumí y otras influencias africanas en Cuba," *Estudios Afrocubanos* 3.1–4 (1939): 76–77. The 1939 date is a

deliberate error; its actual appearance was 1941. The journal, subsidized by the city of Havana, was behind in publication due to funding troubles. See Fernando Ortiz to Rómulo Lachatañeré, 2/15/1941, Carpeta 183, "Correspondencia Varios L," CMFO. On the term *lucumí* as a Yoruba signifier, see George Brandon, *Santería from Africa to the New World: The Dead Sell Memories* (Bloomington: Indiana University Press, 1997).

43. Lachatañeré, "El sistema," 77. In the same issue of *Estudios Afrocubanos*, Ortiz published a reply in agreement with Lachatañeré, historicizing his use of the term in question: "Brujos o santeros," *Estudios Afrocubanos* 3.1–4 (1939): 85–90.

44. Lachatañeré, "El sistema," 28.

45. I take "geopolitics of knowledge" from Walter D. Mignolo, "Capitalism and Geopolitics of Knowledge: Latin American Social Thought and Latino/a American Studies," in *Critical Latin American and Latino Studies*, ed. Juan Poblete, 32–75 (Minneapolis: University of Minnesota Press, 2003).

46. Lachatañeré to Ortiz, 8/28/1940, Carpeta 183, "Correspondencia Varios L," CMFO.

47. Lachatañeré to Ortiz, 11/9/1940, Carpeta 183, "Correspondencia Varios L," CMFO.

48. Lachatañeré to Ortiz, 8/28/1940.

49. Harrison, *Outsider Within*, 12.

50. Moore, *Music and Revolution*, 172.

51. Ortiz to unspecified recipients, 9/9/1940, RLP.

52. Around this time, Lachatañeré called himself Ortiz's "*discípulo*"—his "disciple." Lachatañeré to Ortiz, 3/5/1941, Carpeta 183, "Correspondencia Varios L," CMFO.

53. Lachatañeré to Melville Herskovits, 11/9/1940, African Manuscripts 6, Series 3516, Box 12, Folder 12, Melville J. Herskovits (1895–1963) Papers, 1906–1963, Northwestern University Archives, Evanston, IL (hereafter MHP). As we saw, Eusebia Cosme had performed at Northwestern earlier that year (and the Indiana recording was among Herskovits's materials), suggesting a possible link between the Cosme-Lachatañeré friendship and their respective professional relationships with Herskovits.

54. Such an anthropology focused heavily on the "authenticity" of African-diasporic cultures. See David Scott, *Postcolonial Futures: Criticism after Postcoloniality* (Princeton: Princeton University Press, 1999), 108.

55. Herskovits to Lachatañeré, 1/9/1941, African Manuscripts 6, Series 3516, Box 12, Folder 12, MHP.

56. Ortiz to Franz Boas, 2/15/1941, RLP. A postscript stated that copies had been sent to Herskovits and Benedict.

57. "The Negro Heathenism in Cuba," by R. Lachatanere [*sic*] (Report by W. R. Bascom), African Manuscripts 6, Series 3516, Box 12, Folder 12, MHP. The origin of the English title for the manuscript is unclear.

58. Herskovits to Lachatañeré, 2/18/1941, African Manuscripts 6, Series 3516, Box 12, Folder 12, MHP.

59. Herskovits to Lachatañeré, 2/22/1941, African Manuscripts 6, Series 3516, Box 12, Folder 12, MHP.

60. Herskovits to Lachatañeré, 4/7/1941, and Lachatañeré to Herskovits, 5/14/1941, African Manuscripts 6, Series 3516, Box 12, Folder 12, MHP.

61. Lachatañeré to Ortiz, 3/30/1941, Carpeta 183, "Correspondencia Varios L," CMFO.

62. Lachatañeré's words on *brujería* were "very true," Ortiz admitted, and he promised he would say so in "Brujos o santeros," which he would offer not so much as a "correction [than] as an explanation." Ortiz to Lachatañeré, 5/15/1941, Carpeta 183, "Correspondencia Varios L," CMFO. Two further sections of "El sistema," under the same title, were published in the journal: 4.1–4 (1940): 27–38, and 5 (1945–1946): 190–215. In addition, previously unpublished manuscript pages of the project were published as parts 6, 7, 9, 10, and 11 in the "El sistema" section of Lachatañeré, *El sistema religioso de los afrocubanos.*

63. Lachatañeré to Herskovits, 6/12/1941, African Manuscripts 6, Series 3516, Box 12, Folder 12, MHP.

64. Peter M. Ascoli, *Julius Rosenwald: The Man Who Built Sears, Roebuck and Advanced the Cause of Black Education in the American South* (Bloomington: Indiana University Press, 2006), 399. Some fellowships were granted to Anglo-white Southerners—C. Vann Woodward, for example.

65. Ruth Benedict to Edwin R. Embree, 6/23/1941, and Embree to Benedict, 6/27/1941, RLP.

66. "Plan of Work," n.d., Rosenwald Application, RLP.

67. His three letters of reference for the Rosenwald were written by Benedict, Boas, and Ortiz. RLP.

68. Lachatañeré, *Manual de santería: Estudios afro-cubanos* (Havana: Editorial Caribe, 1942), 72.

69. Ibid., 10.

70. Ibid., 62–63, italics in original. A note on page 62 states that "*mudanzas interiores*" (interior moves) involved "moving furniture around the house to thwart evil spells."

71. The monthly *Norte, Revista Continental* was published in New York City, 1940–1950, and stayed close to a "good-neighbor" editorial line. The monthly *La Nueva Democracia (The New Democracy)*, a Protestant publication, 1920–1963, published articles by and about many of major Latin American writers and intellectuals of the twentieth century.

72. José Martí, "El puente de Brooklyn," in *Obras completas*, vol. 9 (Havana: Editorial de Ciencias Sociales, 1975), 424.

73. Lachatañeré, "Coney Island: El centro de diversiones mayor del mundo," *Norte, Revista Continental* 1.12 (September 1941): 29.

74. Lachatañeré, "El barrio latino de Harlem," *Norte, Revista Continental* 2.4 (January 1942): 20–22.

75. Ibid., 21. Lachatañeré's "Los 'jardines botánicos' de Harlem," *La Nueva Democracia* 23.5 (May 1942): 22–23, continues these themes in its discussion of the alternative economies of healing seen in the *Manual* passage. Another significant article during this period is "Some Aspects of the Negro Problem in Cuba," *Negro Quarterly: A Review of Negro Life and Culture* 1.2 (1942): 145–54. It is unclear whether the article was written in English or translated. Lachatañeré's contribution to this landmark publication by Ralph Ellison and Angelo Herndon revealed his skepticism over Cuban claims to postracial and *mestizo* national harmony.

76. "Cae ante San Juan un avión D-C con 69 personas," *La Prensa*, 4/15/1952: 1; Western Union Telegram to Sara Lachatañeré, 4/12/1952, RLP; Diana Lachatanere, email correspondence, 7/13/2009.

77. Emilio Delgado and Jack Lessinger, "Homenaje Póstumo a Rómulo Lachata-ñeré," RLP; Juan Marinello, "Adhesión a un acto efectuado en Nueva York en honor de Rómulo Lachatañeré," Manuscritos Marinello, Número 804, Sala Cubana, Biblio-teca Nacional José Martí; "One Had Changed Plans," *New York Times*, 4/12/1952: 20. I thank Tomás Fernández Robaina for providing me with a transcription of the Mari-nello document.

78. Delgado and Lessinger, "Homenaje."

79. Grosfoguel, *Colonial Subjects*, 110.

80. Sandoval Sánchez, "Puerto Rican Identity Up in the Air: Air Migration, Its Cul-tural Representations, and Me 'Cruzando el Charco,'" in *Puerto Rican Jam: Rethinking Colonialism and Nationalism*, ed. Frances Negrón-Muntaner and Ramón Grosfoguel, 189–208 (Minneapolis: University of Minnesota Press, 1997), 190.

81. Rafael Hernández, "Tragedia de Viernes Santo," *Lo más selecto del Trio Veg-abajeño*, CD (Disco Hit, 1999).

82. Buscaglia-Salgado, *Undoing Empire*, 299n. 51.

83. Diana Lachatanere, email correspondence, 7/13/2009.

84. Jack Lessinger adds another dimension: that of a culture-front-influenced, Jewish American activism. See Anne Tucker, "The Photo League," in *Illuminations: Women Writing on Photography from the 1850s to the Present*, ed. Liz Heron and Val Williams, 165–69 (Durham: Duke University Press, 1996).

85. Tony Vélez, telephone interview, 5/18/2010. See Vélez, "Portfolio Tony Vélez," *Centro Journal* 9.9 (Winter 1996–1997): 8, 26, 43–45, 86.

86. David Platt, "Lachatanere [*sic*]: Splendid Artist, Fighter for Peace," *Daily Work-er*, 6/8/1952: 7, RLP. On the ASP and African Americans, see *Gerald Horne, Black and Red: W. E. B. Du Bois and the Afro-American Response to the Cold War, 1944–1963* (Albany: SUNY Press, 1986), 107.

87. García, *Arsenio Rodríguez*, 86.

88. Platt, "Lachatanere [*sic*]." Sherry Turner DeCavara, "Celebration," in *The Jazz Cadence of American Culture*, ed. Robert G. O'Meally, 243–63 (New York: Columbia University Press, 1998), 245.

89. The identification of the settings of the Puerto Rico photographs belongs to José Buscaglia-Salgado, who reviewed a representative selection on my behalf. I thank him very much.

90. Deborah Willis, ed., *Picturing Us: African American Identity in Photography* (New York: New Press, 1994); Sara Blair, *Harlem Crossroads: Black Writers and the Photograph in the Twentieth Century* (Princeton: Princeton University Press, 2007).

91. "These Pictures Lived On ... After Puerto Rico Crash," *Daily Compass*, 5/16/1952: 8–9. A copy appears in the Lachatañeré Papers; most of the article's content quotes from the Delgado/Lessinger homage.

92. José Buscaglia-Salgado has helped me locate the setting of this photograph in the Cordillera Central. "The girls eat from a plate made from the fruit of the fig tree (from which *güiros* are made). In Puerto Rico it's called a *dita*. As a rule, this was typical of the mountainous region." José Buscaglia-Salgado, email correspondence, 5/25/2010.

93. Juan Flores, *Puerto Rican Arrival in New York: Narratives of the Migration, 1920–1950* (Princeton, NJ: Markus Wiener, 2005). Another Lachatañeré photograph, an interior shot of a crowd in Harlem, appears inside the book. A 1997 edition of *Puerto Rican Arrival* did not include the Lachatañeré photographs.

94. *Every Child Is Born a Poet: The Life and Work of Piri Thomas*, dir. Jonathan Meyer Robinson, DVD (When In Doubt Productions, 2003).

95. Carmen Hernández, *Puerto Rican Voices in English: Interviews with Writers* (Westport, CT: Praeger, 1997), 173. Based on the age listed for Juan Tomás on his son's birth certificate, Tomás's date of birth is either 1904 or 1905.

96. I suggest an Afro-Cuban American Piri Thomas in the spirit of Lisa Sánchez González's and Frances Negrón-Muntaner's reclaiming of Arturo Schomburg's and Jean-Michel Basquiat's boricua identities, respectively. See Sánchez González, *Boricua Literature*; and Negrón-Muntaner, *Boricua Pop*.

97. Sánchez González, *Boricua Literature*, 132; Antonio Viego, *Dead Subjects: Toward a Politics of Loss in Latino Studies* (Durham: Duke University Press, 2007), 9.

98. Piri Thomas, *Down These Mean Streets* (New York: Vintage, 1997).

99. Luis, "Black Latinos Speak," 28–29.

100. Sánchez González, *Boricua Literature*, 103.

101. Georg Lukács, *The Historical Novel*, trans. Hannah and Stanley Mitchell (Lincoln: University of Nebraska Press, 1983), 42.

102. Handwritten note, Box Three, Manuscripts: *Down These Mean Streets*, Fragments, Piri Thomas Papers, Schomburg Center for Research in Black Culture (hereafter PTP).

103. Iraida H. López, *La autobiografía hispana contemporánea en los estados unidos: A través del caleidoscopio* (Lewiston, NY: Edwin Mellen, 2001), 83n. 9. Monica Brown, *Gang Nation: Delinquent Citizens in Puerto Rican, Chicano, and Chicana Narratives* (Minneapolis: University of Minnesota Press, 2002), is one of the many critical works that recognize the importance of the father's characterization to the text.

104. Hernández, *Puerto Rican Voices in English*; Wolfgang Binder, "An Interview with Piri Thomas," *Minority Voices* 4.1 (1980): 63–78; Piri Thomas, *Savior, Savior, Hold My Hand* (Garden City, NY: Doubleday, 1972), 51. Burgos, *Playing America's Game*, 135, offers information on the baseball career.

105. Birth certificate, Box One, Personal Papers, Biographical Information, PTP; handwritten note, Box Three, Manuscripts: *Down These Means Streets*, Fragments, PTP.

106. Hernández, *Puerto Rican Voices in English*, 173; Binder, "An Interview," 67.

107. Birth certificate, Box One, Personal Papers, Biographical Information, PTP. Thomas's mother, Dolores Montañez from Bayamón, Puerto Rico, is important to the critical narrative of *Streets* in her own right; my relative silence on her role, a result of my focus on the father and his Afro-Cuban American identity, should not suggest otherwise.

108. Both the passage from the first edition and the quotations, all of which come from a variety mainstream newspaper and magazine sources, are found in Box Three, "*Down These Mean Streets* Reviews," PTP.

109. Thomas, *Down These Mean Streets*, 1, 22; subsequent references appear in the text.

110. Arnaldo Cruz-Malavé's "What a Tangled Web! Masculinity, Abjection, and the Foundations of Puerto Rican Literature in the United States," *differences* 8.1 (1996): 132–51, addresses masculinity and the abject in the text's well-known representations of transgender identity and homosexuality.

111. Binder, "An Interview," 76.

112. The account of Casal's 1973 return is "Fragmentos de un diario de viaje," *Nueva Generación* 4.27 (June 1974): 1–11, a guarded, at times critical narrative regarding her experience of Cuban reality (mediated by state-appointed guides). *Nueva Generación* called Casal "the first exile to visit Cuba at the invitation of the ICAP [Instituto Cubano de Amistad con los Pueblos]." "En este número," *Nueva Generación* 4.27 (June 1974): 1.

113. María Cristina Herrera, "Dedicatoria," in *Itinerario ideológico: Antología de Lourdes Casal,* ed. María Cristina Herrera and Leonel Antonio de la Cuesta, 1–2 (Miami: Instituto de Estudios Cubanos, 1982), 1.

114. Víctor Fowler Calzada, *Rupturas y homenajes* (Havana: Ediciones Unión, 1998), 186.

115. Lourdes Casal, "Cubans in the U.S.," *Nueva Generación* 3.24–25/4.26 (December 1972): 6–20; Lourdes Casal and Rafael Prohías, *The Cuban Minority in the U.S.: Preliminary Report on Need Identification and Program Evaluation* (Washington, DC: Cuban National Planning Council, 1974), based on Prohías's unfinished dissertation; Casal and Prieto, "Black Cubans in the United States."

116. Undated clipping from *Chicago San Juan al Día,* Box Two, Programs and Events, 1972–1979, Club Cubano Inter-Americano Papers, Schomburg Center for Research in Black Culture. Casal's talk was entitled "Maceo como pensador" (Maceo as Thinker).

117. Frances Negrón-Muntaner and Yolanda Martínez-San Miguel, "In Search of Lourdes Casal's 'Ana Veldford,'" *Social Text* 25.3 (Fall 2007): 56–84; Josefina de Diego, "Through Other Looking Glasses," in *By Heart/De memoria: Cuban Women's Journeys In and Out of Exile,* ed. María de los Ángeles Torres, 85–102 (Philadelphia: Temple University Press, 2003); Leonel Antonio de la Cuesta, "Perfil Biográfico," in Herrera and de la Cuesta, *Itinerario ideológico,* 3–8; Miguel Barnet, "Testimonios," *Areíto* 7.26 (1981): 15–17. On Casal's Chinese heritage, see her story collection *Los fundadores: Alfonso y otros cuentos* (Miami: Ediciones Universal, 1973).

118. Lourdes Casal, "Memories of a Black Cuban Childhood," *Nuestro* 2.4 (1978): 61–62. I thank Iraida López for bringing me to this text.

119. Ibid., 62.

4 / Around 1979

1. Iván de la Nuez, "Mariel: El espejo roto de la literatura cubana," in *Cuentos desde Miami,* ed. Juan Abreu, 9–16 (Barcelona: Poliedro, 2004), locates *escoria* at the port of Mariel. My personal observation is that, by the summer of 1980, *escoria* had become common in Hialeah and Miami.

2. Lourdes Casal, "Cuba, Abril-Mayo 1980," *Areíto* 6.23 (1980): 22, 23.

3. Vicente S. Pujals, "La 'Face' del exilio," *El Sol de Hialeah,* 9/30/1982: 2.

4. Editorial, *Mariel* 1.1 (Spring 1983): 2.

5. Susana Peña, "'Obvious Gays' and the State Gaze: Cuban Gay Visibility and U.S. Immigration Policy during the 1980 Mariel Boatlift," *Journal of the History of Sexuality* 16.3 (July 2007): 482–514. The primary figure of a gay Mariel, of course, is Reinaldo Arenas.

6. "Estampas del éxodo cubano: De todas las clases," *El Expreso de Miami,* 5/23/1980: 1.

7. Enrique Patterson, "Cuba: Discursos sobre la identidad," *Encuentro de la cultura cubana* 2 (1996): 67.

8. Stephan Palmié, "Spics or Spades? Racial Classification and Ethnic Conflict in Miami," *Amerikastudien* 34 (1989): 211–21.

9. Ramón Grosfoguel with Chloe S. Georas, "'Coloniality of Power' and Racial Dynamics: Notes on a Reinterpretation of Latino Caribbeans in New York City," in Grosfoguel, *Colonial Subjects*, 171.

10. Edna Buchanan, *The Corpse Had a Familiar Face: Covering Miami, America's Hottest Beat* (New York: Random House, 1987), 226.

11. *Cocaine Cowboys*, dir. Billy Corben, DVD (Los Angeles: Magnolia Home Entertainment, 2007).

12. Palmié, *Wizards and Scientists*, 198.

13. Pitbull, "Outro," *El Mariel*, CD (New York: TVT Records, 2006).

14. Marvin Dunn, *Black Miami in the Twentieth Century* (Gainesville: University Press of Florida, 1997), 319; Robert Samuels, "Memories of Liberty City Riots Fade, but Neighborhood Bears Scars," *Miami Herald*, 5/16/2010: A1. The source in this latter article is Dunn.

15. See Tiffany Ana López, "Critical Witnessing in Latina/o and African American Prison Narratives," in *Prose and Cons: Essays on Prison Literature in the United States*, ed. D. Quentin Miller, 62–77 (Jefferson, NC: McFarland, 2005).

16. Jacques Derrida, *Specters of Marx: The State of the Debt, the Work of Mourning, and the New International*, trans. Peggy Kamuf (New York: Routledge, 1994), 9.

17. Buchanan, *The Corpse*, 233.

18. Dunn, *Black Miami*, 267, 271. Hanlon's charges were later dropped.

19. Marvin Dunn and Bruce Porter, *The Miami Riot: Crossing the Bounds* (Lexington, MA: Lexington Books, 1984), 38–39.

20. Ibid.

21. Edna Buchanan, "Hundreds Weep at Funeral for McDuffie," *Miami Herald*, 12/30/1979: 1; Buchanan, *The Corpse*, 223.

22. Dunn, *Black Miami*, 254.

23. Buchanan, *The Corpse*, 226; Patrice Gaines-Carter, "McDuffie: The Case behind Miami's Riots," *Southern Changes: The Journal of the Southern Regional Council* 2.7 (1980): 20–23.

24. "Acquitted Miami Officer Arrested in Drug Case," *Washington Post*, 4/11/1989: A6.

25. Manning Marable, "The Fire This Time," *Black Scholar* (July–August 1980): 3, 11.

26. June Jordan, *Civil Wars* (1981; repr., New York: Simon and Schuster, 1995), 184; Dunn and Porter, *Miami Riot*, xiii.

27. Jordan, *Civil Wars*, 182.

28. Ibid., 184–85.

29. June Jordan, *Affirmative Acts* (New York: Anchor Books, 1998), 28.

30. Dan Williams, "Allapattah Latins Play Dominoes on Front Lines," *Miami Herald*, 5/19/1980: 4B.

31. "Arthur McDuffie's Name to Be Preserved in Song," *Jet*, 6/26/1980: 5.

32. Ella Washington, "The Ballad of Arthur McDuffie," record single (Miami: Kingston Records, 1980).

33. Harold Lee Rush, telephone interview, 8/24/2009. Rush was involved in radical politics leading up to his imprisonment.

34. Hakim Al-Jamil, "Who Killed McDuffie (A Definitive Question)," *Semiotext(e)* 5.13 (1987): 264.

35. A photograph of the image accompanies Sara Rimer, "Smoky Smell Turns Sweet around Riot's Corner," *Miami Herald*, 5/20/1980: 16A.

36. Samuels, "Memories of Liberty City Riots Fade."

37. Buchanan, *The Corpse*, 222–23.

38. Dunn, *Black Miami*, 156–58.

39. Marquis Lewis, telephone interview, 9/3/2009.

40. Román de la Campa, *Cuba on My Mind: Journeys to a Severed Nation* (New York: Verso, 2000), 96; Mark Sawyer, *Racial Politics in Post-Revolutionary Cuba* (New York: Cambridge University Press, 2005), 160.

41. Cristina García, *Havana USA: Cuban Exiles and Cuban Americans in South Florida, 1959–1994* (Berkeley: University of California Press, 1997), 78. García mistakes Paul Muni for James Cagney.

42. Rivera, *New York Ricans*, 118.

43. Todd Boyd, *Am I Black Enough for You? Popular Culture from the 'Hood and Beyond* (Bloomington: Indiana University Press, 1997), 86, 87.

44. Terrie Williams, *Black Pain: It Just Looks Like We're Not Hurting* (New York: Scribner, 2008), 94.

45. John Kobler, *Capone: The Life and World of Al Capone* (New York: Da Capo, 2003), 15, 120.

46. Armitage Trail, *Scarface* (1930; repr., London: Bloomsbury, 1997), 15.

47. Jerome Lawrence, *Actor: The Life and Times of Paul Muni* (New York: Putnam, 1974), 15, 45, 57, 97, 136.

48. Ibid., 160.

49. J. E. Smyth, "Revisioning Modern American History in the Age of *Scarface* (1932)," *Historical Journal of Film, Radio and Television* 24.4 (2004): 553.

50. Frances Negrón-Muntaner, "Feeling Pretty: *West Side Story* and Puerto Rican Identity Discourses," *Social Text* 18.2 (2000): 92.

51. Bernard Weinraub, "20 Years Later, Pacino's *Scarface* Resonates with a Young Audience," *New York Times*, 9/23/2003: E1.

52. Al Pacino, *Al Pacino in Conversation with Lawrence Grobel* (New York: Simon Spotlight Entertainment, 2008), 4, 87.

53. Ibid., 87.

54. Humberto Delgado and Lorna Veraldi, "¿Qué Pasa, USA?," *Television Quarterly* 37.2 (Winter 2007): 47–52. The show was produced by the public television station WPBT (Miami) and was soon broadcast nationally. It went into preproduction in 1975 and ended its run in 1980, with the end of the grant.

55. Pacino, *Al Pacino in Conversation*, 86.

56. Interview on *Scarface*, dir. Brian De Palma, Bonus DVD (Universal City, CA: Universal Studios Home Videos, 2003).

57. Gregory Jaynes, "Miami Official Objects to Cuban Refugee Film," *New York Times*, 8/24/1982: A12; Ken Tucker, *Scarface Nation: The Ultimate Gangster Movie and How It Changed America* (New York: St. Martin's Griffin, 2008), 56.

58. "Fuerte controversia sobre el film *Caracortada*," *El Sol de Hialeah*, 9/2/1982, 3.

59. I draw here on a variety of sources on rap and hip hop: Robin D. G. Kelley, *Race Rebels: Culture, Politics, and the Black Working Class* (New York: Free Press, 1994); Tricia Rose, *Black Noise: Rap Music and Black Culture in Contemporary America* (Hanover, NH: University Press of New England, 1994); S. Craig Watkins, *Representing: Hip Hop Culture and the Production of Black Cinema* (Chicago: University of Chicago Press, 1998); Adam Krims, *Rap Music and the Poetics of Identity* (New York: Cambridge University Press, 2000); and Michael S. Collins, "Biggie Envy and the Gangsta Sublime," *Callaloo* 29.3 (Summer 2006): 911–38. "Speech effusive" comes from Krims.

60. Eithne Quinn, *Nuthin' but a "G" Thang: The Culture and Commerce of Gangsta Rap* (New York: Columbia University Press, 2005), 39.

61. The suicide alternative as a critique of Eurocentric "rationality" among African-diasporic people in slavery historicizes the appeal of a corpse-in-waiting Montana for gangsta artists. See Paul Gilroy, *The Black Atlantic: Modernity and Double Consciousness* (Cambridge: Harvard University Press, 1993), 68.

62. Prince Buster, "Al Capone," *It's Burke's Law*, LP (Blue Beat, 1965).

63. Mark Anthony Neal, "'Memory Lane': On Jazz, Hip-Hop, and Fathers," in *Born to Use Mics: Reading Nas's* Illmatic, ed. Michael Eric Dyson and Sohail Daulatzai, 117–28 (New York: Basic Civitas Books, 2010), 127.

64. Nas, "N.Y. State of Mind," *Illmatic*, CD (Columbia Records, 1994).

65. The Notorious B.I.G., "Respect," *Ready to Die*, CD (Bad Boy Records, 1994).

66. Raekwon, *Only Built 4 Cuban Linx*, CD (Loud Records, 1995).

67. Interview on *Scarface: Origins of a Hip Hop Classic*, dir. Benny Boom, Bonus DVD (Universal City, CA: Universal Studios Home Videos, 2003).

68. Frank Owen, "Censorship Isn't Def America," *Spin* (November 1990): 44.

69. Geto Boys, "Scarface," *Geto Boys*, CD (Def American Records, 1990).

70. The "all I have in / this world / balls" sample goes back to the track "Balls and My Word" on the Geto Boys' first album, *Making Trouble* (1988), before Scarface joined the group. It is revised as the first track on Scarface's *Balls and My Word* (2003), the cover art of which reproduces the iconic black-and-white poster image of the 1983 film, with Scarface in the place of Montana. Among the samples in "Scarface" (1989) is N.W.A.'s "Straight Outta Compton," which, of course, connects the Houston group to the West Coast scene happening simultaneously.

71. Scarface, "Mr. Scarface," *Mr. Scarface Is Back*, CD (Rap-a-Lot Records, 1991).

72. Scarface, "Mr. Scarface, Part III: The Final Chapter," *The World Is Yours* (*Face II Face*), CD (Rap-a-Lot Records, 1993).

73. Cuban Link, "Shakedown," *Chain Reaction*, CD (M.O.B. Records, 2005).

74. Rivera, *New York Ricans*, 191.

75. The major figures of Terror Squad were the Puerto Rican Big Pun and Fat Joe, of Puerto Rican and Cuban descent.

76. Terror Squad, "As the World Turns," *Terror Squad, the Album*, CD (Big Beat Records, 1999).

77. The protagonist, Nino Brown (Wesley Snipes), speaks in Montana brownface as he watches the climactic killing of Montana on a big-screen television that then flashes to a scene from Melvin Van Peebles's *Sweet Sweetback's Baadasssss Song* (1971): a visual sampling that pointedly historicizes (and, indeed, displaces) *Scarface* 1983 in relation to African American film.

78. Cuban Link, "Shakedown."

79. Mirta Ojito, *Finding Mañana: A Memoir of a Cuban Exodus* (New York: Penguin, 2005), 254.

80. Ulla and Villaverde, *Dos filmes*, 114. See also Peña, "'Obvious Gays' and the State Gaze."

81. Ulla and Villaverde, *Dos filmes*, 72.

82. Robert L. Bach, Jennifer B. Bach, and Timothy Triplett, "The Flotilla 'Entrants': Latest and Most Controversial," *Cuban Studies/Estudios Cubanos* 11.2/12.1 (July 1981–January 1982): 29–54.

83. On Krome, see Mark Dow, *American Gulag: Inside U.S. Immigration Prisons* (Berkeley: University of California Press, 2004). On the camp, see Giorgio Agamben, *Homo Sacer: Sovereign Power and Bare Life*, trans. Daniel Heller-Roazen (Stanford: Stanford University Press, 1998).

84. De la Nuez, "Mariel," 15–16.

85. "Biography," in Esteban Luis Cárdenas, *Un café exquisito* (Miami: Ediciones Universal, 2001).

86. I thank Luis de la Paz for putting me in contact with Cárdenas.

87. I am influenced here by Ricardo Ortiz's argument on addiction, nostalgia, and Cuban exile in *Cultural Erotics*.

88. Cárdenas, "Un café exquisito," in *Un café exquisito*, 45; subsequent references appear in the text.

5 / Cosa de Blancos

1. Pablo Medina, *Exiled Memories: A Cuban Childhood* (New York: Persea Books, 2002), x, 118.

2. Alina Troyano, *I, Carmelita Tropicana: Performing between Cultures* (Boston: Beacon, 2000), 59.

3. Large-scale returns to revolutionary Cuba date from 1978, when the Carter administration and the Cuban state reached détente. Examples of a late 1977 return by members of the Antonio Maceo Brigade are found in "Encuentro con los familiares," *Areíto* 4.3–4 (Spring 1978): 37–45. See María de los Ángeles Torres, *In the Land of Mirrors: Cuban Exile Politics in the United States* (Ann Arbor: University of Michigan Press, 1999), 84–126, for the Maceo Brigade and the 1970s and 1980s returns.

4. Emron Esplin, "Cuban Types, Distorted Memory, and a Return to Cuba in Cristina García's *The Agüero Sisters*," *Confluencia: Revista Hispánica de Cultura y Literatura* 20.2 (2005): 96. Jacqueline Stefanko, "New Ways of Telling: Latinas' Narratives of Exile and Return," *Frontiers: A Journal of Women Studies* 17.2 (1996): 67.

5. Ortiz, *Cultural Erotics*, 155.

6. Ariana Hernández-Reguant, "Writing the Special Period: An Introduction," in *Cuba in the Special Period: Culture and Ideology in the 1990s*, ed. Ariana Hernández-Reguant, 1–18 (New York: Palgrave, 2009), 1, 11.

7. Ariana Hernández-Reguant, "Return to Havana: Adio Kerida and the Films of the One-and-a-Half Generation," *Journal of Latin American Anthropology* 9.2 (Fall 2004): 496.

8. Ariana Hernández-Reguant, "Multicubanidad," in Hernández-Reguant, *Cuba in the Special Period*, 72.

9. Roberto Segre, "Hábitat: Tipología y tecnología," in *Tres décadas de reflexiones*

sobre el hábitat latinoamericano, 133–47 (Bogotá: Universidad Nacional de Colombia, 2005), 134.

10. DeGuzmán, *Spain's Long Shadow,* shows how the Spanish "fiction of the hidalgo with *sangre pura* (pure blood), untainted by the blood of *moros* (Moors) or *judíos* (Jews)," ironically encouraged Anglo white supremacy "to do 'the Spaniards' one better" by elaborating "a fantasy of [Anglo] racial purity through the representation of Spaniards as figures of morally blackened alien whiteness or *off-whiteness* and doomed hybridity" (xxiv).

11. On the demographic constructions of Cuban racial identity in the United States, see Pew Hispanic Center, *Cubans in the United States* (Washington, DC: Pew Hispanic Center, 2006), available at www.pewhispanic.org. "Cubans are far more likely than other Hispanics to identify themselves as white when asked about their race. In the 2004 Census data, about 86% of Cubans said they were white, compared with 60% among Mexicans, 53% among other Central and South Americans and 50% among Puerto Ricans" (3). This stands in contrast to estimations of a majority Afro-Cuban island.

12. Pérez Firmat, de la Campa, and Behar were prominent academics in the emergence in the 1990s of Cuban American literary and cultural studies—especially Pérez Firmat's *Life on the Hyphen: The Cuban-American Way* (Austin: University of Texas Press, 1994), de la Campa's essays on Cuban Americans and Latinas/os (for example, "The Latino Diaspora in the United States: Sojourns from a Cuban Past," *Public Culture* 6.2 [1994]: 293–317), and Behar's edited collection *Bridges to Cuba/Puentes a Cuba* (Ann Arbor: University of Michigan Press, 1995).

13. Valerie Babb, *Whiteness Visible: The Meaning of Whiteness in American Literature and Culture* (New York: NYU Press, 1998), 43.

14. Vron Ware and Les Back, *Out of Whiteness: Color, Politics, and Culture* (Chicago: University of Chicago Press, 2002), 3.

15. Silvio Torres-Saillant, "Inventing the Race: Latinos and the Ethnoracial Pentagon," *Latino Studies* 1 (2003): 126. Buscaglia-Salgado, *Undoing Empire,* addresses Spanish whiteness's "uncertain" origins in the religious and proto-racial/national identities of the Afro-Judeo-Islamo-Christian contact zones of the early-modern Iberian peninsula. Mexican American whiteness is an object of inquiry in Martha Menchaca, *Recovering History, Constructing Race: The Indian, Black, and White Roots of Mexican Americans* (Austin: University of Texas Press, 2001). Dominican whiteness is an element in Silvio Torres-Saillant's critique of "negrophobia" in the Dominican Republic and its U.S. diaspora ("The Tribulations of Blackness: Stages in Dominican Racial Identity," *Callaloo* 23.3 [2000]: 1086–1111), while Grosfoguel, *Colonial Subjects,* and Salvador Vidal-Ortiz, "On Being a White Person of Color: Using Autoethnography to Understand Puerto Ricans' Racialization," *Qualitative Sociology* 27.2 (Summer 2004): 179–203, approach island and mainland Puerto Rican whiteness. I discuss Cuban and Cuban American whiteness texts later in this chapter. On critical Anglo-whiteness studies, see Shelley Fisher Fishkin, "Interrogating 'Whiteness,' Complicating 'Blackness': Remapping American Culture," *American Quarterly* 47.3 (1995): 428–66.

16. Ada Ferrer, "The Silence of the Patriots: Race and Nationalism in Martí's Cuba," in *José Martí's "Our America": From National to Hemispheric Cultural Studies,* ed. Jeffrey Belnap and Raúl Fernández, 228–49 (Durham: Duke University Press, 1998).

17. Mirabal, "Scripting Race." For a range of criticism on Afro-Cuban literary figures in white Cuban and Cuban American texts, see William Luis, *Literary Bondage: Slavery in Cuban Narrative* (Austin: University of Texas Press, 1990); Kutzinski, *Sugar's Secrets*; and Edna M. Rodríguez-Mangual, *Lydia Cabrera and the Construction of an Afro-Cuban Cultural Identity* (Chapel Hill: University of North Carolina Press, 2004).

18. Multidisciplinary texts interested in revealing such articulations of Cuban and Cuban American whiteness include Josef Opatrný, "José Antonio Saco's Path toward the Idea of *Cubanidad*," *Cuban Studies* 24 (1994): 39–56; Consuelo Naranjo Orovio, *Racismo e inmigración en Cuba en el siglo XIX* (Madrid: Doce Calles, 1996); Greenbaum, *More Than Black*; Mirabal, "Scripting Race"; Juan Flores, "Life Off the Hyphen: Latino Literature and Nuyorican Traditions," in *From Bomba to Hip-Hop*, 167–88; and Mirta Ojito, "Best of Friends, Worlds Apart," in *How Race Is Lived in America: Pulling Together, Pulling Apart*, ed. Correspondents of the New York Times, 23–39 (New York: Times Books, 2001).

19. Patterson, "Cuba," 67.

20. Isabel Álvarez Borland, *Cuban-American Literature of Exile: From Person to Persona* (Charlottesville: University Press of Virginia, 1998), 62.

21. Sidonie Smith, "Performativity, Autobiographical Practice, Resistance," in *Women, Autobiography, Theory: A Reader*, ed. Sidonie Smith and Julia Watson, 108–15 (Madison: University of Wisconsin Press, 1998), 108.

22. Fritz Gysin, "The Enigma of Return," in *Black Imagination and the Middle Passage*, ed. Maria Diedrich, Henry Louis Gates, Jr., and Carl Pedersen, 183–90 (Oxford: Oxford University Press, 1999), 187.

23. Toni Morrison, *Playing in the Dark: Whiteness and the Literary Imagination* (Cambridge: Harvard University Press, 1992), 7.

24. Ibid., 9.

25. Patterson, "Cuba," 66.

26. Alejandro Portes and Alex Stepick, *City on the Edge: The Transformation of Miami* (Berkeley: University of California Press, 1993), 176–202.

27. De los Ángeles Torres, *In the Land of Mirrors*, 76.

28. Grosfoguel, *Colonial Subjects*, 112, 113, 163, 169; the latter two quotations are from a chapter of the book coauthored with Chloe S. Georas.

29. Dunn, *Black Miami*, 319. As chapter 4 demonstrated, the 1980 Mariel boatlift represented a turning point in the history of Cuban-migrant racialization under discussion here.

30. Ortiz, *Cultural Erotics*, 36.

31. Gustavo Pérez Firmat, *Next Year in Cuba: A Cubano's Coming-of-Age in America* (New York: Anchor Books, 1995), 9; subsequent references appear in the text.

32. Morrison, *Playing in the Dark*, 17, 69.

33. Bruce Robbins, *The Servant's Hand: English Fiction from Below* (New York: Columbia University Press, 1986), 8.

34. Burgos, *Playing America's Game*, 33.

35. See Moore, *Music and Revolution*, 44–46, on the racial and class meanings of the *cha-cha-chá*, and Pérez, *Cuba*, 200–201, on Spanish domination of the Cuban retail industry during the early decades of the republic. The song in question is almost certainly the renowned Afro-Cuban composer and flutist Eduardo "Richard" Egües's

"El bodeguero," composed in 1956, played by the Orquesta Aragón (of which Egües was a member).

36. López, *La autobiografía hispana*, 58.

37. Kutzinski, *Sugar's Secrets*, 12–13.

38. Claudette M. Williams, *Charcoal and Cinnamon: The Politics of Color in Spanish Caribbean Literature* (Gainesville: University Press of Florida, 2000), 1.

39. Buscaglia-Salgado, *Undoing Empire*.

40. An earlier critique of race and gender vis-à-vis Pérez Firmat's critical work is Kutzinski, *Sugar's Secrets*, 172, 176, which focuses on his readings of Guillén's poems.

41. Román de la Campa, "Itinerario de la brigada Antonio Maceo," *Areíto* 4.3–4 (1978): 12–23, is an important account of the late 1977 return that features his first reencounter with what was to become the Afro-Cuban-occupied house in *Cuba on My Mind*. De la Campa has published many articles on Latin American and U.S. Latino culture, theory, and politics, and his books include *Latin Americanism* (1999) and *Nuevas cartografías latinoamericanas* (2006). *Contra viento y marea* (Havana: Casa de las Américas, 1978), edited by Lourdes Casal, Margarita Lejarza, Vicente Dopico, and de la Campa, emerges from the Maceo Brigade and *Areíto* experience.

42. De la Campa devotes a chapter of *Cuba on My Mind*—"A Peter Pan Story"—to this experience.

43. De la Campa, *Cuba on My Mind*, 21; further references appear in the text.

44. López, *La autobiografía hispana*, 159.

45. Here I am drawing on Doris Sommer, *Foundational Fictions: The National Romances of Latin America* (Berkeley: University of California Press, 1991).

46. See Lane, *Blackface Cuba*, 124–25, for the *gallego* and Buscaglia-Salgado, *Undoing Empire*, 195, for the *guajiro* types in Cuba.

47. Behar embarked on the film with little prior training in filmmaking, assisted by two graduate students, Gisela Fosado and Umi Vaughn. There have been several cuts of the film. Ruth Behar, "While Waiting for the Ferry to Cuba," in *Memory, Oblivion, and Jewish Culture in Latin America*, ed. Marjorie Agosín, 221–34 (Austin: University of Texas Press, 2005), 229, 233.

48. Ruth Behar, "Juban América," *Poetics Today* 16.1 (1995): 164. See also her *An Island Called Home: Returning to Jewish Cuba* (New Brunswick: Rutgers University Press, 2007).

49. Ruth Behar, "Temporary Latina," in *Telling to Live: Latina Feminist Testimonios*, ed. Latina Feminist Group, 231–37 (Durham: Duke University Press, 2001), 237.

50. Ruth Behar, "Daughter of Caro," in *Daughters of Caliban: Caribbean Women in the Twentieth Century*, ed. Consuelo López Springfield, 112–20 (Bloomington: Indiana University Press, 1997); Behar, "Honeymoon Nightgowns That a Black Woman Saved for a White Woman: A Perilous Journey into the Cuban Historical Imagination," *American Studies* 41.2–3 (2000): 287–302; Behar, "Yellow Marigolds for Ochún: An Experiment in Feminist Ethnographic Fiction," *International Journal of Qualitative Studies in Education* 14.2 (2001): 107–16.

51. Behar, "Honeymoon Nightgowns," 288.

52. Ibid., 291, 293.

53. Ruth Behar, "Queer Times," in *Bridges to Cuba*, 394–95.

54. Behar, "Honeymoon Nightgowns," 289.

55. Ruth Behar, *Adio Kerida/Goodbye Dear Love*, DVD (New York: Women Make Movies, 2002).

56. The original narrator was Behar herself. Ruth Behar, email correspondence, 4/7/2009.

57. Rosa Linda Fregoso, *MeXicana Encounters: The Making of Social Identities on the Borderlands* (Berkeley: University of California Press, 2003), 64.

58. Ana M. López, "Greater Cuba," in *The Ethnic Eye: Latino Media Arts*, ed. Chon A. Noriega and Ana M. López, 38–58 (Minneapolis: University of Minnesota Press 1996), 44–46. *El súper* is set in upper Manhattan.

59. For the early "illegal" domestic-worker and nanny roles, see the film *Down and Out in Beverly Hills* (1986) and the television series *I Married Dora* (1987).

60. *Cuban Roots/Bronx Stories*, dir. Pam Sporn, DVD (New York: Third World Newsreel, 2000); all quotations are my transcriptions from the video.

61. The biographical information in this paragraph comes from http://www .cubanroots.com.

62. Fernando Ortiz, *Nuevo catauro de cubanismos* (Havana: Editorial de Ciencias Sociales, 1985), 65.

63. De la Fuente, *A Nation for All*, 51–53.

64. Ian Smart, *Central American Writers of West Indian Origin: A New Hispanic Literature* (Washington, DC: Three Continents, 1984), 11–12.

65. In 2006, a Catalonian-produced documentary film on Castillo Bueno was released: *Reyita*, dir. Oliva Acosta and Elena Ortega (Barcelona: CPI, Centre Promotor de la Image).

66. María de los Reyes Castillo Bueno, *Reyita, sencillamente: Testimonio de una negra cubana nonagenaria* (Havana: Instituto Cubano del Libro, Prolibros, 1996), 33–34; further references appear in the text.

67. Patterson, "Cuba," 63, 64.

68. Segre, "Hábitat," 138.

69. Elizabeth Dore, introduction to *Reyita: The Life of a Black Cuban Woman in the Twentieth Century*, by María de los Reyes Castillo Bueno, trans. Anne McLean, 1–18 (Durham: Duke University Press, 2003), 14–15.

70. Her son, Monín, died when a French ship containing arms, *La Coubre*, exploded in Havana harbor in 1960 in a possible act of sabotage.

Conclusion

1. Carlos Ramírez, "El aporte de los inmigrantes afrolatinos," *El Pregonero*, 10/2/2008: 6.

2. Evelio Grillo, *Black Cuban, Black American* (Houston: Arte Público, 2000), back cover.

3. Nicolás Kanellos, telephone interview, 10/24/2007.

4. Evelio Grillo Papers, privately held (hereafter EGP). Maggie Rivas-Rodríguez, Juliana Torres, Melissa Dipiero-D'Sa, and Lindsay Fitzpatrick, *A Legacy Greater Than Words: Stories of U.S. Latinos and Latinas of the WWII Generation* (Austin: University of Texas Press, 2006), 296.

5. Evelio Grillo, interview, Oakland, California, 12/1/2007.

6. Evelio Grillo, "Statement of Personal and Professional Qualifications," and *Aframerican Woman's Journal* (Summer–Fall 1940), EGP. I thank Judge Evelio Grillo, Jr.,

for the way in which he put me in touch with his father, welcomed me into his home, and shared with me his father's papers.

7. Diana Lachatanere, interview, New York City, 3/8/2008.

8. Manuscripts, Box One, Evelio Grillo Papers, Anacostia Community Museum, Smithsonian Institution. Dworkin y Méndez, "Cuban Theater, American Stage," 123. Dworkin y Méndez wrote the introduction to *Black Cuban, Black American*, emphasizing in it the history of Grillo's Tampa origins; see also Greenbaum, *More Than Black*; Evelio Grillo, interview.

9. Evelio Grillo to Alaine Locke, n.d., and Grillo to Locke, 10/14/1942, "Correspondence, Grillo, Evelio," Alaine Locke Papers, Moorland-Spingarn Research Center, Howard University.

10. *Asili: The Journal of Multicultural Heartspeak* 1.3 (April 1997), http://www.asilithejournal.com.

11. Joseph McNair, telephone interview, 4/23/2008.

Index

Page numbers in italics indicate figures.

About the Author

Antonio López is Assistant Professor in the Department of English at George Washington University.